UNIX® for Programmers and Users

A Complete Guide

UNIX® for Programmers and Users

A Complete Guide

GRAHAM GLASS

PRENTICE HALL
Englewood Cliffs, New Jersey 07632

Library of Congress Cataloging-in-Publication Data

Glass, Graham.
    UNIX for programmers and users : a complete guide / Graham Glass.
        p.   cm.
    Includes bibliographical references and index.
    ISBN 0-13-480880-0
    1. Operating systems (Computers) 2. UNIX (Computer file)
  I. Title.
  QA76.76.O63G583   1993
  005.4'3--dc20   92-27320
                                                      CIP

Acquisitions editor: *Bill Zobrist*
Production editor: *Jennifer Wenzel*
Copy editor: *Brenda Melissaratos*
Cover designer: *Karen Noferi*
Fractal image on cover provided by Kerry Mitchell.

Prepress buyer: *Linda Behrens*
Manufacturing buyer: *Dave Dickey*
Supplements editor: *Alice Dworkin*
Editorial assistant: *Danielle Robinson*

© 1993 by Prentice-Hall, Inc.
A Simon & Schuster Company
Englewood Cliffs, New Jersey 07632

The author and publisher of this book have used their best efforts in preparing this book. These efforts include the development, research, and testing of the theories and programs to determine their effectiveness. The author and publisher make no warranty of any kind, expressed or implied, with regard to these programs or the documentation contained in this book. The author and publisher shall not be liable in any event for incidental or consequential damages in connection with, or arising out of, the furnishing, performance, or use of these programs.

Printed in the United States of America

10 9 8 7 6 5 4 3 2 1

ISBN   0-13-480880-0

Prentice-Hall International (UK) Limited, *London*
Prentice-Hall of Australia Pty. Limited, *Sydney*
Prentice-Hall Canada Inc., *Toronto*
Prentice-Hall Hispanoamericana, S.A., *Mexico*
Prentice-Hall of India Private Limited, *New Delhi*
Prentice-Hall of Japan, Inc., *Tokyo*
Simon & Schuster Asia Pte. Ltd., *Singapore*
Editora Prentice-Hall do Brasil, Ltda., *Rio de Janeiro*

TRADEMARK INFORMATION

Apple is a registered trademark of Apple
    Computer Inc.
DEC is a registered trademark of Digital
    Equipment Corp.
Hewlett Packard is a registered trademark of
    the Hewlett Packard Company.
IBM is a registered trademark of International
    Business Machines Corporation.
Microsoft is a registered trademark of
    Microsoft Corporation.
UNIX is a registered trademark of AT&T
    (Bell Laboratories).

to Truth and Beauty,
wherever they are found

Contents

3   THE UNIX SHELLS

8   NETWORKING   288

9   C PROGRAMMING TOOLS   319

Preface

ABOUT THE AUTHOR, BY THE AUTHOR

My name is Graham Glass. I graduated from the University of Southampton, England, with a Bachelor's degree in Computer Science and Mathematics in 1983. I then emigrated to the United States and obtained my Master's degree in Computer Science from the University of Texas at Dallas in 1985. After that, I worked in industry as a UNIX/C systems analyst, and became heavily involved with research in neural networks and parallel distributed processing. Interested in becoming a professor, I then began teaching at the University of Texas at Dallas, covering a wide variety of courses including UNIX, C, assembly language, programming languages, C++, and Smalltalk. I then branched out into industry, cofounded a corporation called "objectSpace," and currently train and consult for companies including DSC Corporation, Texas Instruments, Northern Telecom, J.C. Penney, and Bell Northern Research. I am using my OOP and parallel systems knowledge to design and build a parallel object-oriented computer system and language based on the new Inmos T9000 transputer chip. In my spare time I write music, scuba dive, ski, and occasionally sleep.

ABOUT THIS BOOK

One of my jobs during the past few years has been to teach UNIX to a variety of individuals, including university students, industry C hackers, and occasionally friends and colleagues. During that time I acquired a large amount of knowledge, both in my head as well as in the form of a substantial library, that I often thought would be good to put it into book form. When I began preparing my university lecture series about UNIX, I found that none of the available UNIX text books suited my purpose—they were either too unstructured, too specialized, or lacking in suitable exercises and projects for my students. In response to this situation, I wrote the very first version of this book. After a couple of years of use, I then completely rewrote it, giving careful thought to the organization of the new material. I decided to group the information based on the various typical kinds of UNIX users, allowing the book to be used by a good range of people without completely going over the top (or underneath) anyone's head. One tricky decision concerned the level of detail to include about things like utilities and system calls. Most of these have a large number of specialized options and features that are rarely used, and to document them all and still cover the range of topics that I had targeted would result in a book about two feet thick. Because of this, I've included information only about the most common and useful features of utilities, shells, and system calls. I include page references to other commercially available books for the less useful details. This hybrid-book approach seemed like a good compromise; I hope that you agree.

THE BOOK LAYOUT

UNIX is a big thing. To describe it fully requires an explanation of many different topics from several different angles, which is exactly what I've done. This book is split into several sections, each designed for a particular kind of user:

1. What is UNIX?
2. UNIX For Non-Programmers
3. The UNIX Shells
4. The Bourne Shell
5. The Korn Shell
6. The C Shell
7. Utilities
8. Networking
9. C Programming Tools

10. Systems Programming
11. UNIX Internals
12. System Administration
13. The Future
    Appendix
    Bibliography

I recommend that the various categories of user read the chapters as follows:

Category of user	Chapters
Day-to-day casual users	1, 2
Advanced users	1, 2, 3, 7, 8
Programmers	1 thru 10, 13
System analysts	1 thru 11, 13
Wizards	Everything (of course!)

THE CHAPTER LAYOUT

Every chapter in this book has a standard prologue, as follows:

Motivation

Why it's useful to learn the material that follows.

Prerequisites

What the reader should know in order to successfully negotiate the chapter.

Objectives

A list of the topics that are presented.

Presentation

A description of the method by which the topics are presented.

Utilities

A list of the utilities that are covered in the chapter (when appropriate).

System calls

A list of the system calls that are covered in the chapter (when appropriate).

Shell commands

A list of the shell commands that are covered in the chapter (when appropriate).

In addition, every chapter ends with a review section, which contains the following:

Checklist

A recap of the topics.

Quiz

A quick self-test.

Exercises

A list of exercises, rated *easy, medium,* or *hard.*

Projects

One or more related projects, rated *easy, medium,* or *hard.*

A GUIDE FOR TEACHERS

As I mentioned earlier, this book was originally written for an audience of under-graduate and graduate students. I suggest that a lecture series based on this book could be designed as follows:

- If the students don't know the C language, then a medium-paced course could begin with chapters 1, 2, 3, and 9. The lecturer could then introduce the students to the C language, and use the contents of chapter 10 for class exercises and projects.
- If the students already know the C language, then a medium-paced course could include chapters 1, 2, 3, 6, 9, 10, and 11. Projects focusing on parallel processing and interprocess communication will ensure that the students end up with a good knowledge of UNIX fundamentals.
- If the students know the C language and are enthusiastic, I suggest that all of the chapters with the exception of chapters 4, 5, and 7 can be covered in one semester. I know it's possible, as I've taught it that way!

NOMENCLATURE

There are references throughout this book to UNIX utilities, shell commands, and system calls. It's quite easy to confuse these three things, so I adopted a consistent way to differentiate them:

- UNIX utilities are always written in bold case, like this: "the **mkdir** utility makes a directory."
- System calls are always followed by parentheses, like this: "the fork () system call duplicates a process."
- Shell commands are always written in italics, like this: "the *history* command lists your previous commands."

Formal descriptions of utilities, system calls, and shell commands are supplied in a box, using a modified-for-UNIX Backus-Naur notation. The conventions of this notation are fairly simple, and are described fully in the appendix. As an example, here's a description of the UNIX **man** utility:

Utility: **man** [*chapter*] *word*
            man -k *keyword*

The first usage of **man** displays the manual entry associated with *word*. If no chapter number is specified, the first entry found is displayed. The second usage of **man** displays a list of all the manual entries that contain *keyword*.

All utilities, system calls, and shell commands are fully cross-referenced in the appendix, including the page numbers of the scripts and programs that use them.

Sample UNIX sessions are presented in a courier font. Keyboard input from a user is always displayed in italics, and annotations are always preceded by ellipses (. . .). Here's an example:

```
$ ls                        ... generate a directory listing.
myfile.txt  yourfile.txt
$ whoami
glass
$ _                         ... a new prompt is displayed.
```

REFERENCES TO OTHER BOOKS

For the same reason that it's good to reuse existing code, it's also good to use other people's reference material when it doesn't interfere with the natural flow of the presentation. Information that I consider to be too specialized for this book is referenced by a pair of numbers like this:

"for information concerning a port of UNIX to a 68030 processor, see [14,426]"

The first number in brackets is an index into the bibliography section in the back of this book. In this case, book #14 is titled "UNIX papers." The second number is the page number of the reference. It's always possible that future reprints of these books will have different page numbers. In these cases, the reference will hopefully still remain reasonably close to the quoted page number.

ACKNOWLEDGMENTS

I'd like to thank the following people for reviewing my manuscript: James F. Peters III, Kansas State University; Fadi Deek, New Jersey Institute of Technology; Dr. William Burns, University of Texas at Dallas; and Richard Newman-Wolfe, University of Florida.

I'd also like to thank the following lifeforms for technical and emotional support during the writing of this book: Laura, Mum, Dad, Blair, Beauty, Ross, Agatha, Tim, Howard, Jeff, Tom, Nemo, Danielle, David, Gwen, Bill, Jennifer, and Mike.

Chapter 1

What Is UNIX?

Motivation

UNIX is a popular operating system that a good percentage of the computer industry will be using within a few years. Knowledge of its functions and purpose will help you to understand why so many people choose to use it, and will make your own use of UNIX more effective.

Prerequisites

To fully understand this chapter, you should have a little experience with using a computer and a familiarity with basic computer terms such as *program*, *file*, and *CPU*.

Objectives

In this chapter, I describe the basic components of a computer system, define the term *operating system*, and explain why UNIX is so successful. I also present UNIX from several different perspectives, ranging from that of a non-programmer to that of an advanced systems programmer.

1

Presentation

To begin with, I describe the main bits and pieces that go to make up a typical computer system. I then show how a special program called an *operating system* is needed to control these pieces effectively, and present a short list of operating system facilities. Following this is a description of the basic UNIX philosophy that acts as a framework for the information presented in the rest of this book. Finally, I present a short history of UNIX and a glimpse of where I believe UNIX is heading.

COMPUTER SYSTEMS

A typical single-user computer system is built out of many parts, including a central processing unit (CPU), memory, disks, a monitor, and a keyboard. Small systems like this may be connected together to form larger computer networks, enabling tasks to be distributed among individual computers. Figure 1.1 is an illustration of such a network.

The hardware that goes to make up a computer network is only half the story; the software that runs on the computers is equally important. Let's take a closer look at the various hardware and software components of a computer system...

THE HARDWARE

Computer systems, whether large or small, multi-user or single-user, expensive or cheap, include most of the following pieces of hardware:

A central processing unit (CPU)

This reads machine code (instructions in a form that a computer can understand) from memory and executes it. A CPU is often likened to the "brain" of a computer.

Random access memory (RAM)

This holds the machine code and data that are accessed by the CPU. RAM normally forgets everything it holds when the power is turned off.

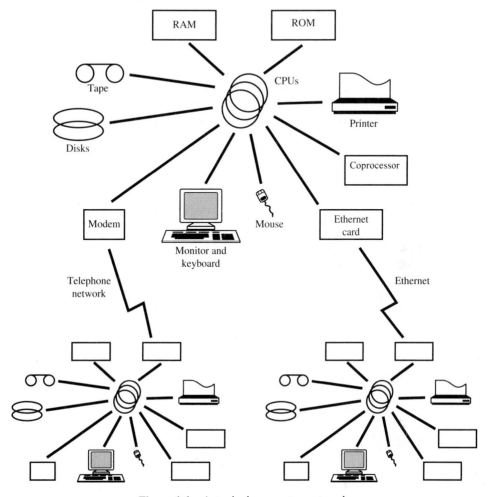

Figure 1.1   A typical computer network

Read only memory (ROM)

This holds both machine code and data. Its contents may not be changed, and are remembered even when the power is turned off.

Disk(s)

These hold large amounts of data and code on a magnetic or optical medium, and remember it all even when the power is turned off. Floppy disks are generally removable, whereas hard disks are not. Hard disks can hold a lot more information than floppy disks.

Monitor(s)

These display information, and come in two flavors: monochrome and color.

Graphics card(s)

These allow the CPU to display information on a monitor. Some graphics cards can display characters only, whereas others support graphics.

Keyboard

This allows a user to enter alphanumeric information. There are several different kinds of keyboards available, depending partly on the language of the user. For example, Japanese keyboards are much larger than Western keyboards, as their alphabet is much larger. The Western keyboards are often referred to as QWERTY keyboards, as these are the first six letters on the upper left-hand side of the keyboard.

Mouse

This allows a user to position things easily on the screen by short movements of the hand. Most mice have "tails" that connect them to the computer, but some have radio connections that make the tail unnecessary. I recommend "radio mice" to anyone who has a cat, as cats tend to get tangled up with a mouse very easily.

Printer(s)

These allow a user to obtain hard copies of information. Some printers print characters only, whereas others may print graphics.

Tape(s)

These are generally used for making backup copies of information stored on disks. They are slower than disks, but store large amounts of data in a fairly cheap way.

Math coprocessor

These are special add-on chips that are designed to speed up mathematical operations. Most computer systems allow a math coprocessor to be added as an option.

Modem

A modem allows you to communicate with other machines across a telephone line. Different modems allow different rates of communication. Some modems even correct for errors that occur due to a poor telephone connection.

Ethernet interface

An Ethernet is a medium (typically some wires) that allows computers to communicate at high speeds. Computers attach to an Ethernet by a special piece of hardware called an *Ethernet interface*.

Other peripherals

There are many other kinds of peripherals that computer systems can support, including graphics tablets, hand scanners, array processors, MIDI cards (**M**usical **I**nstrument **D**igital **I**nterface[1]), voice recognition cards, and synthesizers (to name a few).

You cannot just connect these pieces of hardware together and have a working computer system - you must also have some software that controls and coordinates it all. The ability to share peripherals, to share memory, to communicate between machines, and to run more than one program at a time is made possible by a special kind of program called an *operating system*. You may think of an operating system as being a ''super program'' that allows all of the other programs to operate. Let's take a closer look at operating systems...

OPERATING SYSTEMS

As you've already seen, a computer system can't function without an operating system. There are many different operating systems that are available for PCs, minicomputers, and mainframes, the most common ones being DOS, OS/2, VMS, MVS, MacOS and UNIX. DOS and OS/2 are only available for PCs, VMS is only available for minis and mainframes, and UNIX is available on all platforms. This is one of the first good things about UNIX - it's available on just about any machine. Of the operating systems listed above, only UNIX and VMS allow more than one user to use the computer system at a time, which is an obvious requirement for business systems. Many businesses buy a powerful minicomputer with twenty or more terminals and then use UNIX as the operating system that shares the CPUs, memory, and disks among the users. If we assume that we pick UNIX

[1] I'm a keyboard fan, and own both a Korg M1 and a Roland D-70.

as the operating system for our computer system, what can we do with it? Let's take a look now at the software side of things.

THE SOFTWARE

One way to describe the hardware of a computer system is that it provides a framework for executing programs and storing files. The kinds of programs that run on UNIX platforms vary widely in size and complexity, but tend to share certain common characteristics. Here is a list of useful facts concerning UNIX programs and files:

- A *file* is a collection of data that is usually stored on disk, although some files are stored on tape. UNIX treats peripherals as special files, so that terminals, printers, and other devices are accessible in the same way as disk-based files.
- A *program* is a collection of bytes representing code and data that are stored in a file.
- When a program is started, it is loaded from disk into RAM (actually, only parts of it are loaded, but we'll come to that later). When a program is running it is called a *process*.
- Most processes read and write data from files.
- Processes and files have an *owner*, and may be protected against unauthorized access.
- UNIX supports a hierarchical directory structure.
- Files and processes have a "location" within the directory hierarchy. A process may change its own location and/or the location of a file.
- UNIX provides services for the creation, modification, and destruction of both programs, processes, and files.

Here is an illustration of a tiny UNIX directory hierarchy that contains four files and a process running the "sort" utility:

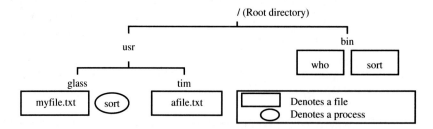

Figure 1.2 Directory hierarchy

SHARING RESOURCES

Another operating system function that UNIX provides is the sharing of limited resources among competing processes. Limited resources in a typical computer system include CPUs, memory, disk space, and peripherals such as printers. Here is a brief outline of how these resources are shared:

- UNIX shares *CPUs* among processes by dividing each second of CPU time into equal-sized "slices" (typically 1/10 second) and then allocating them to processes based on a priority scheme. Important processes are allocated more slices than others.
- UNIX shares *memory* among processes by dividing RAM up into thousands of equal-sized "pages" of memory, and then allocating them to processes based on a priority scheme. Only those portions of a process that actually need to be in RAM are ever loaded from disk. Pages of RAM that are not accessed for a while are saved back to disk so that the memory may be reallocated to other processes.
- UNIX shares *disk space* among users by dividing up the disks into thousands of equal-sized "blocks" and then allocating them to users based on a quota system. A single file is built out of one or more blocks.

Chapter 11 contains more details on how these sharing mechanisms are implemented. We've now looked at every major role that UNIX plays as an operating system except one - as a medium for communication.

COMMUNICATION

The components of a computer system cannot achieve very much when they work in isolation:

- A process may need to talk to a graphics card to display output.
- A process may need to talk to a keyboard to get input.
- A network mail system needs to talk to other computers to send and receive mail.
- Two processes need to talk to each other in order to collaborate on a single problem.

UNIX provides several different ways for processes and peripherals to talk to each other, depending on the type and the speed of the communication. For example, one way that a process can talk to another process is via an interprocess communication mechanism called a "pipe." A pipe is a one-way medium-speed data channel that allows two processes on the same machine to talk. If the processes are on different machines connected by a network, then a mechanism called a "socket" may be used instead. A socket is a two-way high-speed data channel.

It is becoming quite common nowadays for different pieces of a problem to be tackled by different processes on different machines. For example, there is a graphics system called X Windows that works by using something termed a "client-server" model. One computer (the X "server") is used to control a graphics terminal and to draw the various lines, circles, and windows, while another computer (the X "client") generates the data that is to be displayed. Arrangements like this are examples of distributed processing, where the burden of computation is spread among many computers. In fact, a single X server may service many X clients. Here's an illustration of an X-based system:

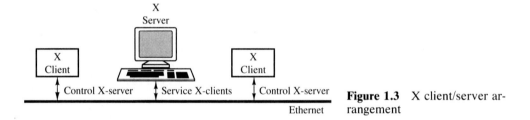

Figure 1.3   X client/server arrangement

For more information on X Windows, consult [10].

UTILITIES

Even the most powerful operating system isn't worth too much to the average user unless there is a good chunk of useful software that is available for it. Due to the relatively old age of UNIX and its perceived market value, there is no shortage of good utilities. Standard UNIX comes complete with at least two hundred small utility programs, including (usually) a couple of editors, a C compiler, a sorting utility, a graphical user interface, some shells, and some text processing tools. Popular packages like spreadsheets, compilers, and desktop publishing tools are also commercially available. There is also plenty of free software that is available from computer sites all over the world via the expansive UNIX networks described in Chapter 8.

PROGRAMMER SUPPORT

UNIX caters very well to programmers. It is an example of an "open" system, which means that the internal software architecture is well documented and available in source code form for a relatively small fee. The features of UNIX such as parallel processing, interprocess communication, and file handling are all easily accessible from a programming language such as C via a set of library routines known as "system calls." Many facilities that were difficult to use on older operating systems are now within the reach of every systems programmer.

STANDARDS

UNIX is a fairly standard operating system, with two main versions that are slowly merging into one. As you'll see shortly, UNIX was created in AT&T's Bell Labs, and evolved from that genesis into what is currently known as "System V" UNIX. The University of California at Berkeley obtained a copy of UNIX early on in its development and spawned another major version, known as BSD UNIX. Both System V and BSD UNIX have their own strengths and weaknesses, as well as a large amount of commonality. Two consortiums of leading computer manufacturers have gathered behind these two versions of UNIX, each believing its own version to be the best. "UNIX International," headed by AT&T and Sun, are backing the latest version of System V UNIX, called System V.4.1. The "Open Software Foundation" (OSF), headed by IBM, Digital Equipment Corporation, and Hewlett-Packard, are constructing the successor to BSD UNIX called OSF/1. Both groups are attempting to comply with a set of standards set by the POSIX (Portable Operating System Interface) committee and other such organizations. It is therefore likely that UNIX will be driven by market pressure to evolve toward a single common standard. UNIX is mostly written in the C language, which makes it relatively easy to port to different platforms. This is an important benefit, and has contributed a great deal to the proliferation and success of UNIX.

LIST OF UNIX FEATURES (A RECAP)

Here is a recap of the features that UNIX provides:

- It allows many users to access a computer system at the same time.
- It supports the creation, modification, and destruction of programs, processes, and files.

- It provides a directory hierarchy that gives a location to processes and files.
- It shares CPUs, memory, and disk space in a fair and efficient manner between competing processes.
- It allows processes and peripherals to talk to each other, even if they're on different machines.
- It comes complete with a large number of standard utilities.
- There are plenty of high-quality commercially available software packages.
- It allows programmers to easily access operating features via a well-defined set of system calls, which are analogous to library routines.
- It is a portable operating system, and thus available on a wide variety of platforms.

Now that we've covered the main features of UNIX, it's time to examine some of the philosophies behind UNIX and explore both its past and its future.

UNIX PHILOSOPHIES

The original UNIX system was lean and mean. It had a very small number of utilities and no network functionality. The original designers of UNIX had some pretty strong notions about how utilities should be written, and built a special mechanism called a "pipe" into the heart of UNIX to support their vision. A pipe allows a user to specify that the output of one process is to be used as the input to another process. Two or more processes may be connected in this fashion, resulting in a "pipeline" of data flowing from the first process through to the last:

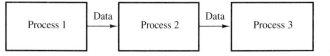

Figure 1.4 A pipeline

The nice thing about pipelines is that many problems can be solved by such an arrangement of processes. Each process in the pipeline performs a set of operations upon the data and then passes the results on to the next process for further processing. For example, imagine that you wish to obtain a sorted list of all the users on the UNIX system. There is a utility called **who** that outputs an unsorted list of the users, and another utility called **sort** that outputs a sorted version of its input. These two utilities may be connected together with a pipe so that the output from **who** passes directly into **sort**, resulting in a sorted list of users:

Figure 1.5 A pipeline that sorts

This is a more powerful approach to solving problems than writing a fresh program from scratch every time.

The UNIX philosophy for solving problems can be stated thus:

- If you can solve the problem by using utilities and pipes, do it; *otherwise*
- ... ask people on the network if they know how to solve it. If they do, great; *otherwise*
- ... if you could solve the problem with the aid of some other hand-written utilities, write the utilities yourself and add them into the UNIX repertoire. Design each utility to do one thing well and one thing only, so that each may be reused to solve other problems. If more utilities won't do the trick
- ... write a program to solve the problem (typically in C or C++.)

Inside UNIX is hidden another more subtle philosophy that is slowly eroding. The original system was designed by guys who liked to have the power to access data or code anywhere in the system, regardless of who owns it. To support this notion, they built the concept of a "super-user" into UNIX, which meant that certain privileged individuals could have special access rights. For example, the system administrator of a UNIX system always has the capability of becoming a super-user so that he/she may perform clean-up tasks such as terminating rogue processes or removing unwanted users from the system. The concept of super-user has security implications that are a little frightening. Anyone with the right password could potentially wipe out an entire system, or extract top-security data with relative ease. Some of the research versions of UNIX do away entirely with the super-user concept, and instead subdivide privileged tasks among several different "slightly super" users.

UNIX YESTERDAY

The first version of UNIX was built by a computer scientist called Ken Thompson at Bell Labs. Ken was interested in building a video game called "Space Wars," which required a fairly fast response time. The operating system that he was using, "MULTICS," didn't give him the performance that he needed, so he decided to build his own operating system. He called it UNIX because the "UNI" part of the name implied that it would do one thing well, as opposed to the "MULTI" part of the "MULTICS" name, which he felt tried to do many things without much success. He wrote it in assembly language, and the first version was very primitive; it was only a single-user system, it had no network capability, and it had a poor memory management system for sharing memory between processes. However, it was efficient, compact, and fast, which was exactly what he wanted.

A few years later, a colleague named Dennis Ritchie suggested that they rewrite UNIX using the C language, which Dennis had recently developed from a language called B. The idea that an operating system could be written in a high-level language was an unusual approach at that time, since most people felt that assembly language was the only language fast enough for such an important component of a computer system. Fortunately, C was slick enough that the conversion was successful, and the UNIX system suddenly had a huge advantage over other operating systems - its source code was understandable. Only a small percentage of the original source code remained in assembly language, which meant that porting the operating system to a different machine was quite easy. As long as the target machine had a C compiler, most of the operating system would work with no changes; only the assembly language component had to be hand-translated.

Bell Labs started using this prototype version of UNIX in its patent department, primarily for text processing, and a number of UNIX utilities that are found in modern UNIX systems were originally designed during this time period. Examples of these utilities are **nroff** and **troff**. Bell Labs allowed universities to obtain a free copy of the UNIX source code, hoping that enterprising students would enhance the system and further its progress into the marketplace. Indeed, graduate students at the University of California at Berkeley took the task to heart and made some huge improvements over the years, including the first good memory management system and the first networking capability. The University started to market its own version of UNIX, called BSD UNIX, to the general public. The differences in the implementation of the Bell Labs UNIX and the BSD UNIX remain to this day.

UNIX TODAY

The currently available versions include offerings from AT&T, Apple®, IBM®, HP, DEC®, Sun, and Apollo. The older versions of UNIX are derived from either System V or BSD 4.3, whereas the newer versions tend to contain features from both. Here is an abbreviated genealogy:

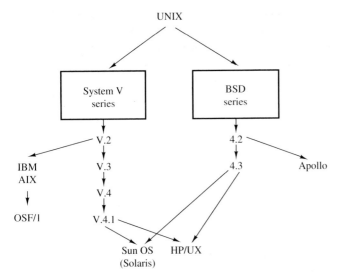

Figure 1.6   An abbreviated UNIX genealogy

For PC users, there are a number of choices that include:

• Sun's Solaris 2.0
• Santa Cruz Operation's SCO UNIX
• Mark Williams Coherent System, a UNIX look-alike

UNIX TOMORROW

It is likely that the future versions of UNIX will follow a philosophy similar to that of the present UNIX systems; for example, the idea that you can build an application from a collection of interconnected utilities. However, there are a couple of global trends that it may not be able to keep up with:

Parallel distributed processing

Solving big problems requires a lot of processing power, and the way to achieve this power is not just to make individual CPUs faster, but to split up the problem so that many CPUs may be used to solve the different pieces. Efficient parallel distributed systems must support rapid communication between a large number of CPUs in a single coherent network. Even in massively parallel architectures, there will still be more processes than CPUs, so it helps if each CPU can switch between runnable processes at a fast rate. Traditional programmers on UNIX systems tend to break a problem down into a few medium-sized pieces, each of which is solved by a program. Research techniques for solving problems using the parallel distributed approach tend to break down the problem into large numbers of very small pieces, each of which is solved by a single function. Current UNIX implementations do not support the parallel execution of single functions very well, and so are not good candidates for this kind of approach to problem solving.

Object-oriented programming

Object-oriented programming (OOP) is currently taking industry by storm, as it allows small groups of programmers to tackle much large projects with greater reuse of code, smaller executable size, and easier maintenance of the overall system. Operating systems that support the next wave of OOP will be required to support the following facilities:

- transparent access to objects stored across networks
- persistent objects
- fast message passing between CPUs

These kind of facilities tend to be ones that are built into the core design of an operating system, rather than being added on later, which is why UNIX might have a bit of a problem handling future OOP trends.

THE REST OF THIS BOOK

As you can probably tell by now, UNIX is a fairly substantial topic, and can only be properly digested in small portions. In order to aid this process, and to allow individual readers to focus on the subjects that they find most applicable, I decided to write this book's chapters based on the different kinds of UNIX user. These users tend to fall into one of several categories:

- *Non-Programmers,* who occasionally want to perform simple tasks like sending and receiving electronic mail, use a spreadsheet, or do some word processing.
- *Shell Users,* who use background processing and write small scripts from within a convenient interface.
- *Advanced Non-Programmers,* who use more complex facilities like file encryption, stream editors, and file processing.
- *Advanced Shell Users,* who write programs in a high-level shell language (a little like JCL) for performing useful tasks such as automatic backups, monitoring disk usage, and performing software installations.

- *Programmers,* who write programs in a general-purpose language such as C for speed and efficiency.
- *System Programmers,* who write programs that require a good knowledge of the underlying computer system, including network communications and advanced file access.
- *System Architects,* who invent better computer systems. These people provide a vision and a framework for the future.
- *System Administrators,* who make sure that the computer system runs smoothly and that the users are generally satisfied.

To begin with, read the chapters that interest you the most. Then go back and fill in the gaps when you have the time. If you're unsure of which chapters are most appropriate for your skill level, read the introductory section "About This Book" for some hints.

CHAPTER REVIEW

Checklist

In this chapter, I mentioned:

- the main hardware components of a computer system
- the purpose of an operating system
- the meaning of the terms *program, process,* and *file*
- the layout of a hierarchical directory structure
- that UNIX shares CPUs, memory, and disk space among competing processes
- that UNIX supports communication between processes and peripherals
- that UNIX comes complete with a multitude of standard utilities
- that most major software packages are available on UNIX systems
- that UNIX is an "open" system
- that UNIX has a rosy future

Quiz

1. What are the two main versions of UNIX, and how did each begin?
2. Write down five main functions of an operating system.
3. What is the difference between a *process* and a *program*?

4. What is the UNIX philosophy?
5. Who created UNIX?
6. What makes UNIX an "open" system?

Projects

1. Investigate the MULTICS system and find the similarities and differences between it and the UNIX system. [level: *medium*]
2. Obtain a list of the other currently popular operating systems and determine whether any of them could be serious contenders to UNIX. [level: *medium*]

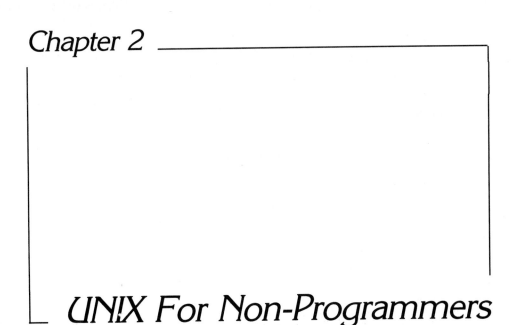

Chapter 2

UNIX For Non-Programmers

Motivation

This section contains the absolute basics that you really need to know in order to be able to do anything useful with UNIX.

Prerequisites

In order to understand this chapter, you must have already read chapter 1. It also helps if you have access to a UNIX system so that you can try out the various UNIX features that I discuss.

Objectives

In this chapter, I'll show you how to log on and off a UNIX system, how to change your password, how to get online help when you're stuck, how to stop a program, and how to use the file system. I'll also introduce you to the mail system so that you can enter the world of computer networking.

Presentation

The information in this section is presented in the form of a couple of sample UNIX sessions. If you don't have access to a UNIX account, march through the sessions anyway and try them out later.

Utilities

This section introduces the following utilities, listed in alphabetical order:

cat	lpr	rm
chgrp	lprm	rmdir
chmod	ls	stty
chown	mail	tail
clear	man	tset
cp	mkdir	vi
date	more	wc
emacs	mv	
file	newgrp	
groups	page	
head	passwd	
lpq	pwd	

Shell command

This section introduces the following shell command:

cd

OBTAINING AN ACCOUNT

This is the tricky part. If you're a student, the best way to get access to a UNIX account is to enroll in a UNIX course or beg one from a professor. If you're a professional, it's likely that your company already has some UNIX facilities, in which case it's a matter of contacting either the training staff or a suitable manager. If you have a little cash and a PC, you can buy a UNIX look-alike system called "Coherent" from a company called Mark Williams for about $100. It's a reasonable system to learn on, although it lacks some of the more advanced features. If you have more cash, you could buy a PC-oriented UNIX from a company like the Santa Cruz Operation, which markets a very nice version of UNIX called SCO UNIX. The good thing about having your own version of

UNIX is that you can be a super-user, since you're the one who owns the system. Most companies won't let a non-guru *near* the super-user password.

LOGGING IN

In order to use a UNIX system, you must first "log in" with a suitable "user id." A user id is a unique name that distinguishes you from the other users of the system. For example, my own user id is "glass." Your user id and initial password are assigned to you by the system administrator, or set to something standard if you bought your own UNIX system. It's sometimes necessary to press the *Enter* key (also known as the *Return* key) a couple of times to make the system give you a login prompt. This effectively tells UNIX that "somebody's waiting to log in." UNIX first asks you for your user id by prompting you with the line "login:," and then asks for your password. When you enter your password, the letters that you type are not displayed on your terminal for security reasons. UNIX is case sensitive, so make sure that the case of the letters is matched exactly. Depending on how your system is set up, you should then see either a $ or a % prompt. Here's an example login:

```
SunOS UNIX

login: glass
Password: ...what I typed here is secret and doesn't show.
SunOS Release 4.1.1 (GENERIC) #1: Sat Oct 13 06:05:48 PDT 1990

$ _
```

It's quite common for the system to immediately ask you which kind of terminal you're using. This is so that it can set special characters like the backspace and cursor movement keys to their correct values. You are usually allowed to press the *Enter* key for the default terminal setting, and I suggest that you do this when you log in for the first time. I'll show you later how to change the terminal type if necessary. Other possible events that might occur when you log in are:

- A help system recognizes that you're a first-time user and asks you whether you'd like a guided tour of UNIX.
- The "news of the day" messages are displayed to your screen, informing you of scheduled maintenance times and other useful information.

Here's an example of a slightly more complex login sequence that asked me what my terminal type was. I pressed the *Enter* key to select the default terminal type, a "vt100":

```
SunOS UNIX

login: glass
Password:              ...secret.
SunOS Release 4.1.1 (GENERIC) #1: Sat Oct 13 07:05:52 PDT 1990
You have mail.      ...the system informs me that I have mail waiting.
Enter your terminal type (default is vt100): ...I pressed Enter.
LOGIN complete      ... go for it!
$ _
```

SHELLS

The $ or % prompt that you see when you first log in is displayed by a special kind of program called a *shell*. A shell is a program that acts as a middleman between you and the raw UNIX operating system. It lets you run programs, build pipelines of processes, save output to files, and run more than one program at the same time. All of the commands that you enter are executed by a shell. The three most popular shells are:

- the Bourne shell
- the Korn shell
- the C shell

All three of these shells share a similar set of core functionality, together with some specialized properties. The Korn shell is a superset of the Bourne shell, and thus users typically choose either the C shell or the Korn shell to work with. I personally favor the Korn shell, as it's easy to program and has the best command line interface. This book contains information on how to use all three shells, separated into four chapters. Chapter 3 describes the core functionality of the three shells and chapters 4 through 6 describe the specialized features of each shell.

Each shell has its own programming language. One reasonable question to ask is: why would you write a program in a shell language rather than a language like C? The answer is that the shell languages are tailored specially for manipulating files and processes in the UNIX system, which makes them more convenient in many situations. In this chapter the only shell facilities that I use are the abilities to run utilities and to save the output of a process to a file. Let's go ahead and run a few simple UNIX utilities...

RUNNING A UTILITY
_____

To run a utility, simply enter its name and press the *Enter* key. From now on, when I mention that you should enter a particular bit of text, I also implicitly mean that you should press the *Enter* key after the text. This tells UNIX that you've entered the command and that you wish it to be executed.

Not all systems have exactly the same utilities, so if a particular example doesn't work, don't be too surprised. I'll try to point out the utilities that vary a lot from system to system. One utility that every system has is called **date**, which displays the current date and time:

```
$ date                                    ... run the date utility.
Thu Nov  7 10:41:50 CST 1991
$ _
```

Whenever I introduce a new utility, I'll write a small synopsis of its typical operation in the format shown below. It's self-explanatory, as you can see. I use a modified-for-UNIX BNF notation for the syntax description, which is fully documented in the appendix. Please note that I do not list every different kind of option or present a particularly detailed description - this is best left to books that focus almost entirely on utilities.

Utility: **date** [*yymmddhhmm* [*.ss*]]

Without any arguments, **date** displays the current date and time. Otherwise, it sets the date to the supplied setting, where *yy* are the last two digits of the year, the first *mm* is the number of the month, *dd* is the number of the day, *hh* is the number of hours (use the 24-hour clock), and the last *mm* is the number of minutes. The optional *ss* is the number of seconds. Only a super-user may set the date.

Another useful utility is **clear**, which clears your screen.

Utility: **clear**

This utility clears your screen.

OBTAINING ONLINE HELP: MAN

There are bound to be many times when you're at your terminal and you can't quite remember how to use a particular utility. Alternatively, you may know what a utility does, but don't remember what it's called. All UNIX systems worth their salt have a utility called **man** (short for manual page), which puts this information at your fingertips. **man** works as follows:

Utility: **man** [*chapter*] *word*
       man -k *keyword*

The manual pages are an online version of the original UNIX documentation, which usually comes as an eight-volume set. They contain information about utilities, system calls, file formats, and shells. When **man** displays help about a given utility, it indicates which chapter the entry is taken from.

    The first usage of **man** displays the manual entry associated with *word*. If no chapter number is specified, the first entry that it finds is displayed. The second usage of **man** displays a list of all the manual entries that contain *keyword*.

There is sometimes more than one manual entry for a particular word. For example, there is a utility called **chmod** and a system call called chmod ( ), and there are manual pages for both. By default, **man** displays the manual pages for the first entry that it finds. In the case that other entries exist, the manual page of the first entry will state: "SEE ALSO..." with the other entries listed, followed by their chapter numbers.

    Here's an example of **man** in action:

```
$ man -k mode        ...search for keyword ''mode''.
chmod (1V)                   - change the permissions mode of a file
chmod, fchmod (2V)           - change mode of file
getty (8)                    - set terminal mode
ieee_flags (3M)              - mode and status function
umask (2V)                   - set file creation mode mask
$ man chmod          ...select the first manual entry.
CHMOD(1V)                USER COMMANDS                        CHMOD (1V)

NAME
     chmod - change the permissions mode of a file
```

```
SYNOPSIS
    chmod [ -fR ] mode filename ...

...the description of chmod goes here.

SEE ALSO
    csh(1), ls(1V), sh(1), chmod(2V), chown(8)
$ man 2 chmod      ...select the manual entry from section 2.
CHMOD(2V)                SYSTEM CALLS                CHMOD(2V)


NAME
    chmod, fchmod - change mode of file

SYNOPSIS
    #include <sys/stat.h>

    int chmod(path, mode)
    char *path;
    mode_t mode;

...the description of chmod () goes here.

SEE ALSO
    chown(2V), open(2V), stat(2V), sticky(8)
$ _
```

SPECIAL CHARACTERS

Some characters are interpreted specially when typed at a UNIX terminal. These characters are sometimes called *metacharacters*, and may be listed by using the **stty** utility with the **all** option. The **stty** utility is discussed fully at the end of this chapter. Here's an example:

```
$ stty all ...obtain a list of terminal metacharacters
erase  kill   werase  rprnt  flush  lnext  susp    intr  quit  stop   eof
^H     ^U     ^W      ^R     ^O     ^V     ^Z/^Y  ^C    ^\    ^S/^Q  ^D
$ _
```

The ^ in front of each letter means that the *Control* key must be pressed at the same time as the letter. The meaning of each option is as follows:

Option	Meaning
erase	Backspace one character.
kill	Erase all of the current line.
werase	Erase the last word.
rprnt	Reprint the line.
flush	Ignore any pending input and reprint the line.
lnext	Don't treat the next character specially.
susp	Suspend the process for a future awakening.
intr	Terminate the foreground job with no core dump.
quit	Terminate the foreground job and generate a core dump.
stop	Stop/restart terminal output.
eof	End-of-input.

Some of these characters won't mean much to you until you read some more chapters of this book, but there are a few worth mentioning immediately: *Control-C, Control-S, Control-Q,* and *Control-D.*

Terminating A Process: Control-C

There are often times when you run a program and then wish to stop it before it's finished. The standard way to do this in UNIX is to press the keyboard sequence *Control-C.* Although there are a few programs that are immune to this form of process termination, most processes are immediately killed, and your shell prompt is returned. Here's an example:

```
$ man chmod
CHMOD(1V)               USER COMMANDS               CHMOD(1V)

NAME
     chmod - change the permissions mode of a file
SYNOPSIS
^C
     ...terminate the job and go back to the shell.
$ _
```

Pausing Output: Control-S/Control-Q

If the output of a process starts to rapidly scroll up the screen, you may pause it by typing *Control-S.* To resume the output, you may either type *Control-S* again or type *Control-Q.* This sequence of control characters is sometimes called XON/XOFF protocol. Here's an example:

```
$ man chmod
CHMOD(1V)                    USER COMMANDS                    CHMOD(1V)


NAME
     chmod - change the permissions mode of a file

^S   ...suspend terminal output.
^Q   ...resume terminal output.

SYNOPSIS
     chmod [ -fR ] mode filename ...

...the rest of the man page is displayed here.

SEE ALSO
     csh(1), ls(1V), sh(1), chmod(2V), chown(8)
$ _
```

End-Of-Input: Control-D

Many UNIX utilities may take their input from either a file or from the keyboard. If you instruct a utility to do the latter, you must tell the utility when the input from the keyboard is finished. To do this, type a *Control-D* on a line of its own after the last line of input. *Control-D* means "end-of-input." For example, the **mail** utility allows you to send mail from the keyboard to a named user:

```
$ mail tim  ...send some mail from the keyboard to my friend tim.
Hi Tim,    ...input is entered from the keyboard.
 I hope you get this piece of mail. How about building a country one
of these days?

- with best wishes from Graham
^D          ...tell the terminal that there's no more input.
$ _
```

The **mail** utility is fully described later in this chapter.

SETTING YOUR PASSWORD: PASSWD

After you first log in to a UNIX system, it's a good idea to change your initial password to something a bit more private. Passwords should generally be at least six letters long, and *should not* be a word from a dictionary or a proper noun. This is because it's quite easy for someone to set up a computer program that runs through all the words in a standard dictionary and tries them as your password. I know this first-hand, as I've had someone break into my account using the very same technique. My password is now something like "GWK145W." Get the idea?

To set your password, use the **passwd** utility, which works as follows:

Utility: **passwd**

passwd allows you to change your password. You are prompted for your old password and then twice for the new one. The new password is stored in an encrypted form in the password file "/etc/passwd."

Here's an example, with the passwords shown. Note that you wouldn't normally be able to see the passwords, as UNIX turns off the keyboard echo when you enter them.

```
$ passwd
Changing password for glass.
Old password: penguin
New password: GWK145W
Retype new password: GWK145W
Password changed
$ _
```

If you forget your password, the only thing to do is to contact your system administrator and ask for a new password.

LOGGING OUT

To leave the UNIX system, type the keyboard sequence *Control-D* at your shell prompt. This tells your login shell that there is no more input for it to process, causing it to disconnect you from the UNIX system. Most systems then display a "login:" prompt and wait for another user to log in. Here's an example:

```
$ ^D      ...I'm done!

SunOS UNIX

login:    ...wait for another user to log in.
```

Congratulations! You've now seen how you can log into a UNIX system, execute a few simple utilities, change your password, and then log out. In the next few sections I'll describe some more utilities that allow you to explore the directory hierarchy and manipulate files.

POETRY IN MOTION: EXPLORING THE FILE SYSTEM

I decided that the best way to illustrate some common UNIX utilities was to describe a session that used them in a natural fashion. One of my hobbies is to compose music, and I often use the UNIX system to write lyrics for my songs. The next few sections of this chapter are a running commentary on the UNIX utilities that I used to create a final version of one of my song's lyrics, called "Heart To Heart." Here is the approximate series of events that took place, together with the utility that I used at each stage:

Action	Utility
I displayed my current working directory.	pwd
I wrote the first draft and stored it in a file called "heart."	cat
I listed the directory contents to see the size of the file.	ls
I displayed the "heart" file using several utilities.	cat, more, page, head, tail
I renamed the first draft "heart.ver1."	mv
I made a directory called "lyrics" to store the first draft.	mkdir
I moved "heart.ver1" into the "lyrics" directory.	mv
I made a copy of "heart.ver1" called "heart.ver2."	cp
I edited the "heart.ver2" file.	vi
I moved back to my home directory.	cd
I made a directory called "lyrics.final."	mkdir
I renamed the "lyrics" directory to "lyrics.draft."	mv
I copied the "heart.ver5" file from "lyrics.draft" to "lyrics.final," renaming it "heart.final."	cp
I removed all the files from the "lyrics.draft" directory.	rm
I removed the "lyrics.draft" directory.	rmdir
I moved into the "lyrics.final" directory.	cd
I printed the "heart.final" file.	lpr
I counted the words in "heart.final."	wc
I listed the file attributes of "heart.final."	ls
I looked at the file type of "heart.final."	file
I obtained a list of my groups.	groups
I changed the group of "heart.final."	chgrp
I changed the permissions of "heart.final."	chmod

PRINTING YOUR SHELL'S CURRENT WORKING DIRECTORY: PWD

Every UNIX process has a location in the directory hierarchy, termed its *current working directory*. When you log into a UNIX system, your shell starts off in a particular directory called your "home directory." In general, every user has a different home directory, which often begins with the prefix "/usr." For example, my own home directory is called "/usr/glass." These home directory values are assigned by the system administrator. To display your shell's current working directory, use the **pwd** utility, which works like this:

Utility: **pwd**

Prints the current working directory.

To illustrate this utility, here's what happened when I logged into UNIX to start work on my song's lyrics:

```
SunOS UNIX

login: glass
Password: ...secret.

$ pwd
/usr/glass
$ _
```

Here's a diagram that indicates the location of my login Korn shell in the directory hierarchy:

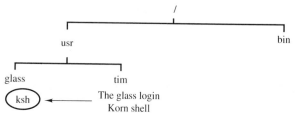

Figure 2.1 The login shell starts at the user's home directory

ABSOLUTE AND RELATIVE PATHNAMES

Before I continue with the sample UNIX session, it's important to introduce you to the idea of *pathnames*.

Two files in the same directory may not have the same name, although it's perfectly OK for several files in *different* directories to have the same name. For example, here's a small hierarchy that contains a "ksh" process and three files called "myFile":

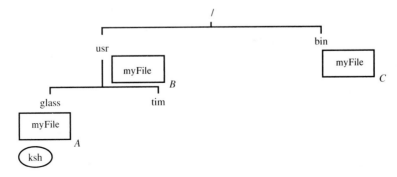

Figure 2.2   Different files may have the same name

Although these files have the same name, they may be unambiguously specified by their *pathname* relative to "/", the root of the directory hierarchy. A pathname is a sequence of directory names that lead you through the hierarchy from a starting directory to a target file. A pathname relative to the root directory is often termed an *absolute* or *full* pathname. Here are the absolute pathnames of the "A," "B," and "C" instances of "myFile":

File	Absolute PathName
A	/usr/glass/myFile
B	/usr/myFile
C	/bin/myFile

A process may also unambiguously specify a file by using a pathname *relative* to its current working directory. The UNIX file system supports the following special fields that may be used when supplying a relative pathname:

Field	Meaning
.	current directory
..	parent directory

For example, here are the pathnames of the three instances of "myFile" relative to the "ksh" process located in the "/usr/glass" directory:

File	Relative PathName
A	myFile
B	../myFile
C	../../bin/myFile

Note that the pathname "myFile" is equivalent to "./myFile," although the second form is rarely used because the leading "." is redundant.

CREATING A FILE

I already had an idea of what the first draft of my song's lyrics would look like, so I decided to store them in a file called "heart." Ordinarily, I would use a UNIX editor such as **vi** or **emacs** to create the file, but this is a beginner's chapter, so I used a simpler utility called **cat** to achieve the same result. Here's how **cat** works:

Utility: **cat** -n { *fileName* }*

The **cat** utility takes its input from standard input or from a list of files and displays them to standard output. The **-n** option adds line numbers to the output. **cat** is short for "catenate," which means "to connect in a series of links."

By default, the standard input of a process is the keyboard and the standard output is the screen. We can send the standard output of a process to a file instead of the screen by making use of a shell facility called *output redirection*. If you follow a command by a > character and the name of a file, the output from the command is saved to the file. If the file doesn't already exist, it is created; otherwise, its previous contents are overwritten. Right now, use this feature without worrying how it works; chapter 3 explains it all in detail. To create the first draft of my lyrics, I entered the following text at the shell prompt:

```
$ cat > heart    ...store keyboard input into a file called ''heart''.
I hear her breathing,
I'm surrounded by the sound.
```

```
$ cat heart                    ...list the contents of the "heart" file.
I hear her breathing,
I'm surrounded by the sound.
Floating in this secret place,
I never shall be found.
$ _
```

cat can actually take any number of files as arguments, in which case they are listed together, one following the other. **cat** is good for listing small files, but doesn't pause between full screens of output. The **more** and **page** utilities are better suited for larger files, and contain advanced facilities such as the ability to scroll backward through a file. Here are some notes on each utility:

Utility: **more** -f [+*lineNumber*] { *fileName* }*

The **more** utility allows you to scroll through a list of files, one page at a time. By default, each file is displayed starting at line 1, although the + option may be used to specify the starting line number. The **-f** option tells **more** not to fold long lines. After each page is displayed, **more** displays the message ''-- More --'' to indicate that it's waiting for a command. To list the next page, press the space bar. To list the next line, press the *Enter* key. To quit from **more,** press the **q** key. To obtain help on the multitude of other commands, press the **h** key.

Utility: **page** -f [+*lineNumber*] { *fileName* }*

The **page** utility works just like **more** except that it clears the screen before displaying each page. This sometimes makes the listing a little quicker.

While we're on the topic of listing files, there are a couple of handy utilities called **head** and **tail** that allow you to peek at the start and end of a file respectively. Here's how they work:

Utility: **head** -n { *fileName* }*

The **head** utility displays the first *n* lines of a file. If *n* is not specified, it defaults to 10. If more than one file is specified, a small header identifying each file is displayed before its contents.

Utility: **tail** -n { *fileName* }*

The **tail** utility displays the last *n* lines of a file. If *n* is not specified, it defaults to 10. If more than one file is specified, a small header identifying each file is displayed before its contents.

In the following example, I displayed the first two lines and last two lines of my "heart" file:

```
$ head -2 heart              ...list the first two lines of "heart."
I hear her breathing,
I'm surrounded by the sound.
$ tail -2 heart              ...list the last two lines of "heart."
Floating in this secret place,
I never shall be found.
$ _
```

RENAMING A FILE: mv

Now that I'd created the first draft of my lyrics, I wanted to create a few more experimental versions. To indicate that the file "heart" was really the first generation of many versions to come, I decided to rename it "heart.ver1" by using the **mv** utility, which works as follows:

Utility: **mv** [-] -i *oldFileName newFileName*
          mv [-] -i { *fileName* }* *directoryName*
          mv [-] -i *oldDirectoryName newDirectoryName*

The first form of **mv** renames *oldFileName* as *newFileName*. If the label *newFileName* already exists, it is replaced. The second form allows you to move a collection of files to a directory, and the third form allows you to move an entire directory. None of these options actually moves the physical contents of a file; instead, they all just move labels around the hierarchy. **mv** is therefore a very fast utility. The **-i** option prompts you for confirmation if *newFileName* already exists. The - option tells **mv** to treat all of the following arguments as filenames, which is handy if the name of a file starts with a minus sign.

Here's how I renamed the file using the first form of the **mv** utility:

```
$ mv heart heart.ver1    ...rename "heart" to "heart.ver1".
$ ls
heart.ver1
$ _
```

The second and third forms of the **mv** utility are illustrated later in this chapter.

MAKING A DIRECTORY: mkdir

Rather than clog up my home directory with the many versions of "heart," I decided to create a subdirectory called "lyrics" in which to keep them all. To do this, I used the **mkdir** utility, which works like this:

Utility: **mkdir** [-p] *newDirectoryName*

The **mkdir** utility creates a directory. The **-p** option creates any parent directories in the *newDirectoryName* pathname that do not already exist. If *newDirectoryName* already exists, an error message is displayed and the existing file is not altered in any way.

Here's how I did it:

```
$ mkdir lyrics        ...create a directory called "lyrics".
$ ls -lF              ...confirm.
-rw-r--r-- 1 glass      106  Jan 30 23:28       heart.ver1
drwxr-xr-x 2 glass      512  Jan 30 19:49       lyrics/
$ _
```

The letter "d" at the start of the permission flags of "lyrics" indicates that it's a directory file.

In general, you should keep related files in their own separate directory. If you name your directories sensibly, it'll make it easy to track down files weeks, or even years after you create them.

Once the "lyrics" directory was created, the next step was to move the "heart.ver1" into its new location. To do this, I used mv, and confirmed the operation using **ls**:

```
$ mv heart.ver1 lyrics     ...move "heart.ver1" into "lyrics"
$ ls                       ...list the current directory.
lyrics/                    ..."heart.ver1" has gone.
$ ls lyrics                ...list the "lyrics" subdirectory.
heart.ver1                 ..."heart.ver1" has moved.
$ _
```

MOVING TO A DIRECTORY: cd

Although I could remain in my home directory and access the various versions of my lyric files by preceding them with the prefix "lyrics/," this would be rather inconvenient. For example, to edit the file "heart.ver1" with the UNIX **vi** editor, I'd have to do the following:

```
$ vi lyrics/heart.ver1  ... invoke the vi editor.
```

In general, it's a good idea to move your shell into a directory if you intend to do a lot of work there. To do this, use the *cd* command. *cd* isn't actually a UNIX utility, but instead is an example of a shell built-in command. Your shell recognizes it as a special keyword and executes it directly. Notice that I write shell commands using italics, in adherence to the nomenclature that I described at the start of this book. Here's how *cd* works:

Shell Command: **cd** [*directoryName*]

The *cd* shell command changes a shell's current working directory to be *directoryName*. If the *directoryName* argument is omitted, the shell is moved to its owner's home directory.

The following example shows how I moved into the "lyrics" directory and confirmed my new location using **pwd**:

```
$ pwd                 ...display where I am.
/usr/glass
$ cd lyrics           ...move into the "lyrics" directory.
$ pwd                 ...display where I'm at now.
/usr/glass/lyrics
$ _
```

Here's an illustration of the shell movement caused by the previous *cd* command:

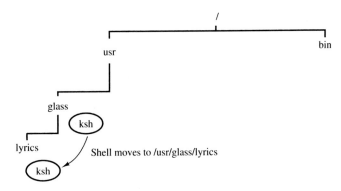

Figure 2.3   cd moves a shell

Since "." and ".." refer to your shell's current working directory and parent directory, respectively, you may move up one directory level by typing "cd ..". Here's an example:

```
$ pwd          ...display where I'm at.
/usr/glass/lyrics
$ cd ..         ...move up one level.
$ pwd          ...display where I'm at now.
/usr/glass
$ _
```

COPYING A FILE: cp

After moving into the "lyrics" directory, I decided to work on a second version of my lyrics. I wanted to keep the first version for posterity, so I copied "heart.ver1" into a new file called "heart.ver2" and then edited the new file. To copy the file I used the **cp** utility, which works as follows:

Utility: **cp** -i *oldFileName newFileName*
       cp -ir { *fileName* }* *directoryName*

The first form of **cp** copies *oldFileName* to *newFileName*. If the label *new-FileName* already exists, it is replaced. The **-i** option prompts you for confirmation if *newFileName* already exists. The second form of **cp** copies a list of files into *directoryName*. The **-r** option causes any source files that are directories to be recursively copied, thus copying the entire directory structure.

cp actually does two things:

- It makes a physical copy of the original file's contents.
- It creates a new label in the directory hierarchy that points to the copied file.

The copy of the original file can therefore be edited, removed, and otherwise manipulated without having any effect on the original file. Here's how I copied the "heart.ver1" file:

```
$ cp heart.ver1 heart.ver2      ...copy "heart.ver1" to "heart.ver2".
$ ls -l heart.ver1 heart.ver2 ...confirm.
-rw-r--r-- 1      glass        106   Jan 30  23:28       heart.ver1
-rw-r--r-- 1      glass        106   Jan 31  00:12       heart.ver2
$ _
```

EDITING A FILE: vi

At this point, I edited the "heart.ver2" file using a UNIX editor called **vi**. The way that the **vi** editor works is described later in this chapter, together with information about another editor called **emacs**. For the time being, assume that I edited "heart.ver2" to look like this:

```
$ vi heart.ver2                         ...edit the file.
... editing session takes place here.
$ cat heart.ver2                        ...list the file.
I hear her breathing,
I'm surrounded by the sound.
Floating in this secret place,
I never shall be found.

She pushed me into the daylight,
I had to leave my home.
But I am a survivor,
And I'll make it on my own.
$ _
```

After creating five versions of my song's lyrics, my work was done. I moved back to my home directory and created a subdirectory called "lyrics.final" in which to store the final version of my lyrics. I also renamed the original "lyrics" directory to "lyrics.draft," which I felt was a better name.

```
$ cd                      ...move back to my home directory.
$ mkdir lyrics.final      ...make the final lyrics directory.
$ mv lyrics lyrics.draft  ...rename the old lyrics directory.
$ _
```

The final version of my lyrics was stored in a file called "heart.ver5" in the "lyrics.draft" directory, which I then copied into a file called "heart.final" in the "lyrics.final" directory:

```
$ cp lyrics.draft/heart.ver5 lyrics.final/heart.final
$ _
```

DELETING A DIRECTORY: rmdir

Although posterity is a good reason for keeping old things around, it can interfere with your disk usage in a multi-user system. I therefore decided to remove the "lyrics.draft" directory to avoid exceeding my modest disk quota. Before I removed it, I archived its contents using the **cpio** utility, which is described in chapter 7. To remove the directory, I used the **rmdir** utility, which works like this:

Utility: **rmdir** { *directoryName* }+

The **rmdir** utility removes all of the directories in the list of directory names. A directory must be empty before it can be removed. To recursively remove a directory and all of its contents, use the **rm** utility with the **-r** option (described shortly).

I tried to remove the "lyrics.draft" directory while it still contained the draft versions, and received the following error message:

```
$ rmdir lyrics.draft
rmdir: lyrics.draft: Directory not empty
$ _
```

To remove the files from the "lyrics.draft" directory, I made use of the **rm** utility, described next.

DELETING A FILE: rm

The **rm** utility allows you to remove a file's label from the hierarchy. When no more labels reference a file, UNIX removes the file itself. In most cases, every file only has one label, so the act of removing the label causes the file's physical contents to be deallocated. However, in chapter 7 I'll show you some occasions where a single file has more than one label. In these cases, a label may be removed without affecting the file that it refers to. Here's a description of **rm**:

Utility: **rm** [-] -fir { *fileName* } *

The **rm** utility removes a file's label from the directory hierarchy. If the filename doesn't exist, an error message is displayed. The **-i** option prompts the user for confirmation before deleting a filename; press **y** to confirm, and **n** otherwise. If *fileName* is a directory, the **-r** option causes all of its contents, including subdirectories, to be recursively deleted. The **-f** option inhibits all error messages and prompts. The **-** option causes all tokens that follow to be treated as filenames, which is handy if a filename begins with a dash.

To remove every file in the "lyrics.draft" directory, I moved into the "lyrics.draft" directory and used **rm**:

```
$ cd lyrics.draft         ...move to the "lyrics.draft" directory.
$ rm heart.ver1 heart.ver2 heart.ver3 heart.ver4 heart.ver5
$ ls                      ...nothing remains.
$ _
```

Now that all the files were erased, I moved back to my home directory and erased the draft directory:

```
$ cd                   ...move to my home directory.
$ rmdir lyrics.draft   ...this time it works.
$ _
```

As you'll see in chapter 3, there's a much easier way to erase a collection of files when you're using a shell. I could have written the following instead:

```
$ cd lyrics.draft  ...move into "lyrics.draft" directory.
$ rm *             ...erase all files in current
                                             directory.
```

Even better, I could have used the more advanced **-r** option of **rm** to delete the "lyrics.draft" directory and all of its contents with just one command:

```
$ cd                    ...move to my home directory.
$ rm -r lyrics.draft   ...recursively delete directory.
$ _
```

PRINTING A FILE: lpr/lpq/lprm

Now that the hard work was done, I wanted to obtain a printout of my lyrics to sing from. I used the UNIX print utility called **lpr**, which works like this:

Utility: **lpr** -m [-P*printer*] [-#*copies*] { *fileName* }*

lpr prints the named files to the printer specified by the **-P** option. If no printer is specified, the printer in the environment variable $PRINTER is used (for more information about environment variables, refer to chapter 3). If no files are specified, standard input is printed instead. By default, one copy of each file is printed, although this may be overridden using the -# option. The **-m** option causes mail to be sent to you when the printing is complete.

---

lpr causes a numbered print job to be started for the specified files. You may find the status of a particular job and/or printer by using the **lpq** utility, which works as follows:

Utility: **lpq** -l [-P*printer*] { *job#* }* { *userId* }*

lpq displays the status of jobs on the printer specified by the **-P** option. If no printer is specified, the printer in the environment variable $PRINTER is used. **lpq** displays information pertaining to the specified jobs and/or the jobs of the specified users. If no jobs or users are specified, the status of all jobs on the specified printer is displayed. The **-l** option generates extra information.

If for some reason you wish to cancel a print job, you may do so by using the **lprm** utility:

Utility: **lprm** [-P*printer*] [-] { *job#* }* { *userId* }*

lprm cancels all of the specified jobs on the printer specified by the **-P** option. If no printer is specified, the printer in the environment variable $PRINTER is used. The **-** option cancels all of the print jobs started by you. If you're a super-user, then you may cancel all of the jobs owned by a particular user by specifying their user id.

You may obtain a list of the printers on your system from your system administrator.

In the following example, I started by ordering a printout of "heart.final" from the "lwcs" printer. I then decided to order two more copies, and obtained a printer status. Finally, I changed my mind and canceled the last print job.

```
$ lpr -Plwcs heart.final        ...order a printout.
$ lpq -Plwcs glass              ...look at the printer status.
lwcs is ready and printing
Rank     Owner   Job   Files         Total Size
active   glass   731   heart.final   213 bytes
$ lpr -#2 -Plwcs heart.final    ...order two more copies.
$ lpq -Plwcs glass              ...look at the printer status again.
lwcs is ready and printing
Rank     Owner   Job   Files         Total Size
active   glass   731   heart.final   213 bytes
active   glass   732   heart.final   426 bytes
$ lprm -Plwcs 732               ...remove the last job.
centaur: dfA732vanguard dequeued
centaur: cfA732vanguard.utdallas.edu dequeued
$ _
```

In the next example, I used the keyboard to compose a quick message for the printer, and requested mail notification of job completion:

```
$ lpr -m -Plwcs          ...print from standard input.
Hi there,
This is a test of the print facility.
- Graham
^D                       ...end of input.
$                        ...wait a little.
$ mail                   ...read my mail.
Mail version SMI 4.0 Sat Oct 13 20:32:29 PDT 1990 Type ? for help.
>N  1 daemon@utdallas.edu Fri Jan 31 16:59  15/502  printer job
& 1                      ...read the first mail message.
From: daemon@utdallas.edu
```

```
To: glass@utdallas.edu
Subject: printer job
Date: Fri, 31 Jan 1992 16:59:17 -0600

Your printer job (stdin)
completed successfully
& q                            ...quit out of mail.
$ _
```

COUNTING THE WORDS IN A FILE: wc

I was quite interested to find out how many characters, words, and lines were in the "heart.final" file. To do this, I used the **wc** utility, which works as follows:

Utility: **wc** -lwc { *fileName* }*

The **wc** utility counts the lines, words, and/or characters in a list of files. If no files are specified, standard input is used instead. The **-l** option requests a line count, the **-w** option requests a word count, and the **-c** option requests a character count. If no options are specified, then all three counts are displayed. A word is defined by a sequence of characters surrounded by tabs, spaces, or newlines.

Here's an example of **wc**:

```
$ wc heart.final         ...obtain a word count.
        9       43      213 heart.final
$ _
```

FILE ATTRIBUTES

Now that I've introduced you to some of the common file-oriented utilities, it's time to look at the various file attributes. I used **ls** to obtain a long listing of "heart.final," and got the following output:

```
$ ls -lgsF heart.final
1 -rw-r--r--  1   glass cs   213  Jan 31 00:12   heart.final
$ _
```

Each field is the value of a file attribute, described by the following table:

Field #	Field value	Meaning
1	1	the number of blocks of physical storage occupied by the file
2	-rw-r--r--	the permission mode of the file, which indicates who can read, write, and execute the file
3	1	the hard link count (discussed in chapter 7)
4	glass	the user id of the owner of the file
5	cs	the group id of the file
6	213	the size of the file, in bytes
7	Jan 31 00:12	the time that the file was last modified
8	heart.final	the name of the file

The next few sections describe the meaning of the individual fields, in increasing order of difficulty.

File Storage

The number of blocks of physical storage is shown in field 1 and is useful if you want to know how much actual disk space a file is using. It's possible to create sparse files that seem to be very large in terms of field 6 but actually take up very little physical storage. Sparse files are discussed in detail in Chapter 10.

Filenames

The name of the file is shown in field 8. A UNIX filename may be up to 14 characters long (up to 255 chararacters in BSD UNIX). You may use any characters you want in a filename, although I recommend that you avoid the use of <, >, and tab characters as these confuse the shells. Unlike some operating systems, there's no requirement that a file has to end in an extension such as ".c" and ".h," although many UNIX utilities such as the C compiler will only accept files that end with a particular suffix. Thus, the filenames "heart" and "heart.final" are both perfectly legal. The only filenames that you definitely *can't* choose are

".." and "..", as these are predefined filenames that correspond to your current working directory and its parent directory, respectively.

File Modification Time

Field 7 shows the time that the file was last modified, and is used by several utilities. For example, the **make** utility, described in chapter 9, uses the last modification time of files to control its dependency checker. The **find** utility, described in chapter 7, may be programmed to find files based on their last modification time.

File Owner

Field 3 tells you the owner of the file. Every UNIX process has an owner, which is typically the same as the user id of the person who started it. For example, my login shell is owned by "glass," which is my user id. Whenever a process creates a file, the file's owner is set to the process's owner. This means that every file that I create from my shell is owned by "glass," the owner of the shell itself. Chapter 10 contains more information on processes and ownership.

File Group

Field 5 shows the file's group. Every UNIX user has a group id, which is initially assigned by the system administrator, and is used as part of the UNIX security mechanism. For example, my group id is "cs." Every UNIX process also has a group id, which is typically the same as the group id of the person who started it. For example, my login shell has the group id "cs," which is my own group id. Whenever a process creates a file, the file's group is set to the process's group. This means that every file that I create from my shell has the group id "cs." Chapter 10 contains more information on processes and groups. The use of groups in relation to the UNIX security mechanism is described in the next few sections.

File Types

Field 2 describes the file's type and permission settings. For convenience, here's the output from the previous **ls** example:

```
1 -rw-r--r--  1    glass cs    213  Jan 31 00:12   heart.final
```

The first character of field 2 indicates the type of the file, which is encoded as follows:

Character	File type
-	regular file
d	directory file
b	buffered special file (such as a disk drive)
c	unbuffered special file (such as a terminal)
l	symbolic link
p	pipe
s	socket

In the example, the type of "heart.final" is indicated as a regular file. You'll encounter symbolic links in chapter 7, pipes and sockets in chapter 10, and buffered/unbuffered special files in chapter 11.

A file's type can often be determined by using the **file** utility, which works like this:

Utility: **file** -L { *fileName* }+

The **file** utility attempts to describe the contents of the *fileName* arguments, including the language that any text is written in. When using **file** on a symbolic link file, the **-L** option tells **file** to describe the file that the link is pointing to, rather than the link itself.

For example, when I ran **file** on "heart.final," I saw this:

```
$ file heart.final        ...determine the file type.
heart.final:     ascii text
$ _
```

File Permissions

The next nine characters of field 2 indicate the file's permission settings. In the current example, the permission settings are "rw-r--r--":

```
1 -rw-r--r--  1   glass cs   213  Jan 31 00:12   heart.final
```

These nine characters should be thought of as being arranged in three groups of three characters, like this:

User (owner)	Group	Others
rw-	r--	r--

Each cluster of three letters has the same format:

Read permission	Write permission	Execute permission
r	w	x

If a dash occurs instead of a letter, then the permission is denied. The meaning of the read, write, and execute permissions depends on the type of the file:

	Regular file	Directory file	Special file
read	The process may read the contents.	The process may read the directory (i.e., list the names of the files that it contains).	The process may read from the file using the read () system call.
write	The process may change the contents.	The process may add or remove files to/ from the directory.	The process may write to the file using the write () system call.
execute	The process may execute the file (which only makes sense if it's a program)	The process may access files in the directory or any of its subdirectories.	No meaning.

When a process executes, it has four values related to file permissions:

1. a *real* user id
2. an *effective* user id
3. a *real* group id
4. an *effective* group id

When you log in, your login shell process has its real and effective user ids set to your own user id, and its real and effective group ids set to your group id. When a process runs, the file permissions apply as follows:

• If the process's effective user id is the same as the owner of the file, the **User** permissions apply.
• If the process's effective user id is different from the owner of the file, but its effective group id matches the file's group id, then the **Group** permissions apply.
• If neither the process's effective user id nor the process's effective group id matches, the **Others** permissions apply.

The permission system is therefore a three-tier arrangement that allows you to protect your files from general users but at the same time allows access by certain groups. Later on in this chapter I'll illustrate the use of permission settings to good effect and describe the utilities that are used to alter them.

Note that only a process's effective user and group ids affect its permissions; its real user and group ids are only used for accounting purposes. Note also that a process's access rights depend ordinarily on who *executes* the process, and not on who *owns* the executable. There are some occasions where this is undesirable. For example, there is a game called **rogue** that comes with most UNIX systems that maintains a file of the best scores of previous players. Obviously, the **rogue** process must have permission to alter this file when it is executing, but the player that executes **rogue** should not. This seems impossible, based on the permission rules that I just described. To get around this problem, the designers of UNIX added two special file permissions called *set-user-id* and *set-group-id*. When an executable with set-user-id permission is exec'ed, the process's effective user id becomes that of the executable. Similarly, when an executable with set-group-id permission is exec'ed, the process's effective group id is copied from the executable. In both cases, the real user/group id is unaffected. In the case of the **rogue** game, the executable and the score file are both owned by the user "rogue," and the **rogue** executable has set-user-id permission. The score file only has write permission for its owner, thus protecting general users from modifying it. When a player executes **rogue**, the player process executes with the effective user id of **rogue**, and thus is able to modify the score file.

set-user-id and set-group-id permissions are indicated by an "s" instead of an "x" in the user and group clusters, respectively. They may be set using the **chmod** utility, described shortly, and by the chmod () system call, described in chapter 10.

Here are a few other notes relating to file permissions:

- When a process creates a file, the default permissions given to that file are modified by a special value called the *umask*. The umask value is usually set a sensible default, so we won't mention it again until chapter 3.
- The super-user automatically has all access rights, regardless of whether they're granted or not.
- It's perfectly possible, although unusual, for the owner of a file to have fewer permissions than the group or anyone else.

Hard Link Count

Field 3 shows the file's hard link count, which indicates how many labels in the hierarchy are pointing to the same physical file. Hard links are rather advanced, and are discussed in conjunction with the **ln** utility in chapter 7.

GROUPS

Now that you've read about file permissions, it's time to see how they can come in handy. Recall that the "heart.final" file's user and group ids were "glass" and "cs," respectively, inherited from my login shell:

```
$ ls -lg heart.final
-rw-r--r--  1   glass   cs   213   Jan 31 00:12    heart.final
$ _
```

The original permission flags allow anyone to read it but only the owner to write it. What I really wanted to do was to set up a new group called "music" and allow anyone in the "music" group to read my work. I, the owner, would retain read and write permissions, and anyone else would be denied all access rights.

The only way to create a new group is to ask the system administrator to add it. The actual way that a new group is added is described in chapter 12. After a new group is added, any user who wants to be a part of that group must also ask the system administrator. At this time, I mailed a request to the system administrator for a new "music" group and asked for myself and my friend Tim to be added to the group. When I received a confirmation of the request, it was time to update my file attributes.

LISTING YOUR GROUPS: GROUPS

Before changing my file's group setting, I wanted to confirm that I was now an official member of the "music" group. The **groups** utility allows you to list all of the groups that you're a member of, and works like this:

Utility: **groups** [*userId*]

When invoked with no arguments, the **groups** utility displays a list of all the groups that you are a member of. If the name of a user is specified, a list of that user's groups are displayed.

Here's what I saw when I executed **groups**:

```
$ groups          ...list my groups.
cs     music
$ _
```

CHANGING A FILE'S GROUP: chgrp

The first step toward protecting my lyrics was to change the group id of "heart-.final" from "cs" to "music." I did this by using the **chgrp** utility, which works as follows:

Utility: **chgrp** -R *groupId* { *fileName* }*

The **chgrp** utility allows a user to change the group of files that he/she owns. A super-user can change the group of any file. All of the files that follow the *groupId* argument are affected. The **-R** option recursively changes the group of the files in a directory.

I used **chgrp** like this:

```
$ ls -lg heart.final
-rw-r--r--  1    glass        cs    213  Jan 31 00:12    heart.final
$ chgrp music heart.final      ...change the group of the file.
$ ls -lg heart.final           ...confirm that it's changed.
-rw-r--r--  1    glass        music 213  Jan 31 00:12    heart.final
$ _
```

You may also use **chgrp** to change the group of a directory.

CHANGING A FILE'S PERMISSIONS: chmod

Now that the file's group was changed, it was necessary to update its permissions to deny all access rights to general users. To do this, I used the **chmod** utility, which works as follows:

Utility: **chmod** -R *change* { , *change* }*{ *fileName* }+

The **chmod** utility changes the modes of the specified files according to the *change* parameters, which may take the following forms:

clusterSelection+newPermissions   (add permissions)
clusterSelection−newPermissions   (subtract permissions)
clusterSelection=newPermissions   (assign permissions absolutely)

where *clusterSelection* is any combination of:

- u (user/owner)
- g (group)
- o (others)
- a (all)

and *newPermissions* is any combination of

- r (read)
- w (write)
- x (execute)
- s (set user id/set group id)

The **-R** option recursively changes the modes of the files in directories. Please see the following text for examples. Changing a directory's permission settings doesn't change the settings of the files that it contains.

To remove read permission from others, I used **chmod** as follows:

```
$ ls -lg heart.final       ...before.
-rw-r--r--  1     glass    music 213  Jan 31 00:12    heart.final
$ chmod o-r heart.final    ...remove read permissions from others.
$ ls -lg heart.final       ...after.
-rw-r-----  1     glass    music 213  Jan 31 00:12    heart.final
$ _
```

Here are some other examples of **chmod**:

Requirement	Change parameters
Add group write permission.	g+w
Remove user read and write permission.	u-rw
Add execute permission for user, group, and others.	a+x
Give the group just read permission.	g=r
Add write permission for user, and remove read from group.	u+w, g-r

I recommend that you protect your login directory from unauthorized access by not granting write permission for anyone but yourself, and by restricting read and execute permission to yourself and members of your group. Here's an example of how to do this:

```
$ cd                  ...change to home directory.
$ ls -ld .            ...list attributes of home directory.
drwxr-xr-x 45 glass      4096 Apr 29 14:35 .
$ chmod o-rx .        ...update permissions.
$ ls -ld .            ...confirm.
drwxr-x--- 45 glass      4096 Apr 29 14:35 .
$ _
```

Note that I used the **-d** option of **ls** to ensure that the attributes of my home directory were displayed, rather than the attributes of its files.

The **chmod** utility allows you to specify the new permission setting of a file as an octal number. Each octal digit represents a permission triplet. For example, if you wanted a file to have the following permission settings:

```
rwxr-x---
```

then the octal permission setting would be 750, calculated as follows:

	User	Group	Others
setting	rwx	r-x	---
binary	111	101	000
octal	7	5	0

The octal permission setting would be supplied to **chmod** as follows:

```
$ chmod 750 .              ...update permissions.
$ ls -ld .                 ...confirm.
drwxr-x--- 45 glass         4096 Apr 29 14:35 .
$ _
```

CHANGING A FILE'S OWNER: chown

If for some reason you ever want to relinquish ownership of a file, you may do so
by using the **chown** utility, which works as follows:

Utility: **chown** -R *newUserId* { *fileName* }+

The **chown** utility allows a super-user to change the ownership of files. All of
the files that follow the *newUserId* argument are affected. The **-R** option
recursively changes the owner of the files in directories.

As you can see, only a super-user can change the ownership of a file. Several
occasions when the system administrator needs to use **chown** are described in
chapter 12.

If I was a super-user, I could have executed the following sequence of
commands to change the ownership of "heart.final" to "tim" and then back to
"glass" again:

```
$ ls -lg heart.final        ...before.
-rw-r----- 1         glass   music 213  Jan 31 00:12    heart.final
$ chown tim heart.final     ...change the owner to "tim".
$ ls -lg heart.final        ...after.
-rw-r----- 1         tim     music 213  Jan 31 00:12    heart.final
$ chown glass heart.final   ...change the owner back to "glass".
$ _
```

CHANGING GROUPS: newgrp

If you're a member of several groups and then you create a file, what is the group
id of the file? Well, although you may be a member of several groups, only one of
them is your *effective* group at any given time. When a process creates a file, the

group id of the file is set to the process's *effective* group id. This means that when you create a file from the shell, the group id of the file is set to the effective group id of your shell. In this example session, I was a member of the "cs" and "music" groups, and my login shell's effective group id was "cs."

The system administrator is the one who chooses which one of your groups is used as your login shell's effective group id. The only way to permanently alter your login shell's effective group id is to ask the system administrator to change it. However, you may create a shell with a different effective group id by using the **newgrp** utility, which works like this:

Utility: **newgrp** [-] [*groupId*]

The **newgrp** utility, when invoked with a group id as an argument, creates a new shell with the specified effective group id. The old shell sleeps until you exit the newly created shell. You must be a member of the group that you specify. If you use a dash (-) instead of a filename as the argument, a shell is created with the same settings as the shell that was created when you logged into the system.

In the following example, I created a file called "test1" from my login shell, which had an effective group id of "cs." I then created a temporary shell with an effective group id of "music" and then created a file called "test2." I then terminated the shell and went back to the original shell, where I obtained a long listing of both files:

```
$ date > test1        ...create "test1" from a "cs" group shell.
$ newgrp music        ...create a temporary "music" group shell.
$ date > test2        ...create "test2" from a "music" group shell.
^D                    ...terminate the new shell and restart the old.
$ ls -lg test1 test2 ...look at each file's attributes.
-rw-r--r--   1    glass cs         29  Jan 31 22:57         test1
-rw-r--r--   1    glass music      29  Jan 31 22:57         test2
$ _
```

POETRY IN MOTION: EPILOGUE

This concludes the "Poetry In Motion" series of examples. During this series, you were introduced to many useful UNIX concepts and utilities. I thoroughly recommend that you try out them out before progressing further through this book, as this will help you retain and understand the UNIX basics. The remainder of this chapter covers the two most popular UNIX editors and explains how you can alter your terminal settings so that they work correctly. It also contains some information on using the UNIX email system.

DETERMINING YOUR TERMINAL'S TYPE: tset

Several UNIX utilities, including the two standard editors **vi** and **emacs**, need to know what kind of terminal you're using so that they can control the screen correctly. The type of your terminal is stored by your shell in something called an *environment variable*. Environment variables are described in more detail in chapter 3; you may think of them as being rather like global variables that hold strings.

Before **vi** or **emacs** can work correctly, your shell's environment variable $TERM must be set to your terminal type. Common settings for this variable include ''vt100'' and ''vt52.'' There are several ways that this variable can be set:

- Your shell startup file, described in the next section, can set $TERM directly by containing a line of the form: 'setenv TERM vt100' (C shell) or 'TERM=vt100; export TERM' (Bourne and Korn shells). This is only practical if you know the type of your terminal in advance and you always log into the same terminal.
- Your shell startup file can invoke the **tset** utility, which looks at the communications port that you're connected to and then examines a special file called ''/etc/ttytab,'' which contains a table of port/terminal mappings. In most cases, **tset** can find out what kind of terminal you're using from this table and set $TERM accordingly. If **tset** can't find the terminal type, it can be programmed to prompt you for the terminal type when you log in.
- You can manually set $TERM from a shell.

The rest of this section describes the operation of **tset**. Before using **vi** or **emacs**, you should also be sure to read the section that follows, which describes the operation of a related utility called **stty**.

The best way to set $TERM is to use **tset** from your login shell. **tset** works as follows:

Utility: **tset** -s [-e*c*] [-i*c*] {-m *portId*:[?]*terminalType*}*

tset is a utility that tries to determine your terminal's type and then resets it for standard operation.

If the **-s** option is not used, **tset** assumes that your terminal type is already stored in the $TERM environment variable, and resets it using information stored in the ''/etc/termcap'' file.

If you use the **-s** option, **tset** examines the "/etc/ttytab" file and tries to map your terminal's port to a terminal type. If found, it initializes your terminal with an appropriate initialization sequence from the "/etc/termcap" file. The **-s** option also causes **tset** to output shell commands to standard output that, when executed, cause the $TERM and $TERMCAP environment variables to be set. **tset** uses the contents of the $SHELL environment variable to determine which kind of shell commands to output. Filename expansion must be temporarily inhibited during the execution of the command sequence that **tset** generates. Examples of this follow shortly.

The **-e** option sets the terminal's erase character to *c* instead of the default *Control-H* setting. Control characters may be indicated by either typing the character directly or by preceding the character by a ˆ (i.e., use ˆh to indicate *Control-H*).

The **-i** option sets the terminal's interrupt character to *c* instead of the default *Control-C* setting. Control characters may be indicated as described in the previous paragraph.

The "/etc/ttytab" mappings may be overridden or supplemented by using the **-m** option. The sequence "-m *pp:tt*" tells **tset** that if the terminal's port type is *pp*, then it should assume that the terminal is of type *tt*. If a ? is placed after the :, **tset** displays *tt* and asks the user to either press *Enter* to confirm that the terminal type is indeed *tt*, or to enter the actual terminal type that **tset** should use.

The "/etc/ttytab" file contains lines of the following form:

```
tty0f "usr/etc getty std.9600"      vt100        off local
ttyp0 none                          network      off secure
ttyp1 none                          network      off secure
```

The first field contains the names of ports, and the third field contains the names of terminal types. For example, if I was logged on via port tty0f, my terminal type would be read from this file as a vt100. In the following example, I found out my actual port name by using the **tty** utility (described in chapter 7) and then examined the output from the **tset** command:

```
$ tty                    ...display my terminal's port id.
/dev/ttyp0
$ tset -s                ...call tset.
set noglob;              ...shell commands generated by tset.
setenv TERM network ;
setenv TERMCAP 'sa|network:li#24:co#80:am:do=ˆJ: ' ;
unset noglob;
Erase is Ctrl-H
$ _
```

The previous example is only provided to illustrate how **tset** does its stuff. To actually make **tset** change the $TERM and $TERMCAP variables, which after all is the reason for using it in the first place, you must 'eval' its output. The *eval* shell command is described fully in the next chapter. Here's a more realistic example of **tset**:

```
$ set noglob          ...temporarily inhibit filename expansion.
$ eval `tset -s`      ...evaluate output from tset.
Erase is Backspace    ...message from tset.
$ unset noglob        ...re-enable filename expansion.
$ echo $TERM          ...look at the new value of TERM.
network               ...this is the terminal type that tset found.
$ _
```

Unfortunately, the terminal type *network* is not very useful, as it assumes that my terminal has almost no capabilities at all. The **tset** command may be presented with a rule that tells it, "If the terminal type is discovered to be network, assume that the terminal is a vt100 and prompt the user for confirmation." Here is the variation of **tset** that does this:

```
$ set noglob              ...disable filename expansion.
$ eval `tset -s -m 'network:vt100'`    ...provide rule.
TERM = (vt100) ⟨Enter⟩ ...I pressed the Enter key to confirm default.
Erase is Backspace
$ unset noglob            ...re-enable filename expansion.
$ echo $TERM              ...display new TERM setting.
vt100                     ...this is the terminal type that tset used.
$ _
```

In summary, it's wise to contain a command in your shell's startup file that calls **tset** to set your terminal type. Shell startup files are described in chapter 3. The simplest form of **tset** is the following:

C shell

```
setenv TERM vt100
tset
```

Bourne/Korn shell

```
TERM=vt100; export TERM
tset
```

The more sophisticated form of **tset** searches the "/etc/ttytab" file for your terminal type, and should look somewhat like this:

C shell

```
set noglob
eval `tset -s -m 'network:?vt100'`
unset noglob
```

Bourne/Korn shell

```
eval `tset -s -m 'network:?vt100'`
```

CHANGING A TERMINAL'S CHARACTERISTICS: stty

All terminals have the ability to process certain characters in a special manner; these characters are sometimes called *metacharacters*. Examples of metacharacters include the backspace character and the *Control-C* sequence, which is used to terminate programs. The default metacharacter settings may be overridden using the **stty** utility, which works as follows:

Utility: **stty -a** { *option* }* { *metacharacterString* ⟨*value*⟩} *

The **stty** utility allows you to examine and set a terminal's characteristics. **stty** supports the modification of over one hundred different settings, so I've only listed the most common ones here. Consult **man** for more details. To list a terminal's current settings, use the **-a** option. To alter a particular setting, supply one or more of the following options:

Option	Meaning
-echo	Don't echo typed characters.
echo	Echo typed characters.
-raw	Enable the special meaning of metacharacters.
raw	Disable the special meaning of metacharacters.
-tostop	Allow background jobs to send output to the terminal.
tostop	Stop background jobs that try to send output to the terminal.
sane	Set the terminal characteristics to sensible default values.

You may also set the mappings of metacharacters by following the name of its corresponding string with its new value. A control character may be indicated by preceding the character with a ˆ or by typing a \ followed by the actual control character itself. Here are the common metacharacter strings together with their meanings:

Option	Meaning
erase	Backspace one character.
kill	Erase all of the current line.
lnext	Don't treat the next character specially.
susp	Suspend the process for a future awakening.
intr	Terminate the foreground job with no core dump.
stop	Stop/restart terminal output.
eof	End-of-input.

Here's an example of **stty** in action:

```
$ stty -a                         ...display current terminal settings.
speed 38400 baud, 24 rows, 80 columns
parenb -parodd cs7 -cstopb -hupcl cread -clocal -crtscts
-ignbrk brkint ignpar -parmrk -inpck istrip -inlcr -igncr icrnl
-iuclc
ixon -ixany -ixoff imaxbel
isig iexten icanon -xcase echo echoe echok -echonl -noflsh -tostop
echoctl -echoprt echoke
opost -olcuc onlcr -ocrnl -onocr -onlret -ofill -ofdel
erase  kill   werase  rprnt  flush  lnext  susp    intr  quit   stop   eof
^H     ^U     ^W      ^R     ^O     ^V     ^Z/^Y ^C    ^\     ^S/^Q ^D
$ stty erase ^b                   ...set erase key to Control-B.
$ stty erase ^h                   ...set erase key to Control-H
$ _
```

Invoke **stty** from your shell's startup file if your favorite metacharacter mappings differ from the norm. **stty** is useful when building shells that need to turn keyboard echoing on and off; an example of such a script is included in chapter 6. Here's an example that uses **stty** to turn off keyboard echoing:

```
$ stty -echo           ...turn echoing off.
$ stty echo            ...turn echoing back on again.
$ _
```

Note that the last line of input (*stty echo*) would not ordinarily be seen due to the inhibition of echoing caused by the preceding line!

Now that you've seen how to set your terminal type and alter its settings, it's time to take a look at the two most popular UNIX editors: **vi** and **emacs**.

EDITING A FILE: vi

The two most popular UNIX text editors are called **vi** and **emacs**. It's handy to be reasonably proficient with both editors so that you'll be able to create and edit files on any UNIX system. This section and the next section contain enough information about each editor to allow you to perform essential editing tasks. They also contain references to other books for obtaining more advanced information.

Starting vi

The **vi** editor was originally developed for BSD UNIX at Berkeley, and was later adopted as a standard utility for System V. It is therefore found on virtually every UNIX system.

To start **vi** with a blank slate, enter the command **vi** without any parameters. To edit an existing file, supply the name of the file as a command line parameter. When your screen is initialized, blank lines are indicated by tilda characters (˜). **vi** then enters *command mode* and awaits instructions. To conserve space, I'll draw screens that are only six lines long. For example, when I executed **vi** with no parameters, I saw this:

```
˜
˜
˜
˜
˜
˜
```

Command mode is one of the two modes that **vi** may be in; the other mode is called *text entry mode*. Since it's easier to describe command mode when there's some text on the screen, I'll start by describing text entry mode.

Text Entry Mode

To enter text entry mode from command mode, press one of the following keys. Each key enters you into text entry mode in a slightly different way:

Key	Action
i	Text is inserted in front of the cursor.
a	Text is added after the cursor.
o	Text is added after the current line.
O	Text is inserted before the current line.
R	Text is replaced (overwritten).

Any text that you enter at this point will be displayed on the screen. To move to the next line, press the *Enter* key. You may use the backspace key to delete the last character that you entered. *You may not move around the screen using the cursor keys when you're in text entry mode.* In text entry mode, cursor keys are interpreted as regular ASCII characters, and their control codes are entered as normal text. This takes many users by surprise, so beware.

To go from command mode to text entry mode, press the *Esc* key.

To enter a short four-line poem, I pressed the **a** key to add characters in text entry mode, entered the text of the poem, and then pressed the *Esc* key to return to command mode. Here's what I ended up with:

```
I always remember standing in the rains,
On a cold and damp september,
Brown Autumn leaves were falling softly to the ground,
Like the dreams of a life as they slide away.
~
~
```

The next section describes the editing features of **vi** that allowed me to change this poem to something a little more appealing.

Command Mode

To edit text, you must enter command mode. To travel from text entry mode to command mode, press the *Esc* key. If you accidentally press the *Esc* key when in command mode, nothing happens.

vi's editing features are selected by pressing special character sequences. For example, to erase a single word, position the cursor over the particular word and press the **d** key followed by the **w** key.

Some editing features require parameters, and are accessed by pressing the colon (:) key, followed by the command sequence, followed by the *Enter* key. When the colon key is pressed, the remainder of the command sequence is displayed at the bottom of the screen. In the following example, the *Enter* key is indicated as ⟨*Enter*⟩. The ⟨ and ⟩ characters act as delimiters and should not be entered. For example, to delete lines 1 through 3, you'd enter the following command sequence:

```
:1,3d⟨Enter⟩
```

Some editing features, such as the block delete command that I just described, act upon a range of lines. **vi** accepts a couple of formats for a line range:

- To select a single line, state its line number.
- To select a block of lines, state the first and last line numbers inclusively, separated by a comma.

vi allows you to use $ to denote the line number of the last line in the file, and . to denote the line number of the line currently containing the cursor. **vi** also allows you to use arithmetic expressions when stating line numbers. For example, the sequence

```
:.,.+2d⟨Enter⟩
```

would delete the current line and the two lines that follow it. Here are some other examples of line ranges:

Range	Selects
1,$	all of the lines in the file
1,.	all of the lines from the start of the file to the current line, inclusive
.,$	all of the lines from the current line to the end of the file, inclusive
.-2	the single line that's two lines before the current line

In what follows, the term ⟨*range*⟩ indicates a range of lines in the format described above.

Common Editing Features

The most common **vi** editing features can be grouped into the following categories:

- cursor movement
- deleting text
- replacing text
- pasting text
- searching text
- search/replace text
- saving/loading files
- miscellaneous (including how to quit **vi**)

These categories are described and illustrated in the subsections that follow, using the sample poem that I entered at the start of this section.

Cursor Movement

Here is a table of the common cursor movement commands:

Movement	Key sequence	
Up one line	⟨cursor up⟩ or **k**	
Down one line	⟨cursor down⟩ or **j**	
Right one character	⟨cursor right⟩ or **l**	(will not wrap around)
Left one character	⟨cursor left⟩ or **h**	(will not wrap around)
To start of line	^	
To end of line	$	
Back one word	**b**	
Forward one word	**w**	
Down a half screen	*Control-D*	
Down one screen	*Control-F*	
Up a half screen	*Control-U*	
Up one screen	*Control-B*	
To line *nn*	:*nn*⟨*Enter*⟩	

For example, to insert the word ''Just'' before the word ''Like'' on the fourth line, I moved the cursor to the fourth line, pressed the **i** key to enter text entry mode, entered the text, and pressed the *Esc* key to return to command mode. To move the cursor to the fourth line, I used the key sequence :4⟨*Enter*⟩.

Deleting Text

Here is a table of the common text deletion commands:

Item to delete	Key sequence
Character	Position the cursor over the character and then press **x**.
Word	Position the cursor at start of word and then press **dw**.
Line	Position the cursor anywhere the line and then press **dd**.
To end of current line	Press *D*.
Block of lines	:⟨*range*⟩**d**⟨*Enter*⟩

For example, to delete the word ''always,'' I typed **:1**<*Enter*> to move to the start of line one, pressed **w** to move forward one word, and then typed the letters **dw**. To delete the trailing ''s'' on the end of ''rains'' on the first line, I moved my cursor over the letter ''s'' and then pressed the **x** key. My poem now looked like this:

```
I remember standing in the rain,
On a cold and damp september,
Brown Autumn leaves were falling softly to the ground,
Just Like the dreams of a life as they slide away.
~
~
```

Replacing Text

Following is a table of the common text replacement commands:

Item to replace	Key sequence
Character	Position the cursor over the character, press **r**, and then type the replacement character.
Word	Position the cursor at start of word, press **cw**, and then type the replacement text followed by *Esc*.
Line	Position the cursor anywhere in line, press **cc**, and then type the replacement text followed by *Esc*.

For example, to replace the word "standing" by "walking," I moved to the start of the word and then typed the letters **cw**. I then typed the word "walking" and pressed the *Esc* key. To replace the lowercase "s" of september by an uppercase "S," I positioned the cursor over the "s," pressed the **r** key, and then pressed the "S" key.

I then performed a few more tidy-up operations, replacing "damp" by "dark," "slide" by "slip," and the "L" of "like" by "l". Here's the final version of the poem:

```
I remember walking in the rain,
On a cold and dark September,
Brown Autumn leaves were falling softly to the ground,
Just like the dreams of a life as they slip away.
~
~
```

Pasting Text

vi maintains a paste buffer that may be used for copying and pasting text between areas of a file. Here is a table of the most common pasting operations:

Action	Key sequence
Copy (**yank**) lines into paste buffer.	**:**<*range*>**y**<*Enter*>
Insert (**put**) paste buffer after current line.	**:pu**<*Enter*> (contents of paste buffer are unchanged)
Insert paste buffer after line *nn*.	**:**nn**pu**<*Enter*> (contents of paste buffer are unchanged)

For example, to copy the first two lines into the paste buffer and then paste them after the third line, I entered the following two commands:

```
:1,2y
:3pu
```

The poem then looked like this:

> I remember walking in the rain,
> On a cold and dark September,
> Brown Autumn leaves were falling softly to the ground,
> I remember walking in the rain,
> On a cold and dark September,
> Just like the dreams of a life as they slip away.

To restore the poem, I typed **:4,5d**<*Enter*>.

Searching

vi allows you to search forward and backward through a file, relative to the current line, for a particular substring. Here is a table of the most common search operations:

Action	Key sequence
Search forward from current position for string *sss*.	/*sss*<*Enter*>
Search backward from current position for string *sss*.	?*sss*<*Enter*>
Repeat last search.	**n**

For example, I searched for the substring ''ark'' from line 1 of the poem by entering the following commands:

```
:1<Enter>
/ark<Enter>
```

vi positioned the cursor at the start of the substring "ark" located in the word "dark" on the second line:

> I remember walking in the rain,
> On a cold and dark September,
> Brown Autumn leaves were falling softly to the ground,
> Just like the dreams of a life as they slip away.
> ~
> ~

Search/Replace

You may perform global "search and replace" operations by using the following commands:

Action	Key sequence
Replace the first occurrence of *sss* on each line with *ttt*.	:*<range>***s**/ *sss*/ *ttt*/*<Enter>*
Relace every occurrence of *sss* on each line with *ttt*.	:*<range>***s**/ *sss*/ *ttt*/**g***<Enter>*

For example, to replace every occurrence of the substring "re" by "XXX," I entered the command displayed below:

> I XXXmember walking in the rain,
> On a cold and dark September,
> Brown Autumn leaves weXXX falling softly to the ground,
> Just like the dXXXams of a life as they slip away.
> ~
>
> :1,$s/re/XXX/g

Saving/Loading Files

Here is a table of the most common save/load file commands:

Action	Key sequence
Save file as <name>.	**:w** <*name*> <*Enter*>
Save file with current name.	**:w**<*Enter*>
Edit file <name> instead of current file.	**:e** <*name*> <*Enter*>
Edit next file on initial command line.	**:n**<*Enter*>

For example, I saved the poem in a file called "rain.doc" by entering the command displayed below:

```
I remember walking in the rain,
On a cold and dark September,
Brown Autumn leaves were falling softly to the ground,
Just like the dreams of a life as they slip away.
~

:w rain.doc
```

vi tells you how many bytes a file occupies when you save it, and won't let you accidentally quit **vi** without saving the current file.

If you place more than one file on the command line when you first invoke **vi**, **vi** starts by loading up the first file. You may edit the next file by using the key sequence **:n.**

Miscellaneous

Here's a list of the most common miscellaneous commands, including the commands for quitting **vi:**

Action	Key sequence
Redraw screen.	*Control-L*
Execute *command* in a subshell and then return to **vi**.	**:!**<*command*> <*Enter*>
Quit **vi** if work is saved	**:q**<*Enter*>
Quit **vi** and discard unsaved work.	**:q!**<*Enter*>

Control-L is particularly useful for refreshing the screen if a message pops up and messes up your screen, or if some static interferes with your modem connection during a **vi** session.

To finally quit **vi** after saving the final version of the poem, I typed the command illustrated below:

```
I remember walking in the rain,
On a cold and dark September,
Brown Autumn leaves were falling softly to the ground,
Just like the dreams of a life as they slip away.
~

:q
```

For More Information

For more information about **vi**, I recommend "The UNIX Operating System, second edition" [8].

EDITING A FILE: emacs

emacs is a popular editor that is commonly present on UNIX systems. It was originally written in 1975 by Richard Stallman, who distributed its source code free in accordance with his objection to copyright and patent laws. **emacs** stands for **E**ditor **Mac**ros.

Starting emacs

To start **emacs** with a blank file, enter the command **emacs** with no parameters. To edit an existing file, specify its name as a command line parameter. Assuming that you supply no parameters, your screen will initially look something like this, depending on your version of **emacs**:

```
GNU Emacs 18.58.1
Copyright (C) 1990 Free Software Foundation, Inc.
Type C-h for help, C-x u to undo changes ('C-' means use CTRL-key)

--- Emacs:  *scratch*                    (Fundamental) --- All ------------
```

I'll draw screens that are only six lines long to conserve space. The second-from-bottom line is called the *mode line*, and contains information in the following left-to-right order:

- If the first three dashes contain a **, it means that the current file has been modified.
- The name that follows "Emacs:" is the name of the current file. If no file is currently loaded, the name *scratch* is used instead.
- The current editing mode is then shown between parentheses. In this case, it's *Fundamental*, which is the standard editing mode.
- The next entry indicates your relative position in the file as a percentage. If the file is very small and fits completely on the screen, then *All* is displayed. If you're at the top or the bottom of a file, then *Top* or *Bot* are displayed, respectively.

emacs Commands

Unlike **vi**, **emacs** doesn't distinguish between text entry mode and command mode. To enter text, simply start typing. The initial **emacs** welcome banner automatically disappears when you type the first letter. Long lines are not automatically broken, so you must press the *Enter* key when you wish to start a new line. Lines longer than the screen width are indicated by a \ character at the end of the screen:

```
This is a very long line that illustrates the way that unbroken lines a \
re displayed.
This is a much shorter line.

--- Emacs:  *scratch*                   (Fundamental) --- All -------------
```

emacs's editing features are accessed via either a control sequence or a meta-sequence. I'll indicate control sequences by prepending the name of the key with the prefix *Control-*. For example, the sequence

```
Control-H t
```

means "Press and hold the *Control* key and then press the **H** key (for control sequences, it doesn't matter whether you use uppercase or lowercase, so I suggest that you use lowercase, as it's easier). Then release both keys and press the **t** key on its own." Similarly, meta-sequences use the *Esc* key. For example, the sequence:

    Esc x

means "Press the *Esc* key (but don't hold it) and then press the **x** key." The next few sections contain many examples of **emacs** command sequences. If you ever accidentally press *Esc* followed by *Esc*, **emacs** warns you that you're trying to do something advanced and suggests that you press the **n** key to continue. Unless you're a seasoned **emacs** user, it's good advice.

Getting Out of Trouble

Whenever you're learning a new editor, it's quite easy to get lost and confused. Here are a couple of useful command sequences to return you to a sane state:

- The command sequence *Control-G* terminates any **emacs** command, even if it's only partially entered, and returns **emacs** to the state where it's waiting for a new command.
- The command sequence *Control-X* **1** closes all **emacs** windows except your main file window. This is useful, as several **emacs** options create a new window to display information, and it's important to know how to close them once you've read their contents.

Getting Help

There are several ways to obtain help information about **emacs**. One of the best ways to get started with **emacs** is to read the self-describing help tutorial. I suggest that you do this before anything else. To read the tutorial, use the command sequence *Control-H* **t**. The tutorial will appear and give you directions on how to proceed.

Leaving emacs

To leave **emacs** and save your file, use *Control-X Control-C*. If you haven't saved your file since it was last modified, you'll be asked whether you want to save it.

emacs Modes

emacs supports several different modes for entering text, including Fundamental, Lisp Interaction, and C. Each mode supports special features that are customized for the particular kind of text that you're editing. **emacs** starts in Fundamental mode by default, which is the mode that I'll be using during my description of **emacs**. For more information about modes, consult the **emacs** tutorial.

Entering Text

To enter text, simply start typing. For example, here's a short four-line poem:

```
There is no need for fear in the night,
You know that your Mommy is there,
To watch over her babies and hold them tight,
When you are in her arms you can feel her sigh all night.
--- Emacs:  *scratch*                    (Fundamental) --- All ------------
```

The next section describes the editing features of **emacs** that allowed me to change this poem to something a little better.

Common Editing Features

The most common **emacs** editing features can be grouped into the following categories:

- cursor movement
- deleting, pasting, and undoing text
- searching text
- search/replace text
- saving/loading files
- miscellaneous

These categories are described and illustrated in the subsections that follow, using the sample poem that I entered at the start of this section.

Moving the Cursor

Here's a table of the common cursor movement commands:

Movement	Key sequence
Up one line	*Control-P* (previous)
Down one line	*Control-N* (next)
Right one character	*Control-F* (forward, wraps around)
Left one character	*Control-B* (backward, wraps around)
To start of line	*Control-A* (a is first letter)
To end of line	*Control-E* (end)
Back one word	*Esc* **b** (back)
Forward one word	*Esc* **f** (forward)
Down one screen	*Control-V*
Up one screen	*Esc* **v**
Start of file	*Esc* <
End of file	*Esc* >

For example, to insert the words "worry or" before the word "fear" on the first line, I moved the cursor to the first line of the file by typing *Esc* < and then moved forward several words by using the *Esc* **f** sequence. I then typed in the words, which were automatically inserted at the current cursor position.

Deleting, Pasting, and Undoing

Here is a table of the common deletion commands:

Item to delete	Key sequence
Character before cursor	<delete> key
Character after cursor	*Control-D*
Word before cursor	*Esc* <delete>
Word after cursor	*Esc* **d**
To end of current line	*Control-K*
Sentence	*Esc* **k**

Whenever an item is deleted, **emacs** remembers it in an individual "kill buffer." A list of kill buffers is maintained so that deleted items may be retrieved long after they have been removed from the display. To retrieve the last killed item, use *Control-Y*. After you have typed *Control-Y*, you may type *Esc* **y** to replace the retrieved item with the previously deleted item. Every time you type *Esc* **y**, the retrieved item moves one step back through the kill buffer list.

   You may append the next deleted item onto the end of the last kill buffer rather than create a new one by typing *Esc Control-W* immediately prior to the delete command. This is useful if you wish to cut different bits and pieces out of a file and then paste them all together back into one place.

   You may undo editing actions one at a time by typing *Control-X* **u** for each action that you wish to undo.

   Here is a summary of the kill buffer and undo commands:

Action	Key sequence
Insert last kill buffer.	*Control-Y*
Retrieve previous kill.	*Esc* **y**
Append next kill.	*Esc Control-W*
Undo.	*Control-X* **u**

Searching

emacs allows you to perform something called an *incremental search*. To search forward from your current cursor position for a particular sequence of letters, type *Control-S*. The prompt "I-search:" is displayed on the bottom line of the screen, indicating that **emacs** wants you to enter the string that you wish to search for. As you enter the character sequence, **emacs** searches to find the first string from your initial cursor position that matches what you've entered so far; in other words, partial substrings are found as you enter the full string. To terminate the search and leave your cursor at its current position, press *Esc*. If you delete characters in the full string before pressing the *Esc* key, **emacs** moves back to the first match of the remaining substring. To repeat a search, don't press *Esc*, but instead press *Control-S* to search forward or *Control-R* to search backward. Here is a summary of the searching commands:

Action	Key sequence
Search foward for *str*.	*Control-S str*
Search backward for *str*.	*Control-R str*
Repeat last search forward.	*Control-S*
Repeat last search backward.	*Control-R*
Leave search mode.	*Esc*

Search/Replace

To perform a global search/replace, type *Esc* **x** followed by the string "repl s" followed by *Enter*. **emacs** then prompts you for the string to replace. Enter the string and press *Enter*. **emacs** then prompts you for the replacement string. Enter the string and press *Enter*. **emacs** then performs the global text substitution.

Saving/Loading Files

To save your current work to a file, type *Control-X Control-S*. If your work hasn't been associated with a filename yet, you are prompted for a filename. Your work is then saved into its associated file.

To edit another file, type *Control-X Control-F*. You are prompted for the new filename. If the file already exists, its contents are loaded into **emacs**; otherwise, the file is created.

To save your file and then quit out of **emacs**, type *Control-X Control-C*.

Here's a summary of the save/load commands:

Action	Key sequence
Save current work.	*Control-X Control-S*
Edit another file.	*Control-X Control-F*
Save work and then quit.	*Control-X Control-C*

Miscellaneous

To redraw the screen, type *Control-L*. To place **emacs** into auto-wrap mode, which automatically inserts line breaks when words flow past the end of a line, type *Esc* **x** auto-fill-mode and press *Enter*. To leave this mode, repeat the command again.

For More Information

For more information about **emacs**, I recommend "UNIX Desktop Guide To emacs" [19].

ELECTRONIC MAIL: mail

This is the last section of this chapter, and contains information about how to use the UNIX electronic mail system. It's handy to be able to use **mail** from the very beginning, as it's a convenient way to ask the system administrator and other seasoned users questions about UNIX. The name of the email facility on BSD systems is **mail**; on System V it is called **mailx**. Fortunately, their functionalities are very similar. For the purposes of this section, I shall refer to both of them as **mail**.

   mail has a large number of features, so in accordance with the initial aim of this book, I shall only describe what I consider to be the most useful; consult **man** for more information. Here's a description of **mail**:

Utility: **mail** -H [-f *fileName*] { *userId* }*

mail allows you to send and read mail. If a list of user ids is supplied, **mail** reads standard input, mails it to the specified users, and then terminates. User ids can be a combination of the following forms:

   • a local user name (i.e., login name)
   • an Internet address of the form name@domain
   • a filename
   • a mail group

   Internet addresses are described in chapter 8, and mail groups are described shortly.

   If no user ids are specified, **mail** assumes that you wish to read mail from a mail folder. The folder "/usr/spool/mail/<user Id>" is read by default, where <user Id> is your own user id, although this may be overridden by using the **-f** option. **mail** prompts you with an & and then awaits commands. The **-H** option lists the headers from your mail folder but does not

---

enter the command mode. A list of the most useful command mode options is contained in the next few pages.

When **mail** is invoked, it begins by reading the contents of the mail startup file, which may contain statements that customize the **mail** utility. By default, **mail** reads the file ".mailrc" in your home directory, although the name of this file may be overridden by setting the environment variable $MAILRC. Environment variables are discussed in chapter 3.

There are a large number of customizable options. The most important option is the ability to define *mail groups*, which are variables that denote a group of users. To specify a mail group, place a line of the form:

```
group name { userId }+
```

into the **mail** startup file. You may then use *name* as an alias for the specified list of users, either on the command line or in command mode.

Here is a list of the most useful **mail** commands that are available from command mode:

Command	Meaning
?	Display help.
copy [*mesgList*] [*fileName*]	Copy messages into *fileName* without marking them as "saved."
delete [*mesgList*]	Delete specified messages from system mailbox.
file [*fileName*]	Read mail from mailbox *fileName*. If no filename is given, display the name of the current mailbox together with the number of bytes and messages that it contains.
headers [*message*]	Display page of message headers that include *message*.
mail { *userId* }+	Send mail to specified users.
print [*mesgList*]	Display specified messages using **more**.
quit	Exit **mail**.
reply [*mesgList*]	Mail response back to senders of message list.
save [*mesgList*] [*fileName*]	Save specified messages to *fileName*. If no filename is given, save them in a file called "mbox" in your home directory by default.

where *mesgList* describes a collection of one or more mail messages using the following syntax:

Syntax	Meaning
.	current message
nn	message number *nn*
^	first undeleted message
$	last message
*	all messages
nn-mm	messages numbered *nn* through *mm* inclusive
user	all messages from user

As you'll see in the examples that follow, these **mail** commands may be invoked by their first letter only; i.e., you can use ''p'' instead of ''print.''

Sending Mail

The easiest way to send mail is to enter the mail directly from the keyboard and terminate the message by pressing *Control-D* on a line of its own:

```
$ mail tim              ...send some mail to the local user tim.
Subject: Mail Test      ...enter the subject of the mail
Hi Tim,
   How is Amanda doing?

- with best regards from Graham
^D                      ...end of input; standard input is sent as mail.
$ _
```

I wanted to create a mail group called ''music'' that would allow me to send mail to all of the people in my band. To do this, I created a file called ''.mailrc'' in my home directory to look like this:

```
group music jeff richard kelly bev
```

This allowed me to send mail as follows:

```
$ mail music              ...send mail to each member of the group.
Subject: Music
Hi guys
  How about a jam sometime?

- with best regards from Graham.
^D                        ...end of input.
$ _
```

For mail messages that are more than just a few lines long, it's a good idea to compose the message using a text editor, save it in a named file, and then redirect the input of **mail** from the file:

```
$ mail music < jam.txt       ...send jam.txt as mail.
$ _
```

To send mail to users on the Internet, use the standard Internet addressing scheme described in chapter 8:

```
$ mail glass@utdallas < mesg.txt      ...send mail via the Internet.
$ _
```

Reading Mail

When mail is sent to you, it is stored in a file called "/usr/spool/mail/<user id>", where <user id> is equal to your own user id. Files that hold mail are termed "mail folders." For example, my own incoming mail is held in the mail folder "/usr/spool/mail/glass." To read a mail folder, type **mail** followed by an optional folder specifier. You are notified if no mail is currently present:

```
$ mail           ...try reading my mail from the default folder.
No mail for glass
$ _
```

If mail is present, **mail** displays a list of the incoming mail headers and then prompts you with an ampersand. Press *Enter* to read each message in order, and press **q**(uit) to exit mail. The mail that you read is appended by default to the mail folder "mbox" in your home directory, which may be read at a later time by typing the following in your home directory:

```
$ mail -f mbox     ...read mail saved in the mbox mail folder.
```

In the examples that follow, I've deleted some of **mail**'s verbose information so that the output fits in a reasonable amount of space. In the following example, I read two pieces of mail from my friend Tim and then exited **mail**:

```
$ ls -l /usr/spool/mail/glass        ...list mail file; mail is present!
-rw-------  1 glass         738 May  2 14:32 /usr/spool/mail/glass
$ mail                               ...read mail from default folder.
Mail version SMI 4.0 Thu Oct 11 12:59:09 PDT 1990  Type ? for help.
"/usr/spool/mail/glass": 2 messages 2 unread
>U  1 tim@utdallas.edu Sat May  2 14:32 11/382    Mail test
 U  2 tim@utdallas.edu Sat May  2 14:32 11/376    Another mail test
& <Enter>                            ...press enter to read message #1.
From tim@utdallas.edu Sat May  2 14:32:33 1992
To: glass@utdallas.edu
Subject: Mail test
hi there
& <Enter>                            ...press enter to read message #2.
From tim@utdallas.edu Sat May  2 14:32:33 1992
To: glass@utdallas.edu
Subject: Another mail test
hi there again
& <Enter>                            ...press enter to read next message.
At EOF                               ...there are none!
& q                                  ...quit mail.
Saved 2 messages in /home/csservr2/glass/mbox
$ _
```

To see the headers of the messages in your mail folder but not enter mail's command mode, use the **-H** option:

```
$ mail -H                       ...peek at my mail folder.
  U  1 tim@utdallas.edu Sat May 2  14:32    11/382     Message 2
  U  2 tim@utdallas.edu Sat May 2  14:32    11/376     Message 1
$ _
```

To respond to a message after reading it, use the **r**(eply) option. To save a message to a file, use the **s**(ave) option. If you don't specify a message list, **mail** selects the previous message by default. Here's an example:

```
& 15                         ...read message #15.
From ssmith@utdallas.edu Tue Aug  7 23:27:11 1990
To: glass@utdallas.edu
Subject: Re:  come to a party
The SIGGRAPH party begins Thursday NIGHT at 10:00 PM!!
Hope you don't have to teach Thursday night.
& r                          ...reply to ssmith.
```

```
To: ssmith@utdallas.edu
Subject: Re:  come to a party
Thanks for the invitation.
- see you there
^D                                  ...end of input.
& s ssmith.party                    ...save the message from ssmith to me.
"ssmith.party" New file 27/1097
& q                                 ...quit from mail.
$ _
```

It's quite possible that you'll receive quite a bit of ''junk mail''; to delete messages that aren't worth reading, use the d(elete) option:

```
& d1-15          ...delete messages 1 thru 15 inclusive.
& d*             ...delete all remaining messages.
```

Contacting the System Administrator

The system administrator's mailing address is usually ''root'' and/or ''sysadmin.''

CHAPTER REVIEW

Checklist

In this chapter, I described:

- how to obtain a UNIX account
- how to log in and out of a UNIX system
- the importance of changing your password
- the function of a shell
- how to run a utility
- how to obtain online help
- the special terminal metacharacters
- the most common file-oriented utilities
- two UNIX editors
- how to set up your terminal correctly
- how to send electronic mail

Quiz

1. What is one way that hackers try to break UNIX security?
2. What's the best kind of password?
3. Is UNIX case-sensitive?
4. Name the three most common shells.
5. Why are shells better suited than C programs for some tasks?
6. How do you terminate a process?
7. How do you indicate the end-of-input when entering text from the keyboard?
8. How do you terminate a shell?
9. What term is given to the current location of a process?
10. What attributes does every file have?
11. What is the purpose of groups?
12. How do permission flags relate to directories?
13. Who may change the ownership of a file?
14. What does "case-sensitive" mean?

Exercises

1. Design a file security mechanism that alleviates the need for the set-user-id feature. [level: *hard*]
2. Why may a process have only *one* current group? [level: *medium*]
3. Even seeming trivial inventions such as a flashing cursor and a scrolling window have been granted patents. Many software designers construct programs only to find that they have unintentionally re-invented someone else's patented invention. Do you think that patents are fair, and if not, can you think of a better philosophy? [level: *hard*]
4. Obtain the Internet mailing address of an acquaintance in another country and send them email. How long does it take to get there? Does the travel time seem reasonable? [level: *easy*]

Project

1. Send mail to the system administrator and set up two new groups for yourself. Experiment with the group-related utilities and explore the permissions system. [level: *easy*]

Chapter 3

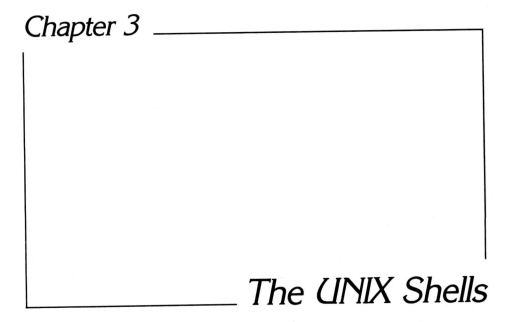

The UNIX Shells

Motivation

A shell is a program that sits between you and the raw UNIX operating system. There are three shells that are commonly available—the Bourne shell, the Korn shell, and the C shell. All three of these shells share a common core set of operations that make life in the UNIX system a little easier. For example, all shells allow the output of a process to be stored in a file or "piped" to another process. They also allow the use of wildcards in filenames, so it's easy to say things like "list all of the files whose name ends with the suffix '.c'." This chapter describes all of the common core shell facilities, whereas chapters 4 through 6 describe the special features of each individual shell.

Prerequisites

In order to understand this chapter, you must have already read chapters 1 and 2. Some of the utilities that I mention are described fully in chapter 7. It also helps if you have access to a UNIX system so that you can try out the various UNIX features that I discuss.

Objectives

In this chapter, I'll explain and demonstrate the common shell features, including I/O redirection, piping, command substitution, and simple job control.

Presentation

The information in this section is presented in the form of several sample UNIX sessions. If you don't have access to a UNIX account, march through the sessions anyway and hopefully you'll be able to try them out later.

Utilities

This section introduces the following utilities, listed in alphabetical order:

chsh	kill	ps
echo	nohup	sleep

Shell Commands

This section introduces the following shell commands, listed in alphabetical order:

echo	kill	umask
eval	login	wait
exec	shift	
exit	tee	

INTRODUCTION

A shell is a program that is an interface between a user and the raw operating system. It makes basic facilities such as multitasking and piping easy to use, as well as adding useful file-specific features such as wildcards and I/O redirection. There are three common shells in use:

- the Bourne shell
- the Korn shell
- the C shell

The shell that you use is a matter of taste, power, and compatibility. For example, the C shell is better than the Bourne shell for interactive work, but slightly worse in some respects for script programming. The Korn shell was designed to be upward compatible with the Bourne shell, and incorporates the best features of the Bourne and C shells plus some more of its own. Unfortunately, it's not as widely available as the other two shells. If you don't have much time to learn a particular shell, I'd recommend starting with the Bourne shell and then upgrading to the Korn shell when you can. I personally use the Korn shell.

SHELL FUNCTIONALITY

This chapter describes the common core of functionality that all three shells provide. Here is a diagram that illustrates the relationship among the three shells:

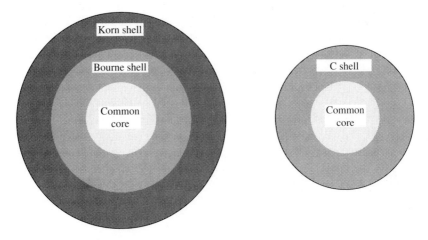

Figure 3.1   The relationship of shell functionality

A hierarchy diagram is a useful way to illustrate the features shared by the three shells, so nice, in fact, that I use the same kind of hierarchy chart throughout the rest of this book:

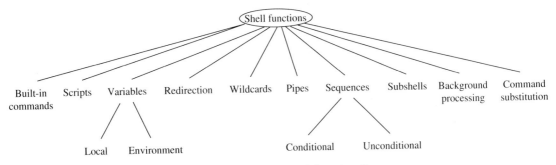

Figure 3.2   Core shell functionality

The rest of this chapter describes each component of the hierarchy in detail.

SELECTING A SHELL

When you are granted a UNIX account, the system administrator chooses a shell for you. To find out which shell was chosen for you, look at your prompt. If you have a $ prompt, you're probably in a Bourne shell or a Korn shell. If you have a % prompt, you're probably in a C shell. When I wrote this chapter, I used a Bourne shell, but it really doesn't matter, since the facilities that I'm about to describe are common to all three shells. However, in later chapters you will want to select the particular shell that the chapter is about.

To change your default login shell, use the **chsh** utility, which works as follows:

Utility: **chsh**

chsh allows you to change your default login shell. It prompts you for the full pathname of the new shell, which is then used as your shell for subsequent logins.

In order to use **chsh,** you must know the full pathnames of the three shells. Here they are:

Shell	Full pathname
Bourne	/bin/sh
Korn	/bin/ksh
C	/bin/csh

In the following example, I changed my default login shell from a Bourne shell to a Korn shell:

```
% chsh                   ...change the login shell from Bourne to Korn.
Changing login shell for glass
Old shell: /bin/sh       ...full pathname of old shell is displayed.
New shell: /bin/ksh      ...enter the full pathname of the new shell.
% ^D                     ...terminate login shell.

login: glass             ...log back in again.
Password:                ...secret.
$ _                      ...this time I'm in a Korn shell.
```

Another way to find out the full pathname of your login shell is to type the following:

```
$ echo $SHELL   ...display the name of my login shell.
/bin/ksh        ...full pathname of the Korn shell program.
$ _
```

This example illustrated the *echo* shell command and a shell variable called $SHELL. Both of these new facilities—echoing and variables—are discussed later in this chapter.

SHELL OPERATIONS

When a shell is invoked, either automatically during a login, or manually from a keyboard or script, it follows a preset sequence:

1. It reads a special startup file, typically located in the user's home directory, that contains some initialization information. Each shell's startup sequence is different, so I'll leave the specific details to later chapters.
2. It displays a prompt and waits for a user command.
3. If the user enters a *Control-D* character on a line of its own, this is interpreted by the shell as meaning "end-of-input," and causes the shell to terminate; otherwise, the shell executes the user's command and returns to step 2.

Commands range from simple utility invocations like this:

```
$ ls
```

to complex-looking pipeline sequences like this:

```
$ ps -ef | sort | ul -tdumb | lpr
```

If you ever need to enter a command that is longer than a line on your terminal, you may terminate a portion of a command by a backslash (\) character, and the shell allows you to continue the command on the next line:

```
$ echo this is a very long shell command and needs to be extended \
with the line continuation character. Note that a single command may \
be extended for several lines
this is a very long shell command and needs to be extended with the line
```

```
continuation character. Note that a single command may be extended for
several lines
$ _
```

EXECUTABLE FILES VERSUS BUILT-IN COMMANDS

Most UNIX commands invoke utility programs that are stored in the directory hierarchy. Utilities are stored in files that have execute permission. For example, when you type:

```
$ ls
```

the shell locates the executable program called "ls," which is typically found in the "/bin" directory, and executes it. The way that the shell finds a utility is described later in this chapter. In addition to its ability to locate and execute utilities, the shell contains several built-in commands, which it recognizes and executes internally. I'll describe two of the most useful ones now: *echo* and *cd*.

Displaying Information: Echo

The built-in *echo* command displays its arguments to standard output, and works like this:

Shell Command: **echo** -n {*arg*}*

echo is a built-in shell command that displays all of its arguments to standard output. By default, it appends a newline to the output; the **-n** option inhibits this behavior.

The Bourne shell does not contain this built-in function, but invokes the utility called **echo** instead, which performs the same actions. Here's an example:

```
$ echo this is a sample line of output
this is a sample line of output
$ _
```

The *echo* command is most often used by shell programs (described shortly) to display information.

Changing Directories: cd

The built-in *cd* command changes the current working directory of the shell to a new location, and was described fully in chapter 2.

METACHARACTERS

Some characters are processed specially by the shell, and are known as *metacharacters*. All three shells share a core set of common metacharacters, whose meanings are as follows:

Symbol	Meaning
>	Output redirection; writes standard output to a file.
>>	Output redirection; appends standard output to a file.
<	Input redirection; reads standard input from a file.
*	File substitution wildcard; matches zero or more characters.
?	File substitution wildcard; matches any single character.
[...]	File substitution wildcard; matches any character between brackets.
\`command\`	Command substitution; replaced by the output from *command*.
|	Pipe symbol; sends the output of one process to the input of another.
;	Used to sequence commands.
||	Conditional execution; executes a command if the previous one failed.
&&	Conditional execution; executes a command if the previous one succeeded.
(...)	Groups commands.
&	Runs a command in the background.
#	All characters that follow up to a newline are a comment.
$	Accesses a variable.
<<*tok*	Input redirection; reads standard input from script up to *tok*.

When you enter a command, the shell scans it for metacharacters and processes them specially. When all metacharacters have been processed, the command is finally executed. To turn off the special meaning of a metacharacter, precede it by a \ character. Here's an example:

```
$ echo hi > file      ...store output of echo in "file".
$ cat file            ...look at the contents of "file".
hi
$ echo hi \> file     ...inhibit > metacharacter.
hi > file             ...> is treated like a regular character.
$ _
```

This chapter describes the meaning of each metacharacter in the order that it was listed in the preceding table.

REDIRECTION

The shell redirection facility allows you to:

- store the output of a process to a file (*output redirection*)
- use the contents of a file as input to a process (*input redirection*)

Let's have a look at each facility, in turn.

Output Redirection

Output redirection is handy because it allows you to save a process's output into a file so it can be listed, printed, edited, or used as input to a future process. To redirect output, use either the > or >> metacharacters. The sequence

```
$ command > fileName
```

sends the standard output of *command* to the file with name *fileName*. The shell creates the file with name *fileName* if it doesn't already exist, or overwrites its previous contents if it already exists. If the file already exists and doesn't have write permission, an error occurs. In the following example, I created a file called "alice.txt" by redirecting the output of the **cat** utility. Without parameters, **cat** simply copies its standard input—which in the case is the keyboard—to its standard output.

```
$ cat > alice.txt                    ...create a text file.
In my dreams that fill the night,
I see your eyes,
^D                                   ...end-of-input.
$ cat alice.txt                      ...look at its contents.
In my dreams that fill the night,
I see your eyes,
$ _
```

The sequence

```
$ command >> fileName
```

appends the standard output of *command* to the file with name *fileName*. The shell creates the file with name *fileName* if it doesn't already exist. In the following example, I appended some text to the existing "alice.txt" file:

```
$ cat >> alice.txt                   ...append to the file.
And I fall into them,
Like Alice fell into Wonderland.
^D                                   ...end-of-input.
$ cat alice.txt                      ...look at the new contents.
In my dreams that fill the night,
I see your eyes,
And I fall into them,
Like Alice fell into Wonderland.
$ _
```

By default, both forms of output redirection leave the standard error channel connected to the terminal. However, both shells have variations of output redirection that allow them to redirect the standard error channel. The C and Korn shells also provide protection against accidental overwriting of a file due to output redirection. These facilities are described in later chapters.

Input Redirection

Input redirection is useful because it allows you to pre-prepare a process's input and store it in a file for later use. To redirect input, use either the < or << metacharacters. The sequence:

```
$ command < fileName
```

executes *command* using the contents of the file *fileName* as its standard input. If the file doesn't exist or doesn't have read permission, an error occurs. In the following example, I sent myself the contents of "alice.txt" via the **mail** utility:

```
$ mail glass < alice.txt                 ...send myself mail.
$ mail                                   ...look at my mail.
Mail version SMI 4.0 Sat Oct 13 20:32:29 PDT 1990   Type ?
for help.
>N  1 glass@utdallas.edu Sun Feb  2 13:29   17/550
& 1                                      ...read message #1.
From: Graham Glass <glass@utdallas.edu>
To: glass@utdallas.edu
In my dreams that fill the night,
I see your eyes,
And I fall into them,
Like Alice fell into Wonderland
& q                                      ...quit mail.
$ _
```

When the shell encounters a sequence of the form:

```
$ command << word
```

it copies its standard input up to but not including the line starting with *word* into a temporary file, and then executes *command* using the contents of the temporary file as its standard input. This facility is used almost exclusively to allow shell programs (*scripts*) to supply the standard input to other commands as inline text, and is revisited in more detail later on in this chapter.

FILENAME SUBSTITUTION (WILDCARDS)

All shells support a wildcard facility that allows you to select files from the file system that satisfy a particular name pattern. Any word on the command line that contains at least one of the wildcard metacharacters is treated as a pattern, and is replaced by an alphabetically sorted list of all the matching filenames. This act of pattern replacement is sometimes known as *globbing*. The wildcards and their meanings are as follows:

Wildcard	Meaning
*	Matches any string, including the empty string.
?	Matches any single character.
[..]	Matches any one of the characters between the brackets. A range of characters may be specified by separating a pair of characters by a dash.

You may prevent the shell from processing the wildcards in a string by surrounding the string by single or double quotes. See the "quoting" section later in this chapter for more details. A / character in a filename must be matched explicitly. Here are some examples of wildcards in action:

```
$ ls -FR            ...recursively list my current directory.
a.c    b.c    cc.c  dir1/  dir2/

dir1:
d.c  e.e

dir2:
f.d  g.c
$ ls *.c            ...anything number of characters followed by ".c".
a.c    b.c    cc.c
$ ls ?.c            ...one character followed by ".c".
a.c    b.c
$ ls [ac]*          ...either "a" or "c" followed by anything.
a.c    cc.c
$ ls [A-Za-z]*      ...alphabetic character followed by any # of chars.
a.c    b.c    cc.c
$ ls dir*/*.c       ...all files ending in ".c" in a "dir*" directory.
dir1/d.c  dir2/g.c
$ ls */*.c          ...all files ending in ".c" in a subdirectory.
dir1/d.c  dir2/g.c
$ ls *2/?.? ?.?
a.c    b.c    dir2/f.d  dir2/g.c
$ _
```

The result of a pattern that has no matches is shell-specific. Some shells have a mechanism for turning off wildcard replacement.

PIPES

The shell allows you to use the standard output of one process as the standard input of another process by connecting the processes together using the pipe (|) metacharacter. The sequence

```
$ command1 | command2
```

causes the standard output of *command1* to "flow through" to the standard input of *command2*. Any number of commands may be connected by pipes. A sequence of commands chained together in this way is called a *pipeline*.

Pipelines support one of the basic UNIX philosophies, which is that large problems can often be solved by a chain of smaller processes, each performed by a relatively small, reusable utility.

The standard error channel is not piped through a standard pipeline, although some shells support this capability.

In the following example, I piped the output of the **ls** utility to the input of the **wc** utility to count the number of files in the current directory. See chapter 2 for a description of **wc**.

```
$ ls                              ...list the current directory.
a.c    b.c    cc.c    dir1    dir2
$ ls | wc -w                      ...count the entries.
        5
$ _
```

Here's an illustration of the pipeline:

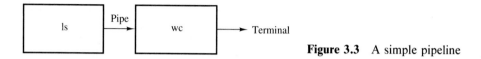

Figure 3.3 A simple pipeline

In the next example, I piped the contents of the "/etc/passwd" file into the **awk** utility to extract the first field of each line. The output of **awk** was then piped to the **sort** utility, which sorted the lines alphabetically. The result was a sorted list of every user on the system. The **awk** utility is described fully in chapter 7.

```
$ head -4 /etc/passwd              ...look at the password file.
root:eJ2S10rVe8mCg:0:1:Operator:/:/bin/csh
nobody:*:65534:65534::/:
daemon:*:1:1::/:
sys:*:2:2::/:/bin/csh
$ cat /etc/passwd | awk -F: '{ print $1 }' | sort ...list user ids.
audit
bin
daemon
glass
ingres
news
nobody
root
sync
sys
tim
uucp
$ _
```

Here's an illustration of the pipeline:

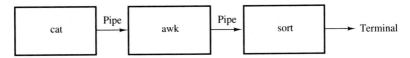

Figure 3.4 A pipeline that sorts

There's a very handy utility called **tee** that allows you to copy the output of a pipe to a file and still allow it to flow down the pipeline. As you might have guessed, the name of this utility comes from the "T" connections that plumbers use. Here's how **tee** works:

Utility: **tee** -ia { *fileName* }+

The **tee** utility copies its standard input to the specified files and to its standard output. The **-a** option causes the input to be appended to the files rather than overwriting them. The **-i** option causes interrupts to be ignored.

In the following example, I copied the output of **who** to a file called "who.capture," and also let it pass through to **sort:**

```
$ who | tee who.capture | sort      ...use tee to copy pipe data.
glass    ttyp0    May  3 18:49 (bridge05.utdalla)
posey    ttyp2    Apr 23 17:44 (blackfoot.utdall)
posey    ttyp4    Apr 23 17:44 (blackfoot.utdall)
$ cat who.capture                   ...look at the captured data.
glass    ttyp0    May  3 18:49 (bridge05.utdalla)
posey    ttyp2    Apr 23 17:44 (blackfoot.utdall)
posey    ttyp4    Apr 23 17:44 (blackfoot.utdall)
$_
```

COMMAND SUBSTITUTION

A command surrounded by grave accents (`) is replaced by its standard output. Any newlines in the output are replaced by spaces. For example:

```
$ echo the date today is `date`
the date today is Mon Feb 3 00:41:55 CST 1992
$ _
```

It's possible to do some crafty things by combining pipes and command substitution. For example, the **who** utility (described in chapter 8) outputs a list of all the users on the system, and the **wc** utility (described in chapter 2) counts the number of words/lines in its input. By piping the output of **who** to the **wc** utility, it's possible to count the number of users on the system:

```
$ who                ...look at the output of who.
posey     ttyp0    Jan 22 15:31    (blackfoot:0.0)
glass     ttyp3    Feb  3 00:41    (bridge05.utdalla)
huynh     ttyp5    Jan 10 10:39    (atlas.utdallas.e)
$ echo there are `who | wc -l` users on the system
there are 3 users on the system
$ _
```

The result of command substitution may be used as part of another command. For example, the **vi** utility allows you to specify a list of files to be edited on the command line, which are then visited by the editor one after the other. The **grep** utility, described in chapter 7, has a **-l** option that returns a list of all the files on the command line that contain a specified pattern. By combining these two features using command substitution, it's possible to specify using a single command that **vi** be invoked upon all files ending in ".c" that contain the pattern "debug":

```
$ vi `grep -l debug *.c`
```

SEQUENCES

If you enter a series of simple commands or pipelines separated by semicolons, the shell will execute them in sequence, from left to right. This facility is useful for type-ahead (and think-ahead) addicts who like to specify an entire sequence of actions at once. Here's an example:

```
$ date; pwd; ls                 ...execute three commands in sequence.
Mon Feb  3 00:11:10 CST 1992
/tmp_mnt/home/csservr2/glass/wild
a.c    b.c    cc.c    dir1    dir2
$ _
```

Each command in a sequence may be individually I/O redirected:

```
$ date > date.txt; ls; pwd > pwd.txt        ...redirect 1st and 3rd.
a.c         b.c         cc.c      date.txt   dir1      dir2
$ cat date.txt                              ...look at output of date.
Mon Feb  3 00:12:16 CST 1992
```

```
$ cat pwd.txt                                        ...look at output of pwd.
/usr/glass
$ _
```

Conditional Sequences

Every UNIX process terminates with an exit value. By convention, an exit value of 0 means that the process completed successfully, and a non-zero exit value indicates failure. All built-in shell commands return 1 if they fail. You may construct sequences that make use of this exit value:

- If you specify a series of commands separated by && tokens, the next command is executed only if the previous command returns an exit code of 0.
- If you specify a series of commands separated by ‖ tokens, the next command is executed only if the previous command returns a non-zero exit code.

The && and ‖ metacharacters therefore mirror the operation of their counterpart C operators.

For example, if the C compiler **cc** compiles a program without fatal errors, it creates an executable program called "a.out" and returns an exit code of 0; otherwise, it returns a non-zero exit code. The following conditional sequence compiles a program called "myprog.c" and only executes the "a.out" file if the compilation succeeds:

```
$ cc myprog.c && a.out
```

The following example compiles a program called "myprog.c" and displays an error message if the compilation fails:

```
$ cc myprog.c || echo compilation failed.
```

Exit codes are discussed in more detail toward the end of this chapter.

GROUPING COMMANDS

Commands may be grouped by placing them between parentheses, which causes them to be executed by a child shell (*subshell*). The group of commands shares the same standard input, standard output, and standard error channels, and may be redirected and piped as if it were a simple command. Here are some examples:

```
$ date; ls; pwd > out.txt        ...execute a sequence
Mon Feb  3 00:33:12 CST 1992     ...output from date.
a.c          b.c                 ...output from ls.
$ cat out.txt                    ...only pwd was redirected.
/usr/glass
$ (date; ls; pwd) > out.txt      ...group and then redirect.
$ cat out.txt                    ...all output was redirected.
Mon Feb  3 00:33:28 CST 1992
a.c
b.c
/usr/glass
$ _
```

BACKGROUND PROCESSING

If you follow a simple command, pipeline, sequence of pipelines, or group of
commands by the & metacharacter, a subshell is created to execute the commands as a background process. The background process runs concurrently with
the parent shell, and does not take control of the keyboard. Background processing is therefore very useful for performing several tasks simultaneously, as long as
the background tasks do not require keyboard input. In windowed environments,
it's more common to run each command within its own window than to run many
commands in one window using the background facility. When a background
process is created, the shell displays some information that may be used to control
the process at a later stage. The exact format of this information is shell-specific.

In the following example, I executed a **find** command in the foreground to
locate the file called "a.c". This command took quite a while to execute, so I
decided to run the next **find** command in the background. The shell displayed the
background process's unique process id number and then immediately gave me
another prompt, allowing me to continue my work. Note that the output of the
background process continued to be displayed at my terminal, which was inconvenient. In the next few sections, I'll show you how you can use the process id
number to control the background process, and how to prevent background processes from messing up your terminal.

```
$ find . -name a.c -print        ...search for "a.c" in the foreground.
./wild/a.c                       ...output from foreground "find".
./reverse/tmp/a.c                ...output from foreground "find".
$ find . -name b.c -print &      ...search for "a.c" in the background.
27174                            ...process id number of background process.
$ date                           ...run "date" in the foreground.
./wild/b.c                       ...output from background "find".
Mon Feb  3 18:10:42 CST 1992     ...output from date.
```

```
$ ./reverse/tmp/b.c          ...more output from background "find".
$ _
```

You may specify several background commands on a single line by separating each command by an ampersand:

```
$ date & pwd &               ...create two background processes.
27310                        ...process id of "date".
27311                        ...process id of "pwd".
/usr/glass                   ...output from "date".
$ Mon Feb  3 18:37:22 CST 1992  ...output from "pwd".
$ _
```

REDIRECTING BACKGROUND PROCESSES

Redirecting Output

To prevent the output from a background process from arriving at your terminal, redirect its output to a file. In the following example, I redirected the standard output of the **find** command to a file called "find.txt". As the command was executing, I watched it grow using the **ls** command:

```
$ find . -name a.c -print > find.txt &   ...create background process.
27188                                     ...process id of "find".
$ ls -l find.txt                          ...look at "find.txt".
-rw-r--r-- 1 glass      0 Feb  3 18:11 find.txt
$ ls -l find.txt                          ...watch it grow.
-rw-r--r-- 1 glass     29 Feb  3 18:11 find.txt
$ cat find.txt                            ...list "find.txt".
./wild/a.c
./reverse/tmp/a.c
$ _
```

Another alternative is to mail it to yourself:

```
$ find . -name a.c -print / mail glass &  ...run "find" in background.
27193
$ cc program.c                            ...do other useful work.
$ mail                                    ...read my mail.
Mail version SMI 4.0 Sat Oct 13 20:32:29 PDT 1990  Type ? for help.
>N  1 glass@utdallas.edu Mon Feb  3 18:12  10/346
& 1
```

```
From: Graham Glass <glass@utdallas.edu>
To: glass@utdallas.edu
./wild/a.c                                    ...the output from "find".
./reverse/tmp/a.c
& q
$ _
```

Some utilities also produce output on the standard error channel, which must be redirected *in addition* to standard output. The next chapter describes in detail how this is done, but I'll supply an example now just in case you're interested:

```
$ man ps > ps.txt &         ...save documentation in background.
27203
$ Reformatting page.  Wait...   ...standard error output from "man".
$ done                      ...standard error output from "man".
$ man ps > ps.txt 2>&1 &    ...redirect error channel too.
27212
$ _                         ...all output is redirected.
```

Redirecting Input

When a background process attempts to read from a terminal, the terminal automatically sends it an error signal which causes it to terminate. In the following example, I ran the **chsh** utility in the background. It immediately issued the "Login shell unchanged" message and terminated, never bothering to wait for any input. I then ran the **mail** utility in the background, which similarly issued the message "No message !?!":

```
$ chsh &                            ...run "chsh" in background.
27201
$ Changing NIS login shell for glass on csservr1.
Old shell: /bin/sh
New shell: Login shell unchanged. ...don't wait for keyboard input.

$ mail glass &                      ...run "mail" in background.
27202
$ No message !?!                    ...don't wait for keyboard input.
$ _
```

SHELL PROGRAMS: SCRIPTS

Any series of shell commands may be stored inside a regular text file for later execution. A file that contains shell commands is called a *script*. Before you can run a script, you must give it execute permission by using the **chmod** utility.

Then, to run it, you only need to type its name. Scripts are useful for storing commonly used sequences of commands, and range in complexity from simple one-liners to fully blown programs. The control structures supported by the languages built into the shells are sufficiently powerful to enable scripts to perform a wide variety of tasks. System administrators find scripts particularly useful for automating repetitive administrative tasks such as warning users when their disk usage goes beyond a certain limit.

When a script is run, the kernel determines which shell the script was written for, and then executes the shell using the script as its standard input. The UNIX kernel decides which shell the script is written for by examining the first line of the script. Here are the rules that it uses:

- If the first line is just a #, then the script is interpreted by a C shell.
- If the first line is of the form #! *pathName*, then the executable program *pathName* is used to interpret the script.
- If neither rule 1 nor rule 2 applies, then the script is interpreted by a Bourne shell.

If a # appears on any other line apart from the first line, all characters up to the end of that line are treated as a comment. Scripts should be liberally commented in the interests of maintainability.

When you write your own scripts, I recommend that you use the #! form to specify which shell the script is designed for, as it's completely unambiguous and doesn't require the reader to be aware of the default rules.

Here is an example that illustrates the construction and execution of two scripts, one for the C shell, and the other for the Korn shell:

```
$ cat > script.csh                    ...create the C shell script.
# This is a sample C shell script.
echo -n the date today is
date            # output today's date.
^D                                    ...end-of-input.
$ cat > script.ksh                    ...create the Korn shell script.
#! /bin/ksh
# This is a sample Korn shell
script.
echo -n the date today is
date            # output today's date.
^D                                    ...end-of-input.
$ chmod +x script.csh script.ksh   ...make them executable.
$ ls -1F script.csh script.ksh     ...look at their attributes.
-rwxr-xr-x  1 glass         59 Feb  2 22:46 script.csh*
-rwxr-xr-x  1 glass         72 Feb  2 22:47 script.ksh*
$ script.csh                          ...execute the C shell script.
the date today is Sat Feb  1 19:50:00 CST 1992
```

```
$ script.ksh                          ...execute the Korn shell script.
the date today is Sat Feb  1 19:50:05 CST 1992
$ _
```

The ".csh" and ".ksh" extensions of my scripts are used only for clarity; scripts can be called anything at all, and don't even need an extension.

SUBSHELLS

When you log into UNIX, it supplies you with an initial login shell. Any simple commands that you enter are executed by this initial shell. However, there are several circumstances when your current (*parent*) shell creates a new (*child*) shell to perform some tasks:

- When a grouped command is executed, such as (ls; pwd; date), the parent shell creates a child shell to execute the grouped commands. If the command is not executed in the background, the parent shell sleeps until the child shell terminates.
- When a script is executed, the parent shell creates a child shell to execute the commands in the script. If the script is not executed in the background, the parent shell sleeps until the child shell terminates.
- When a background job is executed, the parent shell creates a child shell to execute the background commands. The parent shell continues to run concurrently with the child shell.

A child shell is sometimes called a *subshell*. Just like any other UNIX process, a subshell has its own current working directory, and so *cd* commands executed in a subshell do not affect the working directory of the parent shell:

```
$ pwd            ...display my login shell's current working directory.
/usr/glass
$ (cd /; pwd)    ...the subshell moves and executes pwd.
/                ...output comes from the subshell.
$ pwd            ...my login shell never moved.
/usr/glass
$ _
```

Every shell contains two data areas: an environment space and a local variable space. A child shell inherits a copy of its parent's environment space and a clean local variable space:

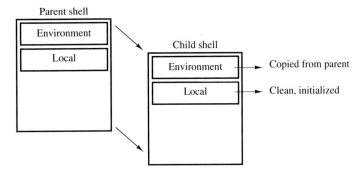

Figure 3.5   Child shell data spaces

VARIABLES

The shell supports two kinds of variables—*local* and *environment*. Both kinds of variables hold data in a string format. The main difference between them is that when a shell invokes another shell (called a *subshell*), the child shell gets a copy of its parent shell's environment variables, but not its local variables. Environment variables are therefore used for transmitting useful information between parent shells and their children.

Every shell has a set of predefined environment variables that are usually initialized by the startup files described in later chapters. Similarly, every shell has a set of predefined local variables that have special meanings to the shell. Other environment and local variables may be created by shell users as needed, and are particularly useful when writing scripts. Here is a list of the predefined environment variables that are common to all shells:

Name	Meaning
$HOME	the full pathname of your home directory
$PATH	a list of directories to search for commands
$MAIL	the full pathname of your mailbox
$USER	your user id
$SHELL	the full pathname of your login shell
$TERM	the type of your terminal

The syntax for assigning variables differs between shells, but the way that you access them is the same; if you write a $ followed by the name of a variable, this token sequence is replaced by the shell with the value of the named variable.

To create a variable, simply assign it a value; a variable does not have to be declared. The details of how variables are assigned are left to the specific shell chapters, but for now it's enough to know that the syntax for assigning a variable in the Bourne and Korn shells is as follows:

```
variableName=value   ...place no spaces around the = character.
```

In the following example, I displayed the values of some common shell environment variables:

```
$ echo HOME = $HOME, PATH = $PATH              ...list two variables.
HOME = /usr/glass, PATH = :/usr/ucb:/bin:/usr/bin
$ echo MAIL = $MAIL                            ...list another.
MAIL = /usr/spool/mail/glass
$ echo USER = $USER, SHELL = $SHELL, TERM=$TERM ...list three more.
USER = glass, SHELL = /bin/sh, TERM=vt100
$ _
```

The next example illustrates the difference between local and environment variables. I assigned values to two local variables and then made one of them an environment variable by using the Bourne shell *export* command (described fully in chapter 4). I then created a child Bourne shell and displayed the values of the variables that I had assigned in the parent shell. Note that the value of the environment variable was copied into the child shell, but the value of the local variable was not. Finally, I typed a *Control-D* to terminate the child shell and restart the parent shell, and then displayed the original variables:

```
$ firstname=Graham        ...set a local variable.
$ lastname=Glass          ...set another local variable.
$ echo $firstname $lastname ...display their values.
Graham Glass
$ export lastname         ...make "lastname" an environment variable.
$ sh                      ...start a child shell; the parent sleeps.
$ echo $firstname $lastname ...display their values again.
Glass                     ...note that firstname wasn't copied.
$ ^D                      ...terminate child; the parent awakens.
$ echo $firstname $lastname ...the parent shell remains unchanged.
Graham Glass
$ _
```

There are several common built-in variables that have a special meaning:

Name	Meaning
$$	The process id of the shell.
$0	The name of the shell script (if applicable).
$1..$9	$n refers to the nth command line argument (if applicable).
$*	A list of all the command line arguments.

The first special variable is especially useful for creating temporary filenames, and the rest are handy for accessing command line arguments in shell scripts. Here's an example that illustrates all of the common special variables:

```
$ cat script.sh                        ...list the script.
echo the name of this script is $0
echo the first argument is $1
echo a list of all the arguments is $*
echo this script places the date into a temporary file called $1.$$
date > $1.$$        # redirect the output of date.
ls $1.$$            # list the file.
rm $1.$$            # remove the file.
$ script.sh paul ringo george john  ...execute the script.
the name of this script is script.sh
the first argument is paul
a list of all the arguments is paul ringo george john
this script places the date into a temporary file called paul.24321
paul.24321
$ _
```

QUOTING

There are often times when you want to inhibit the shell's wildcard replacement, variable substitution, and/or command substitution mechanisms. The shell's quoting system allows you to do just that. Here's the way that it works:

- Single quotes (') inhibit wildcard replacement, variable substitution, and command substitution.
- Double quotes (") inhibit wildcard replacement only.
- When quotes are nested, it's only the outer quotes that have any effect.

The following example illustrates the difference between the two different kinds of quotes:

```
$ echo 3 * 4 = 12        ...remember, * is a wildcard.
3 a.c b b.c c.c 4 = 12
$ echo "3 * 4 = 12"      ...double quotes inhibit wildcards.
3 * 4 = 12
$ echo '3 * 4 = 12'      ...single quotes inhibit wildcards.
3 * 4 = 12
$ name=Graham
$ echo 'my name is $name and the date is `date`'      ...inhibit all.
my name is $name and the date is `date`
$ echo "my name is $name and the date is `date`"      ...no effect.
my name is Graham and the date is Mon Feb  3 23:14:56 CST 1992
$ _
```

HERE DOCUMENTS

Earlier in the chapter, I briefly mentioned the << metacharacter. I delayed its full description until now, as it's only really used in conjunction with scripts and variables. When the shell encounters a sequence of the form:

```
$ command << word
```

it copies its own standard input up to but not including the line starting with *word* into a temporary file, and then executes *command* using the contents of the temporary file as its standard input. Obviously, you should choose a sensible value for *word* that is unusual enough not to occur naturally in the text that follows. If no line containing just *word* is encountered, the Bourne and Korn shells stop copying input when they reach the end of the script, whereas the C shell issues an error message. All references to shell variables are replaced by their values. The most common use of the << metacharacter is to allow scripts to supply the standard input of other commands as inline text, rather than having to use auxiliary files. Scripts that use << are sometimes called *here documents*. Here's an example of a here document:

```
$ cat here.sh             ...look at an example of a "here" doc.
mail $1 << ENDOFTEXT
Dear $1,
  Please see me regarding some exciting news!

- $USER
ENDOFTEXT
echo mail sent to $1
$ here.sh glass           ...send mail to myself using the script.
```

```
mail sent to glass
$ mail                          ...look at my mail.
Mail version SMI 4.0 Sat Oct 13 20:32:29 PDT 1990  Type ? for help.
>N  1 glass@utdallas.edu Sun Feb  2 13:34   12384
& 1                             ...read message #1.
From: Graham Glass <glass@utdallas.edu>
To: glass@utdallas.edu

Dear glass,
  Please see me regarding some exciting news!

- glass

& q                             ...quit out of mail.
$ _
```

JOB CONTROL

Convenient multitasking is one of UNIX's best features, so it's important to be able to obtain a listing of your current processes and control their behavior. There are two utilities and one built-in command that allow you to do this:

- **ps,** which generates a list of processes and their attributes, including their name, process id number, controlling terminal, and owner
- **kill,** which allows you to terminate a process based on its id number
- **wait,** which allows a shell to wait for one of its child processes to terminate

The next few sections describe these facilities in more detail.

Process Status: ps

The **ps** utility allows you to monitor the status of processes, and works as follows:

Utility: **ps** -arux

ps generates a listing of process status information. By default, the output is limited to processes created by your current shell. The **-a** option instructs **ps** to include processes owned by other users. The **-x** option causes **ps** to include processes that don't have controlling terminals, such as unfinished background processes created during a previous login session. The **-r** option restricts the output to processes that are running. The **-u** option produces a long user-oriented output that includes the owner of each process. The meaning of each **ps** column is described in the text that follows.

In the following example, I made use of the **sleep** utility to delay a simple *echo* statement, and placed the command in the background. I then executed the **ps** utility to obtain a list of my shell's associated processes. Each "sh" process was a Bourne shell process; one of them was my login shell, and the other one was the subshell created to execute the command group.

```
$ (sleep 10; echo done) &          ...place a delayed echo in the background.
27387                              ...the process id number.
$ ps                               ...obtain a status list.
  PID TT STAT   TIME COMMAND
27355 p3 S      0:00 -sh (sh) ...the login shell.
27387 p3 S      0:00 -sh (sh) ...the subshell.
27388 p3 S      0:00 sleep 10 ...the sleep.
27389 p3 R      0:00 ps       ...the ps command itself!
$ done                             ...the output from the background process.
$_
```

For the record, here's a description of the **sleep** utility:

Utility: **sleep** *seconds*

The **sleep** utility sleeps for the specified number of seconds and then terminates.

The meanings of the common column headings of **ps** output are as follows:

Column	Meaning
USER	the user id of the owner of the process
PID	the process id
%CPU	the percentage of CPU time that the process used in the last minute
%MEM	the percentage of real RAM that the process used in the last minute
SZ	the size of the process's data and stack in kilobytes
RSS	the amount of real RAM currently used by the process in kilobytes
TT	the process's controlling terminal (t3 = /dev/tty3, etc.)
STAT	the process status
START	the time the process was created, or the date if created before today
TIME	the amount of CPU time used so far (MM:SS)
COMMAND	the name of the command

The STAT field encodes the process's status as follows:

Letter	Meaning
R	runnable/running
T	suspended
P	waiting for page-in
D	in non-interruptible wait, such as waiting for disk I/O
S	short-term sleep, less than 20 seconds
I	long-term sleep, greater than 20 seconds
Z	zombie process

The meanings of most of these terms are described later in the book; only the R and S fields will make sense right now. If an 'N' precedes the STAT entry, this means that the process is running at a modified priority level. See the description of *nice* in chapter 5 for more details. Here's an example of some user-oriented output from **ps:**

```
$ (sleep 10; echo done) &
27462
$ ps -u                 ...request user-oriented output.
USER        PID %CPU %MEM   SZ  RSS TT STAT START  TIME COMMAND
glass     27460  0.0  1.1   40   80 p3 S    20:46  0:00 -sh (sh)
glass     27464  0.0  6.5  192  464 p3 R    20:46  0:00 ps -u
glass     27462  0.0  1.1   40   80 p3 S    20:46  0:00 -sh (sh)
glass     27463  0.0  2.6   24  184 p3 S    20:46  0:00 sleep 10
$ done
$ _
```

If you're interested in tracking the movements of other users on your system, try the **-a** option of **ps:**

```
$ ps -a             ...list all user's processes.
  PID TT STAT TIME COMMAND
 3823 p0 I    0:00 -sh (csh)
 7094 p1 I    0:01 -csh (csh)
  465 p2 T    0:04 latex test.tex
 1018 p5 T    0:00 mail
 1019 p5 T    0:00 sh -c /usr/ucb/more
... other processes are listed here.
 1020 p5 T    0:01 /usr/ucb/more
$ _
```

In chapter 5 I describe a utility called "track" that makes use of this option to monitor other users. Background processes are automatically terminated by the Bourne and Korn shells when you log out, whereas the C shell allows them to continue. If you're using a Bourne or Korn shell and you want to make a background process immune from this effect, use the **nohup** utility to protect it. **nohup** works like this:

Utility: **nohup** *command*

The **nohup** utility executes *command* and makes it immune to the hangup (HUP) and terminate (TERM) signals. The standard output and error channels of *command* are automatically redirected to a file called "nohup.out," and the process's priority value is increased by 5, thereby reducing its priority. This utility is ideal for ensuring that background processes are not terminated when your login shell is exited.

If you execute a command using **nohup,** log out, and then log back in again; you won't see the command on the output of a regular **ps.** This is because a process loses its control terminal when you log out, and continues to execute without it. To include a list of all the processes without control terminals in a **ps** output, use the **-x** option.

Here's an example of this effect:

```
$ nohup sleep 10000 &           ...nohup a background process.
27406
Sending output to 'nohup.out'  ...message from "nohup".
$ ps                            ...look at processes.
  PID TT STAT   TIME COMMAND
27399 p3 S     0:00 -sh (sh)
27406 p3 S N   0:00 sleep 10000
27407 p3 R     0:00 ps
$ ^D                            ...log out.

SunOS

login: glass                    ...log back in.
Password:                       ...secret.
$ ps                            ...the background process it not seen.
  PID TT STAT   TIME COMMAND
27409 p3 S     0:00 -sh (sh)
27411 p3 R     0:00 ps
$ ps -x                         ...the background process may be seen.
  PID TT STAT   TIME COMMAND
27406 ?  I N   0:00 sleep 10000
```

```
27409 p3 S      0:00 -sh (sh)
27412 p3 R      0:00 ps -x
$ _
```

For more information about control terminals, consult chapter 10.

Signalling Processes: kill

If you wish to terminate a process before it completes, use the **kill** command. The Korn and C shells contain a built-in command called **kill,** whereas the Bourne shell invokes the standard utility instead. Both versions of **kill** support the following functionality:

> *Utility/Shell Command:* **kill** [*-signalId*] { *pid* }+
> **kill** -l
>
> **kill** sends the signal with code *signalId* to the list of numbered processes. *signalId* may be the number or name of a signal. By default, **kill** sends a TERM signal (number 15), which causes the receiving processes to terminate. To obtain a list of the legal signal names, use the **-l** option. To send a signal to a process, you must either own it or be a super-user. For more information about signals, refer to chapter 10.
> Processes may protect themselves from all signals except for the KILL signal (number 9). Therefore, to ensure a kill, send signal number 9.
> The **kill** utility (as opposed to the Korn and C shell built-ins) allows you to specify 0 as the *pid*, which causes all of the processes associated with the shell to be terminated. Chapter 5 contains information on the advanced features of the built-in **kill** command.

In the following example, I created a background process and then killed it. To confirm the termination, I obtained a **ps** listing:

```
$ (sleep 10; echo done) &      ...create a background process.
27390                          ...process id number.
$ kill 27390                   ...kill the process.
$ ps                           ...it's gone!
  PID TT STAT   TIME COMMAND
27355 p3 S      0:00 -sh (sh)
27394 p3 R      0:00 ps
$ _
```

The following example illustrates the use of the **-l** option and a named signal. The signal names are listed in numeric order, starting with signal #1.

```
$ kill -l                          ...list the signal names.
HUP INT QUIT ILL TRAP ABRT EMT FPE KILL BUS SEGV SYS PIPE ALRM TERM URG
STOP TSTP CONT CHLD TTIN TTOU IO XCPU XFSZ VTALRM PROF WINCH LOST USR1
USR2
$ (sleep 10; echo done) &          ...create a background process.
27490                              ...process id number.
$ kill -KILL 27490                 ...kill the process with signal #9.
$ _
```

Finally, here's an example of the **kill** utility's ability to kill all of the processes associated with the current shell:

```
$ sleep 30 & sleep 30 & sleep 30 &  ...create three background processes.
27429
27430
27431
$ kill 0                           ...kill them all.
27431 Terminated
27430 Terminated
27429 Terminated
$ _
```

Waiting For Child Processes: wait

A shell may wait for one or more of its child processes to terminate by executing the built-in **wait** command, which works as follows:

Shell Command: **wait** [*pid*]

wait causes the shell to suspend until the child process with the specified process id number terminates. If no arguments are supplied, the shell waits for all of its child processes.

In the following example, the shell waited until both background child processes had terminated before continuing:

```
$ (sleep 30; echo done 1) &        ...create a child process.
24193
$ (sleep 30; echo done 2) &        ...create a child process.
24195
$ echo done 3; wait; echo done 4   ...wait for children between echoes.
done 3
```

```
done 1                              ...output from first child.
done 2                              ...output from second child.
done 4
$ _
```

This facility is generally useful only in advanced shell scripts.

FINDING A COMMAND: $PATH

When a shell processes a command, it first checks to see whether it's a built-in; if it is, the shell executes it directly. *echo* is an example of a built-in shell command:

```
$ echo some commands are executed directly by the shell
some commands are executed directly by the shell
$ _
```

If it isn't a built-in command, the shell looks to see if the command begins with a / character. If it does, it assumes that the first token is the absolute pathname of a command, and tries to execute the file with the stated name. If the file doesn't exist or isn't an executable, an errors occurs:

```
$ /bin/ls                           ...full pathname of the ls utility.
script.csh   script.ksh
$ /bin/nsx                          ...a non-existent filename.
/bin/nsx: not found
$ /etc/passwd                       ...the name of the password file.
/etc/passwd: Permission denied      ...because it's not executable.
$ _
```

If it isn't a built-in command or a full pathname, the shell searches the directories whose names are stored in the $PATH environment variable, from left to right, until a file whose name matches the command is found. If a match is found, the file is executed. If a match isn't found or the file that matches is not executable, an error occurs. If $PATH is not set or is equal to the empty string, then only the current directory is searched. The contents of the $PATH variable may be changed using the methods described in later chapters, thereby allowing you to tailor the search path to your needs. The original search path is usually initialized by the shell's startup file, and typically includes all of the standard UNIX directories that contain executable utilities. Here are some examples:

```
$ echo $PATH
:/usr/ucb:/bin:/usr/bin              ...the directories that are searched.
$ ls                                 ...located in the "/bin" directory.
```

```
script.csh   script.ksh
$ nsx                        ...not located anywhere.
nsx: not found
$ _
```

OVERLOADING STANDARD UTILITIES

Users often create a "bin" subdirectory in their home directory and place this subdirectory *before* the traditional "bin" directories in their $PATH setting. This allows them to overload default UNIX utilities with their own "homebrewed" versions, since they will be located by the search process in preference to their standard counterparts. Such practices are not recommended however, as scripts run from a shell expect to use standard utilities and might be confused by the non-standard utilities that actually get executed. In the following example, I inserted my own "bin" directory into the search path sequence, and then overrode the standard "ls" utility with my own version:

```
$ mkdir bin              ...make my own personal "bin" directory.
$ cd bin                 ...move into the new directory.
$ cat > ls               ...create a script called "ls".
echo my ls
^D                       ...end-of-input.
$ chmod +x ls            ...make it executable.
$ echo $PATH             ...look at the current PATH setting.
:/usr/ucb:/bin:/usr/bin
$ echo $HOME             ...look at the pathname of my home directory.
/home/csservr2/glass
$ PATH=:/home/csservr2/glass/bin:/usr/ucb:/bin:/usr/bin   ...update.
$ ls                     ...call "ls".
my ls                    ...my own version overrides "/bin/ls".
$ _
```

Note that only this shell and its child shells would be affected by the change to $PATH; all other shells in the system would be unaffected.

TERMINATION AND EXIT CODES

Every UNIX process terminates with an exit value. By convention, an exit value of 0 means that the process completed successfully, and a non-zero exit value indicates failure. All built-in commands return 1 if they fail. In the Bourne and

Korn shells, the special shell variable $? always contains the value of the previous command's exit code. In the C shell, the $status variable holds the exit code. In the following example, the **date** utility succeeded, whereas the **cc** and **awk** utilities failed:

```
$ date                          ...date succeeds.
Mon Feb  3 22:13:38 CST 1992
$ echo $?                       ...display its exit value.
0                               ...indicates success.
$ cc prog.c                     ...compile a non-existent program.
cpp: Unable to open source file 'prog.c'.
$ echo $?                       ...display its exit value.
1                               ...indicates failure.
$ awk                           ...use awk illegally.
awk: Usage: awk [-f source | 'cmds'] [files]
$ echo $?                       ...display its exit value.
2                               ...indicates failure.
$ _
```

Any script that you write should always explicitly return an exit code. To terminate a script, use the built-in *exit* command, which works as follows:

Shell Command: **exit** *number*

exit terminates the shell and returns the exit value *number* to its parent process. If *number* is omitted, the exit value of the previous command is used.

If a shell doesn't include an explicit *exit* statement, the exit value of the last command is returned by default. The script in the following example returned an exit value of 3:

```
$ cat script.sh             ...look at the script.
echo this script returns an exit code of 3
exit 3
$ script.sh                 ...execute the script.
this script returns an exit code of 3
$ echo $?                   ...look at the exit value.
3
$ _
```

The next chapter contains some examples of scripts that make use of a command's exit value.

COMMON CORE BUILT-INS

There are a large number of built-in commands that are supported by the three shells, of which only a few are common to all. This section describes the most useful common core built-in commands.

eval

> *Shell Command:* **eval** *command*
>
> The *eval* shell command executes the output of *command* as a regular shell command. It is useful when for processing the output of utilities, such as **tset,** which generate shell commands.

In the following example, I executed the result of the *echo* command, which caused the variable $x to be set:

```
$ echo set x=5              ...first execute an echo directly.
set x=5
$ eval `echo set x=5`       ...execute the result of the echo.
$ echo $x                   ...confirm that x was set to 5.
5
$ _
```

For a more complex example, see the description of **tset** in chapter 2.

exec

> *Shell Command:* **exec** *command*
>
> The *exec* shell command causes the shell's process to be replaced by a process that executes *command*. If *command* is successfully executed, the shell that performed the *exec* ceases to exist. If this shell was a login shell, then the login session is terminated.

In the following example, I exec'ed the **date** command from my login shell, which caused the **date** utility to run and then my login process to terminate:

```
$ exec date                      ...replace shell process by date process.
Sun May  3 18:55:01 CDT 1992     ...output from date utility.

login: _                         ...login shell is terminated.
```

shift

> *Shell Command:* **shift**
>
> The *shift* shell command causes all of the positional parameters $1..$n to be renamed $2..$(n-1), and $1 to be lost. It's particularly handy in shell scripts when cycling through a series of command line parameters. If there are no positional arguments left to shift, an error message is displayed.

In the following example, I wrote a C shell script to display its arguments before and after a shift.

```
$ cat shift.csh                        ...list the script.
#! /bin/csh
echo first argument is $1, all args are $*
shift
echo first argument is $1, all args are $*
$ shift.csh a b c d                    ...try with four arguments.
first argument is a, all args are a b c d
first argument is b, all args are b c d
$ shift.csh a                          ...try with one argument.
first argument is a, all args are a
first argument is , all args are
$ shift.csh                            ...try with no arguments.
first argument is , all args are
shift: No more words.                  ...error message.
$ _
```

umask

When a C program creates a file, it supplies the file's original permissions settings as an octal parameter to the system call open (). For example, to create a file with read and write permission for the owner, group, and others, it would execute a system call like this:

```
fd = open ("myFile", O_CREAT | O_RDWR, 0666);
```

For information on the encoding of permissions as octal numbers, see chapter 2. For information on the open () system call, see chapter 10. When the shell performs redirection using >, it uses a system call sequence similar to the one shown above to construct a file with octal permission 0666. However, if you try creating a file using >, you'll probably end up with a file that has a permission setting of 644 octal:

```
$ date > date.txt
$ ls -l date.txt
-rw-r--r--  1 glass       29 May  3 18:56 date.txt
$ _
```

The reason for this is that every UNIX process contains a special quantity called a *umask* value, which is used to restrict the permission settings that it requests when a file is created. The default umask value of a shell is 0022 octal. The set bits of a umask value mask out the set bits of a requested permission setting. In the example shown above, the requested permission 0666 was masked with 0022 to produce the final permission 0644:

	r	w	x	r	w	x	r	w	x
original	1	1	0	1	1	0	1	1	0
mask	0	0	0	0	1	0	0	1	0
final	1	1	0	1	0	0	1	0	0

If a file already exists before it is redirected to, the original file's permission values are retained and the umask value is ignored.

Here's how the *umask* command may be used to manipulate the umask value:

Shell Command: **umask** [*octalValue*]

The *umask* shell command sets the shell's umask value to the specified octal number, or displays the current umask value if the argument is omitted. A shell's umask value is retained until changed. Child processes inherit their umask value from their parent.

In the following example, I changed the umask value to 0 and then created a new file to illustrate its effect:

```
$ umask                    ...display current umask value.
22                         ...mask write permission of group/others.
$ umask 0                  ...set umask value to 0.
$ date > date2.txt         ...create a new file.
$ ls -l date2.txt
-rw-rw-rw-  1 glass    29 May  3 18:56 date2.txt
$ _
```

CHAPTER REVIEW

Checklist

In this chapter, I described:

- the relationship between the functionalities of the major three shells
- the common shell metacharacters
- output and input redirection
- filename substitution
- pipes
- command substitution
- command sequences
- grouped commands
- the construction of scripts
- the difference between local and environment variables
- the two different kinds of quotes
- basic job control
- the mechanism that the shell uses to find commands
- several core built-in commands

Quiz

1. Can you change your default shell?
2. How can you enter commands that are longer than one line?
3. What is the difference between a built-in command and a utility?
4. How can you make a script executable?
5. What is the strange term that is sometimes given to filename substitution?
6. Describe a common use for command substitution.

7. Describe the meaning of the terms *parent shell*, *child shell*, and *subshell*.

8. How do you think the *kill* command got its name?

9. Describe a way to override a standard utility.

10. What is a good *umask* value, and why?

Exercises

1. Write a script that prints the current date, your user name, and the name of your login shell. [level: *easy*]

2. Experiment with the *exec* command by writing a series of three shell scripts called "a.sh," "b.sh," and "c.sh" that each display their name, execute **ps,** and then *exec* the next script in the sequence. Observe what happens when you start the first script by executing exec a.sh. [level: *medium*]

3. Why is the file that is created in the following session unaffected by the umask value? [level: *medium*]

```
$ ls -l date.txt
-rw-rw-rw-  1 glass       29 Aug 20 21:04 date.txt
$ umask 0077
$ date > date.txt
$ ls -l date.txt
-rw-rw-rw-  1 glass       29 Aug 20 21:04 date.txt
$ _
```

4. Write a script that creates three background processes, waits for them all to complete, and then displays a simple message. [level: *medium*]

Project

1. Compare and contrast the UNIX shell features against the graphical shells available on Windows and OS/2. Which do you think is better? [level: *medium*]

Chapter 4

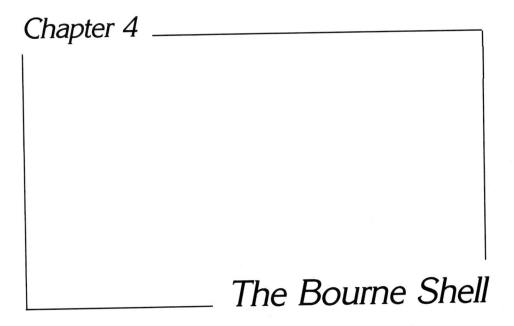

The Bourne Shell

Motivation

The Bourne shell, written by Stephen Bourne, was the first popular UNIX shell, and is available on all UNIX systems. It supports a fairly versatile programming language, and is a subset of the more powerful Korn shell that is described in chapter 5. Knowledge of the Bourne shell will therefore allow you to understand the operation of many scripts that have already been written for UNIX, as well as preparing you for the more advanced Korn shell.

Prerequisites

You should have already read chapter 3 and experimented with some of the core shell facilities.

Objectives

In this chapter, I'll explain and demonstrate the Bourne-specific facilities, including the use of environment and local variables, the built-in programming language, and advanced redirection.

Presentation

The information in this section is presented in the form of several sample UNIX sessions.

Utilities

This section introduces the following utilities, listed in alphabetical order:

    expr   test

Shell commands

This section introduces the following shell commands, listed in alphabetical order:

break	for..in..do..done	set
case..in..esac	if..then..elif..fi	trap
continue	read	while..do..done
export	readonly	

INTRODUCTION

The Bourne shell supports all of the core shell facilities described in chapter 3 plus the following new facilities:

- several ways to set and access variables
- a built-in programming language that supports conditional branching, looping, and interrupt handling
- extensions to the existing redirection and command sequence operations
- several new built-in commands

These new facilities are described by this chapter, and are illustrated by the following hierarchy diagram:

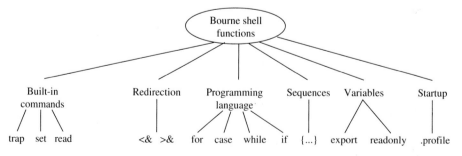

Figure 4.1 Bourne shell functionality

STARTUP

The Bourne shell is a regular C program whose executable file is stored as "/bin/sh". If your chosen shell is "/bin/sh," an interactive Bourne shell is invoked automatically when you log into UNIX. You may also invoke a Bourne shell manually from a script or from a terminal by using the command **sh. sh** has several command line options that are described at the end of this chapter.

When an interactive Bourne shell is started, it searches for a file called ".profile" in its owner's home directory. If it finds the file, it executes all of the shell commands that it contains. Then, regardless of whether ".profile" was found or not, an interactive Bourne shell displays its prompt and awaiting user commands. The standard Bourne shell prompt is $, although it may be changed by setting the local variable $PS1 described later in this chapter.

Non-interactive Bourne shells do not read any startup files.

One common use of ".profile" is to initialize environment variables such as $TERM, which contains the type of your terminal, and $PATH, which tells the shell where to search for executable files. Here's an example of a Bourne shell ".profile" startup file:

```
TERM=vt100                                       # Set terminal type.
export TERM                                      # Copy to environment.
stty erase "^?" kill "^U" intr "^C" eof "^D"     # Set metacharacters.
PATH='.:~/bin:/bin:/usr/ucb:/usr/bin:/usr/local/bin'  # Set path.
```

VARIABLES

The Bourne shell can perform the following variable-related operations:

- simple assignment and access
- testing of a variable for existence
- reading a variable from standard input
- making a variable read-only
- exporting of a local variable to the environment

The Bourne shell also defines several local and environment variables in addition to those mentioned in chapter 3.

The next few sections describe each feature in turn.

Creating/Assigning A Variable

The Bourne shell syntax for assigning a value to a variable is:

```
{name=value}+
```

If a variable doesn't exist, it is implicitly created; otherwise, its previous value is overwritten. A newly created variable is always local, although it may be turned into an environment variable using a method that I'll describe shortly. To assign a value that contains spaces, surround the value by quotes. Here's an example:

```
$ firstName=Graham lastName=Glass age=29 ...assign three variables.
$ echo $firstName $lastName is $age
Graham Glass is 29                        ...simple access.
$ name=Graham Glass                       ...syntax error.
Glass: not found
$ name="Graham Glass"                     ...use quotes to built strings.
$ echo $name                              ...now it works.
Graham Glass
$ _
```

Accessing A Variable

The Bourne shell supports the following access methods:

Syntax	Action
$name	Replaced by the value of name.
${name}	Replaced by the value of name. This form is useful if the expression is immediately followed by an alphanumeric that would otherwise be interpreted as part of the variable name.
${name-word}	Replaced by the value of name if set, and word otherwise.
${name+word}	Replaced by word if name is set, and nothing otherwise.
${name=word}	Assigns word to the variable name if name is not already set, and then is replaced by the value of name.
${name?word}	Replaced by name if name is set. If name is not set, word is displayed to the standard error channel and the shell is exited. If word is omitted, then a standard error message is displayed instead.

If a variable is accessed before it is assigned a value, it returns a null string.

I personally find these variable access techniques to be "hack" methods of dealing with certain conditions, and hardly ever user them. However, it's good to be able to understand code that uses them. The following examples illustrate each access method. In the first example, I used braces to append a string to the value of a variable:

```
$ verb=sing              ...assign a variable.
$ echo I like $verbing   ...there's no variable called "verbing".
I like
$ echo I like ${verb}ing ...now it works.
I like singing
$ _
```

Here's an example that uses command substitution to set the variable $startDate to the current date if it's not already set:

```
$ startDate=${startDate-`date`}  ...if not set, assign to `date`.
$ echo $startDate                ...look at its value.
Tue Feb 4 06:56:51 CST 1992
$ _
```

In the next example, I set the variable $x to a default value and printed its value, all at the same time:

```
$ echo x = ${x=10}    ...assign a default value.
x = 10
$ echo $x             ...confirm the variable was set.
10
$ _
```

In the following example, I displayed messages based on whether certain variables were set or not:

```
$ flag=1                        ...assign a variable.
$ echo ${flag+'flag is set'}    ...conditional message #1.
flag is set
$ echo ${flag2+'flag2 is set'}  ...conditional message #2.
$_
```

In the next example, I tried to access an undefined variable called $grandTotal and received an error message instead:

```
$ total=10                              ...assign a variable.
$ value=${total?'total not set'}        ...accessed OK.
$ echo $value                           ...look at its value.
10
$ value=${grandTotal?'grand total not set'}  ...not set.
grandTotal: grand total not set
$ _
```

In the final example, I ran a script that used the same access method as the previous example. Note that the script terminated when the access error occurred:

```
$ cat script.sh                        ...look at the script.
value=${grandTotal?'grand total is not set'}
echo done         # this line is never executed.
$ script.sh                            ...run the script.
script.sh: grandTotal: grand total is not set
$ _
```

Reading A Variable From Standard Input

The *read* command allows you to read variables from standard input, and works
like this:

Shell Command: **read** { *variable* }+

read reads one line from standard input and then assigns successive words
from the line to the specified variables. Any words that are left over are
assigned to the last named variable.

If you specify just one variable, the entire line is stored in the variable. Here's an
example script that prompts a user for his or her full name:

```
$ cat script.sh                        ...list the script.
$ echo -n "Please enter your name: "
read name                 # read just one variable.
echo your name is $name   # display the variable.
$ script.sh                            ...run the script.
Please enter your name: Graham Walker Glass
your name is Graham Walker Glass     ...the whole line is in "name".
$ _
```

Here's an example that illustrates what happens when you specify more than one
variable:

```
$ cat script.sh                    ...list the script.
echo -n "Please enter your name: "
read firstName lastName      # read two variables.
echo your first name is $firstName
echo your last name is $lastName
$ script.sh                        ...run the script.
Please enter your name: Graham Walker Glass
your first name is Graham          ...first variable holds first word.
your last name is Walker Glass     ...last variable holds the rest.
$ script.sh                        ...run the script again.
Please enter your name: Graham
your first name is Graham          ...first variable holds first word.
your last name is                  ...last variable is empty.
$
```

Exporting Variables

The *export* command allows you to mark local variables for export to the environment, and works as follows:

Shell Command: **export** { *variable* }+

export marks the specified variables for export to the environment. If no variables are specified, a list of all the variables marked for export during the shell session is displayed.

Although it's not necessary, I tend to use uppercase letters to name environment variables. The **env** utility allows you to modify and list environment variables:

Utility: **env** { *variable=value* }* [*command*]

env assigns values to specified environment variables, and then executes an optional command using the new environment. If no variables or command are specified, a list of the current environment is displayed.

In the following example, I created a local variable called $DATABASE, which I then marked for export. When I created a subshell, a copy of the environment variable was inherited:

```
$ export                        ...list my current exports.
export TERM                     ...set in my ".profile" startup file.
$ DATABASE=/dbase/db            ...create a local variable.
$ export DATABASE               ...mark it for export.
$ export                        ...note that it's been added.
export DATABASE
export TERM
$ env                           ...list the environment.
DATABASE=/dbase/db
HOME=/home/csservr2/glass
LOGNAME=glass
PATH=:/usr/ucb:/bin:/usr/bin
SHELL=/bin/sh
TERM=vt100
USER=glass
$ sh                            ...create a subshell.
$ echo $DATABASE                ...a copy was inherited.
/dbase/db
$ ^D                            ...terminate subshell.
$ _
```

Read-only Variables

The *readonly* command allows you to protect variables against modification, and
works like this:

Shell Command: **readonly** { *variable* }*

readonly makes the specified variables read-only, protecting them against
future modification. If no variables are specified, a list of the current read-
only variables is displayed. Copies of exported variables do not inherit their
read-only status.

In the following example, I protected a local variable from modification. I then
exported the variable and showed that its copy did not inherit the read-only status:

```
$ password=Shazam            ...assign a local variable.
$ echo $password             ...display its value.
Shazam
$ readonly password          ...protect it.
$ readonly                   ...list all readonly variables.
readonly password
$ password=Phoombah          ...try to modify it.
password: is read only
$ export password            ...export the variable.
$ password=Phoombah          ...try to modify it.
password: is read only
$ sh                         ...create a subshell.
$ readonly                   ...the exported password is not readonly.
$ echo $password             ...its value was copied correctly.
Shazam
$ password=Alacazar          ...its value may be changed.
$ echo $password             ...echo its value.
Alacazar
$ ^D                         ...terminate the subshell.
$ echo $password             ...echo original value.
Shazam
$ _
```

Predefined Local Variables

In addition to the core predefined local variables, the Bourne shell defines the
following:

Name	Value
$@	an individually quoted list of all the positional parameters
$#	the number of positional parameters
$?	the exit value of the last command
$!	the process id of the last background command
$-	the current shell options assigned from the command line or by the built-in set command—discussed later

Here's a small shell script that illustrates the first three variables. In this example, the **cc** compiler was invoked on a file that didn't exist, and therefore returned a failure exit code.

```
$ cat script.sh                      ...list the script.
echo there are $# command line arguments: $@
cc $1                                # compile the first argument.
echo the last exit value was $?      # display the exit code.
$ script.sh nofile tmpfile           ...execute the script.
there are 2 command line arguments: nofile tmpfile
cc: Warning: File with unknown suffix (nofile) passed to ld
ld: nofile: No such file or directory
the last exit value was 4            ...cc errored.
$ _
```

The next example illustrates how $! may be used to kill the last background process:

```
$ sleep 1000 &        ...create a background process.
29455                 ...process id of background process.
$ kill $!             ...kill it!
29455 Terminated
$ echo $!             ...the process id is still remembered.
29455
$ _
```

Predefined Environment Variables

In addition to the core predefined environment variables, the Bourne shell defines the following:

Name	Value
$IFS	When the shell tokenizes a command line prior to its execution, it uses the characters in this variable as delimiters. $IFS usually contains a space, a tab, and a newline character.
$PS1	This contains the value of the command line prompt, and is $ by default. To change the command line prompt, simply set $PS1 to a new value.
$PS2	This contains the value of the secondary command line prompt that is displayed when more input is required by the shell, and is > by default. To change the prompt, set $PS2 to a new value.
$SHENV	If this variable is not set, the shell searches the user's home directory for the ".profile" startup file when a new shell is created. If this variable is set, then the shell searches the directory specified by $SHENV.

Here's a small example that illustrates the first three predefined environment variables. I set my prompt to something different by assigning a new value to $PS1, and changed the delimiter character to a colon, saving the previous value in a local variable. Finally, I set $PS2 to a new value and illustrated an occasion where the secondary prompt is displayed.

```
$ PS1="sh? "               ...set a new primary prompt.
sh? oldIFS=$IFS            ...remember the old value of IFS.
sh? IFS=":"                ...change the word delimiter to a colon.
sh? ls:*.c                 ...this executes OK!
badguy.c    number.c    open.c      trunc.c     writer.c
fact2.c     number2.c   reader.c    who.c
sh? IFS=$oldIFS            ...restore the old value of IFS.
sh? string="a long\        ...assign a long string (\ quotes the newline).
>  string"                 ...">" is the default secondary prompt.
sh? echo $string           ...look at the value of "string".
a long string
sh? PS2="??? "             ...change the secondary prompt.
sh? string="a long\        ...assign a long string.
??? string"                ..."???" is the new secondary prompt.
sh? echo $string           ...look at the value of "string".
a long string
sh? _
```

ARITHMETIC

Although the Bourne shell doesn't support arithmetic directly, it may be performed by using the **expr** utility, which works like this:

Utility: **expr** *expression*

expr evaluates *expression* and sends the result to standard output. All of the components of *expression* must be separated by blanks, and all of the shell metacharacters must be escaped by a \. *expression* may yield a numeric or string result, depending on the operators that it contains. The result of *expression* may be assigned to a shell variable by appropriate use of command substitution.

expression may be constructed by applying the following binary operators to integer operands, grouped in decreasing order of precedence:

OPERATOR	MEANING
* / %	multiplication, division, remainder
+ -	addition, subtraction
=\>\>=\<\<=!=	comparison operators
\&	logical and
|	logical or

Escaped parentheses \(and \) may be used to explicitly control the order of evaluation. **expr** also supports a few string operators:

OPERATOR	MEANING
string : *regularExpression* **match** *string regularExpression*	Both forms return the length of string if both sides match, and 0 otherwise.
substr *string start length*	Returns the substring of *string* starting from index *start* and consisting of *length* characters.
index *string charList*	Returns the index of the first character in *string* that appears in *charList*.
length *string*	Returns the length of *string*.

where the format of *regularExpression* is defined in the appendix.

The following example illustrates some of the functions of **expr,** and makes plentiful use of command substitution:

```
$ x=1                           ...initial value of x.
$ x=`expr $x + 1`               ...increment x.
$ echo $x
```

```
2
$ x=`expr 2 + 3 \* 5`                          ...* before +.
$ echo $x
17
$ echo `expr \( 2 + 3 \) \* 5`                 ...regroup.
25
$ echo `expr length "cat"`                     ...find length of "cat".
3
$ echo `expr substr "donkey" 4 3`              ...extract a substring.
key
$ echo `expr index "donkey" "ke"`              ...locate a substring.
4
$ echo `expr match "smalltalk" '.*lk'`         ...attempt a match.
9
$ echo `expr match "transputer" '*.lk'`        ...attempt a match.
0
$ echo `expr "transputer" : '*.lk'`            ...attempt a match.
0
$ echo `expr \( 4 \> 5 \)`                      ...is 4 > 5 ?
0
$ echo `expr \( 4 \> 5 \) \| \( 6 \< 7 \)`     ...is 4 > 5 or 6 < 7?
1
$ _
```

CONDITIONAL EXPRESSIONS

The control structures described in the next section often branch based on the value of a logical expression; that is, an expression that evaluates to true or false. The **test** utility supports a substantial set of UNIX-oriented expressions suitable for most occasions, and works like this:

Utility: **test** *expression*
    [*expression*]   (equivalent form on some UNIX systems)

test returns a zero exit code if *expression* evaluates to true; otherwise, it returns a non-zero exit status. The exit status is typically used by shell control structures for branching purposes.

Some Bourne shells support **test** as a built-in command, in which case they support the second form of evaluation as well. The brackets of the second form must be surrounded by spaces in order to work.

See the following text for a description of the syntax of *expression*.

A **test** expression may take the following forms:

Form	Meaning
-b *filename*	True if *filename* exists as a block special file.
-c *filename*	True if *filename* exists as a character special file.
-d *filename*	True if *filename* exists as a directory.
-f *filename*	True if *filename* exists as a non-directory.
-g *filename*	True if *filename* exists as a set-group-id file.
-h *filename*	True if *filename* exists as a symbolic link.
-k *filename*	True if *filename* exists and has its sticky bit set.
-l *string*	The length of *string*.
-n *string*	True if *string* contains at least one character.
-p *filename*	True if *filename* exists as a named pipe.
-r *filename*	True if *filename* exists as a readable file.
-s *filename*	True if *filename* contains at least one character.
-t *fd*	True if file descriptor *fd* is associated with a terminal.
-u *filename*	True if *filename* exists as a set-user-id file.
-w *filename*	True if *filename* exists as a writeable file.
-x *filename*	True if *filename* exists as an executable file.
-z *string*	True if *string* contains no characters.
str1 = *str2*	True if *str1* is equal to *str2*.
str1 != *str2*	True if *str1* is not equal to *str2*.
string	True if *string* is not null.
int1 -eq *int2*	True if integer *int1* is equal to integer *int2*.
int1 -ne *int2*	True if integer *int1* is not equal to integer *int2*.
int1 -gt *int2*	True if integer *int1* is greater than integer *int2*.
int1 -ge *int2*	True if integer *int1* is greater than or equal to integer *int2*.
int1 -lt *int2*	True if integer *int1* is less than integer *int2*.

Form	Meaning
int1 -le *int2*	True if integer *int1* is less than or equal to integer *int2*.
! *expr*	True if *expr* is false.
expr1 -a *expr2*	True if *expr1* and *expr2* are both true.
expr1 -o *expr2*	True if *expr1* or *expr2* are true.
\(*expr* \)	Escaped parentheses are used for grouping expressions.

test is very picky about the syntax of expressions; the spaces shown in this table are *not* optional. For examples of **test,** please consult the next section, which uses them in a natural context.

CONTROL STRUCTURES

The Bourne shell supports a wide range of control structures that make it suitable as a high-level programming tool. Shell programs are usually stored in scripts and are commonly used to automate maintenance and installation tasks. The next few subsections describe the control structures in alphabetical order. They assume that you are already familiar with at least one high-level programming language.

case .. in .. esac

The *case* command supports multi-way branching based on the value of a single string, and has the following syntax:

```
case expression in
pattern { | pattern }* )
 list
 ;;
esac
```

where *expression* is an expression that evaluates to a string, *pattern* may include wildcards, and *list* is a list of one or more shell commands. You may include as many pattern/list associations as you wish. The shell evaluates *expression* and then compares it to each pattern in turn, from top to bottom. When the first matching pattern is found, its associated list of commands is executed and then the shell skips to the matching **esac**. A series of patterns separated by pipe symbols (|) are all associated with the same list. If no match is found, then the shell skips to the matching **esac**.

Here's an example of a script called "menu.sh" that makes use of a *case* control structure:

```
#! /bin/sh
echo menu test program
stop=0                          # reset loop termination flag.
while test $stop -eq 0          # loop until done.
do
  cat << ENDOFMENU              # display menu.

  1   : print the date.
  2, 3: print the current working directory.
  4   : exit
ENDOFMENU
  echo
  echo -n 'your choice? '       # prompt.
  read reply                    # read response.
  echo
  case $reply in                # process response.
    "1")
       date                     # display date.
       ;;
    "2"|"3")
       pwd                      # display working directory.
       ;;
    "4")
       stop=1                   # set loop termination flag.
       ;;
    *)                          # default.
       echo illegal choice      # error.
       ;;
  esac
done
```

Here's the output from the "menu.sh" script:

```
$ menu.sh
menu test program

  1   : print the date.
  2, 3: print the current working directory.
  4   : exit

your choice? 1
```

```
Wed Feb  5 07:09:13 CST 1992

  1   : print the date.
  2, 3: print the current working directory.
  4   : exit

your choice? 2

/usr/glass

  1   : print the date.
  2, 3: print the current working directory.
  4   : exit

your choice? 5

illegal choice

  1   : print the date.
  2, 3: print the current working directory.
  4   : exit

your choice? 4

$ _
```

for .. do .. done

The *for* command allows a list of commands to be executed several times, using a
different value of the loop variable during each iteration. Here's the syntax:

```
for name [ in { word } * ]
do
  list
done
```

The *for* command loops the value of the variable *name* through each *word* in the
word list, evaluating the commands in *list* after each iteration. If no word list is
supplied, $@ ($1..) is used instead. A *break* command causes the loop to immediately end, and a *continue* command causes the loop to immediately jump to the
next iteration. Here's an example of a script that uses a *for* control structure:

```
$ cat for.sh                            ...list the script.
for color in red yellow green blue
```

```
do
   echo one color is $color
done
$ for.sh                              ...execute the script.
one color is red
one color is yellow
one color is green
one color is blue
$ _
```

if .. then .. fi

The *if* command supports nested conditional branches, and has the following syntax:

> **if** *list1*
> **then**
>   *list2*
> **elif** *list3*   ...optional, **elif** part may be repeated several times.
> **then**
>   *list4*
> **else**   ...optional, **else** part may occur zero or one times.
>   *list5*
> **fi**

The *if* command works as follows:

- The commands in *list1* are executed.
- If the last command in *list1* succeeds, the commands in *list2* are executed.
- If the last command in *list1* fails and there are one or more *elif* components, then a successful command list following an *elif* causes the commands following the associated *then* to be executed.
- If no successful lists are found and there is an *else* component, the commands following the *else* are executed.

Here's an example of a script that uses an *if* control structure:

```
$ cat if.sh                          ...list the script.
echo -n 'enter a number: '
read number
if [ $number -lt 0 ]
then
   echo negative
elif [ $number -eq 0 ]
```

```
then
  echo zero
else
  echo positive
fi
$ if.sh                              ...run the script.
enter a number: 1
positive
$ if.sh                              ...run the script again.
enter a number: -1
negative
$ _
```

trap

The *trap* command allows you to specify a command that should be executed when the shell receives a signal of a particular value. Here's the syntax:

---

trap [[*command*] { *signal* } +]

The *trap* command instructs the shell to execute *command* whenever any of the numbered signals *signal* are received. If several signals are received, they are trapped in numeric order. If a signal value of 0 is specified, then *command* is executed when the shell terminates. If *command* is omitted, then the traps of the numbered signals are reset to their original values. If *command* is an empty string, then the numbered signals are ignored. If *trap* is executed with no arguments, a list of all the signals and their *trap* settings are displayed. For more information on signals and their default actions, see chapter 10.

Here's an example of a script that uses the *trap* control structure. When a *Control-C* was typed, the shell executed the *echo* command followed by the *exit* command:

```
$ cat trap.sh                    ...list the script.
trap 'echo Control-C; exit 1' 2  # trap Control-C (signal #2).
while 1
do
  echo infinite loop
  sleep 2                        # sleep for two seconds.
done
$ trap.sh                        ...execute the script.
infinite loop
infinite loop
^C                               ...I typed a Control-C here.
Control-C                        ...displayed by the echo command.
$ _
```

until .. do .. done

The *until* command executes one series of commands as long as another series of commands fails, and has the following syntax:

```
until list1
do
  list2
done
```

The *until* command executes the commands in *list1* and ends if the last command in *list1* succeeds; otherwise, the commands in *list2* are executed and the process is repeated. If *list2* is empty, the *do* keyword should be omitted. A *break* command causes the loop to immediately end, and a *continue* command causes the loop to immediately jump to the next iteration.

Here's an example of a script that uses an *until* control structure:

```
$ cat until.sh                     ...list the script.
x=1
until [ $x -gt 3 ]
do
   echo x = $x
   x=`expr $x + 1`
done
$ until.sh                         ...execute the script.
x = 1
x = 2
x = 3
$ _
```

while .. done

The *while* command executes one series of commands as long as another series of commands succeeds. Here's the syntax:

```
while list1
do
  list2
done
```

The *while* command executes the commands in *list1* and ends if the last command in *list1* fails; otherwise, the commands in *list2* are executed and the process is repeated. If *list2* is empty, the *do* keyword should be omitted. A *break* command causes the loop to end immediately, and a *continue* command causes the loop to jump immediately to the next iteration.

Here's an example of a script that uses a *while* control structure to generate a small multiplication table:

```
$ cat multi.sh                          ...list the script.
x=1                                     # set outer loop value
while [ $x -le $1 ]                     # outer loop
do
  y=1                                   # set inner loop value
  while [ $y -le $1 ]
  do
    echo -n `expr $x \* $y` "    "      # generate one table entry
    y=`expr $y + 1`                     # update inner loop count
  done
  echo                                  # blank line
  x=`expr $x + 1`                       # update outer loop count
done
$ multi.sh 7                            ...execute the script.
1       2       3       4       5       6       7
2       4       6       8       10      12      14
3       6       9       12      15      18      21
4       8       12      16      20      24      28
5       10      15      20      25      30      35
6       12      18      24      30      36      42
7       14      21      28      35      42      49
$ _
```

SAMPLE PROJECT: TRACK

To illustrate a good percentage of the Bourne shell capabilities, I'll present a small project that I call "track." This script tracks a user's logins and logouts, generating a simple report of their sessions. It uses the following utilities:

- **who,** which displays a listing of the current users of the system
- **grep,** which filters text for lines that match a specified pattern
- **diff,** which displays the differences between two files
- **sort,** which sorts a text file
- **sed,** which performs pre-programmed edits on a file
- **expr,** which evaluates an expression
- **cat,** which lists a file
- **date,** which displays the current time

- **rm,** which removes a file
- **mv,** which moves a file
- **sleep,** which pauses for a specified number of seconds

grep, diff, sort, and **sed** are described in chapter 7. **who** is described in chapter 8. The usage of **track** is as follows:

Script: **track** [-n*count*] [-t*pause*] *userId*

track monitors the specified user's login and logout sessions. Every *pause* number of seconds, **track** scans the system and makes a note of who is currently logged on. If the specified user has logged on or logged off since the last scan, this information is displayed to standard output. **track** operates until *count* scans have completed. By default, *pause* is 20 seconds and *count* is 10,000 scans. **track** is usually executed in the background with its standard output redirected.

Here's an example of **track** at work:

```
$ track -n3 ivor -t200   ...track ivor's sessions.
track report for ivor:   ...initial output.
login       ivor         ttyp3   Feb  5 06:53
track report for ivor:   ...ivor logged out.
logout      ivor         ttyp3   Feb  5 06:55
^C                       ...terminate program using Control-C.
stop tracking            ...termination message.
$ _
```

The implementation of **track** consists of three files:

- "track," the main Bourne shell script
- "track.sed," a **sed** script for editing the output of the **diff** utility
- "track.cleanup," a small script that cleans up temporary files at the end

The operation of **track** may be divided into three pieces:

- It parses the command line and sets the values of three local variables: $user, $pause, and $loopCount. If any errors occur, a usage message is displayed and the script terminates.

- It then sets two traps: one to trap the script's termination, and the other to trap an INT (*Control-C*) or QUIT (*Control-*) signal. The latter trap invokes the former trap by executing an explicit *exit*, so the cleanup script *always* gets called regardless of how the script terminates. The cleanup script takes the process id of the main script as its single argument, and removes the temporary files that **track** uses for its operation.

- The script then loops the specified number of times, storing a filtered list of the current users in a temporary file called ".track.new.$$," where $$ is the process id of the script itself. This file is then compared against the last version of the same output, stored in ".track.old.$$." If a line is in the first file but not the second, the user must have logged in, and if a line is in the second file but not the first, the user must have logged out. If the output file from **diff** is non-zero length, it is massaged into a suitable form by **sed** and then displayed. The script then pauses for the specified number of seconds and continues to loop.

The output from two **diff**'ed **who** outputs is illustrated by the following session:

```
$ cat track.new.1112                       ...the new output from who.
gglass              ttyp0      Feb  4 23:04
gglass              ttyp2      Feb  4 23:04
$ cat track.old.1112                       ...the old output from who.
gglass              ttyp0      Feb  4 23:04
gglass              ttyp1      Feb  4 23:06
$ diff track.new.1112 track.old.1112       ...the changes.
2c2
< gglass                ttyp2        Feb  4 23:04
---
> gglass                ttyp1        Feb  4 23:06
$ _
```

The **sed** script "track.sed" removes all lines that start with a digit or "---", and then substitutes "<" for login and ">" for logout. Here is a listing of the three source files:

Track.sed

```
/^[0-9].*/d
/^---/d
s/^</login/
s/^>/logout/
```

track.cleanup

```
echo stop tracking
rm -f .track.old.$1 .track.new.$1 .track.report.$1
```

track

```
pause=20         # default pause between scans
loopCount=10000  # default scan count
error=0          # error flag
for arg in $*    # parse command line arguments
do
  case $arg in
    -t*)         # time
      pause=`expr substr $arg 3 10`      # extract number
      ;;
    -n*)         # scan count
      loopCount=`expr substr $arg 3 10` # extract number
      ;;
    *)
      user=$arg                         # user name
      ;;
  esac
done
if [ ! "$user" ]        # check a user id was found
then
  error=1
fi
if [ $error -eq 1 ]     # display error message if error(s) found
then
  cat << ENDOFERROR     # display usage message
usage: track [-n#] [-t#] userId
ENDOFERROR
  exit 1                # terminate shell
fi
trap 'track.cleanup $$; exit $exitCode' 0      # trap on exit
trap 'exitCode=1; exit' 2 3                    # trap on INT/QUIT
echo -n > .track.old.$$ # zero the old track file.
count=0                 # number of scans so far
while [ $count -lt $loopCount ]
do
  who | grep $user | sort > .track.new.$$      # scan systen
  diff .track.new.$$ .track.old.$$ | sed -f track.sed > .track.report.$$
  if [ -s .track.report.$$ ]           # only report changes
  then                                 # display report
    echo track report for ${user}:
    cat .track.report.$$
  fi
  mv .track.new.$$ .track.old.$$                # remember current state
  sleep $pause                                  # wait a while
  count=`expr $count + 1`                       # update scan count
done
exitCode=0                                      # set exit code
```

MISCELLANEOUS BUILT-INS

The Bourne shell supports several specialized built-in commands. I described several of them in other sections of this chapter, such as those related to control structures and job control. This section contains an alphabetical list of the rest, together with a brief description.

Read Command: .

To execute the contents of a text file from within a shell's environment, use a period followed by the name of the file. The file does not have to have execute permission. This command is handy if you make modifications to your ".profile" file and wish to re-execute it.

```
$ cat .profile        ...assume ".profile" was just edited.
TERM=vt100
export TERM
$ . .profile          ...re-execute it.
$ _
```

Note that since a subshell is not created to execute the contents of the file, any local variables that the file sets are those of the current shell.

null Command

The *null* command is usually used in conjunction with the control structures listed earlier in this chapter, and performs no operation. It is often used in case structures to denote an empty set of statements associated with a particular switch.

> *Shell Command:* **null**
>
> The *null* command performs no operation.

Setting Shell Options: set

The *set* command allows you to control several shell options:

> *Shell Command:* **set** -ekntuvx { *arg* }*
>
> *set* allows you to choose the shell options that are displayed in the table below. Any remaining arguments are assigned to the positional parameters $1, $2, etc., overwriting their current values.

Here is a list of the *set* options:

Option	Meaning
e	If the shell is not executing commands from a terminal or a startup file, and a command fails, then execute an ERR trap and exit.
n	Accept but do not execute commands. This flag does not affect interactive shells.
t	Execute the next command and then exit.
u	Generate an error when an unset variable is encountered.
v	Echo shell commands as they are read.
x	Echo shell commands as they are executed.
-	Turns off the x and v flags and treat further - characters as arguments.

Here's a small example of a script that makes use of these options. The **-x** and **-v** options are very useful when debugging a shell script, as they cause the shell to display lines before and after the variable, wildcard, and command substitition metacharacters are processed. I recommend that you always use these options when testing scripts. Here's an example:

```
$ cat script.sh                          ...look at the script.
set -vx a.c          # set debug trace and overwrite $1.
ls $1                # access first positional parameter.
set -                # turn off trace.
echo goodbye $USER
echo $notset
set -u               # unset variables will generate an error now.
echo $notset         # generate an error.
$ script.sh b.c                           ...execute the script.
ls $1                                     ...output by -v option.
+ ls a.c                                  ...output by -x option.
a.c                                       ...regular output.
set -                                     ...output by -v option.
+ set -                                   ...output by -x option.
goodbye glass                             ...regular output.

script.sh: notset: parameter not set      ...access unset variable.
$ _
```

ENHANCEMENTS

In addition to the new facilities that have already been described, the Bourne shell also enhances the following areas of the common core:

- redirection
- sequenced commands

This section describes each enhancement.

Redirection

In addition to the common core redirection facilities, the Bourne shell allows you to duplicate, close, and redirect arbitrary I/O channels. You may associate the standard input file descriptor (0) with file descriptor n by using the following syntax:

```
$ command <& n   ...execute command after associating standard input.
```

Similarly, you may associate the standard output file descriptor (1) with file descriptor n by using the following syntax:

```
$ command >&n   ...execute command after associating standard output.
```

To close the standard input and standard output channels, use the following syntax:

```
$ command <&-   ...execute command after closing standard input.
$ command >&-   ...execute command after closing standard output.
```

You may precede any redirection metacharacters, including the Bourne-specific ones described above, by a digit to indicate the file descriptor that should be used instead of 0 (for input redirection) or 1 (for output redirection). It's fairly common to redirect file descriptor 2, which corresponds to the standard error channel.

The following example illustrates the use of these redirection facilities. The **man** utility always outputs a couple of lines to the standard error channel: "Reformatting page. Wait" when it begins, and "done" when it ends. If you only redirect standard output, these messages are seen on the terminal. To redirect the standard error channel to a separate file, use the "2>" redirection sequence, and to send it to the same place as standard output, use the "2>&1" sequence.

```
$ man ls > ls.txt                      ...send standard output to "ls.txt".
Reformatting page.  Wait... done   ...from standard error.
$ man ls > ls.txt 2> err.txt           ...send error channel to "err.txt".
$ cat err.txt                          ...look at the file.
Reformatting page.  Wait... done
$ man ls > ls.txt 2>&1                  ...associate stderr with stdout.
```

```
$ head -1 ls.txt                      ...look at first line of "ls.txt".
Reformatting page.
$ _
```

Sequenced Commands

When a group of commands is placed between parentheses, they are executed by a subshell. The Bourne shell also lets you group commands by placing them between braces, in which case they are still redirectable and "pipeable" as a group, but are executed directly by the parent shell. A space must be left after the opening brace, and a semicolon must precede the closing brace.

In the following example, the first *cd* command didn't affect the current working directory of my login shell, since it executed inside a subshell, but the second *cd* command *did*:

```
$ pwd                           ...display current working directory.
/usr/glass
$ (cd /; pwd; ls | wc -1)       ...count files in /, execute in subshell.
/
        22
$ pwd                           ...my shell didn't move; just the subshell.
/usr/glass
$ { cd /; pwd; ls | wc -1; }    ...count files in /, execute in shell.
/
        22
$ pwd                           ...my shell moved.
/
$ _
```

COMMAND LINE OPTIONS

The Bourne shell supports several command line options:

Option	Meaning
-c *string*	Create a shell to execute the command *string*.
-s	Create a shell that reads commands from standard input and sends shell messages to the standard error channel.
-i	Create an interactive shell; like the **-s** option except that the SIGTERM, SIGINT, and SIGQUIT signals are all ignored. For information about signals, consult chapter 10.

CHAPTER REVIEW

Checklist

In this chapter, I described:

- the creation of a Bourne shell startup file
- the creation and access of shell variables
- arithmetic
- conditional expressions
- six control structures
- a sample project for tracking user login sessions
- some miscellaneous built-in commands
- several enhancements to the core facilities

Quiz

1. Who wrote the Bourne shell?
2. Describe a common use of the built-in variable $$.
3. What is the easiest way to re-execute your ''.profile'' file?
4. What debugging features does the Bourne shell provide?

Exercises

1. Write a utility called **junk** that satisfies the following specification:

Utility: **junk** -lp { *fileName* }*

junk is a replacement for the **rm** utility. Rather than removing files, it moves them into the subdirectory ''.junk'' in your home directory. If ''.junk'' doesn't exist, it is automatically created. The **-l** option lists the current contents of the ''.junk'' directory, and the **-p** option purges ''.junk''.

Here's an example of **junk** at work:

```
$ ls -l reader.c                 ...list existing file.
-rw-r--r--  1 glass      2580 May  4 19:17 reader.c
$ junk reader.c                  ...junk it!
$ ls -l reader.c                 ...confirm that it was moved.
reader.c not found
$ junk badguy.c                  ...junk another file.
$ junk -l                        ...list contents of "junk" directory.
-rw-r--r--  1 glass        57 May  4 19:17 badguy.c
-rw-r--r--  1 glass      2580 May  4 19:17 reader.c
$ junk -p                        ...purge junk.
$ junk -l                        ...list junk.
$ _
```

Remember to comment your script liberally. [level: *medium*]

2. Modify the **junk** script to be menu-driven. [level: *easy*]

3. Write a **shhelp** utility that works as follows:

Utility: **shhelp** -k { *command* }*

shhelp lists help about the specified Bourne shell command. The **-k** option lists every command that **shhelp** knows about.

Here's an example of **shhelp** in action:

```
$ shhelp null                              ...ask for help about null.
The null command performs no operation.
$ _
```

Make sure that your utility displays a suitable error message if *command* is not a legal command. I suggest that the text of each command's help message is kept in a separate file, rather than storing it inside the **shhelp** script. If you do decide to place it all inside a script, try using the here document facility. [level: *easy*]

4. Write a crafty script called **ghoul** that is difficult to kill; when it receives a SIGINT (from a *Control-C*), it should create a copy of itself before dying. Thus, every time an unwary user tries to kill a ghoul, another ghoul is created to take its place! Of course, **ghoul** can still be killed by a SIGKILL (-9) signal. [level: *medium*]

Projects

1. Build a phonebook utility that allows you to access and modify an alphabetical list of names, addresses, and telephone numbers. Use the utilities described in chapter 7, such as **awk** and **sed,** to maintain and edit the file of phonebook information. [level: *hard*]

2. Build a process management utility that allows you to kill processes based on their CPU usage, user id, total elapsed time, etc. This kind of utility would be especially useful to system administrators (see chapter 12). [level: *hard*]

Chapter 5:

The Korn Shell

Motivation

The Korn shell, written by David Korn, is a powerful superset of the Bourne shell, and offers improvements in job control, command line editing, and programming features. It's rapidly becoming the industry favorite, and looks likely to be the UNIX shell of choice for many years to come.

Prerequisites

You should already have read chapter 4 and experimented with the Bourne shell.

Objectives

In this chapter, I explain and demonstrate the Korn-specific facilities.

Presentation

The information in this section is presented in the form of several sample UNIX sessions.

Shell Commands

This section introduces the following shell commands, listed in alphabetical order:

alias	jobs	select
bg	kill	typeset
fc	let	unlimit
fg	print	unalias
function	return	

INTRODUCTION

The Korn shell supports all of the Bourne shell facilities described in chapter 4 plus the following new features:

- command customization using aliases
- access to previous commands via a history mechanism.
  vi- and emacs-like command line editing features
- functions
- advanced job control
- several new built-in commands and several enhancements to existing commands

These new facilities are described by this chapter and are illustrated by the following hierarchy diagram:

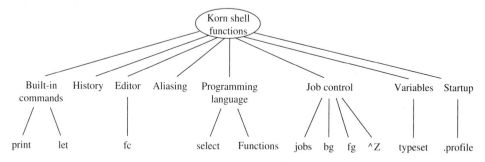

Figure 5.1   Korn shell functionality

STARTUP

The Korn shell is a regular C program whose executable file is stored as ''/bin/ksh.'' If your chosen shell is ''/bin/ksh,'' an interactive Korn shell is invoked automatically when you log into UNIX. You may also invoke a Korn shell manually from a script or from a terminal by using the command **ksh. ksh** has several command line options that are described at the end of this chapter.

When a Korn shell is invoked, the startup sequence is different for interactive shells and non-interactive shells:

Step	Shell type	Action
1	interactive only	Execute commands in ''/etc/profile'' if it exists.
2	interactive only	Execute commands in $HOME/.profile if it exists.
3	both	Execute commands in $ENV if it exists.

The value of $ENV is usually set to $HOME/.kshrc in the $HOME/.profile script. After reading the startup files, an interactive Korn shell then displays its prompt, awaiting user commands. The standard Korn shell prompt is $, although it may be changed by setting the local variable $PS1 described in the previous chapter. Here's an example of a Korn shell ''.profile'' script, which is executed exactly once at the start of every login session:

```
TERM=vt100; export TERM            # my terminal type.
ENV=~/.kshrc; export ENV           # environment filename.
HISTSIZE=100; export HISTSIZE      # remember 100 commands.
MAILCHECK=60; export MAILCHECK     # seconds between mail checks.
set -o ignoreeof                   # don't let Control-D log me out.
set -o trackall                    # speed up file searches.
stty erase '^H'                    # set backspace character.
tset                               # set terminal.
```

Some of these commands won't mean much to you right now, but their meaning will become clear as the chapter progresses.

Here's an example of a Korn shell ''.kshrc'' script, which typically contains useful Korn-shell specific information required by all shells, including those that are created purely to execute scripts:

```
PATH='.:~/bin:/bin:/usr/ucb:/usr/bin:/usr/local/bin:bin:/com:/gnuemacs'
PS1='! $ ';export PS1    # include command number in prompt.
alias h="fc -l"          # set up useful aliases.
alias ll="ls -l"
alias rm="rm -i"
alias cd="cd_x"
alias up="cd_x .."
alias dir="/bin/ls"
alias ls="ls -aF"
alias env="printenv|sort"
function cd_x      # function to display path and directory when moving
```

```
{
  if 'cd' "$@"
  then
    echo $PWD
    ls -aF
  fi
}
```

This script is executed by every Korn shell when it begins, including all subshells.

ALIASES

The Korn shell allows you to create and customize your own commands by using the *alias* command, which works like this:

Shell Command: **alias** [-tx] [*word* [= *string*]]

alias supports a simple form of command line customization. If you alias *word* to be equal to *string* and then later enter a command beginning with *word*, the first occurrence of *word* is replaced by *string* and then the command is reprocessed. If you don't supply *word* or *string*, a list of all the current shell aliases is displayed. If you only supply *word*, then the string currently associated with the alias *word* is displayed. If you supply *word* and *string*, the shell adds the specified alias to its collection of aliases. If an alias already exists for *word*, it is replaced. If the replacement string begins with *word*, it is not reprocessed for aliases to prevent infinite loops. If the replacement string ends with a space, then the first word that follows is processed for aliases.

Here's an example of *alias* in action:

```
$ alias dir='ls -aF'        ...register an alias.
$ dir                       ...same as typing "ls -aF".
./          main2.c         p.reverse.c        reverse.h
../         main2.o         palindrome.c       reverse.old
$ dir *.c                   ...same as typing "ls -aF *.c".
main2.c     p.reverse.c     palindrome.c
$ alias dir                 ...look at the value associated with "dir".
dir=ls -aF
$ _
```

In the following example, I defined a command in terms of itself:

```
$ alias ls='ls -aF'        ...define "ls" in terms of itself; no problem.
$ ls *.c                   ...same as typing "ls -aF *.c".
main2.c      p.reverse.c         palindrome.c
$ alias dir='ls'           ...define "dir" in terms of "ls".
$ dir                      ...same as typing "ls -aF".
./           main2.c      p.reverse.c      reverse.h
../           main2.o      palindrome.c     reverse.old
$ _
```

Aliasing Built-in Commands

All built-in commands may be aliased except for the following: *case, do, done, elif, else, esac, fi, for, function, if, select, then, time, until, while, {, }.*

Removing An Alias

To remove an alias, use the *unalias* command, which works as follows:

Shell Command: **unalias** { *word* } +

unalias removes all the specified aliases.

Here's an example of *unalias*:

```
$ alias dir          ...look at an existing alias.
dir=ls
$ unalias dir        ...remove the alias.
$ alias dir          ...try looking at the alias again.
dir alias not found
$ _
```

Predefined Aliases

For convenience, the shell predefines the following aliases:

Alias	Value
false	let 0
functions	typeset -'
history	fc -l
integer	typeset -i
nohup	nohup
r	fc -e -
true	:
type	whence -v
hash	alias -t

The uses of these aliases will become more apparent as the chapter progresses. For example, the "r" alias is particularly useful, as it allows you to recall previous commands without having to use the tedious sequence "fc -e -".

Some Useful Aliases

Here's a grab-bag of useful aliases that I've gathered from various sources:

Alias	Value
rm	rm -i This causes **rm** to prompt for confirmation.
mv	mv -i This causes **mv** to prompt for confirmation.
ls	ls -aF This causes **ls** to display more information.
env	printenv |sort This displays a sorted list of the environment variables.
ll	ls -l This allows you to obtain a long directory listing more conveniently.

For some other interesting aliases, please see "Aliases" in chapter 6.

Tracked Aliases

One common use of aliases is as a shorthand for full pathnames, to avoid the lookup penalty of the standard search mechanism as it scans the directories specified by $PATH. You may arrange for the full pathname replacement to occur automatically by making use of the *tracked alias* facility. All aliases listed with the **-t** option are flagged as tracked aliases, and the standard search mechanism is used to set their initial value. From then on, a tracked alias is replaced by its value, thereby avoiding the search time. If no aliases follow the **-t** option, a list of all the currently tracked aliases is displayed.

```
$ alias -t page        ...define a tracked alias for page.
$ alias -t             ...look at all tracked aliases.
page=/usr/ucb/page     ...its full pathname is stored.
$ _
```

The "-o trackall" option of *set* (described later in this chapter) tells the shell to track all commands automatically.

```
$ set -o trackall      ...all commands are now tracked.
$ date                 ...execute date.
Thu Feb  6 00:54:44 CST 1992
$ alias -t             ...look at all tracked aliases.
date=/bin/date         ...date is now tracked.
page=/usr/ucb/page
$ _
```

Since the value of a tracked alias is dependent on the value of $PATH, the values of all tracked aliases are re-evaluated every time the $PATH variable is changed. If $PATH is unset, the values of all tracked aliases are set to null, but remain tracked.

Sharing Aliases

To make an alias available to a child shell, you must mark it as an *export alias* by using the **-x** option of *alias*. All aliases listed with the **-x** option are flagged as export aliases. If no aliases follow the **-x** option, a list of all currently exported aliases is displayed. Note that if the value of an alias is changed in a child shell, it does not affect the value of the original alias in the parent shell.

```
$ alias -x mroe='more'  ...add an export alias.
$ alias -x              ...list exported aliases.
autoload=typeset -fu    ...a standard alias.
...                     ...other aliases are listed here.
```

```
ls=ls -F
mroe=more                      ...the alias I just added.
...                            ...other aliases are listed here.
type=whence -v
vi=/usr/ucb/vi
$ cat test.ksh                 ...list a script that uses the new alias.
mroe main2.c
$ test.ksh                     ...execute the script. mroe works!
/* MAIN2.C */

#include <stdio.h>
#include "palindrome.h"

main ()

{
  printf ("palindrome (\"cat\") = %d\n", palindrome ("cat"));
  printf ("palindrome (\"noon\") = %d\n", palindrome ("noon"));
}
$ _
```

HISTORY

The Korn shell keeps a record of commands entered from the keyboard so that they may be edited and re-executed at a later stage. This facility is sometimes known as a *history* mechanism. The built-in command *fc* (**fix c**ommand) gives you access to history. There are two forms of *fc*. The first, simpler form allows you to re-execute a specified set of previous commands, and the second more complex form allows you edit them before re-execution.

Numbered Commands

When you're using history, it's very handy to arrange for your prompt to contain the "number" of the command that you're about to enter. To do this, set the primary prompt $PS1 to contain a ! character:

```
$ PS1='! $ '                   ...set PS1 to contain a !.
103 $ _                        ...prompt for command #103.
```

Storage Of Commands

The Korn shell records the last $HISTSIZE commands in the file $HISTFILE. If the environment variable $HISTSIZE is not set, a default value of 128 is used. If $HISTFILE is not set, or the named file is not writeable, then the file $HOME/

.sh_history is used by default. A history file is shared by all the Korn shells that specify it as their history file. Therefore, as long as you don't change the value of $HISTFILE during a login session, the commands entered during that session are available as history at the next session. In the following example, I examined the history file where commands are stored:

```
$ echo $HISTSIZE            ...I set HISTSIZE to 100 in ".profile".
100
$ echo $HISTFILE            ...I didn't set HISTFILE anywhere.

$ tail -3 $HOME/.sh_history ...display last 3 lines of history file.
echo $HISTSIZE
echo $HISTFILE
tail -3 $HOME/.sh_history
$ _
```

Command Re-execution

The *fc* command allows you to re-execute previous commands. The first, simpler form of *fc* works as follows:

Shell Command: **fc** -e - [*old=new*] *prefix*

This form of the **fc** command re-executes the last command beginning with *prefix* after optionally replacing the first occurrence of the string *old* by the string *new*. *prefix* may be a number, in which case the numbered event is re-executed.

Here's an example of *fc* in action:

```
360 $ fc -e - ech              ...execute last command with prefix "ech".
echo $HISTFILE

361 $ fc -e - FILE=SIZE ech     ...replace "FILE" by "SIZE".
echo $HISTSIZE
100
362 $ fc -e - 360              ...execute command # 360.
echo $HISTFILE

$ _
```

The token "r" is a predefined alias for "fc -e -", which allows for a more convenient way to re-execute commands:

```
364 $ alias r               ...look at "r"'s alias.
r=fc -e -
```

```
365 $ r 364                      ...execute command # 364.
alias r
r=fc -e -
366 $ _
```

Editing Commands

The Korn shell allows you to pre-edit commands before they are re-executed by
using a more advanced form of the *fc* command, which works as follows:

Shell Command: **fc** [-e *editor*] [-nlr] [*start*] [*end*]

This form of **fc** invokes the editor called *editor* upon the specified range of
commands. When the editor is exited, the edited range of commands is then
executed. If *editor* is not specified, then the editor whose pathname is
stored in the environment variable $FCEDIT is used. The value of
$FCEDIT is "/bin/ed" by default, and I *don't* recommend that you use this
default. I personally prefer "/usr/ucb/vi" (the full pathname of the **vi** editor
on my system), as I'm most familiar with the UNIX **vi** editor. If no other
options are specified, the editor is invoked upon the last command.

When you enter the editor, you may edit the command(s) as you wish
and then save the text. When you exit the editor, the Korn shell automatically echoes and executes the saved version of the command(s).

To specify a particular command either by its index or by its prefix,
supply the number or the prefix as the value of *start* but don't supply a value
for *end*. To specify a range of commands, set the value of *start* to select the
first command in the series, and set the value of *end* to select the last
command in the series. If a negative number is supplied, it's interpreted as
an offset to the current command.

The **-l** option causes the selected commands to be displayed but not
executed. In this case, if no command series is specified, the last sixteen
commands are listed. The **-r** option reverses the order of the selected commands, and the **-n** option inhibits the generation of command numbers when
they are listed.

The following example illustrates the method of editing and re-execution:

```
371 $ whence vi                  ...find the location of the "vi" editor.
/usr/ucb/vi
372 $ FCEDIT=/usr/ucb/vi         ...set FCEDIT to full path.
373 $ fc 371                     ...edit command # 371.
...enter vi, edit the command to say "whence ls", save, and quit vi
whence ls                        ...display edited commands.
```

```
/bin/ls                          ...output from edited command.
374 $ fc 371 373                 ...edit commands # 371..373.
...enter vi and edit a list of the last three commands.
...assume that I deleted the first line, changed the remaining lines
...to read "echo -n hi" and "echo there", and then quit.
echo -n "hi "                    ...display edited commands.
echo there
hi there                         ...output from edited commands.
$ _
```

Here's an example of the **-l** option:

```
376 $ fc -l 371 373     ...list commands # 371 .. 373, with numbers.
371 $ whence vi
372 $ FCEDIT=/usr/ucb/vi
373 $ fc 371
377 $ fc -6              ...edit command # 371.
...edit command to say "whence ls" and then quit.
whence ls               ...display edited command.
/bin/ls                 ...output by command.
$ _
```

EDITING COMMANDS

The Korn shell contains simplified built-in versions of the **vi, gmacs,** and **emacs** editors that may be used to edit the current command or previous commands. To select one of these built-in editors, set either the $VISUAL or the $EDITOR variable to a string that ends in the name of one of these editors. In the following example, I selected the **vi** editor:

```
380 $ VISUAL=vi          ...select the built-in "vi" editor.
381 $ _
```

Each built-in editor is now described separately.

The Built-in vi Editor

This description assumes that you are familiar with the **vi** editor. If you're not, please consult the description of the **vi** editor in chapter 2.

To edit the current line, press the *Esc* key to enter the built-in **vi** editor's control mode and make the required changes. To enter append or insert mode from control mode, press the **a** key or the **i** key, respectively. To go back to control mode from either of these modes, press the *Esc* key. To re-execute the command, press the *Enter* key. Be warned—if you type a *Control-D* inside the editor, it terminates the shell, not just the editor.

When in control mode, key sequences fall into one of several categories:

- standard **vi** key sequences (described in chapter 2).
- additional movement.
- additional searching.
- filename completion.
- alias replacement.

The last four categories of key sequences are described in the following subsections.

Additional movement

The cursor up (**k** or -) and cursor down (**j** or +) keys select the previous and next commands in the history list, respectively. This allows you to easily access history from within the built-in editor. To load a command with a particular number, enter command mode and then enter the number of the command followed by the **G** key. Here's an example:

```
125 $ echo line 1
line 1
126 $ echo line 2
line 2
127 $ ...at this point, I pressed the Esc key followed by
      ...k twice (up, up). This loaded command #125 onto the command
      ...line, which I then executed by pressing the Enter key.
line 1
128 $ ...at this point, I pressed the Esc key followed by 125G.
      ...This loaded command #125 onto the command line, which I then
      ...executed by pressing the Enter key.
line 1
129 $_
```

Additional searching

The standard search mechanisms */string* and *?string* search backward and forward through history, respectively. Here's an example:

```
127 $ echo line 1
line 1
138 $ echo line 2
line 2
```

```
139 $ ...at this point, I pressed the Esc key followed by /ech, which
      ...loaded the last command containing "ech" onto the command line.
      ...Then I pressed n to continue the search to the next command
      ...that matched. Finally, I pressed the Enter key to execute the
      ...command.
line 1
$ _
```

Filename completion

If you type a * in control mode, a * is appended to the word that the cursor is over and then processed as if it were a wildcard by the filename substitution mechanism. If no match occurs, a beep is sounded—otherwise, the word is replaced by an alphabetical list of all the matching filenames and the editor enters input mode automatically. Here's an example:

```
$ ls m*
m              m3            main.c           mbox
m1             madness.c     main.o           mon.out
m2             main          makefile         myFile
115 $ ls ma   ...at this point I pressed the Esc key, the * key,
              ...and then the Enter key.
115 $ ls madness.c main main.c main.o makefile
madness.c      main.c                 makefile
main           main.o
$ _
```

If you type an = in control mode, the editor displays a numbered list of all the files that have the current word as a prefix and then redraws the command line:

```
116 $ ls ma ...at this point I pressed the Esc key and then the = key.
1) madness.c
2) main
3) main.c
4) main.o
5) makefile
116 $ ls ma_         ...back to the original command line.
```

If you type a \ in control mode, the editor attempts to complete the current filename in an unambiguous way. If a completed pathname matches a directory, a / is appended; otherwise, a space is appended. Here's an example:

```
116 $ ls ma   ...at this point I pressed the Esc key and then the \ key.
              ...No completion was performed, since "ma" is a prefix of
              ...more than one file.
```

```
116 $ ls mak   ...at this point I pressed the Esc key and then the \ key.
              ...The editor completed the name to be "makefile"
116 $ ls makefile _
```

Alias Replacement

If you find yourself typing the same pattern again and again from the editor, you can make good use of the alias replacement mechanism. If you give _letter an alias of *word*, the sequence @*letter* is replaced by *word* when you're in command mode. In the following example, the letter **i** at the start of the alias causes the built-in editor to go into insert mode, and the literal *Esc* at the end of the string causes it to leave **vi** mode:

```
123 $ alias _c='icommon text^['     ...^[ was Control-V followed by Esc
124 $ echo ...at this point I pressed Esc followed by @c.
124 $ echo common text_
```

The Built-in emacs/gmacs Editor

This description assumes that you are familiar with the **emacs** editor. If you're not, please consult the description of the **emacs** editor in chapter 2.

Most of the **emacs** key sequences are supported. You may move the cursor and manipulate text using the standard **emacs** key sequences. To re-execute the command, press the *Enter* key.

The main difference between the built-in editor and standard **emacs** is that the cursor-up, cursor-down, search forward, and search backward key sequences operate on the history list. For example, the cursor-up key sequence, *Control-P*, displays the previous command on the command line. Similarly, the search backward key sequence *Control-R string* displays the last command that contains *string*.

ARITHMETIC

The *let* command allows you to perform arithmetic, and works like this:

Shell Command: **let** *expression*

The *let* command performs double-precision integer arithmetic, and supports all of the basic math operators using the standard precedence rules. Here they are, grouped in descending order of precedence:

OPERATOR	MEANING
-	unary minus
!	logical negation
* / %	multiplication, division, remainder
+ -	addition, subtraction
<= >= < >	relational operators
== !=	equality, inequality
=	assignment

All of the operators associate from left to right except for the assignment operator. Expressions may be placed between parentheses to modify the order of evaluation. The shell doesn't check for overflow, so beware! Operands may be integer constants or variables. When a variable is encountered, it is replaced by its value, which in turn may contain other variables. You may explicitly override the default base (10) of a constant by using the format *base#number* where *base* is a number between 2 and 36. You must not put spaces or tabs between the operands or operators. You must not place a $ in front of variables that are part of an expression.

Here are some examples:

```
$ let x = 2 + 2          ...expression contains spaces.
ksh: =: syntax error     ...no spaces or tabs allowed!
$ let x=2+2              ...OK.
$ echo $x
4
$ let y=x*4              ...don't place $ before variables.
$ echo $y
16
$ let x=2#100+2#100       ...add two numbers in base 2.
$ echo $x
4                        ...number is displayed in base 10.
$ _
```

Preventing Metacharacter Interpretation

Unfortunately, the shell interprets several of the standard operators such as <, >, and * as metacharacters, so they must be quoted or preceded by a \ to inhibit their special meaning. To avoid this inconvenience, there is an equivalent form of *let* that automatically treats all of the tokens as if they were surrounded by double quotes, and allows you to use spaces around tokens. The token sequence:

```
(( list ))
```

is equivalent to:

```
let " list "
```

Note that double quotes do not prevent the expansion of variables. I personally *always* use the (( )) syntax instead of *let*. Here's an example:

```
$ (( x = 4 ))                  ...spaces are OK.
$ (( y = x * 4 ))
$ echo $y
16
$ _
```

Return Values

If an expression evaluates to zero, its return code is one, otherwise it is zero. The return code may be used by decision-making control structures, such as an *if* statement:

```
$ (( x = 4 ))           ...assign x to 4.
$ if (( x > 0 ))        ...OK to use in a control structure.
> then
>    echo x is positive
> fi
x is positive           ...output from control structure.
$ _
```

For simple arithmetic tests, I recommend using ((..)) instead of **test** expressions.

TILDE SUBSTITUTION

Any token of the form ~*name* is subject to *tilde substitution*. The shell checks the password file ''/etc/passwd'' to see if *name* is a valid user name, and if it is, replaces the ~*name* sequence with the full pathname of the user's home directory. If it isn't, the ~*name* sequence is left unchanged. Tilde subsitution occurs *after* aliases are processed. Here's a table of the tilde substitutions, including the special cases ~+ and ~-:

Tilde sequence	Replaced by
~	$HOME
~*user*	home directory of *user*
~/*pathname*	$HOME/*pathname*
~+	$PWD (current working directory)
~-	$OLDPWD (previous working directory)

The predefined local variables $PWD and $OLDPWD are described later in this chapter. Here are some examples of tilde subsitition:

```
$ pwd
/usr/glass        ...current working directory.
$ echo ~
/usr/glass        ...my home directory.
$ cd /            ...change to root directory.
$ echo ~+
/                 ...current working directory.
$ echo ~-
/usr/glass        ...previous working directory.
$ echo ~dcox
/usr/dcox         ...another user's home directory.
$ _
```

MENUS: SELECT

The *select* command allows you to create simple menus, and has the following syntax:

```
select name [ in {word }+ ]
do
  list
done
```

The *select* command displays a numbered list of the words specified by the *in* clause to the standard error channel, displays the prompt stored in the special variable $PS3, and then waits for a line of user input. When the user enters a line, it's stored in the predefined variable $REPLY and then one of three things occurs:

- If the user entered one of the listed numbers, *name* is set to that number, the commands in list are executed, and then the user is prompted for another choice.
- If the user entered a blank line, the selection is displayed again.
- If the user entered an illegal choice, *name* is set to null, the commands in *list* are executed, and then the user is prompted for another choice.

The next example is a recoding of the menu selection example from the Bourne shell chapter. It replaces the while loop and termination logic with a simpler *select* command.

```
$ cat menu.ksh              ...list the script.
echo menu test program
select reply in "date" "pwd" "pwd" "exit"
do
  case $reply in
    "date")
       date
       ;;
    "pwd")
       pwd
       ;;
    "exit")
       break
       ;;
    *)
       echo illegal choice
       ;;
  esac
done
$ menu.ksh                  ...execute the script.
menu test program
1) date
2) pwd
3) pwd
4) exit
#? 1
Thu Feb  6 21:49:33 CST 1992
#? 5
illegal choice
#? 4
$ _
```

FUNCTIONS

The Korn shell allows you to define functions that may be invoked as shell commands. Parameters passed to functions are accessible via the standard positional parameter mechanism. Functions must be defined before they are used. There are two ways to define a function:

function *name*
{
  list of commands
}

or alternatively,

name ( )
{
  list of commands.
}

I personally favor the second form because it looks more like the C language. To invoke a function, supply its name followed by the appropriate parameters. For obvious reasons, the shell does not check the number or type of the parameters.

Here's an example of a script that defines and uses a function that takes no parameters:

```
$ cat func1.ksh            ...list the script.
message ()  # no-parameter function.
{
  echo hi
  echo there
}
i=1
while (( i <= 3 ))
do
  message    # call the function.
  let i=i+1 # increment loop count.
done
$ func1.ksh                ...execute the script.
hi
there
```

```
hi
there
hi
there
$ _
```

Using Parameters

As I mentioned previously, parameters are accessible via the standard positional
mechanism. Here's an example of a script that passes parameters to a function:

```
$ cat func2.ksh              ...list the script.
f ()
{
  echo parameter 1 = $1      # display first parameter.
  echo parameter list = $*   # display entire parameter list.
}
# main program.
f 1                          # call f () with one parameter.
f cat dog goat               # call f () with three parameters.
$ func2.ksh                  ...execute the script.
parameter 1 = 1
parameter list = 1
parameter 1 = cat
parameter list = cat dog goat
$ _
```

Returning From A Function

The *return* command returns the flow of control back to the caller, and has the
following syntax:

return [*value*]

When *return* is used without an argument, the function call returns immediately
with the exit code of the last command that was executed in the function; otherwise, it returns with its exit code set to *value*. If a *return* command is executed
from the main script, it's equivalent to an *exit* command. The exit code is accessible from the caller via the $? variable. Here's an example function that multiplies
its arguments and returns the result:

```
$ cat func3.ksh        ...list the script.
f ()  # two-parameter function.
```

```
{
    (( returnValue = $1 * $2 ))
    return $returnValue
}
# main program.
f 3 4                        # call function.
result=$?                    # save exit code.
echo return value from function was $result
$ func3.ksh                      ...execute the script.
return value from function was 12
$ _
```

Context

A function executes in the same context as the process that calls it. This means that it shares the same variables, current working directory, and traps. The only exception to this is the "trap on exit"; a function's "trap on exit" executes when the function returns.

Local Variables

The *typeset* command (described in more detail later in this chapter) has some special function-oriented facilities. Specifically, a variable created using the *typeset* function is limited in scope to the function in which it's created and all of the functions that the defining function calls. If a variable of the same name already exists, its value is overwritten and replaced when the function returns. This property is similar (but not identical) to the scoping rules in most traditional high-level languages. Here's an example of a function that declares a local variable using *typeset*:

```
$ cat func4.ksh          ...list the script.
f ()  # two-parameter function.
{
    typeset x                # declare local variable.
    (( x = $1 * $2 ))        # set local variable.
    echo local x = $x
    return $x
}
# main program.
x=1                          # set global variable.
echo global x = $x           # display value of global before function call.
f 3 4                        # call function.
result=$?                    # save exit code.
```

```
echo return value from function was $result      # display result.
echo global x = $x       # display value of global after function call.
$ func4.ksh              ...execute the script.
global x = 1
local x = 12
return value from function was 12
global x = 1
$ _
```

Recursion

With careful thought, it's perfectly possible to write recursive functions. Here are
two example scripts that implement a recursive version of factorial ( ). The first
uses the exit code to return the result, and the second uses standard output to
echo the result.

Recursive Factorial, Using Exit Code

```
factorial ()       # one-parameter function
{
  if (( $1 <= 1 ))
  then
    return 1                        # return result in exit code.
  else
    typeset tmp                     # declare two local variables.
    typeset result
    (( tmp = $1 - 1 ))
    factorial $tmp                  # call recursively.
    (( result = $? * $1 ))
    return $result                  # return result in exit code.
  fi
}
# main program.
factorial 5                         # call function
echo factorial 5 = $?               # display exit code.
```

Recursive Factorial, Using Standard Output

```
factorial ()       # one-parameter function
{
  if (( $1 <= 1 ))
  then
    echo 1                          # echo result to standard output.
  else
    typeset tmp                     # declare two local variables.
```

```
     typeset result
     (( tmp = $1 - 1 ))
     (( result = `factorial $tmp` * $1 ))
     echo $result                # echo result to standard output.
  fi
}
#
echo factorial 5 = `factorial 5`      # display result.
```

Sharing Functions

To share the source code of a function between several scripts, place it in a separate file and then read it using the ".." built-in command at the start of the scripts that use the function. In the following example, assume that the source code of one of the previous factorial scripts was saved in a file called "fact.ksh":

```
$ cat func6.ksh               ...list the script.
. fact.ksh                    # read function source code.
echo factorial 5 = `factorial 5`    # call the function.
$ func6.ksh                   ...execute the script.
factorial 5 = 120
$ _
```

ENHANCED JOB CONTROL

In addition to the Bourne shell job control facilities, the Korn shell supports the following commands:

Command	Function
jobs	lists your jobs
bg	places a specified job into the background
fg	places a specified job into the foreground
kill	sends an arbitrary signal to a process or job

These facilities are only available on UNIX systems that support job control. The next few sections contain a description of each job control facility and examples of their use. The job control features of the Korn shell that are about to be described are identical to those of the C shell.

Jobs

> *Shell Command:* **jobs** [-l]
>
> *jobs* displays a list of all the shell's jobs. When used with the **-l** option, process ids are added to the listing. The syntax of each line of output is:
>
>   *job#   [+|-]   PID   Status   Command*
>
> where a + means that the job was the last job to be placed into the background, and a - means that it was the second-to-last job to be placed into the background. *Status* may be one of the following:
>
> * Running
> * Stopped (suspended)
> * Terminated (killed by a signal)
> * Done (zero exit code)
> * Exit (non-zero exit code)
>
> The only real significance of the + and - is that they may be used when specifying the job in a later command (see: "Specifying A Job").

Here's an example of *jobs* in action:

```
$ jobs                               ...no jobs right now.
$ sleep 1000 &                       ...start a background job.
[1]    27128
$ man ls | ul -tdumb > ls.txt &      ...start another background job.
[2]    27129
$ jobs -l                            ...list current jobs.
[2] + 27129   Running                man ls | ul -tdumb > ls.txt &
[1] - 27128   Running                sleep 1000 &
$ _
```

Specifying A Job

The *bg*, *fg*, and *kill* commands that I'm about to describe allow you to specify a job using one of several forms:

Form	Specifies
%integer	the job number *integer*
%prefix	the job whose name starts with *prefix*
%+	the job that was last referenced
%%	same as *%+*
%-	the job that was referenced second to last

The descriptions that follow contain examples of job specification.

bg

> *Shell Command:* **bg** [*%job*]
>
> *bg* resumes the specified job as a background process. If no job is specified, the last referenced job is resumed.

In the following example, I started a foreground job and then decided it would be better to run it in the background. I suspended the job using *Control-Z* and then restarted it in the background.

```
$ man ksh | ul -tdumb > ksh.txt        ...start a foreground job.
^Z                                     ...suspend it.
[1] + Stopped                  man ksh | ul -tdumb > ksh.txt
$ bg %1                                ...restart it in the background.
[1]    man ksh | ul -tdumb > ksh.txt&
$ jobs                                 ...list current jobs.
[1] +  Running                 man ksh | ul -tdumb > ksh.txt
$ _
```

fg

> *Shell Command:* **fg** [*%job*]
>
> *fg* resumes the specified job as the foreground process. If no job is specified, the last referenced job is resumed.

In the following example, I brought a background job into the foreground using *fg*:

```
$ sleep 1000 &                          ...start a background job.
[1]    27143
$ man ksh | ul -tdumb > ksh.txt &    ...start another background job.
[2]    27144
$ jobs                                  ...list the current jobs.
[2] +  Running              man ksh | ul -tdumb > ksh.txt &
[1] -  Running              sleep 1000 &
$ fg %ma                                ...restart job in foreground.
man ksh | ul -tdumb > ksh.txt       ...command is redisplayed.
$ _
```

kill

> *Shell Command:* **kill** [-l] [-*signal*] { *process* | *job* } +
>
> *kill* sends the specified signal to the specified job or processes. A process is specified by its PID number. A signal may be specified by either its number or symbolically, by removing the ''SIG'' prefix from its symbolic constant in ''/usr/include/signal.h.'' To obtain a list of the signal names, use the **-l** option. If no signal is specified, the TERM signal is sent. If the TERM or HUP signals are sent to a suspended process, it is sent the CONT signal, which causes it to resume.

The following example contains a couple of kills:

```
$ kill -l                              ...list all kill signals.
 1) HUP          12) SYS          23) CHLD
 2) INT          13) PIPE         24) TTIN
 3) QUIT         14) ALRM         25) TTOU
 4) ILL          15) TERM         26) TINT
 5) TRAP         16) USR1         27) XCPU
 6) IOT          17) USR2         28) XFSZ
 7) EMT          18) CLD          29) VTALRM
 8) FPE          19) APOLLO       30) PROF
 9) KILL         20) STOP         31) URG
10) BUS          21) TSTP         32) WINCH
11) SEGV         22) CONT
```

```
$ man ksh | ul -tdumb > ksh.txt &    ...start a background job.
[1]   27160
$ kill -9 %1                         ...kill it via a job id.
[1] + Killed                man ksh | ul -tdumb > ksh.txt &
$ man ksh | ul -tdumb > ksh.txt &    ...start a background job.
[1]   27164
$ kill -KILL 27164                   ...kill it via a process id.
[1] + Killed                man ksh | ul -tdumb > ksh.txt &
$ _
```

ENHANCEMENTS

In addition to the new facilities that have already been described, the Korn shell also offers some enhancements to the Bourne shell in the following areas:

- redirection.
- pipes.
- command substitution.
- variable access.
- extra built-in commands.

This section describes each enhancement.

Redirection

The Korn shell supplies a minor extra redirection facility - the ability to strip leading tabs off "here" documents. Here is the augmented syntax:

---

command << [-] *word*

If *word* is preceded by a -, then leading tabs are removed from the lines of input that follow. Here's an example:

```
$ cat <<- ENDOFTEXT
>            this input contains
>     some leading tabs
> ^D
this input contains
some leading tabs
$ _
```

Pipes

The |& operator supports a simple form of concurrent processing. When a command is followed by |&, it runs as a background process whose standard input and output channels are connected to the original parent shell via a two-way pipe. When the original shell generates output using a *print -p* command (discussed later in this chapter), it is sent to the child shell's standard input channel, and when the original shell reads input using a *read -p* command (discussed later in this chapter), it is taken from the child shell's standard output channel. Here's an example:

```
$ date |&                    ...start child process.
[1]    8311
$ read -p theDate            ...read from standard output of child
                                process.
[1] + Done    date |&        ...child process terminates.
$ echo $theDate              ...display the result.
Sun May 10 21:36:57 CDT 1992
$ _
```

Command Substitution

In addition to the older method of command substitution—surrounding the command with grave accents—the Korn shell also allows you to perform command substitution using the following syntax:

```
$( command )
```

Note that the $ that immediately precedes the open parentheses is part of the syntax, and is *not* a prompt. Here's an example:

```
$ echo there are $(who | wc -l) users on the system
there are 6 users on the system
$ _
```

To substitute the contents of a file into a shell command, you may use **$(<file)** as a faster form of **$(cat file)**.

Variables

The Korn shell supports the following additional variable facilities:

- more flexible access methods
- more predefined local variables

- more predefined environment variables
- simple arrays
- a *typeset* command for formatting the output of variables

The next few subsections describe each feature.

Flexible access methods

In addition to the variable access methods supported by the Bourne shell, the Korn shell supports some more complex access methods, as follows:

Syntax	Action
${#name}	Replaced by the length of the value of *name*.
${#name[*]} }	Replaced by the number of elements in the array *name*.
${name:+word} ${name:=word } ${name:?word} ${name:+word}	Work like their counterparts that do not contain a :, except that *name* must be set *and* non-null instead of just set.
${name#pattern} ${name##pattern}	Removes a leading *pattern* from *name*. The expression is replaced by the value of *name* if name doesn't begin with *pattern*, and with the remaining suffix if it does. The first form removes the smallest matching pattern, and the second form removes the largest matching pattern.
${name%pattern} ${name%%pattern}	Removes a trailing *pattern* from *name*. The expression is replaced by the value of *name* if *name* doesn't end with *pattern*, and with the remaining suffix if it does. The first form removes the smallest matching pattern, and the second form removes the largest matching pattern.

Here are some examples of these features:

```
$ fish='smoked salmon'        ...set a variable.
$ echo ${#fish}               ...display the length of the variable.
13
$ cd dir1                     ...move directory.
$ echo $PWD                   ...display the current working directory.
/usr/glass/dir1
$ echo $HOME
/usr/glass
$ echo ${PWD#$HOME/}          ...remove leading $HOME/
dir1
$ fileName=menu.ksh           ...set a variable.
```

```
$ echo ${fileName%.ksh}.bak  ...remove trailing ".ksh", add ".bak".
menu.bak
$ _
```

Predefined local variables

In addition to the common predefined local variables, the Korn shell supports the following:

Name	Value
$_	The last parameter of the previous command.
$PPID	The process id number of the shell's parent.
$PWD	The current working directory of the shell.
$OLDPWD	The previous working directory of the shell.
$RANDOM	A random integer.
$REPLY	Set by a *select* command.
$SECONDS	The number of seconds since the shell was invoked.
$CDPATH	Used by the *cd* command.
$COLUMNS	Sets the width of the edit window for the built-in editors.
$EDITOR	Selects the built-in editor type.
$ENV	Selects the name of the Korn shell startup file.
$FCEDIT	Defines the editor that is invoked by the *fc* command.
$HISTFILE	The name of the history file.
$HISTSIZE	The number of history lines to remember.
$LINES	Used by *select* to determine how to display the selections.
$MAILCHECK	Tells the shell how many seconds to wait between mail checks. The default value is 600.
$MAILPATH	This should be set to a list of filenames, separated by colons. The shell checks these files for modification every $MAILCHECK seconds.
$PS3	The prompt used by the *select* command, #? by default.
$TMOUT	If set to a number greater than zero and more than $TMOUT seconds elapse between commands, the shell terminates.
$VISUAL	Selects the built-in editor type.

Here are some examples of these predefined variables:

```
$ echo hi there      ...display a message to demonstrate $_.
hi there
$ echo $_             ...display the last argument of the last command.
there
$ echo $PWD           ...display the current working directory.
/usr/glass
$ echo $PPID          ...display the shell's parent process id number.
27709
$ cd /                ...move to the root directory.
$ echo $OLDPWD        ...display the shell's last working directory.
/usr/glass
$ echo $PWD           ...display the shell's current working directory.
/
$ echo $RANDOM $RANDOM  ...display two random numbers.
32561 8323
$ echo $SECONDS       ...display the number of seconds since the shell
                         began.
918
$ echo $TMOUT         ...display the timeout value
0                     ...no timeout selected.
$ _
```

One-dimensional arrays

The Korn shell supports simple one-dimensional arrays. To create an array, simply assign a value to a variable name using a subscript between 0 and 511 in brackets. The syntax is this:

> *name[subscript]=value*

Array elements are created when needed. To access an array element, use the following syntax:

> ${*name[subscript]*}

If you omit *subscript*, the value of 0 is used by default. Here's an example that uses a script to display the squares of the numbers between 0 and 9:

```
$ cat squares.ksh                    ...list the script.
i=0
while (( i < 10 ))
do
  (( squares[$i] = i * i ))          ...assign an individual element.
  (( i = i + 1 ))                    ...increment loop counter.
done
```

```
echo 5 squared is ${squares[5]}           ...display one element.
echo list of all squares is ${squares[*]} ...display all elements.
$ squares.ksh                             ...execute the script.
5 squared is 25
list of all squares is 0 1 4 9 16 25 36 49 64 81
$ _
```

typeset

Shell Command: **typeset** { - HLRZfilprtux [*value*] [*name* [=*word*]]}*

typeset allows the creation and manipulation of variables. It allows variables to be formatted, converted to an internal integer representation for speedier arithmetic, made read-only, made exportable, and switched between lowercase and uppercase.

Every variable has an associated set of flags that determine its properties. For example, if a variable has its "uppercase" flag set, it will always map its contents to uppercase, *even when they are changed*. The options to *typeset* operate by setting and resetting the various flags associated with named variables.When an option is preceded by -, it causes the appropriate flag to be turned *on*. To turn a flag *off* and reverse the sense of the option, precede the option by a + instead of a -.

There now follows a list of the options to *typeset* with illustrations of their usage. I've split the descriptions up into related sections to make things a little easier.

Formatting

In all of the formatting options, the field width of *name* is set to *value* if present; otherwise, it is set to the width of *word*.

Option	Meaning
L	Turn the L flag on and turn the R flag off. Left justify *word* and remove leading spaces. If the width of *word* is less than *name's* field width, then pad it with trailing spaces. If the width of *word* is greater than *name's* field width, then truncate its end to fit. If the Z flag is set, leading zeroes are also removed.
R	Turn the R flag on and turn the L flag off. Right justify *word* and remove trailing spaces. If the width of *word* is less than *name's* field width, then pad it with leading spaces. If the width of *word* is greater than *name's* field width, then truncate its end to fit.
Z	Right justify word and pad with zeroes if the first non-space character is a digit and the L flag is off.

Case

Option	Meaning
l	Turn the l flag on and turn the u flag off. Convert word to lowercase.
u	Turn the u flag on and turn the l flag off. Convert word to uppercase.

Here's an example that left justifies all the elements in an array and then displays them in uppercase:

```
$ cat justify.ksh        ...list the script.
wordList[0]='jeff'       # set three elements.
wordList[1]='john'
wordList[2]='ellen'
typeset -uL7 wordList    # typeset all elements in array.
echo ${wordList[*]}      # beware! shell removes non-quoted spaces
echo "${wordList[*]}"    # works OK.
$ justify.ksh            ...execute the script.
JEFF JOHN ELLEN
JEFF     JOHN     ELLEN
$ _
```

Type

Option	Meaning
i	Store *name* internally as an integer for arithmetic speed. Set the output base to *value* if specified; otherwise, use the *base* of *word*.
r	Flag the named variables as read-only.
x	Flag the named variables as exportable.

In the following example, I modified a previous example by declaring the squares array to be an array of integers. This made the script run faster.

```
$ cat squares.ksh           ...list the script.
typeset -i squares          # declare the array to be integers (for speed).
i=0
while (( i < 10 ))
do
  (( squares[$i] = i * i ))
  (( i = i + 1 ))
done
```

```
echo 5 squared is ${squares[5]}
echo list of all squares is ${squares[*]}
$ squares.ksh              ...execute the script.
5 squared is 25
list of all squares is 0 1 4 9 16 25 36 49 64 81
$ _
```

Miscellaneous

Option	Meaning
f	The only flags that are allowed in conjunction with this option are **t**, which sets the trace option for the named functions, and **x**, which displays all functions with the x attribute set.
p	Causes any output of the *typeset* command to go to the two-way pipe.
t	Tags *name* with the token *word*.

In the following example, I selected the function factorial ( ) to be traced using the **-ft** option, and then ran the script:

```
$ cat func5.ksh              ...list the script.
factorial ()                 # one-parameter function
{
  if (( $1 <= 1 ))
  then
    return 1
  else
    typeset tmp
    typeset result
    (( tmp = $1 - 1 ))
    factorial $tmp
    (( result = $? * $1 ))
    return $result
  fi
}
#
typeset -ft factorial    ...select a function trace.
factorial 3
echo factorial 3 = $?
$ func5.ksh                ...execute the script.
+ let  3 <= 1              ...debugging information.
+ typeset tmp
+ typeset result
+ let  tmp = 3 - 1
```

```
+ factorial 2
+ let  2 <= 1
+ typeset tmp
+ typeset result
+ let  tmp = 2 - 1
+ factorial 1
+ let  1 <= 1
+ return 1
+ let  result = 1 * 2
+ return 2
+ let  result = 2 * 3
+ return 6
factorial 3 = 6
$ _
```

typeset With No Named Variables

If no variables are named, then the names of all the parameters that have the specified flags set are listed. If no flags are specified, then a list of all the parameters and their flag settings are listed. Here's an example:

```
$ typeset            ...display a list of all typeset variables.
export NODEID
export PATH
...
leftjust 7 t
export integer MAILCHECK
$ typeset -i         ...display a list of integer typeset variables.
LINENO=1
MAILCHECK=60
...
$ _
```

Built-ins

The Korn shell enhances the following built-in commands:

- *cd*
- *set*
- *print* (an enhancement of the Bourne shell *echo* command)
- *read*
- *test*
- *trap*

The next few subsections contain a description of each built-in.

cd

The Korn shell's version of *cd* supports several new features, and works like this:

Shell Command: **cd** { *name* }
                  cd *oldName newName*

The first form of the *cd* command is processed as follows:

- If *name* is omitted, the shell moves to the home directory specified by $HOME.
- If *name* is equal to -, the shell moves to the previous working directory that is kept in $OLDPWD.
- If *name* begins with a /, the shell moves to the directory whose full name is *name*.
- If *name* begins with anything else, the shell searches through the directory sequence specified by $CDPATH for a match, and moves the shell to the matching directory. The default value of $CDPATH is null, which causes *cd* to search only the current directory.

If the second form of *cd* is used, the shell replaces the first occurrence of the token *oldName* by the token *newName* in the current directory's full pathname, and then attempts to change to the new pathname. The shell always stores the full pathname of the current directory in the variable $PWD. The current value of $PWD may be displayed by using the built-in command *pwd*.

Here's an example of *cd* in action:

```
$ CDPATH=.:/usr   ...set my CDPATH.
$ cd dir1         ...move to "dir1", located under ".".
$ pwd
/usr/glass/dir1
$ cd include      ...move to "include", located under "/usr".
$ pwd             ...display the current working directory.
/usr/include
$ cd -            ...move to my previous directory.
$ pwd             ...display the current working directory.
/usr/glass/dir1
$ _
```

set

The *set* command allows you to set and unset flags that control shell-wide characteristics:

Shell Command: **set** [-aefhkmnostuvx] [-o *option*] { *arg* } *

The Korn shell version of *set* supports all of the Bourne *set* features plus a few more. The various features of *set* do not fall naturally into categories, so I'll just list each one together with a brief description. An option preceded by a + instead of a - reverses the sense of the description.

Here is a list of the options to *set*:

Option	Meaning
a	All variables that are created are automatically flagged for export.
f	Disable filename substitution.
h	All non-built-in commands are automatically flagged as tracked aliases.
m	Place all background jobs in their own unique process group and display notification of completion. This flag is automatically set for interactive shells.
n	Accept but do not execute commands. This flag has no effect on interactive shells.
o	This option is described separately below.
p	Set $PATH to its default value, cause the startup sequence to ignore the $HOME/.profile file and read ''/etc/suid_profile'' instead of the $ENV file. This flag is set automatically whenever a shell is executed by a process in ''set-user-id'' or ''set-group-id'' mode. For more information on ''set-user-id'' processes, consult chapter 10.
s	Sort the positional parameters.
--	Do not change any flags. If no arguments follow, all of the positional parameters are unset.

The o Option

The **o** option of *set* takes an argument. The argument frequently has the same effect as one of the other flags to *set*. If no argument is supplied, the current settings are displayed. Here is a list of the valid arguments and their meanings:

Option	Meaning
allexport	Equivalent to the a flag.
errexit	Equivalent to the e flag.
bgnice	Background processes are executed at a lower priority.
emacs	Invokes the built-in **emacs** editor.
gmacs	Invokes the built-in **gmacs** editor.
ignoreeof	Don't exit on *Control-D*. **exit** must be used instead.
keyword	Equivalent to the k flag.
markdirs	Append trailing / to directories generated by filename substitution.
monitor	Equivalent to the m flag.
noexec	Equivalent to the n flag.
noglob	Equivalent to the f flag.
nounset	Equivalent to the u flag.
protected	Equivalent to the p flag.
verbose	Equivalent to the v flag.
trackall	Equivalent to the h flag.
vi	Invokes the built-in **vi** editor.
viraw	Characters are processed as they are typed in **vi** mode.
xtrace	Equivalent to the x flag.

I set the **ignoreeof** option in my ''.profile'' script to protect myself against accidental *Control-D* logouts:

```
set -o ignoreeof
```

print

The *print* command is a more sophisticated version of *echo*, and allows you to send output to a arbitrary file descriptor. It works like this:

Shell Command: **print** -npsuR [*n*] { arg }*

By default, *print* displays its arguments to standard output, followed by a newline. The **-n** option inhibits the newline, and the **-u** option allows you to specify a single digit file descriptor *n* for the output channel. The **-s** option causes the output to be appended to the history file instead of an output channel. The **-p** option causes the output to be sent to the shell's two-way pipe channel. The **-R** option causes all further words to be interpreted as arguments.

Here's an example:

```
121 $ print -u2 hi there        ...send output to standard error channel.
hi there
122 $ print -s echo hi there    ...append output to history.
124 $ r 123                     ...recall command #123.
echo hi there
hi there
125 $ print -R -s hi there      ...treat "-s" as an argument.
-s hi there
126 $ _
```

read

The Korn shell's *read* command is a superset of the Bourne shell's *read* command, and works like this:

Shell Command: **read** -prsu [*n*] [*name?prompt*] { *name* }*

The Korn shell *read* works just like the Bourne shell *read*, except for the following new features:

- The **-p** option causes the input line to be read from the shell's two-way pipe.
- The **-u** option causes the file descriptor *n* to be used for input.
- If the first argument contains a ?, the remainder of the argument is used as a prompt.

Here's an example:

```
$ read 'name?enter your name '
enter your name Graham
```

```
$ echo $name
Graham
$ _
```

test

The Korn shell version of *test* accepts several new operators:

Operator	Meaning
-L *fileName*	Return true if *fileName* is a symbolic link.
file1 -nt *file2*	Return true if *file1* is newer than *file2*.
file1 -ot *file2*	Return true if *file1* is older than *file2*.
file1 -ef *file2*	Return true if *file1* is the same file as *file2*.

The Korn shell also supports a more convenient syntax for *test*:

[[*testExpression*]]

is equivalent to:

test *textExpression*

I prefer the more modern form of *test* that uses the double brackets, as it allows me to write more readable programs. Here's an example of this newer form of *test* in action:

```
$ cat test.ksh          ...list the script.
i=1
while [[ i -le 4 ]]
do
  echo $i
  (( i = i + 1 ))
done
$ test.ksh              ...execute the script.
1
2
3
4
$ _
```

trap

The Korn shell's *trap* command is a superset of the Bourne shell's *trap* command, and works as follows:

Shell Command: **trap** [*command*] [*signal*]

The Korn shell *trap* works just like the Bourne shell *trap*, except for the following features:

- If arg is -, then all of the specified signal actions are reset to their initial values.
- If an EXIT or 0 signal value is given to a *trap* inside a function, then *command* is executed when the function is exited.

In the following example, I set the EXIT trap inside a function to demonstrate local function traps:

```
$ cat trap.ksh                        ...list the script.
f ()
{
  echo 'enter f ()'
  trap 'echo leaving f...' EXIT  # set a local trap
  echo 'exit f ()'
}
# main program.
trap 'echo exit shell' EXIT       # set a global trap.
f                                 # invoke the function f ().
$ trap.ksh                        ...execute the script.
enter f ()
exit f ()
leaving f...                      ...local EXIT is trapped.
exit shell                        ...global EXIT is trapped.
$ _
```

SAMPLE PROJECT: JUNK

To illustrate some of the Korn shell capabilities, I present a Korn shell version of the "junk" script project that was suggested at the end of the Bourne shell chapter. Here's the definition of the **junk** utility about to be described:

> *Utility*: **junk** -lp { *fileName* }*
>
> **junk** is a replacement for the **rm** utility. Rather than removing files, it moves
> them into the subdirectory ".junk" in your home directory. If ".junk"
> doesn't exist, it is automatically created. The **-l** option lists the current
> contents of the ".junk" directory, and the **-p** option purges ".junk".

The Korn shell script that is listed below uses a function to process error messages, and uses an array to store filenames. The rest of the functionality should be
pretty easy to follow from the embedded comments.

junk

```
#! /bin/ksh
# junk script
# Korn shell version
# author: Graham Glass
# 9/25/91
#
# Initialize variables
#
fileCount=0        # the number of files specified.
listFlag=0         # set to 1 if the list option (-) is used.
purgeFlag=0        # set to 1 if the purge (-p) option is used.
fileFlag=0         # set to 1 if at least one file is specified.
junk=~/.junk          # the name of the junk directory.
#
error ()
{
#
# Display error message and quit
#
cat << ENDOFTEXT
Dear $USER, the usage of junk is as follows:
  junk -p means "purge all files"
  junk -l means "list junked files"
  junk <list of files> to junk them
ENDOFTEXT
exit 1
}
#
# Parse command line
#
for arg in $*
```

```
do
  case $arg in
    "-p")
      purgeFlag=1
      ;;

    "-l")
      listFlag=1
      ;;

    -*)
      echo $arg is an illegal option
      ;;

    *)
      fileFlag=1
      fileList[$fileCount]=$arg # append to list
      let fileCount=fileCount+1
      ;;
  esac
done
#
# Check for too many options
#
let total=$listFlag+$purgeFlag+$fileFlag
if (( total != 1 ))
then
  error
fi
#
# If junk directory doesn't exist, create it
#
if [[ ! (-d $junk) ]]
then
  'mkdir' $junk                 # quoted just in case it's aliased.
fi
#
# Process options
#
if (( listFlag == 1 ))
then
  'ls' -lgF $junk        # list junk directory.
  exit 0
fi
#
if (( purgeFlag == 1 ))
```

```
then
  'rm' $junk/*                  # remove files in junk directory.
  exit 0
fi
#
if (( fileFlag == 1 ))
then
  'mv' ${fileList[*]} $junk     # move files to junk directory.
  exit 0
fi
#
exit 0
```

Here's some sample output from **junk**:

```
$ ls *.ksh                          ...list some files to junk.
fact.ksh*    func5.ksh*         test.ksh*    trap.ksh*
func4.ksh*   squares.ksh*       track.ksh*
$ junk func5.ksh func4.ksh      ...junk a couple of files.
$ junk -l                       ...list my junk.
total 2
-rwxr-xr-x   1 gglass    apollo_cl    205 Feb  6 22:44 func4.ksh*
-rwxr-xr-x   1 gglass    apollo_cl    274 Feb  7 21:02 func5.ksh*
$ junk -p                       ...purge my junk.
$ junk -z                       ...try a silly option.
-z is an illegal option
Dear glass, the usage of junk is as follows:
  junk -p means "purge all files"
  junk -l means "list junked files"
  junk <list of files> to junk them
$ _
```

THE RESTRICTED SHELL

There is a variation of the Korn shell called the *restricted* Korn shell that provides every Korn shell feature except for the following:

- You may not change directory.
- You may not redirect output using > or >>.
- You may not set the $SHELL, $ENV, or $PATH environment variables.
- You may not used absolute pathnames.

These restrictions only become active *after* the shell's ".profile" and $ENV files have been executed. Any scripts executed by the restricted Korn shell are interpreted by their associated shell, and are not restricted in any way.

The restricted Korn shell is a regular C program whose executable file is stored as "/bin/rksh". If your chosen shell is "/bin/rksh", an interactive restricted Korn shell is invoked automatically when you log into UNIX. You may also invoke a restricted Korn shell manually from a script or from a terminal by using the command **rksh**.

System administrators use the restricted shell to provide users with a limited access to UNIX features as follows:

- They write a series of regular Korn shell scripts that provide access to the features that the particular restricted user wishes to use.
- They place these scripts into a read-only directory, typically called something like "/usr/local/rbin".
- They set up the restricted user's ".profile" file so that $PATH contains only "/usr/local/rbin" and a few other select directories.
- They change the user's "/usr/passwd" file (discussed in chapter 12) so that the user's login shell is "/bin/rksh".

COMMAND LINE OPTIONS

If the first command line argument is a -, the Korn shell is started as a login shell. In addition to this, the Korn shell supports the Bourne shell command line options, the flags of the built-in *set* command (including **-x** and **-v**), and the following:

Option	Meaning
-r	Make the Korn shell a restricted Korn shell.
fileName	Execute the shell commands in *fileName* if the -s option is not used. *fileName* is $0 within the *fileName* script.

CHAPTER REVIEW

Checklist

In this chapter, I described:

- the creation of a Korn shell startup file
- aliases and the history mechanism
- the builtin **vi** and **emacs** line editors

- arithmetic
- functions
- advanced job control
- several enhancements to inherited Bourne shell commands

Quiz

1. Who wrote the Korn shell?
2. Why is the alias mechanism useful?
3. How can you re-edit and re-execute previous commands?
4. Does the Korn shell support recursive functions?
5. Describe the modern syntax of the test command.

Exercises

1. Rewrite the **junk** script of this chapter to be menu-driven. Use the *select* command. [level: *easy*]
2. Write a function called **dateToDays** that takes three parameters—a month string such as Sep, a day number such as 18, and a year number such as 1962—and returns the number of days from Jan 1 1900 to the date. [level: *medium*]
3. Write a set of functions that emulate the directory stack facilities of the C shell (described in the next chapter). Use environment variables to hold the stack and its size. [level: *medium*]
4. Build a script called **pulse** that takes two parameters; the name of a script and an integer. **pulse** should execute the specified script for the specified number of seconds, suspend it for the same number of seconds, and continue this cycle until the specified script is finished.

Projects

1. Write an alias manager script that allows you to choose either DOS emulation, VMS emulation, or none. [level: *medium*]
2. Write a script that allows system administration tasks to be performed automatically from a menu-driven interface. Useful tasks to automate include:

   - automatic deletion of core files
   - automatic warnings to users that use a lot of CPU time or disk space
   - automatic archiving

   [level: *hard*]

Chapter 6

The C Shell

Motivation

The C shell was written after the Bourne shell, and adheres more closely to the C language syntax and control structures. The C shell was the first shell to support advanced job control, and became a favorite of early UNIX developers. Many C shell users are changing over to the Korn shell due to the Korn shell's more powerful command editor, but it still remains popular.

Prerequisites

You should already have read chapter 3 and experimented with some of the core shell facilities.

Objectives

In this chapter, I explain and demonstrate the C shell-specific facilities.

Presentation

The information in this section is presented in the form of several sample UNIX sessions and a small project.

Shell Commands

This section introduces the following shell commands, listed in alphabetical order:

alias	nice	source
chdir	nohup	stop
dirs	notify	suspend
foreach..end	onintr	switch..case..endsw
glob	popd	unalias
goto	pushd	unhash
hashstat	rehash	unset
history	repeat	unsetenv
if..then..else..endif	set	while..end
logout	setenv	

INTRODUCTION

The C shell supports all of the core shell facilities described in chapter 3 plus the following new features:

- several ways to set and access variables
- a built-in programming language that supports conditional branching, looping, and interrupt handling
- command customization using aliases
- access to previous commands via a history mechanism
- advanced job control
- several new built-in commands and several enhancements to existing commands

These new facilities are described by this chapter, and are illustrated by the following hierarchy diagram:

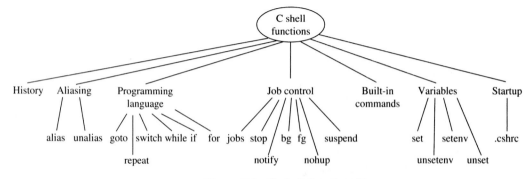

Figure 6.1 C shell functionality

STARTUP

The C shell is a regular C program whose executable file is stored as "/bin/csh". If your chosen shell is "/bin/csh", an interactive C shell is invoked automatically when you log into UNIX. You may also invoke a C shell manually from a script or from a terminal by using the command **csh**. **csh** has several command line options that are described at the end of this chapter.

When a C shell is invoked, the startup sequence is different for login shells and non-login shells:

Step	Shell type	Action
1	both	Execute commands in $HOME/.cshrc if it exists.
2	login only	Execute commands in "/etc/login" if it exists.
3	login only	Execute commands in $HOME/.login if it exists.

An interactive shell then displays its prompt, awaiting user commands. The standard C shell prompt is %, although it may be changed by setting the local variable $prompt, described shortly.

The ".login" file typically contains commands that set environment variables such as $TERM, which contains the type of your terminal, and $PATH, which tells the shell where to search for executable files. Here's an example of a ".login" file:

```
echo -n "Enter your terminal type (default is vt100): "
set termtype = $<
set term = vt100
if ("$termtype" != "") set term = "$termtype"
unset termtype
set path=(. /usr/ucb /usr/bin /usr/local/bin /bin /gnuemacs)
stty erase "^?" kill "^U" intr "^C" eof "^D" crt crterase
set cdpath = (~)
set history = 40
set notify
set prompt = "! % "
set savehist = 32
```

The ".cshrc" file generally contains commands that set common aliases (discussed later). The "rc" suffix stands for "**run c**ommands." Here's an example of a ".cshrc" file:

```
alias emacs /gnuemacs/emacs
alias h history
```

```
alias ll ls -l
alias print prf -pr pb1-2236-lp3
alias ls ls -F
alias rm rm -i
alias t more
```

VARIABLES

The C shell supports local and environment variables. A local variable may hold
either one value, in which case it's called a *simple* variable, or more than one
value, in which case it's termed a *list*. This section describes the C shell facilities
that support variables.

Creating/Assigning Simple Variables

To assign a value to a simple variable, use the built-in *set* command as follows:

---

set {*name* [=*word*] }*

If no arguments are supplied, a list of all the local variables is displayed. If *word* is
not supplied, *name* is set to a null string. If the variable *name* doesn't exist, it is
implicitly created. Here are some examples:

```
% set flag                ...set "flag" to a null string.
echo $flag                ...nothing is printed, as it's null.
% set color = red         ...set "color" to the string "red".
% echo $color
red
% set name = Graham Glass  ...beware! You must use quotes.
% echo $name               ...only the first string was assigned.
Graham
% set name = "Graham Glass" ...now it works as expected.
% echo $name
Graham Glass
% set                     ...display a list of all local variables.
argv  ()
cdpath      /usr/glass
color       red
cwd         /usr/glass
flag
...
```

```
name        Graham Glass
term        vt100
user        glass
% _
```

Accessing A Simple Variable

In addition to the simple variable access syntax ($*name*), the C shell supports the following complex access methods:

Syntax	Action
${*name*}	Replaced by the value of *name*. This form is useful if the expression is immediately followed by an alphanumeric that would otherwise be interpreted as part of the variable's name.
${*?name*}	Replaced by 1 if *name* is set, and 0 otherwise.

Here are some examples that illustrate these access methods. In the first example, I used braces to append a string to the value of a variable:

```
% set verb = sing
% echo I like $verbing
verbing: Undefined variable.
% echo I like ${verb}ing
I like singing
% _
```

In the following example, I used a variable as a simple flag in a conditional expression:

```
% cat flag.csh           ...list the script.
#
set flag                 ...set "flag" to a null string.
if (${?flag}) then       ...branch if "flag" is set.
  echo flag is set
endif
% flag.csh               ...execute the script.
flag is set
% _
```

Creating/Assigning List Variables

To assign a list of values to a variable, use the built-in *set* command with the following syntax:

---

set{ *name* = ({ *word* }*) }*

If the named variable doesn't exist, it is implicitly created. The named variable is assigned to a copy of the specified list of words. Here's an example:

```
% set colors = ( red yellow green )  ...set "colors" to a list.
% echo $colors                        ...display entire list.
red yellow green
% _
```

Accessing A List Variable

The C shell supports a couple of ways to access a list variable. Both of these methods have two forms, the second of which is surrounded by braces. The second form is useful if the expression is immediately followed by an alphanumeric that would otherwise be interpreted as part of the variable's name. Here is a description of the access methods:

Syntax	Action
$name[selector] ${name[selector]}	Both forms are replaced by the element of *name* whose index is specified by the value of *selector*. *selector* may either be a single number, a range of numbers in the format *start-end*, or a *. If *start* is omitted, 1 is assumed. If *end* is omitted, the index of the last element is assumed. If a * is supplied, then all of the elements are selected. The first element of a list has index 1.
$#name ${#name}	Both forms are replaced by the number of elements in *name*.

Here are some examples:

```
% set colors = ( red yellow green )  ...set "colors" to a list.
% echo $colors[1]                     ...display first element.
red
% echo $colors[2-3]                   ...display 2nd and 3rd.
yellow green
% echo $colors[4]                     ...illegal access.
Subscript out of range.
% echo $#colors                       ...display size of list.
3
% _
```

Building Lists

To add an element onto the end of a list, set the original list equal to itself plus the new element, surrounded by parentheses; if you try to assign the new element directly, you'll get an error message. The following example illustrates some list manipulations:

```
% set colors = ( red yellow green )    ...set "colors" to a list.
% set colors[4] = pink                 ...try to set the 4th.
Subscript out of range.
% set colors = ( $colors blue )        ...add to the list.
% echo $colors                         ...it works!
red yellow green blue
% set colors[4] = pink                 ...OK, since 4th exists.
% echo $colors
red yellow green pink
% set colors = $colors black           ...don't forget to use ().
% echo $colors                         ...only the first was set.
red
$ set girls = ( sally georgia )        ...build one list.
$ set boys = ( harry blair )           ...build another.
$ set both = ( $girls $boys )          ...add the lists.
$ echo $both                           ...display the result.
sally georgia harry blair
% _
```

Predefined Local Variables

In addition to the common predefined local variables, the C shell defines the following:

Name	Value
$?0	1 if the shell is executing commands from a named file, and 0 otherwise.
$<	The next line of standard input, fully quoted.
$argv	A list that contains all of the positional parameters: $argv[1] is equal to $1.
$cdpath	The list of alternate directories that *chdir* uses for searching purposes.
$cwd	The current working directory.
$echo	Set if the -x command line option is active.

Name	Value
$histchars	May be used to override the default history metacharacters. The first character is used in place of ! for history substitutions, and the second is used in place of ^ for quick command re-execution.
$history	The size of the history list.
$home	The shell's home directory.
$ignoreeof	Prevents the shell from terminating when it gets a *Control-D*.
$mail	A list of the files to check for mail. By default, the shell checks for mail every 600 seconds (10 minutes). If the first word of $mail is a number, the shell uses this value instead.
$noclobber	Prevents existing files from being overridden by >, and non-existent files from being appended to by >>.
$noglob	Prevents wildcard expansion.
$nonomatch	Prevents an error from occurring if no files match a wildcard filename.
$notify	By default, the shell notifies you of job status changes just before a new prompt is displayed. If $notify is set, the status change is displayed immediately when it occurs.
$path	Used by the shell for locating executable files.
$prompt	The shell prompt.
$savehist	The number of commands to save in the history file.
$shell	The full pathname of the login shell.
$status	The exit code of the last command.
$time	If this is set, any process that takes more than this number of seconds will cause a message to be displayed that indicates process statistics.
$verbose	Set if the -v command line option is used.

Here's a small shell script that uses the $< variable to obtain a user response:

```
% cat var5.csh                                    ...list the script.
#
echo -n "please enter your name: "
set name = $<      # take a line of input.
echo hi $name, your current directory is $cwd
% var5.csh                                        ...execute the script.
```

```
please enter your name: Graham
hi Graham, your current directory is /usr/glass
% _
```

Creating/Assigning Environment Variables

To assign a value to an environment variable, use the built-in command *setenv* as follows:

---

setenv *name word*

If the named variable doesn't exist, it is implicitly created; otherwise, it is over-written. Note that environment variables always hold exactly one value; there is no such thing as an environment list. Here's an example of *setenv:*

```
% setenv TERM vt52         ...set my terminal type.
% echo $TERM               ...confirm.
vt52
% _
```

Predefined Environment Variables

In addition to the common predefined environment variables, the C shell supports the following:

Name	Value
$LOGNAME	the shell owner's user id

EXPRESSIONS

The C shell supports string, arithmetic, and file-oriented expressions. Let's take a look at each kind of expression....

String Expressions

The C shell supports the following string operators:

Operator	Meaning
==	Return true if the string operands are exactly equal.
!=	Return true if the string operands are unequal.
=~	Like ==, except that the right operand may contain wildcards.
!~	Like !=, except that the right operand may contain wildcards.

If either operand is a list, then the first element of the list is used for the comparison. The script in the following example used the string-matching technique to infer a users's response:

```
% cat expr1.csh                              ...list the script.
#
echo -n "do you like the C shell? " # prompt.
set reply = $<                               # get a line of input.
if ($reply == "yes") then                    # check for exact match.
   echo you entered yes
else if ($reply =~ y*) then                  # check for inexact match.
   echo I assume you mean yes
endif
% expr1.csh                                  ...execute the script.
do you like the C shell? yeah
I assume you mean yes
% _
```

Arithmetic Expressions

The C shell supports the following arithmetic operators, in descending order of precedence:

Operator (s)	Meaning
-	unary minus
!	logical negation
* / %	multiplication, division, remainder
+ -	addition, subtraction
<< >>	bitwise left shift, bitwise right shift
<= >= < >	relational operators

Operator (s)	Meaning
== !=	equality, inequality
& ^ |	bitwise and, bitwise xor, bitwise or
|| &&	logical or, logical and

These operators work just like their standard C counterparts, except that they can only operate on integers. Expressions may be surrounded by parentheses to control the order of evaluation. When an arithmetic expression is evaluated, a null string is equivalent to zero. Any expression that uses the &, &&, ||, |, <, >, or >> operators must be surrounded by parentheses to prevent the shell from interpreting these characters specially. Here's a sample script that uses a couple of operators:

```
% cat expr3.csh                              ...list the script.
#
set a = 3
set b = 5
if ($a > 2 && $b > 4) then
  echo expression evaluation seems to work
endif
% expr3.csh                                  ...execute the script.
expression evaluation seems to work
% _
```

To assign the result of an expression to a variable, you may not use the *set* command. Instead, use the built-in @ command, which has the following forms:

```
@                              ...list all of the shell variables.
@ variable op expression       ...set variable to expression.
@ variable[index] op expression ...set indexth element of variable to ex-
                                  pression.
```

where *op* is =, +=, −=, *=, or /=. Here are some examples:

```
% set a = 2 * 2           ...you can't use set for assignment.
set: Syntax error.
% @ a = 2 * 2             ...use @ instead.
% echo $a
4
% @ a = $a + $a           ...add two variables.
% echo $a
8
```

```
% set flag = 1
% @ b = ($a && $flag) ...need parentheses because of &&.
% echo $b
1
% @ b = ($a && $flag)
% echo $b
0
% _
```

You may also increment or decrement a variable by using ++ or −−. For example:

```
% set value = 1
% @ value ++
% echo $value
2
% _
```

File-oriented Expressions

To make file-oriented decisions a little easier to program, the C shell supports several file-specific expressions. Each expression is of the form:

-option *fileName*

where 1 (true) is returned if the selected option is true, and 0 (false) otherwise. If *fileName* does not exist or is inaccessible, all options return 0. Here is a description of each option:

Option	Meaning
r	Shell has read permission for *fileName*.
w	Shell has write permission for *fileName*.
x	Shell has execute permission for *fileName*.
e	*fileName* exists.
o	*fileName* is owned by the same user as the shell process.
z	*fileName* exists and is zero bytes in size.
f	*fileName* is a regular file (not a directory or special file).
d	*fileName* is a directory file (not a regular or special file).

Here's an example script that uses the **-w** option to determine whether a file is writeable or not:

```
% cat expr4.csh                    ...list the script.
#
echo -n "enter the name of the file you wish to erase: "
set filename = $<              # get a line of input.
if (! (-w "$filename")) then   # check I have access.
   echo you do not have permission to erase that file.
else
   rm $filename
   echo file erased
endif
% expr4.csh                        ...execute the script.
enter the name of the file you wish to erase: /
you do not have permission to erase that file.
% _
```

ALIASES

The C shell allows you to create and customize your own commands by using the built-in command *alias*, which works like this:

Shell Command: **alias** [*word* [*string*]]

alias supports a simple form of command line customization. If you alias *word* to be equal to *string* and then later enter a command beginning with *word*, the first occurrence of *word* is replaced by *string* and then the command is reprocessed.

If you don't supply *word* or *string*, a list of all the current shell aliases is displayed. If you only supply *word*, then the string currently associated with the alias *word* is displayed. If you supply *word* and *string*, the shell adds the specified alias to its collection of aliases. If an alias already exists for *word*, it is replaced.

If the replacement string begins with *word*, it is not reprocessed for aliases to prevent infinite loops. If the replacement string contains *word* elsewhere, an error message is displayed when the alias is executed.

Here's an example of *alias* in action:

```
$ alias dir 'ls -aF'     ...register an alias.
$ dir                    ...same as typing "ls -aF".
```

```
./           main2.c       p.reverse.c        reverse.h
../           main2.o       palindrome.c       reverse.old
$ dir *.c                   ...same as typing "ls -aF *.c".
main2.c       p.reverse.c        palindrome.c
$ alias dir                 ...look at the value associated with "dir".
ls -aF
$ _
```

In the following example, I aliased a word in terms of itself:

```
% alias ls 'ls -aF'         ...define "ls" in terms of itself.
% ls *.c                    ...same as typing "ls -aF *.c".
main2.c       p.reverse.c        palindrome.c
% alias dir 'ls'            ...define "dir" in terms of "ls".
% dir                       ...same as typing "ls -aF".
./           main2.c       p.reverse.c        reverse.h
../           main2.o       palindrome.c       reverse.old
% alias who 'date; who'     ...infinite loop problem.
% who
Alias loop.
% alias who 'date; /bin/who'  ...full pathname of "who" avoids error
% who                         ...works fine now.
Thu Feb 13 23:33:37 CST 1992
glass                    ttyp0        Feb 13 23:30    (xyplex_2)
% _
```

Removing An Alias

To remove an alias, use the built-in command *unalias*, which works as follows:

Shell Command: **unalias** *pattern*

unalias removes all of the aliases that match *pattern*. If *pattern* is *, then all aliases are removed.

Useful Aliases

Here's a list of the useful aliases that I keep in my ''.cshrc'' file, together with a brief description:

Alias	Value
cd	cd \!*; set prompt = "$cwd \! > "; ls This changes your prompt to contain both the current working directory and the lastest command number (see history for more details).
ls	ls -F This causes **ls** to include extra file information.
rm	rm -i This causes **rm** to ask for confirmation.
rm	mv \!* ~/tomb This causes **rm** to move a file into a special "tomb" directory instead of removing it.
h	history This allows you to obtain history information by typing just one letter.
vi	(mesg n; /bin/vi \!*; mesg y) This stops people from sending you messages while you're in the **vi** editor.
mroe	more This corrects a common spelling error.
ls-l	ls -l This corrects a common spelling error.
ll	ls -l This allows you to obtain a long directory listing more conveniently.

Sharing Aliases

To make an alias available to a subshell, place its definition in the shell's ".cshrc" file.

Parameterized Aliases

An alias may refer to arguments in the original pre-aliased command by using the history mechanism which is described in the next section. The pre-aliased command is treated as if it were the previous command. The useful alias for *cd* that I mentioned in the previous section makes good use of this facility; the \!* part of the alias is replaced by all of the arguments in the pre-aliased command. The ! is preceded by a \ to inhibit its special meaning during the assignment of the alias:

```
alias cd 'cd \!*; set prompt = "$cwd \! > "; ls'
```

HISTORY

The C shell keeps a record of the commands that you enter from the keyboard so that they may be edited and re-executed at a later stage. This facility is sometimes known as a *history* mechanism. The ! metacharacter gives you access to history.

Numbered Commands

When you're using history, it's very handy to arrange for your prompt to contain the "number" of the command that you're about to enter. To do this, insert the \! character sequence into your prompt:

```
% set prompt = '\! % '      ...include the event number in my prompt.
1 % echo Genesis            ...this command is event #1.
Genesis
2 % _                       ...the next command will be event #2.
```

Storage Of Commands

A C shell records the last $history commands during a particular session. If $history is not set, a default value of 1 is used. If you want these commands to be accessible from the next session, set the $savehist variable. If you do this, the last $savehist commands are maintained in the file $HOME/.history. A history file is shared by all of the interactive C shells created by the same user. In the following example, I instructed my shell to remember the last 40 commands in my history list and to store the last 32 commands between sessions:

```
2 % set history = 40        ...remember the last 40 commands.
40
3 % set savehist = 32       ...save 32 commands across sessions.
32
4 % _
```

Reading History

To obtain a listing of a shell's history, use the built-in command *history*, which works like this:

> *Shell Command:* **history** [-rh] [*number*]
>
> *history* allows you to access a shell's history list. If no parameters are
> supplied, this command lists the last $history commands. The **-r** option
> causes the history list to be listed in reverse order, and the **-h** option inhibits
> the display of event numbers. "history" is usually aliased to "h" for speed.

Here's an example:

```
4 % alias h history          ...make a useful alias.
5 % h                        ...list current history.
  1 set prompt = '\! % '
  2 set history = 40
  3 set savehist = 32
  4 alias h history
  5 h
6 % h -r 3                    ...list last 3 commands in reverse order.
  6 h 3
  5 h
  4 alias h history
7 % _
```

Command Re-execution

To re-execute a previous command, use the ! metacharacter in one of the following forms:

Form	Action
!!	Replaced with the text of the last command.
!*number*	Replaced with the text of the command with the specified event number.
!*prefix*	Replaced with the text of the last command that started with *prefix*.
!?*substring*?	Replaced with the text of the last command that contained *substring*.

These sequences may be used anywhere in a command line, although they're
usually used in isolation. The recalled command is echoed to the terminal before
it is executed. The value of *prefix* or *substring* may not contain a space. The
special meaning of ! is not inhibited by any kind of quote, but may be inhibited by
preceding it with a space, tab, =, (, or \. Here are some examples:

```
41 % echo event 41      ...a simple echo.
event 41
42 % echo event 42      ...another simple echo.
event 42
43 % !!                 ...re-execute last command.
echo event 42           ...echo command before re-execution.
event 42
44 % !41                ...re-execute command #41.
echo event 41           ...echo command before re-execution.
event 41
45 % !ec                ...re-execute command starting with "ec".
echo event 41           ...echo command before re-execution.
event 41
46 % _
```

Accessing Pieces Of History

You may access a portion of a previous command by using history *modifiers*. These are a collection of options that may immediately follow an event specifier. Each modifier returns a single token or range of tokens from the specified event. Here is a list of the modifiers:

Modifier	Token(s) returned
:0	first
:number	(number+1)th
:start-end	(*start*+1) th through to (*end*+1)th
:^	first
:$	last
:*	second through to last

The colon before the ^, $, and * options is optional. To use one of these modifiers on the last command, you may precede the modifier by "!!" or just "!". Here are some examples:

```
48 % echo I like horseback riding    ...original line.
I like horseback riding
49 % !!:0 !!:1 !!:2 !!:4              ...access specified arguments.
echo I like riding
I like riding
```

```
50 % echo !48:1-$          ...access range of arguments.
echo I like horseback riding
I like horseback riding
51 % _
```

Accessing Portions Of Filenames

If a history modifier refers to a filename, it may be further modified in order to access a particular portion of the name. The existing modifiers may be followed immediately by the following filename modifiers:

Modifier	Part of file	Portion of the specified fileName that is returned
:h	head	the filename minus the trailing pathname
:r	root	the filename minus the trailing .* suffix
:e	extension	the trailing .* suffix
:t	tail	the filename minus the leading directory path

In the following example I accessed various portions of the original filename by using this filename access facility:

```
53 % ls /usr/include/stdio.h        ...the original filename.
/usr/include/stdio.h
54 % echo !53:1:h                   ...access head.
echo /usr/include
/usr/include
55 % echo !53:1:r                   ...access root.
echo /usr/include/stdio
/usr/include/stdio
56 % echo !53:1:e                   ...access extension.
echo h
h
57 % echo !53:1:t                   ...access tail.
echo stdio.h
stdio.h
% _
```

History Substitution

The substitution modifier is replaced by the specified portion of a previous event after a textual subsitution is performed. Here is the syntax:

> *!event*:s/*pat1*/*pat2*/

This sequence is replaced by the specified event after replacing the first occurrence of *pat1* by *pat2*. Here's an example:

```
58 % ls /usr/include/stdio.h        ...the original filename.
/usr/include/stdio.h
58 % echo !58:1:s/stdio/signal/  ...perform substitution.
echo /usr/include/signal.h
/usr/include/signal.h
59 % _
```

CONTROL STRUCTURES

The C shell supports a wide range of control structures that make it suitable as a high-level programming tool. Shell programs are usually stored in scripts and are commonly used to automate maintenance and installation tasks.

Several of the control structures require several lines to be entered. If such a control structure is entered from the keyboard, the shell prompts you with a ? for each additional line until the control structure is ended, at which point it executes.

There now follows a description of each control structure, in alphabetical order. I made the C shell examples correspond closely to the Bourne shell examples so that you can compare and contrast the two shells.

foreach .. end

The *foreach* command allows a list of commands to be repeatedly executed, each time using a different value for a named variable. Here's the syntax:

> **foreach** *name* (*wordList*)
>   *commandList*
> **end**

The *foreach* command iterates the value of *name* through each variable in *wordList*, executing the list of commands *commandList* after each assignment. A *break* command causes the loop to immediately end, and a *continue* command causes the loop to jump immediately to the next iteration. Here's an example of a script that uses a *foreach* control structure:

```
% cat foreach.csh                          ...list the script.
#
foreach color (red yellow green blue)      # loop through four colors.
  echo one color is $color
end
% foreach.csh                              ...execute the script.
one color is red
one color is yellow
one color is green
one color is blue
% _
```

goto

The *goto* command allows you to jump unconditionally to a named label. The label may precede or follow the goto statement, even if the command is entered from the keyboard. To declare a label, simply start a line with the name of the label followed immediately by a colon. Here's the syntax of a *goto* command:

> **goto** *name*

Here's the syntax of a label:

> *name*:

Use gotos sparingly, to avoid nasty spaghetti-like code (even if you like spaghetti). Here's an example of a simple *goto*:

```
% cat goto.csh                     ...list the script.
#
echo gotta jump!
goto endOfScript                   # jump
echo I'll never echo this
endOfScript:                       # label
echo the end
% goto.csh                         ...execute the script.
gotta jump!
the end
% _
```

if .. then .. else .. endif

There are two forms of *if* command. The first form supports a simple one-way branch, and has the following syntax:

> **if** (*expr*) *command*

The first form of the *if* command evaluates *expr*, and if it is true (non-zero), executes *command*:

```
% if (5 > 3) echo five is greater than 3
five is greater than three
% _
```

The second form of the *if* command supports alternative branching. Here's the general syntax:

> **if** (*expr1*) **then**
> *list1*
> **else if** (*expr2*) **then**
> *list2*
> **else**
> *list3*
> **endif**

The *else* and *else if* portions of this command are optional, but the terminating *endif* is not. The second form of the *if* command works as follows:

- *expr1* is executed.
- If *expr1* is true, the commands in *list1* are executed and the *if* command is done.
- If *expr1* is false and there are one or more *else if* components, then a true expression following an *else if* causes the commands following the associated *then* to be executed and the *if* command to finish.
- If no true expressions are found and there is an *else* component, the commands following the *else* are executed.

Here's an example:

```
% cat if.csh                    ...list the script.
#
```

```
echo -n 'enter a number: '      # prompt user.
set number = $<                 # read a line of input.
if ($number < 0) then
  echo negative
else if ($number == 0) then
  echo zero
else
  echo positive
endif
% if.csh                        ...execute the script.
enter a number: -1
negative
% _
```

onintr

The *onintr* command allows you to specify a label that should be jumped to when the shell receives a SIGINT signal. This signal is typically generated by a *Control-C* from the keyboard, and is described in more detail in chapter 10. Here's the syntax:

---

onintr [- | *label*]

The *onintr* command instructs the shell to jump to *label* when SIGINT is received. If the - option is used, SIGINTs are ignored. If no options are supplied, it restores the shell's original SIGINT handler. Here's an example:

```
% cat onintr.csh                ...list the script.
#
onintr controlC                 # set Control-C trap.
while (1)
  echo infinite loop
  sleep 2
end
controlC:
echo control C detected
% onintr.csh                    ...execute the script.
infinite loop
infinite loop
^C                              ...press Control-C.
control C detected
% _
```

repeat

The *repeat* command allows you to execute a single command a specified number of times. Here's the syntax:

> **repeat** *expr command*

The *repeat* command evaluates *expr*, and then executes *command* the resultant number of times:

```
% repeat 2 echo hi there              ...display two lines.
hi there
hi there
% _
```

switch .. case .. endsw

The *switch* command supports multi-way branching based on the value of a single expression. Here's the general form of a *switch* construct:

> **switch** (*expr*)
> **case** *pattern1:*
>   *list*
>   **breaksw**
> **case** *pattern2:*
> **case** *pattern3:*
>   *list2*
>   **breaksw**
> **default:**
>   *defaultList*
> **endsw**

expr is an expression that evaluates to a string, *pattern1/pattern2/pattern3* may include wildcards, and *list1/list2/defaultList* are lists of one or more shell commands. The shell evaluates *expr* and then compares it to each pattern in turn, from top to bottom. When the first matching pattern is found, its associated list of commands is executed and then the shell skips to the matching *endsw*. If no match is found and a default condition is supplied, then *defaultList* is executed. If no match is found and no default condition exists, then execution continues from after the matching *endsw*.

Here's an example of a script called "menu.csh" that makes use of a *switch* control structure:

```
#
echo menu test program
set stop = 0                  # reset loop termination flag
while ($stop == 0)            # loop until done
  cat << ENDOFMENU            # display menu

  1   : print the date.
  2, 3: print the current working directory
  4   : exit
ENDOFMENU
  echo
  echo -n 'your choice? '     # prompt
  set reply = $<              # read response
  echo ""
  switch ($reply)             # process response
    case "1":
      date                    # display date
      breaksw
    case "2":
    case "3":
      pwd                     # display working directory
      breaksw
    case "4":
      set stop = 1            # set loop termination flag
      breaksw
    default:                  # default
      echo illegal choice     # error
      breaksw
  endsw
end
```

Here's the output from the "menu.csh" script:

```
% menu.csh
menu test program

  1   : print the date.
  2, 3: print the current working directory
  4   : exit

your choice? 1
```

```
Fri Feb 14 00:50:26 CST 1992

    1   : print the date.
    2, 3: print the current working directory
    4   : exit

your choice? 2

/usr/glass

    1   : print the date.
    2, 3: print the current working directory
    4   : exit

your choice? 5

illegal choice

    1   : print the date.
    2, 3: print the current working directory
    4   : exit

your choice? 4

% _
```

while .. end

The built-in *while* command allows a list of commands to be repeatedly executed as long as a specified expression evaluates to true (non-zero). Here's the syntax:

---
while (*expr*)
  commandlist
end

The *while* command evalutes the expression *expr*, and if it is true, proceeds to execute every command in *commandlist* and then repeats the process. If *expr* is false, the while loop terminates and the script continues to execute from the command following the *end*. A *break* command causes the loop to end immediately, and a *continue* command causes the loop to jump immediately to the next iteration.

Here's an example of a script that uses a *while* control structure to generate a small multiplication table:

```
% cat multi.csh                    ...list the script.
#
set x = 1                          # set outer loop value
while ($x <= $1)                   # outer loop
  set y = 1                        # set inner loop value
  while ($y <= $1)                 # inner loop
    @ v = $x * $y                  # calculate entry
    echo -n $v "         "         # display entry
    @ y ++                         # update inner loop counter
  end
  echo ""                          # newline
  @ x ++                           # update outer loop counter
end
% multi.csh 7                      ...execute the script.
1        2        3        4        5        6        7
2        4        6        8       10       12       14
3        6        9       12       15       18       21
4        8       12       16       20       24       28
5       10       15       20       25       30       35
6       12       18       24       30       36       42
7       14       21       28       35       42       49
% _
```

SAMPLE PROJECT: JUNK

To illustrate some of the C shell capabilities, I present a C shell version of the "junk" script project that was suggested at the end of the Bourne shell chapter. Here's the definition of the **junk** utility about to be described:

Utility: **junk** -lp { *fileName* }*

junk is a replacement for the **rm** utility. Rather than removing files, it moves them into the subdirectory ".junk" in your home directory. If ".junk" doesn't exist, it is automatically created. The **-l** option lists the current contents of the ".junk" directory, and the **-p** option purges ".junk".

The C shell script that is listed below uses a list variable to store filenames. The rest of the functionality should be pretty easy to follow from the embedded comments.

Junk

```
#! /bin/csh
# junk script
# author: Graham Glass
# 9/25/91
#
# Initialize variables
#
set fileList = ()        # a list of all specified files.
set listFlag = 0         # set to 1 if -l option is specified.
set purgeFlag = 0        # set to 1 if -p option is specified.
set fileFlag = 0         # set to 1 if at least one file is specified.
set junk = ~/.junk       # the junk directory.
#
# Parse command line
#
foreach arg ($*)
  switch ($arg)
    case "-p":
      set purgeFlag = 1
      breaksw

    case "-l":
      set listFlag = 1
      breaksw

    case -*:
      echo $arg is an illegal option
      goto error
      breaksw

    default:
      set fileFlag = 1
      set fileList = ($fileList $arg) # append to list
      breaksw
  endsw
end
#
# Check for too many options
#
@ total = $listFlag + $purgeFlag + $fileFlag
if ($total != 1) goto error
#
# If junk directory doesn't exist, create it
#
if (!(-e $junk)) then
  'mkdir' $junk
endif
```

```
#
# Process options
#
if ($listFlag) then
  'ls' -lgF $junk                # list junk directory.
  exit 0
endif
#
if ($purgeFlag) then
  'rm' $junk/*                   # remove contents of junk directory.
  exit 0
endif
#
if ($fileFlag) then
  'mv' $fileList $junk           # move files to junk directory.
  exit 0
endif
#
exit 0
#
# Display error message and quit
#
error:
cat << ENDOFTEXT
Dear $USER, the usage of junk is as follows:
  junk -p means "purge all files"
  junk -l means "list junked files"
  junk <list of files> to junk them
ENDOFTEXT
exit 1
```

ENHANCEMENTS

In addition to the new facilities that have already been described, the C shell also enhances the common core shell facilities in the following areas:

- a shortcut for command re-execution
- the {} metacharacters
- filename substitution
- redirection
- piping
- job control

The following subsections describe each enhancement.

Command Re-execution: A Shortcut

It's quite common to want to re-execute the previous command with a slight modification. For example, say you misspelled the name of a file. Instead of typing "fil.txt", you meant to type "file.txt". There's a convenient shorthand way to correct such a mistake. If you type the command:

```
^pat1^pat2
```

then the previous command is re-executed after the first occurrence of *pat1* is replaced by *pat2*. This shortcut procedure applies only to the previous command. Here's an example:

```
% cc fil.txt              ...whoops!
ld crt0.o fatal: Can't open file fil.txt for input
% ^fil^file               ...quick correction.
cc file.txt               ...OK.
% _
```

Metacharacters: {}

You may use braces around filenames to save typing common prefixes and suffixes. The notation:

```
a{b,c}d
```

is textually replaced with:

```
abd acd
```

In the following example, I copied the files "/usr/include/stdio.h" and "/usr/include/signal.h" (which have a common prefix and suffix) into my home directory:

```
% cp /usr/include/{stdio,signal}.h . ...copy two header files.
% _
```

Filename Substitution

In addition to the common filename substitution facilities, the C shell supports two new features—the ability to disable filename substitution and the ability to specify what action should be taken if a pattern has no matches.

Disabling filename substitution

To disable filename substitution, set the $noglob variable. If this is done, wild-cards lose their special meaning. The $noglob variable is not set by default. Here's an example:

```
% echo a* p*                ...one wildcard pair matches: p*
prog1.c      prog2.c        prog3.c       prog4.c
% set noglob                ...inhibit wildcard processing.
% echo a* p*
a* p*
% _
```

No match situations

If several patterns are present in a command and at least one of them has a match, then no error occurs. However, if none of the patterns has a match, the shell issues an error message by default. If the $nonomatch variable is set and no matches occur, then the original patterns are used as is. The $nonomatch variable is not set by default. Here's an example:

```
% echo a* p*                ...one wildcard pair matches: p*.
prog1.c      prog2.c        prog3.c       prog4.c
% echo a* b*                ...no wildcards match.
echo: No match.             ...error occurs by default.
% set nonomatch             ...set special nonomatch variable.
% echo a* b*                ...wildcards lose their special meaning.
a* b*                       ...no error occurs.
% _
```

Redirection

In addition to the common redirection facilities, the C shell supports a couple of enhancements—the ability to redirect the standard error channel, and the ability to protect files against accidental overwrites.

Redirecting the standard error channel

To redirect the standard error channel in addition to the standard output channel, simply append an & character to the > or >> redirection operator:

```
% cc a.c > errors               ...cc sends errors to standard error.
 printf (1\n");
******** Line 8 of "a.c": Improper expression; "BAD CHAR: '\'
 scanf ("%d", &i);
******** Line 9 of "a.c": Improper argument list; "scanf" found.
% cc a.c >& errors              ...redirect standard error too.
% _
```

Although there's no easy way to redirect just the error channel, it can be done using the following "trick":

```
(process1 > file1) >& file2
```

This trick works by redirecting all of the standard output from *process1* to *file1* (which can be "/dev/null" if you don't want to save the output), allowing only the standard errors to leave the command group. The command group's output and error channels are then redirected to *file2*.

Protecting files against accidental overwrites

You may protect existing files from accidental overwrites, and non-existent files from accidental appends, by setting the $noclobber variable. If a shell command tries to perform either action, it fails and issues an error message. Note that regular system calls such as write () are unaffected. $noclobber is not set by default. Here's an example:

```
% ls -l errors              ...look at existing file.
-rw-r-xr-x   1 glass      225 Feb 14 10:59 errors
% set noclobber             ...protect files.
% cc a.c >& errors          ...cannot overwrite.
errors: File exists.
% _
```

To temporarily override the effect of $noclobber, append a ! character to the redirection operator:

```
% cc a.c >&! errors         ...existing file is overwritten.
% _
```

Piping

In addition to the common piping facilities, the C shell also allows you to pipe the standard output *and* standard error channel from *process1* to *process2* using the following syntax:

> *process1* **|&** *process2*

In the following example I piped the standard output and error channels from the **cc** utility to **more**:

```
% cc a.c |& more         ...pipe standard and error channels.
 printf (1\n");
******** Line 8 of "a.c": Improper expression; "BAD CHAR: '\'
 scanf ("%d", &i);
******** Line 9 of "a.c": Improper argument list; "scanf" found.
% _
```

Although there's no direct way to pipe *just* the error channel, it can be done using the following "trick":

(*process1* > *file*) |& *process2*

This trick works by redirecting all of the standard output from *process1* to *file* (which can be "/dev/null" if you don't want to save the output), allowing only the standard errors to leave the command group. The command group's output and error channels are then piped to *process2*.

Job Control

The job control facilities of the C shell are the same as the Korn shell's, with the following additional built-in commands:

- *stop*
- *suspend*
- *nice*
- *nohup*
- *notify*

There now follows a description of these commands.

Stop

To suspend a specified job, use the *stop* command as follows:

Shell Command: **stop** { *%job* }*

stop suspends the jobs that are specified using the standard job specifier format described in the Korn shell chapter. If no arguments are supplied, the last referenced job is suspended.

Suspend

> *Shell Command:* **suspend**
>
> *suspend* suspends the shell that invokes it. It only makes sense to do this when the shell is a subshell of the login shell, and is most commonly done to suspend a shell invoked by the **su** or **script** utilities.

Nice

To set the priority level of the shell or a command, use the *nice* command as follows:

> *Shell Command:* **nice** [+/− *number*] [*command*]
>
> *nice* runs *command* with priority level *number*. In general, the higher the priority, the slower the process will run. Only a super-user can specify a negative priority level. If the priority level is omitted, 4 is assumed. If no arguments are specified, the shell's priority level is set.

For more information about process priorities, consult chapter 10.

Nohup

To protect a command from hangup conditions, use the built-in *nohup* command as follows:

> *Shell Command:* **nohup** [*command*]
>
> *nohup* executes *command* and protects it from hangup conditions. If no arguments are supplied, then all further commands executed from the shell are nohup'ed. Note that all background commands are automatically nohup'ed.

Notify

The shell normally notifies you of a change in a job's state just before it displays a new prompt. If you want immediate (asynchronous) notification of job state changes, use the built-in *notify* command as follows:

Shell Command: **notify** { *%job* }*

notify instructs the shell to inform you immediately when the specified jobs change state. Jobs must be specified following the standard job specifier format described in the Korn shell chapter. If no job is specified, the last referenced job is used. To enable immediate notification of all jobs, set the $notify variable.

Terminating A Login Shell

The *logout* command terminates a login shell. Unlike *exit*, it cannot be used to terminate an interactive subshell. You may therefore terminate a login C shell in one of three ways:

- Type a *Control-D* on a line by itself (as long as $ignoreeof is not set).
- Use the built-in *exit* command.
- Use the built-in *logout* command.

Here's an example:

```
% set ignoreeof        ...set special variable to prevent ^D exit.
% ^D                   ...won't work now.
Use "logout" to logout.
% logout               ...a better way to log out.

Session disconnected
```

When a login C shell is terminated, it searches for two finish-up files. The commands in each file, if found, are executed in sequence. Here is a list of the finish-up files, in the sequence that they are searched for:

Name	Directory
".logout"	$HOME
"logout"	/etc

A finish-up file typically contains commands for cleaning up temporary directories, other such clean-up operations, and a goodbye message.

If a non-login C shell is terminated using *exit* or *Control-D*, no finish-up files are searched for.

BUILT-INS

The C shell provides the following extra built-ins:

- *chdir*
- *glob*
- *source*

The next few subsections contain a description of each built-in.

chdir

> *Shell Command:* **chdir** [*path*]
>
> *chdir* works the same as *cd*.

glob

> *Shell Command:* **glob** { *arg* }
>
> *glob* works the same as *echo*, outputting a list of *args* after they have been processed by the shell metacharacter mechanisms. The difference is that the list of args are delimited by nulls (ASCII 0) in the final output instead of spaces. This makes the output ideally suited for use by C programs, which like strings to be terminated by null characters.

source

When a script is executed, it is interpreted by a subshell. Any aliases and/or local variable assignments performed by the script therefore have no effect on the original shell. If you want a script to be interpreted by the current shell, and thus affect it, use the built-in *source* command as follows:

> *Shell Command:* **source** [-h] *fileName*
>
> *source* causes a shell to execute every command in the script called *fileName* without invoking a subshell. The commands in the script are only placed in the history list if the **-h** option is used. It is perfectly legal for *fileName* to contain further *source* commands. If an error occurs during the execution of *fileName*, control is returned to the original shell.

In the following example, I used *source* to re-execute an edited ".login" file. The only other way to re-execute it would have been to log out and then log back in again.

```
% vi .login                                ...edit my .login file.
...
% source .login                            ...re-execute it.
Enter your terminal type (default is vt100): vt52
% _
```

THE DIRECTORY STACK

The C shell allows you to create and manipulate a directory stack, which makes life a little easier when you're flipping back and forth between a small working set of directories. To push a directory onto the directory stack, use the *pushd* command:

> *Shell Command:* **pushd** [+*number* | *name*]
>
> *pushd* pushes the specified directory onto the directory stack, and works like this:
>
> - When *name* is supplied, the current working directory is pushed onto the stack and the shell moves to the named directory.
> - When no arguments are supplied, the top two elements of the directory stack are swapped.
> - When *number* is supplied, the *number*th element of the directory stack is rotated to the top of the stack and becomes the current working directory. The elements of the stack are numbered in ascending order, with the top as number 0.

To pop a directory from the directory stack, use the *popd* command, which works as follows:

Shell Command: **popd** [+*number*]

popd pops a directory from the directory stack, and works like this:

- When no argument is supplied, the shell moves to the directory that's on the top of the directory stack and then pops it.
- When a *number* is supplied, the shell moves to the *number*th directory on the stack and discards it.

The *dirs* command is also useful:

Shell Command: **dirs**

dirs lists the current directory stack.

Here are some examples of directory stack manipulation:

```
% pwd                     ...I'm in my home directory.
/usr/glass
% pushd /                 ...move to root directory, push home directory.
/ ~                       ...displays directory stack automatically.
% pushd /usr/include      ...push another directory.
/usr/include / ~
% pushd                   ...swap two stack elements, move back to root.
/ /usr/include ~
% pushd                   ...swap them again, move back to "/usr/include".
/usr/include / ~
% popd                    ...pop a directory, move back to root.
/ ~
% popd                    ...pop a directory, move back to home.
~
% _
```

The Hash Table

As described in chapter 3, the $PATH variable is used when searching for an executable file. To speed up this process, the C shell stores an internal data structure, called a *hash table*, that allows the directory hierarchy to be searched more quickly. The hash table is constructed automatically whenever the ".cshrc" file is read. In order for the hash table to work correctly, however, it must be reconstructed whenever $PATH is changed, or whenever a new executable file is added to any directory in the $PATH sequence. The C shell takes care of the first case automatically, but *you* must take care of the second.

If you add or rename an executable in any of the directories in the $PATH sequence except your current directory, you should use the *rehash* command to instruct the C shell to reconstruct the hash table. If you wish, you may use the *unhash* command to disable the hash table facility, thereby slowing down the search process.

The *hashstat* command may be used to examine the effectiveness of the hashing system. The output of this command doesn't mean anything unless you're familiar with hashing algorithms.

In the following example, I added a new executable into the directory "~/bin", which was in my search path. The shell couldn't find it until I performed a *rehash*.

```
% pwd                          ...I'm in my home directory.
/usr/glass
% echo $PATH                   ...list my PATH variable.
.:/usr/glass/bin:/usr/ucb:/usr/bin:/usr/local/bin:/bin:/gnuemacs
% cat > bin/script.csh         ...create a new script.
#
echo found the script
~D                             ...end-of-input.
% chmod +x bin/script.csh      ...make the script executable.
% script.csh                   ...try to run it.
script.csh: Command not found.
% rehash                       ...make the shell rehash.
% script.csh                   ...try to run it again.
found the script               ...success!
% hashstat                     ...display hash statistics.
5 hits, 6 misses, 45%
% _
```

COMMAND LINE OPTIONS

If the first command line argument is a -, the C shell is started as a login shell. In addition to this, the C shell supports the following command line options:

Option	Meaning
-c *string*	Create a shell to execute the command *string*.
-e	Shell terminates if any command returns a non-zero exit code.
-f	Start shell but don't search for or read commands from ".cshrc".
-i	Create an interactive shell; like the **-s** option except that the SIGTERM, SIGINT, and SIGQUIT messages are all ignored.
-n	Parse commands but do not execute them; for debugging only.
-s	Create a shell that reads commands from standard input and sends shell messages to the standard error channel.
-t	Read and execute a single line from standard input.
-v	Causes $verbose to be set, which was described earlier.
-V	Like -v, except that $verbose is set before ".cshrc" is executed.
-x	Causes the $echo variable to be set, which was described earlier.
-X	Like -x, except that $echo is set before ".cshrc" is read.
fileName	Execute the shell commands in *fileName* if none of the -c, -i, -s, or -t options are used. *fileName* is $0 within the *fileName* script.

CHAPTER REVIEW

Checklist

In this chapter, I described:

- the creation of a C shell startup file
- simple variables and lists
- expressions, including integer arithmetic
- aliases and the history mechanism
- several control structures
- enhanced job control
- several new built-in commands

Utilities

This section introduces the following utilities, listed in alphabetical order:

at	crontab	grep	tar
awk	crypt	ln	tr
biff	diff	mount	ul
cmp	dump	od	umount
compress	egrep	sed	uncompress
cpio	fgrep	sort	uniq
cron	find	su	whoami

INTRODUCTION

In this chapter, I introduce about thirty useful utilities. Rather than describe them in alphabetical order, I've grouped them into fairly logical sets, as follows:

Section	Utilties
filtering files	egrep, fgrep, grep, uniq
sorting files	sort
comparing files	cmp, diff
archiving files	tar, cpio, dump
searching for files	find
scheduling commands	at, cron, crontab
programmable text processing	awk
hard and soft links	ln
switching users	su
checking for mail	biff
transforming files	compress, crypt, sed, tr, ul, uncompress
looking at raw file contents	od
mounting file systems	mount, umount
identifying shells	whoami
document preparation	nroff, spell, style, troff

The remainder of this chapter goes through each group in turn, describing the utilities using worked examples.

FILTERING FILES

There are many times when it's handy to be able to filter the contents of a file, selecting only those lines that match some kind of criteria. The utilities that do this include the following:

- **egrep, fgrep,** and **grep,** which filter out all lines that do not contain a specified pattern
- **uniq,** which filters out duplicate adjacent lines

The next few subsections describe these utilities.

Filtering Patterns: egrep/fgrep/grep

egrep, fgrep, and **grep** allow you to scan a file and filter out all of the lines that don't contain a specified pattern. They are very similar in nature, the main difference being the kind of text patterns that each can filter. I'll begin by describing the common features of all three, and then finish up by illustrating the differences. Here's a brief synopsis of the three utilities:

Utility: **grep** -hilnvw *pattern* { *fileName* } *
       fgrep -hilnvwx *string* { *fileName* } *
       egrep -hilnvw *pattern* { *fileName* } *

grep is a utility that allows you to search for a pattern in a list of files. If no files are specified, it searches standard input instead. *pattern* may be a regular expression. All lines that match the pattern are displayed to standard output. If more than one file is specified, each matching line is preceded by the name of the file unless the **-h** option is specified. The **-n** option precedes each matching line by its line number. The **-i** option causes the case of the patterns to be ignored. The **-l** option displays a list of the files that contain the specified pattern. The **-v** option causes **grep** to display all of the lines that don't match the pattern. The **-w** option restricts matching to occur on whole words only. **fgrep** is a fast version of **grep** that can only search for fixed strings. **egrep** is an extended version of **grep** that supports regular expressions. **fgrep** supports an additional option; the **-x** option outputs only lines that are exactly equal to *string*. For more information about regular expressions, consult the appendix.

To obtain a list of all the lines in a file that contain a string, follow **grep** by the string and the name of the file to scan. Here's an example:

```
$ cat grepfile              ...list the file to be filtered.
Well you know it's your bedtime,
So turn off the light,
Say all your prayers and then,
Oh you sleepy young heads dream of wonderful things,
Beautiful mermaids will swim through the sea,
And you will be swimming there too.
$ grep the grepfile        ...search "grepfile" for the word "the".
So turn off the light,
Say all your prayers and then,
Beautiful mermaids will swim through the sea,
And you will be swimming there too.
$ _
```

Notice that words that contain the string "the" also satisfied the matching condition. Here's an example of the **-w** and **-n** options:

```
$ grep -wn the grepfile ...be more particular this time!
2:So turn off the light,
5:Beautiful mermaids will swim through the sea,
$ _
```

To display only those lines in a file that don't match, use the **-v** option:

```
$ grep -wnv the grepfile        ...reverse the sense of the filter.
1:Well you know it's your bedtime,
3:Say all your prayers and then,
4:Oh you sleepy young heads dream of wonderful things,
6:And you will be swimming there too.
$ _
```

If you specify more than one file to search, each selected line is preceded by the name of the file in which it appears. In the following example, I searched my C source files for the string "x". Please consult chapter 3 for a description of the shell file wildcard mechanism.

```
$ grep -w x *.c              ...search all files ending in ".c".
a.c:test (int x)
fact2.c:long factorial (x)
fact2.c:int x;
fact2.c:  if ((x == 1) || (x == 0))
fact2.c:    result = x * factorial (x-1);
$ grep -wl x *.c          ...list the names of the matching files.
a.c
fact2.c
$ _
```

fgrep, grep, and **egrep** all support the options that I've described so far. The difference between them is that each allows a different kind of text pattern to be matched:

Utility	Kind of pattern that may be searched for
fgrep	fixed string only
grep	regular expression
egrep	extended regular expression

For information about regular expressions and extended regular expressions, consult the appendix.

To illustrate the use of **grep** and **egrep** regular expressions, here is a piece of text followed by the lines of text that would match various regular expressions. When using **egrep** or **grep**, regular expressions should be placed inside single quotes to prevent interference from the shell. The portion of each line that satisfies the regular expression is italicized.

```
Well you know it's your bedtime,
So turn off the light,
Say all your prayers and then,
Oh you sleepy young heads dream of wonderful things,
Beautiful mermaids will swim through the sea,
And you will be swimming there too.
```

Matching Patterns

grep Pattern	Lines that match
.nd	Say all your prayers *and* then, Oh you sleepy young heads dream of *wonder*ful things, *And* you will be swimming there too.
^.nd	*And* you will be swimming there too.
sw.*ng	And you will be *swimming* there too.
[A-D]	*B*eautiful mermaids will swim through the sea, *A*nd you will be swimming there too.
\.	And you will be swimming there too.
a.	*Say* all your prayers and then, Oh you sleepy young he*ad*s dream of wonderful things, Bea*ut*iful mermaids will swim through the sea,

grep Pattern	Lines that match
a.$	Beautiful mermaids will swim through the se*a*,
[a-m]nd	Say all your prayers *and* then,
[^a-m]nd	Oh you sleepy young heads dream of w*ond*erful things, *And* you will be swimming there too.

egrep Pattern	Lines that match
s.*w	Oh you *sleepy young heads dream of* w*onderful things, Beautiful mermaids *will swim* through the sea, And you will be *sw*imming there too.
s.+w	Oh you *sleepy young heads dream of* w*onderful things, Beautiful mermaid*s *will* *sw*im through the sea,
off|will	So turn *off* the light, Beautiful mermaids *will* swim through the sea, And you *will* be swimming there too.
im*ing	And you will be swimming there too.
im?ing	\<no matches\>

Removing Duplicate Lines: uniq

The **uniq** utility displays a file with all of its identical adjacent lines replaced by a single occurrence of the repeated line, and works like this:

Utility: **uniq** -c -*number* [*inputfile* [*outputfile*]]

uniq is a utility that displays its input file with all adjacent repeated lines collapsed to a single occurrence of the repeated line. If an input file is not specified, standard input is read. The **-c** option causes each line to be preceded by the number of occurrences that were found. If *number* is specified, then *number* fields of each line are ignored.

Here's an example:

```
$ cat animals          ...look at the test file.
cat   snake
monkey   snake
dolphin   elephant
```

```
dolphin  elephant
goat  elephant
pig  pig
pig  pig
monkey  pig
$ uniq animals          ...filter out duplicate adjacent lines.
cat  snake
monkey  snake
dolphin  elephant
goat  elephant
pig  pig
monkey  pig
$ uniq -c animals       ...display a count with the lines.
   1 cat  snake
   1 monkey  snake
   2 dolphin  elephant
   1 goat  elephant
   2 pig  pig
   1 monkey  pig
$ uniq -1 animals       ...ignore the first field of each line.
cat  snake
dolphin  elephant
pig  pig
$ _
```

SORTING FILES: SORT

The **sort** utility sorts a file in ascending or descending order based on one or more *sort fields*, and works as follows:

Utility: **sort** -tc -r { *sortField* -bfMn }* { *fileName* }*

sort is a utility that sorts one or more files based on a sorting criteria. By default, lines are sorted into ascending order. The **-r** option specifies descending order instead. Input lines are split into fields separated by spaces and/or tabs. To specify a different field separator, use the **-t** option. By default, all of a line's fields are considered when the sort is being performed. This may be overridden by specifying one or more sort fields, whose format is described later in this section. Individual sort fields may be customized by following them by one or more options. The **-f** option causes **sort** to ignore the case of the field. The **-M** option sorts the field in month order. The **-n** option sorts the field in numeric order. The **-b** option ignores leading spaces.

Individual fields are ordered lexographically, which means that corresponding characters are compared based on their ASCII value. Two consequences of this are that an uppercase letter is "less" than its lowercase equivalent, and a space is "less" than a letter. In the following example, I sorted a text file in ascending order and descending order using the default ordering rule:

```
$ cat sortfile                ...list the file to be sorted.
jan  Start chapter 3  10th
Jan  Start chapter 1  30th
  Jan  Start chapter 5  23rd
  Jan  End chapter 3  23rd
Mar  Start chapter 7  27
  may  End chapter 7  17th
Apr  End Chapter 5  1
  Feb  End chapter 1  14
$ sort sortfile               ...sort it.
  Feb  End chapter 1  14
  Jan  End chapter 3  23rd
  Jan  Start chapter 5  23rd
  may  End chapter 7  17th
Apr  End Chapter 5  1
Jan  Start chapter 1  30th
Mar  Start chapter 7  27
jan  Start chapter 3  10th
$ sort -r sortfile            ...sort it in reverse order.
jan  Start chapter 3  10th
Mar  Start chapter 7  27
Jan  Start chapter 1  30th
Apr  End Chapter 5  1
  may  End chapter 7  17th
  Jan  Start chapter 5  23rd
  Jan  End chapter 3  23rd
  Feb  End chapter 1  14
$ _
```

To sort on a particular field, you must specify the starting field number using a + prefix, followed by the non-inclusive stop field number using a − prefix. Field numbers start at index 0. If you leave off the stop field number, all fields following the start field are included. In the next example, I sorted the same text file on the first field only, which is number zero:.

```
$ sort +0 -1 sortfile      ...sort on the first field only.
  Feb  End chapter 1  14
  Jan  End chapter 3  23rd
  Jan  Start chapter 5  23rd
  may  End chapter 7  17th
Apr  End Chapter 5  1
```

```
Jan  Start chapter 1  30th
Mar  Start chapter 7  27
jan  Start chapter 3  10th
$ _
```

Note that the leading spaces were counted as being part of the first field, which resulted in a strange sorting sequence. Additionally, I would have preferred the months to be sorted in correct order, with "Jan" before "Feb", etc. The **-b** option ignores leading blanks and the **-M** option sorts a field based on a month order. Here's an example that worked better:

```
$ sort +0 -1 -bM sortfile     ...sort on the first month field.
  Jan  End chapter 3  23rd
  Jan  Start chapter 5  23rd
Jan  Start chapter 1  30th
jan  Start chapter 3  10th
  Feb  End chapter 1  14
Mar  Start chapter 7  27
Apr  End Chapter 5  1
  may  End chapter 7  17th
$ _
```

The example text file was correctly sorted by month, but the dates were still out of order. You may specify multiple sort fields on the command line to deal with this problem. The **sort** utility first sorts all of the lines based on the first sort specifier, and then uses the second sort specifier to order lines that compared equally by the first specifier. Therefore, to sort the example text file by month and date, it had to be sorted based on the first field and then the fifth. In addition, the fifth field had to be sorted numerically by using the **-n** option.

```
$ sort +0 -1 -bM +4 -n sortfile
jan  Start chapter 3  10th
  Jan  End chapter 3  23rd
  Jan  Start chapter 5  23rd
Jan  Start chapter 1  30th
  Feb  End chapter 1  14
Mar  Start chapter 7  27
Apr  End Chapter 5  1
  may  End chapter 7  17th
$ _
```

Fields are often delimited by characters other than spaces. For example, the "/etc/passwd" file contains user information stored in fields separated by colons. You may use the **-t** option to specify an alternative field separator. In the following example, I sorted a file based on fields separated by : characters.

```
$ cat sortfile2                           ...look at the test file.
jan:Start chapter 3:10th
Jan:Start chapter 1:30th
Jan:Start chapter 5:23rd
Jan:End chapter 3:23rd
Mar:Start chapter 7:27
may:End chapter 7:17th
Apr:End Chapter 5:1
Feb:End chapter 1:14
$ sort -t: +0 -1 -bM +2 -n sortfile2 ...delimit using colons.
jan:Start chapter 3:10th
Jan:End chapter 3:23rd
Jan:Start chapter 5:23rd
Jan:Start chapter 1:30th
Feb:End chapter 1:14
Mar:Start chapter 7:27
Apr:End Chapter 5:1
may:End chapter 7:17th
$ _
```

sort contains several other options that are too detailed to describe here; I suggest that you use the **man** utility to find out more about them.

COMPARING FILES

There are two utilities that allow you to compare the contents of two files:

- **cmp,** which finds the first byte that differs between two files
- **diff,** which displays all the differences and similarities between two files

The next few subsections describe these utilities.

Testing For Sameness: cmp

The **cmp** utility determines whether two files are the same, and works as follows:

Utility: **cmp** -ls *fileName1 fileName2 offset1 offset2*

cmp is a utility that tests two files for equality. If *fileName1* and *fileName2* are exactly equal, then **cmp** returns the exit code 0 and displays nothing; otherwise, it returns the exit code 1 and displays the offset and line number of the first mismatched byte. If one file is a prefix of the other, then the EOF message is displayed for the file that is shorter. The **-l** option displays the offset and values of all mismatched bytes. The **-s** option causes all output to be inhibited. The optional values *offset1* and *offset2* specify the starting offset in *fileName1* and *fileName2*, respectively, that the comparison should begin.

In the following example, I compared the files "lady1," "lady2," and "lady3":

```
$ cat lady1                      ...look at the first test file.
Lady of the night,
I hold you close to me,
And all those loving words you say are right.
$ cat lady2                      ...look at the second test file.
Lady of the night,
I hold you close to me,
And everything you say to me is right.
$ cat lady3                      ...look at the third test file.
Lady of the night,
I hold you close to me,
And everything you say to me is right.
It makes me feel,
I'm so in love with you.
Even in the dark I see your light.
$ cmp lady1 lady2                ...files differ.
lady1 lady2 differ: char 48, line 3
$ cmp lady2 lady3                ...file2 is a prefix of file3.
cmp: EOF on lady2
$ cmp lady3 lady3                ...files are exactly the same.
$ _
```

The **-l** option displays the byte offset and values of every byte that doesn't match:

```
$ cmp -l lady1 lady2     ...display all bytes that don't match.
    48 141 145
    49 154 166
    ...
    81 145  56
    82  40  12
cmp: EOF on lady2        ...lady2 is smaller than lady1.
$ _
```

File Differences: diff

The **diff** utility compares two files and displays a list of editing changes that would convert the first file into the second file. It works as follows:

Utility: **diff** -i -d*flag fileName1 fileName2*

diff is a utility that compares two files and outputs a description of their differences. See the rest of this section for information on the format of this output. The **-i** flag makes **diff** ignore the case of the lines. The **-D** option causes **diff** to generate output designed for the C preprocessor.

There are three kinds of editing changes: adding lines (a), changing lines (c), and deleting lines (d). Here is the format that **diff** uses to describe each kind of edit:

Additions

---

firstStart **a** secondStart, secondStop
> lines from the second file to add to the first file

Deletions

---

firstStart, firstStop **d** lineCount
< lines from the first file to delete

Changes

---

firstStart, firstStop **c** secondStart, secondStop
< lines in the first file to be replaced

> lines in the second file to be used for the replacement

---

where *firstStart* and *firstStop* denote line numbers in the first file, and *secondStart* and *secondStop* denote line numbers in the second file.

In the following example, I compared several text files to observe their differences:

```
$ cat lady1              ...look at the first test file.
Lady of the night,
I hold you close to me,
And all those loving words you say are right.
$ cat lady2              ...look at the second test file.
```

```
Lady of the night,
I hold you close to me,
And everything you say to me is right.
$ cat lady3              ...look at the third test file.
Lady of the night,
I hold you close to me,
And everything you say to me is right.
It makes me feel,
I'm so in love with you.
Even in the dark I see your light.
$ cat lady4              ...look at the fourth test file.
Lady of the night,
I'm so in love with you.
Even in the dark I see your light.
$ diff lady1 lady2       ...compare lady1 and lady2.
3c3
< And all those loving words you say are right.
---
> And everything you say to me is right.
$ diff lady2 lady3       ...compare lady2 and lady3.
3a4,6
> It makes me feel,
> I'm so in love with you.
> Even in the dark I see your light.
$ diff lady3 lady4       ...compare lady3 and lady4.
2,4d1
< I hold you close to me,
< And everything you say to me is right.
< It makes me feel,
$ _
```

The **-D** option of **diff** is useful for merging two files into a single file that contains C preprocessor directives. Each version of the file can be re-created by using the **cc** compiler with suitable options and macro definitions.

```
$ diff -Dflag lady3 lady4            ...look at the output.
Lady of the night,
#ifndef flag                         ...preprocessor directive.
I hold you close to me,
And everything you say to me is right.
It makes me feel,
#endif flag                          ...preprocessor directive.
I'm so in love with you.
Even in the dark I see your light.
$ diff -Dflag lady2 lady4 > lady.diff ...store the output in a file.
$ cc -P lady.diff                    ...invoke the preprocessor.
$ cat lady.i                         ...look at the output.
Lady of the night,
```

```
I hold you close to me,
And everything you say to me is right.

$ cc -Dflag -P lady.diff          ...obtain the other version.
$ cat lady.i                      ...look at the output.
Lady of the night,

I'm so in love with you.
Even in the dark I see your light.
$ _
```

ARCHIVES

There are several occasions that you'll want to save some files to a secondary storage medium such as a disk or tape:

- for daily, weekly, or monthly backups
- for transport between non-networked UNIX sites
- for posterity

There is a family of three utilities that allows you to archive files, each of which has its own strengths and weaknesses. In my opinion, it would be much better to have a single, powerful, general-purpose archive utility, but no standard utility has these qualities. Here is a list of the utilities, together with a brief description:

- **cpio,** which allows you to save directory structures onto a single backup volume. It's handy for saving small quantities of data, but the single-volume restriction makes it useless for large backups.
- **tar,** which allows you to save directory structures onto a single backup volume. It's specially designed to save files onto tape, so it always archives files onto the end of the storage medium. As before, the single-volume restriction makes it unusable for large backups.
- **dump,** which allows you to save a file system onto multiple backup volumes. It's specially designed for doing total and incremental backups, but it's tricky to restore individual files.

The next few subsections describe these utilities.

Copying Files: cpio

The **cpio** utility allows you to create and access special cpio-format files. These special format files are useful for backing up small subdirectories, thereby avoiding the heavy-duty **dump** utility. Unfortunately, the **cpio** utility is unable to write special format files to multiple volumes, so the entire backup file must be able to reside on a single storage medium. If the backup is larger than this, use the **dump** utility instead. **cpio** works like this:

Utility: **cpio** -ov
             cpio -idtu *patterns*
             cpio -pl *directory*

cpio allows you to create and access special cpio-format files.

The **-o** option takes a list of filenames from standard input and creates a cpio-format file that contains a backup of the files. The **-v** option causes the name of each file to be displayed as it's copied.

The **-i** option reads a cpio-format file from standard input and re-creates all of the files from the input channel whose name matches a specified pattern. By default, older files are not copied over younger files. The **-u** option causes unconditional copying. The **-d** option causes directories to be created if they are needed during the copy process. The **-t** option causes a table of contents to be displayed instead of performing the copy.

The **-p** option takes a list of filenames from standard input and copies their contents to a named directory. This option is useful for copying one subdirectory to another place, although most uses of this option can be performed more easily using the **cp** utility with the **-r** (recursive) option. The **-l** option creates links instead of performing physical copies whenever possible.

To demonstrate the **-o** and **-i** options, I created a backup version of all the C source files in my current directory, deleted the source files, and then restored them.

```
$ ls -l *.c                     ...list the files to be saved.
-rw-r--r--  1 glass          172 Jan  5 19:44 main1.c
-rw-r--r--  1 glass          198 Jan  5 19:44 main2.c
-rw-r--r--  1 glass          224 Jan  5 19:44 palindrome.c
-rw-r--r--  1 glass          266 Jan  5 23:46 reverse.c
$ ls *.c | cpio -ov > backup  ...save them in a file called "backup".
main1.c
main2.c
palindrome.c
reverse.c
3 blocks
$ ls -l backup                  ...examine "backup".
-rw-r--r--  1 glass         1536 Jan9 18:34 backup
$ rm *.c                        ...remove the original files.
$ cpio -it < backup             ...restore the files.
```

```
main1.c
main2.c
palindrome.c
reverse.c
3 blocks
$ ls -l *.c                          ...confirm their restoration.
-rw-r--r--   1 glass       172 Jan  5 19:44 main1.c
-rw-r--r--   1 glass       198 Jan  5 19:44 main2.c
-rw-r--r--   1 glass       224 Jan  5 19:44 palindrome.c
-rw-r--r--   1 glass       266 Jan  5 23:46 reverse.c
$ _
```

To backup all of the files that match the pattern "*.c", including subdirectories, use the output from the **find** utility as the input to **cpio**. The **-depth** option of **find** recursively searches for matching patterns. In the following example, note that I escaped the * character in the argument to the **-name** option so that it was not expanded by the shell:

```
$ find . -name \*.c -depth -print | cpio -ov > backup2
main1.c
main2.c
palindrome.c
reverse.c
tmp/b.c
tmp/a.c
3 blocks
$ rm -r *.c                          ...remove the original files.
$ rm tmp/*.c                         ...remove the lower-level files.
$ cpio -it < backup2                 ...restore the files.
main1.c
main2.c
palindrome.c
reverse.c
tmp/b.c
tmp/a.c
3 blocks
$ _
```

To demonstrate the **-p** option, I obtained a list of all the files in my current directory that were modified in the last two days (using the **find** utility) and then copied them into the parent directory. Without the **-l** option, the files were physically copied, resulting in a total increase in disk usage of 153 blocks. With the **-l** option, however, the files were linked, resulting in no disk usage at all.

```
$ find . -mtime -2 -print | cpio -p ..      ...copy by copying.
153 blocks
```

```
$ ls -l ../reverse.c                        ...look at the copied file.
-rw-r--r--  1 glass          266 Jan  9 18:42 ../reverse.c
$ find . -mtime -2 -print | cpio -pl ..   ...copy by linking.
0 blocks
$ ls -l ../reverse.c                        ...look at the linked file.
-rw-r--r--  2 glass          266 Jan  7 15:26 ../reverse.c
$ _
```

Tape Archiving: tar

The **tar** utility was designed specifically for maintaining an archive of files on a
magnetic tape. When you add a file to an archive file using **tar,** the file is *always*
placed on the end, since you cannot modify the middle of a file that is stored on
tape. If you're not archiving files onto a tape, I suggest that you use the **cpio**
utility instead. Here's how **tar** works:

Utility: **tar** -cfrtuvx [*tarFileName*] *fileList*

tar allows you to create and access special tar-format archive files. The **-c**
option creates a tar-format file. The name of the tar-format file is
''/dev/rmt8'' by default, although this may be overridden by setting the
$TAPE environment variable or by using the **-f** option followed by the re-
quired filename. The **-v** option encourages verbose output. The **-x** option
allows you to extract named files, and the **-t** option generates a table of
contents. The **-r** option unconditionally appends the listed files to the archive file. The **-u** option appends only files that are more recent than those
already archived. If the file list contains directory names, the contents of the
directories are appended/extracted recursively.

In the following example, I saved all of the files in the current directory to the
archive file ''tarfile'':

```
$ ls                      ...look at the current directory.
main1*       main2        palindrome.c       reverse.h
main1.c      main2.c      palindrome.h       tarfile
main1.make   main2.make   reverse.c          tmp/
$ ls tmp                  ...look in the "tmp" directory.
a.c          b.c
$ tar -cvf tarfile .      ...archive the current directory.
a ./main1.c 1 blocks
a ./main2.c 1 blocks
...
a ./main2 48 blocks
```

```
a ./tmp/b.c 1 blocks
a ./tmp/a.c 1 blocks
$ ls -l tarfile      ...look at the archive file "tarfile".
-rw-r--r-- 1 glass          65536 Jan 10 12:44 tarfile
$ _
```

To obtain a table of contents of a **tar** archive, use the **-t** option:

```
$ tar -tvf tarfile                ...look at the table of contents.
rwxr-xr-x496/62      0 Jan 10 12:44 1992 ./
rw-r--r--496/62    172 Jan 10 12:41 1992 ./main1.c
rw-r--r--496/62    198 Jan  9 18:36 1992 ./main2.c
...
rw-r--r--496/62  24576 Jan  7 15:26 1992 ./main2
rwxr-xr-x496/62      0 Jan 10 12:42 1992 ./tmp/
rw-r--r--496/62      9 Jan 10 12:42 1992 ./tmp/b.c
rw-r--r--496/62      9 Jan 10 12:42 1992 ./tmp/a.c
$ _
```

To unconditionally append a file to the end of a tar archive, use the **-r** option followed by a list of files and/or directories to append. Notice in the following example that the tar archive ended up holding two copies of ''reverse.c'':

```
$ tar -rvf tarfile reverse.c       ...unconditionally append a file.
a reverse.c 1 blocks
$ tar -tvf tarfile                 ...look at the table of contents.
rwxr-xr-x496/62      0 Jan 10 12:44 1992 ./
rw-r--r--496/62    172 Jan 10 12:41 1992 ./main1.c
...
rw-r--r--496/62    266 Jan  9 18:36 1992 ./reverse.c
...
rw-r--r--496/62    266 Jan 10 12:46 1992 reverse.c
$ _
```

To append a file only if it isn't in the archive or if it has been modified since it was last archived, use the **-u** option instead of **-r**. In the following example, note that ''reverse.c'' was not archived because it hadn't been modified:

```
$ tar -rvf tarfile reverse.c     ...unconditionally append.
a reverse.c 1 blocks
$ tar -uvf tarfile reverse.c     ...conditionally append.
$ _
```

To extract a file from an archive file, use the **-x** option followed by a list of files and/or directories. If a directory name is specified, it is recursively extracted:

```
$ rm tmp/*                    ...remove all files from "tmp".
$ tar -vxf tarfile ./tmp      ...extract archived "tmp" files.
x ./tmp/b.c, 9 bytes, 1 tape blocks
x ./tmp/a.c, 9 bytes, 1 tape blocks
$ ls tmp                      ...confirm restoration.
a.c          b.c
$ _
```

Unfortunately, **tar** doesn't support pattern matching of the name list, so to extract files that match a particular pattern, be crafty and use **grep** as part of the command sequence like this:

```
$ tar -xvf tarfile `tar -tf tarfile | grep '.*\.c'`
x ./main1.c, 172 bytes, 1 tape blocks
x ./main2.c, 198 bytes, 1 tape blocks
x ./palindrome.c, 224 bytes, 1 tape blocks
x ./reverse.c, 266 bytes, 1 tape blocks
x ./tmp/b.c, 9 bytes, 1 tape blocks
x ./tmp/a.c, 9 bytes, 1 tape blocks
$ _
```

If you change into another directory and then extract files that were stored using relative pathnames, the names are interpreted as being relative to the current directory. In the following example, I restored "reverse.c" from the previously created tar file to a new directory "tmp2". Note that each copy of "reverse.c" overwrote the previous one, so that the latest version was the one that was left intact:

```
$ mkdir tmp2                     ...create a new directory.
$ cd tmp2                        ...move there.
$ tar -vxf ../tarfile reverse.c  ...restore a single file.
x reverse.c, 266 bytes, 1 tape blocks
x reverse.c, 266 bytes, 1 tape blocks
$ ls -l                          ...confirm restoration.
total 1
-rw-r--r--  1 glass         266 Jan 10 12:48 reverse.c
$ _
```

Incremental Backups: dump/restore

Here's a system administrator's typical backup strategy:

- Perform a weekly total file system backup.
- Perform a daily incremental backup, storing only those files that were changed since the last incremental backup.

This kind of backup strategy is supported nicely by the **dump** and **restore** utilities. **dump** works like this:

Utility: **dump** [*level*] [f *dumpFile*] [v] [w] *fileSystem*
      dump [*level*] [f *dumpFile*] [v] [w] { *fileName* }+

The **dump** utility has two forms. The first form of the **dump** utility copies files from the specified file system to *dumpFile*, which is "/dev/rmt8" by default. If the dump level is specified as *n*, then all of the files that have been modified since the last dump at a lower level than *n* are copied. For example, a level 0 dump will always dump *all* files, whereas a level 2 dump will dump all of the files modified since the last level 0 or level 1 dump. If no dump level is specified, it is set to 9. The **v** option causes **dump** to verify each volume of media after it is written. The **w** option causes **dump** to display a list of all the file systems that need to be dumped instead of performing a backup.

The second form of **dump** allows you to specify the names of files to be dumped.

Both forms prompt the user to insert and/or remove dump media when necessary. For example, a large system dump to a tape drive often requires an operator to remove a full tape and replace it with an empty one.

When a dump is performed, information about the dump is recorded in the "/etc/dumpdates" file for use by future invocations of **dump**.

Here's an example of **dump:**

```
$ dump 0 fv /dev/rmt0 /dev/da0    ...perform level 0 dump of file
                                  ...system /dev/da0 to the tape drive
                                  .../dev/rmt0, with verification.
$ _
```

The **restore** utility allows you to restore files from a **dump** backup, and works as follows:

Utility: **restore** -irtx [f *dumpFile*] { *fileName* }*

The **restore** utility allows you to restore a set of files from a previous dump file. If *dumpFile* is not specified, "/dev/rtm8" is used by default. The **-r** option causes every file on *dumpFile* to be restored into the current directory, so use this option with care. The **-t** option causes a table of contents of *dumpFile* to be displayed instead of restoring any files. The **-x** option causes **restore** to restore only the specified filenames from *dumpFile*. If a filename is the name of a directory, its contents are recursively restored.

> The **-i** option causes **restore** to read the table of contents of *dumpFile* and then enter an interactive mode that allows you to choose the files that you wish to restore. For more information on this interactive mode, consult **man.**

In the following example, I used **restore** to extract a couple of previously saved files from the dump device "/dev/rmt0":

```
$ restore -x f /dev/rmt0 wine.c hacking.c ...restore two named files.
$ _
```

FINDING FILES: FIND

The **find** utility can do much more than simply locate a named file; it can perform actions on a set of files that satisfy specific conditions. For example, you can use **find** to erase all of the files belonging to a user *tim* that haven't been modified for 3 days. Here's a formal description:

> *Utility:* **find** *pathList expression*
>
> The **find** utility recursively descends through *pathList* and applies *expression* to every file. The syntax of *expression* is described below, together with some examples of **find**.

Here is a table that describes the syntax of *expression*:

Expression	Value/action
-name *pattern*	True if the file's name matches *pattern*, which may include the shell metacharacters *, [ ], and ?.
-perm *oct*	True if the octal description of the file's permission flags are exactly equal to *oct*.
-type *ch*	True if the type of the file is *ch* (b = block, c = char, etc.).
-user *userId*	True if the owner of the file is *userId*.
-group *groupId*	True if the group of the file is *groupId*.
-atime *count*	True if the file has been accessed within *count* days.

Expression	Value/action
-mtime *count*	True if the contents of the file have been modified within *count* days.
-ctime *count*	True if the contents of the file have been modified within *count* days or if any of its attributes have been altered.
-exec *command*	True if the exit code from executing *command* is 0. *command* must be terminated by an escaped semicolon (\;). If you specify {} as a command line argument, it is replaced by the name of the current file.
-print	Prints out the name of the current file and returns true.
-ls	Displays the current file's attributes and returns true.
-cpio *device*	Writes the current file in cpio format to *device* and returns true.
!expression	Returns the logical negation of *expression*.
expr1 [-a] *expr2*	Short-circuiting and; if *expr1* is false, it returns false and *expr2* is not executed. If *expr1* is true, it returns the value of *expr2*.
expr1 -o *expr2*	Short-circuiting or; if *expr1* is true, it returns true. If *expr1* is false, it returns the value of *expr2*.

Here are some examples of **find** in action:

```
$ find . -name '*.c' -print     ...print the names of all c source files
                                ...in the current directory or any of its
                                ...subdirectories.
./proj/fall.89/play.c
./proj/fall.89/referee.c
./proj/fall.89/player.c
./rock/guess.c
./rock/play.c
./rock/player.c
./rock/referee.c
$ find . -mtime 14 -ls          ...ls files that have been modified
                                ...during the last 14 days.
  53791    14 -rw-r--r--    1 glass    cs    14151 May   1 16:58 ./stty.txt
  53847     1 -rw-r--r--    1 glass    cs       48 May   1 14:02 ./myFile.doc
  53877     1 -rw-r--r--    1 glass    cs       10 May   1 14:02 ./rain.doc
  53879    15 -rw-r--r--    1 glass    cs    14855 May   1 16:58 ./tset.txt
  53883    47 -rw-r--r--    1 glass    cs    47794 May   2 10:56 ./mail.txt
$ find . -name '*.bak' -ls -exec rm {} \;
                                ...ls and then remove all files
                                ...that end with ".bak".
```

```
53915    1 -rw-r--r--   1 glass   cs        9 May 16 12:01 ./a.bak
53916    1 -rw-r--r--   1 glass   cs        9 May 16 12:01 ./b.bak
58196   16 -rw-r--r--   1 glass   cs 15630 Jan 26 00:14 ./sys6/gosh.bak
58188   19 -rw-r--r--   1 glass   cs 18481 Jan 26 12:59 ./sys6/gosh2.bak
$ find . \( -name '*.c' -o -name '*.txt' \) -print
                            ...print the names of all files that
                            ...end in ".c" or ".txt".
./proj/fall.89/play.c
./proj/fall.89/referee.c
./proj/fall.89/player.c
./rock/guess.c
./rock/play.c
./rock/player.c
./rock/referee.c
./stty.txt
./tset.txt
./mail.txt
$ _
```

SCHEDULING COMMANDS

There are two utilities that allow you to schedule commands to be executed at a later point in time:

- **crontab,** which allows you to create a scheduling table that describes a series of jobs to be executed on a periodic basis
- **at,** which allows you to schedule jobs to be executed on a one-time basis

The next couple of subsections describe each utility.

Periodic Execution: Cron/Crontab

The **crontab** utility allows you to schedule a series of jobs to be executed on a periodic basis, and works as follows:

Utility: **crontab** *crontabName*
     crontab -ler [*userName*]

crontab is the user interface to the UNIX **cron** system. When used without any options, the crontab file called *crontabName* is registered and its commands are executed according to the specified timing rules. The **-l** option

---

> lists the contents of a registered crontab file. The **-e** option edits and then registers a registered crontab file. The **-r** option un-registers a registered crontab file. The **-l, -e,** and **-r** options may be used by a super-user to access another user's crontab file by supplying the user's name as an optional argument. The anatomy of a crontab file is described shortly.

To use **crontab,** you must prepare an input file that contains lines of the format:

```
minute    hour    day    month    weekday    command
```

where the values of each field are as follows:

Field	Valid value
minute	0-59
hour	0-23
day	1-31
month	1-12
weekday	1-7 (1=Mon, 2=Tue, 3=Wed, 4=Thu, 5=Fri, 6=Sat, 7=Sun)
command	any UNIX command

Files of this nature are called "crontab" files. Whenever the current time matches a line's description, the associated command is executed by the shell specified in the $SHELL environment variable. A Bourne shell is used if this variable is not set. If any of the first five fields contain an * instead of a number, the field always matches. The standard output of the command is automatically sent to the user via **mail**. Any characters following a % are copied into a temporary file and used as the command's standard input. Here is a sample crontab file that I created in my home directory and called "crontab.cron":

```
$ cat crontab.cron              ...list the crontab file.
0       8       *       *       1       echo Happy Monday Morning
*       *       *       *       *       echo One Minute Passed > /dev/tty1
30      14      1       *       1       mail users % Jan Meeting At 3pm
$ _
```

The first line mails me "Happy Monday Morning" at 8 am every Monday. The next line echoes "One Minute Passed" every minute to the device "/dev/tty1", which happens to be my terminal. The last line sends mail to all users on the first of January at 2:30 pm to remind them of an impending meeting.

There is a single process called "cron" that is responsible for executing the commands in registered crontab files in a timely fashion. It is started when the UNIX system is booted and does not stop until the UNIX system is shut down. Copies of all registered crontab files are stored in the directory "/var/spool/cron/ crontabs".

To register a crontab file, use the **crontab** utility with the name of the crontab file as the single argument:

```
$ crontab crontab.cron         ...register the crontab file.
$ _
```

If you already have a registered crontab file, the new one is registered in place of the old one. To list the contents of your registered crontab, use the **-l** option. To list someone else's, add their name as an argument. Only a super-user can use this option. In the example that follows, note that one of my previously registered crontab file entries triggered coincidentally after I used the **crontab** utility.

```
$ crontab -l            ...list the contents of the crontab file.
0     8    *    *    1    echo Happy Monday Morning
*     *    *    *    *    echo One Minute Passed > /dev/tty1
30    14   1    *    1    mail users % Jan Meeting At 3pm
$ One Minute Passed      ...output from one of my crontab commands.
$ _
```

To edit your crontab file and then resave it, use the **-e** option. To un-register a crontab file, use the **-r** option:

```
$ crontab -r             ...un-register my crontab file.
$ _
```

A super-user may create files called "cron.allow" and "cron.deny" in the "/var/ spool/cron" directory to enable and inhibit individual users from using the crontab facility. Each file consists of a list of user names on separate lines. If neither of the files exist, only a super-user may use **crontab.** If "cron.deny" is empty and "cron.allow" doesn't exist, all users may use **crontab.**

One-time Execution: At

The **at** utility allows you to schedule one-time commands or scripts, and works like this:

Utility: **at** -csm *time* [*date* [, *year*]] [+*increment*] [*script*]
       at -r { *jobId* }+
       at -l { *jobId* }*

at allows you to schedule one-time commands and/or scripts. It supports a flexible format for time specification. The **-c** and **-s** options allow you to specify that commands are run by a C shell or Bourne shell, respectively. The **-m** option instructs **at** to send you mail when then the job is completed. If no script name is specified, **at** takes a list of commands from standard input. The **-r** option removes the specified jobs from the **at** queue, and the **-l** option lists the pending jobs. A job is removed from the **at** queue after it has executed.

    time is in the format HH or HHMM followed by an optional am/pm specifier, and *date* is spelled out using the first three letters of the day and/or month. The keyword "now" may be used in place of the time sequence. The keywords "today" and "tomorrow" may be used in place of *date*. If no *date* is supplied, then **at** uses the following rules:

- If *time* is after the current time, then *date* is assumed to be "today".
- If *time* is before the current time, then *date* is assumed to be "tomorrow".

The stated time may be augmented by an *increment*, which is a number followed by "minutes," "hours," "days," "weeks," "months," or "years".

    A script is executed by the shell specified by the $SHELL environment variable, or a Bourne shell if this variable is not set. All standard output from an **at** script is mailed to the user.

In the following example, I scheduled an **at** script to send a message to my terminal "/dev/tty1":

```
$ cat at.csh                    ...look at the script to be scheduled.
#! /bin/csh
echo at done > /dev/tty1        ...echo output to my terminal.
$ date                          ...look at the current time.
Fri Jan 10 17:27:42 CST 1992
$ at now + 2 minutes at.csh     ...schedule script to execute in 2 minutes
job 2519 at Fri Jan 10 17:30:00 1992
$ at -l                         ...look at the at schedule.
     2519 a     Fri Jan 10 17:30:00 1992
$
at done                         ...output from the scheduled script.
```

```
$ at 17:35 at.csh             ...schedule the script again.
job 2520 at Fri Jan 10 17:35:00 1992
$ at -r 2520                  ...deschedule.
$ at -l                       ...look at the at schedule.
$ _
```

Here are some more examples of legal **at** time formats:

```
0934am Sep 18 at.csh
9:34 Sep 18 , 1994 at.csh
11:00pm tomorrow at.csh
now + 1 day at.csh
9pm Jan 13 at.csh
10pm Wed at.csh
```

If you omit the command name, **at** displays a prompt and then waits for a list of commands to be entered from standard input. To terminate the command list, press a *Control-D*. Here's an example:

```
$ at 8pm              ...enter commands to be scheduled from the keyboard.
at> echo at done > /dev/ttyp1
at> ^D                ...end-of-input.
job 2530 at Fri Jan 10 17:35:00 1992
$ _
```

You may program a script to reschedule itself by calling **at** within the script:

```
$ cat at.csh              ...a script that reschedules itself.
#! /bin/csh
date > /dev/tty1
# Reschedule script
at now + 2 minutes at.csh
$ _
```

A super-user may create files called "at.allow" and "at.deny" in the "/var/spool/ cron" directory to enable and inhibit individual users from using the **at** facility. Each file should consist of a list of user names on separate lines. If neither of the files exist, only a super-user may use **at.** If "at.deny" is empty and "at.allow" doesn't exist, all users may use **at.**

PROGRAMMABLE TEXT PROCESSING: awk

The **awk** utility scans one or more files and performs an action on all of the lines that match a particular condition. The actions and conditions are described by an **awk** program, and range from the very simple to the complex.

awk got its name from the combined first letters of its authors surnames: Aho, Weinberger, and Kernighan. It borrows its control structures and expression syntax from the C language. If you already know C, then learning **awk** is quite straightforward.

awk is a comprehensive utility, so comprehensive in fact that there's a book on it! Because of this, I've attempted to describe only the main features and options of **awk;** however, I think that the material that I describe in this section will allow you to write a good number of useful **awk** applications. Here's a synopsis of **awk:**

Utility: **awk** -Fc [-f *fileName*] *program* { *variable=value* }* { *fileName* }*

awk is a programmable text processing utility that scans the lines of its input and performs actions on every line that matches a particular criteria. An **awk** program may be included on the command line, in which case it should be surrounded by single quotes; alternatively, it may be stored in a file and specified using the **-f** option. The initial values of variables may be specified on the command line. The default field separators are tabs and spaces. To override this, use the **-F** option followed by the new field separator. If no filenames are specified, **awk** reads from standard input.

The next few subsections describe the various **awk** features and include many examples.

awk Programs

An **awk** program may be supplied on the command line, but it's much more common to place it in a text file and specify the file using the **-f** option. If you decide to place an **awk** program on the command line, surround it by single quotes.

When **awk** reads a line, it breaks it into fields that are separated by tabs and/ or spaces. The field separator may be overridden by using the **-F** option, as you'll see later in this section. An **awk** program is a list of one or more commands of the form:

```
[ condition ] [ \{ action \} ]
```

where *condition* is one of the following:

- the special token BEGIN or END
- an expression involving logical operators, relational operators, and/or regular expressions

and *action* is a list of one or more of the following kinds of C-like statements, terminated by semicolons:

- **if** (conditional) statement [**else** statement]
- **while** (conditional) statement
- **for** (expression; conditional; expression) statement
- **break**
- **continue**
- variable=expression
- **print** [list of expressions] [> expression]
- **printf** format [, list of expressions] [> expression]
- **next** (skips the remaining patterns on the current line of input)
- **exit** (skips the rest of the current line)
- { list of statements }

action is performed on every line that matches *condition*. If *condition* is missing, *action* is performed on every line. If *action* is missing, then all matching lines are simply sent to standard output. The statements in an **awk** program may be indented and formatted using spaces, tabs, and newlines.

Accessing Individual Fields

The first field of the current line may be accessed by $1, the second by $2, etc. $0 stands for the entire line. The built-in variable **NF** is equal to the number of fields in the current line. In the following example, I ran a simple **awk** program on the text file "float" to insert the number of fields into each line:

```
$ cat float                          ...look at the original file.
Wish I was floating in blue across the sky,
My imagination is strong,
And I often visit the days
When everything seemed so clear.
Now I wonder what I'm doing here at all...
$ awk '{ print NF, $0 }' float       ...execute the command.
9 Wish I was floating in blue across the sky,
4 My imagination is strong,
6 And I often visit the days
5 When everything seemed so clear.
9 Now I wonder what I'm doing here at all...
$ _
```

BEGIN And END

The special condition BEGIN is triggered before the first line is read, and the special condition END is triggered after the last line has been read. When expressions are listed in a print statement, no space is placed between them, and a newline is output by default. The built-in variable FILENAME is equal to the name of the input file. In the following example, I ran a program that displayed the first, third, and last fields of every line:

```
$ cat awk2                     ...look at the awk script.
BEGIN { print "Start of file:", FILENAME }
{ print $1 $3 $NF }            ...print first, third, and last field.
END { print "End of file" }
$ awk -f awk2 float            ...execute the script.
Start of file: float
Wishwassky,
Myisstrong,
Andoftendays
Whenseemedclear.
Nowwonderall...
End of file
$ _
```

Operators

When commas are placed between the expressions in a **print** statement, a space is output. All of the usual C operators are available in **awk.** The built-in variable **NR** contains the line number of the current line. In the next example, I ran a program that displayed the first, third, and last fields of lines 2..3 of "float":

```
$ cat awk3               ...look at the awk script.
NR > 1 && NR < 4 { print NR, $1, $3, $NF }
$ awk -f awk3 float      ...execute the script.
2 My is strong,
3 And often days
$ _
```

Variables

awk supports user-defined variables. There is no need to declare a variable. A variable's initial value is a null string or zero, depending on how you use it. In the next example, the program counted the number of lines and words in a file as it echoed the lines to standard output:

```
$ cat awk4              ...look at the awk script.
BEGIN { print "Scanning file" }
{
  printf "line %d: %s\n", NR, $0;
  lineCount++;
  wordCount += NF;
}
END { printf "lines = %d, words = %d\n", lineCount, wordCount }
$ awk -f awk4 float     ...execute the script.
Scanning file
line 1: Wish I was floating in blue across the sky,
line 2: My imagination is strong,
line 3: And I often visit the days
line 4: When everything seemed so clear.
line 5: Now I wonder what I'm doing here at all...
lines = 5, words = 33
$ _
```

Control Structures

awk supports most of the standard C control structures. In the following example, I printed the fields in each line backward:

```
$ cat awk5              ...look at the awk script.
{
  for (i = NF; i >= 1; i--)
    printf "%s ", $i;

  printf "\n";
}
$ awk -f awk5 float     ...execute the script.
sky, the across blue in floating was I Wish
strong, is imagination My
days the visit often I And
clear. so seemed everything When
all... at here doing I'm what wonder I Now
$ _
```

Extended Regular Expressions

The condition for line matching can be an extended regular expression, which is defined in the appendix of this book. Regular expressions must be placed between / characters. In the next example, I displayed all of the lines that contained a "t" followed by an "e," with any number of characters in between. For the sake of clarity, I've italicized the character sequences of the output lines that satisfied the condition.

```
$ cat awk6              ...look at the script.
/t.*e/ { print $0 }
$ awk -f awk6 float     ...execute the script.
Wish I was floating in blue across the sky,
And I often visit the days
When everything seemed so clear.
Now I wonder what I'm doing here at all...
$ _
```

Condition Ranges

A condition may be two expressions separated by a comma. In this case, **awk** performs *action* on every line from the first line that matches the first condition to the next line that satisfies the second condition:

```
$ cat awk7              ...look at the awk script.
/strong/ , /clear/ { print $0 }
$ awk -f awk7 float     ...execute the script.
My imagination is strong,
And I often visit the days
When everything seemed so clear.
$ _
```

Field Separators

If the field separators are not spaces, use the **-F** option to specify the separator character. In the next example, I processed a file whose fields were separated by colons:

```
$ cat awk3                     ...look at the awk script.
NR > 1 && NR < 4 { print $1, $3, $NF }
$ cat float2                   ...look at the input file.
Wish:I:was:floating:in:blue:across:the:sky,
My:imagination:is:strong,
And:I:often:visit:the:days
When:everything:seemed:so:clear.
Now:I:wonder:what:I'm:doing:here:at:all...
$ awk -F: -f awk3 float2       ...execute the script.
My is strong,
And often days
$ _
```

Built-in Functions

awk supports several built-in functions, including exp ( ), log ( ), sqrt ( ), int ( ), and substr ( ). The first four functions work just like their standard C counterparts. substr (str, x, y) returns the substring of *str* from the *x*th character to the *y*th character. Here's an example of these functions:

```
$ cat test              ...look at the input file.
1.1 a
2.2 at
3.3 eat
4.4 beat
$ cat awk8              ...look at the awk script.
{
  printf "$1 = %g ", $1;
  printf "exp = %.2g ", exp ($1);
  printf "log = %.2g ", log ($1);
  printf "sqrt = %.2g ", sqrt ($1);
  printf "int = %d ", int ($1);
  printf "substr (%s, 1, 2) = %s\n", $2, substr ($2, 1, 2);
}
$ awk -f awk8 test      ...execute the script.
$1 = 1.1 exp = 3 log = 0.095 sqrt = 1 int = 1 substr (a, 1, 2) = a
$1 = 2.2 exp = 9 log = 0.79 sqrt = 1.5 int = 2 substr (at, 1, 2) = at
$1 = 3.3 exp = 27 log = 1.2 sqrt = 1.8 int = 3 substr (eat, 1, 2) = ea
$1 = 4.4 exp = 81 log = 1.5 sqrt = 2.1 int = 4 substr (beat, 1, 2) = be
$ _
```

HARD AND SOFT LINKS: ln

The **ln** utility allows you to create both hard links and symbolic (soft) links between files, and works like this:

> *Utility:* **ln** -sf *original* [*newLink*]
>   **ln** -sf { *original* }+ *directory*

ln is a utility that allows you to create hard links or symbolic (soft) links to existing files.

To create a hard link between two regular files, specify the existing file label as the *original* filename and the new file label as *newLink*. Both labels will then refer to the same physical file, and this arrangement will be reflected in the hard link count shown by the **ls** utility. The file can then be accessed via either label, and is removed from the file system only when all of its associated labels are deleted. If *newLink* is omitted, the last component of *original* is assumed. If the last argument is the name of a directory, then hard links are made from that directory to all of the specified original filenames. Hard links may not span file systems.

The **-s** option causes **ln** to create symbolic links, which may span file systems. The **-f** option allows a super-user to create a hard link to a directory.

In the following example, I added a new label "hold" to the file referenced by the existing label "hold.3". Note that the hard link count field incremented from one to two when the hard link was added, and then back to one again when the hard link was deleted:

```
$ ls -l                    ...look at the current directory contents.
total 3
-rw-r--r--  1 glass          124 Jan 12 17:32 hold.1
-rw-r--r--  1 glass           89 Jan 12 17:34 hold.2
-rw-r--r--  1 glass           91 Jan 12 17:34 hold.3
$ ln hold.3 hold           ...create a new hard link.
$ ls -l                    ...look at the new directory contents.
total 4
-rw-r--r--  2 glass           91 Jan 12 17:34 hold
-rw-r--r--  1 glass          124 Jan 12 17:32 hold.1
-rw-r--r--  1 glass           89 Jan 12 17:34 hold.2
-rw-r--r--  2 glass           91 Jan 12 17:34 hold.3
$ rm hold                  ...remove one of the links.
$ ls -l                    ...look at the updated directory contents.
total 3
-rw-r--r--  1 glass          124 Jan 12 17:32 hold.1
-rw-r--r--  1 glass           89 Jan 12 17:34 hold.2
-rw-r--r--  1 glass           91 Jan 12 17:34 hold.3
$ _
```

A series of hard links may be added to an existing directory if the directory's name is specified as the second argument to **ln.** In the following example, I created links in the "tmp" directory to all of the files matched by the pattern "hold.*":

```
$ mkdir tmp                ...create a new directory.
$ ln hold.* tmp            ...create a series of links in "tmp".
$ ls -l tmp                ...look at the contents of "tmp".
total 3
-rw-r--r--  2 glass          124 Jan 12 17:32 hold.1
-rw-r--r--  2 glass           89 Jan 12 17:34 hold.2
-rw-r--r--  2 glass           91 Jan 12 17:34 hold.3
$ _
```

A hard link may not be created from a file on one file system to a file on a different file system. To get around this problem, create a *symbolic* link instead. A sym-

bolic link may span file systems. To create a symbolic link, use the **-s** option to
ln. In the following example, I tried to create a hard link from my home directory
to the file ''/usr/include/stdio.h''. Unfortunately, that file was on a different file
system, and so **ln** failed. However, **ln** with the **-s** option succeeded. When **ls** is
used with the **-F** option, symbolic links are preceded by an @ character. By
default, **ls** displays the contents of the symbolic link; to obtain information about
the file that the link refers to, use the **-L** option.

```
$ ln /usr/include/stdio.h stdio.h        ...try to create a hard link.
ln: stdio.h: Cross-device link
$ ln -s /usr/include/stdio.h stdio.h     ...use a symbolic link.
$ ls -l stdio.h                          ...examine the file.
lrwxrwxrwx  1 glass  20 Jan 12 17:58 stdio.h -> /usr/include/stdio.h
$ ls -F                                  ...@ indicates a sym. link.
stdio.h@
$ ls -lL stdio.h                         ...look at the link itself.
-r--r--r--  1 root        1732 Oct 13  1990 stdio.h
$ cat stdio.h                            ...look at the file.
# ifndef FILE
#define    BUFSIZ     1024
#define _SBFSIZ     8
extern     struct     _iobuf {
...
$ _
```

SUBSTITUTING A USER: su

A lot of people think that **su** stands for ''super-user,'' but it doesn't. Instead, it
stands for ''substitute user,'' and allows you to create a subshell owned by another user. It works like this:

Utility: **su** [-] [*userName*] [*args*]

su creates a temporary shell with *userName*'s real and effective user/group
ids. If *userName* is not specified, ''root'' is assumed and the new shell's
prompt is set to a # as a reminder. While you're in the subshell, you are
effectively logged on as that user; when you terminate the shell with a
Control-D, you are returned to your original shell. Of course, you must
know the other user's password to use this utility. The $SHELL and
$HOME environment variables are set from *userName*'s entry in the ''/etc/
passwd'' password file. If *userName* is not ''root,'' the $USER environ-
ment variable is also set. The new shell does not go through its login sequence unless the - option is supplied. All other arguments are passed as
command line arguments to the new shell.

Here's an example of **su:**

```
$ whoami           ...find out my current user id.
glass
$ su               ...substitute user.
Password: <enter super-user password here>
$ whoami           ...confirm that my current user id has changed.
root
$ ... perform super-user tasks here
$ ^D               ...terminate the child shell.
$ whoami           ...confirm that current user id is restored.
glass
$ _
```

CHECKING FOR MAIL: biff

The UNIX shells check for incoming mail periodically. This means that several minutes may pass between the reception of mail at your mailbox and the shell's notification to your terminal. To avoid this delay, you may enable instant mail notification by using the **biff** utility, which works as follows:

Utility: **biff** [y | n]

The **biff** utility allows you to enable and disable instant mail notification. To see your current biff setting, use **biff** with no parameters. Use **y** to enable instant notification and **n** to disable it. Why is this utility called **biff**? I have no idea!

Here's an example of **biff:**

```
$ biff           ...display current biff setting.
biff is n
$ biff y         ...enable instant mail notification.
$ biff           ...confirm new biff setting.
biff is y
$ _
```

TRANSFORMING FILES

There are several utilities that perform a transformation on the contents of a file, including the following:

- **compress/uncompress,** which convert a file into a space-efficient intermediate format and then back again. This utility is useful for saving disk space.
- **crypt,** which encodes a file so that other users can't understand it.
- **sed,** a general-purpose programmable stream editor that edits a file according to a pre-prepared set of instructions.
- **tr,** which maps characters from one set to another. This utility is useful for performing simple mappings such as converting a file from uppercase to lowercase.
- **ul,** which converts embedded underline sequences in a file to a form suitable for a particular terminal.

The next few subsections contain a description of each utility.

Compressing Files: Compress/Uncompress

The **compress** utility encodes a file into a more compact format, to be later decoded using the **uncompress** utility. The utilities work as follows:

Utility: **compress** -cv { *fileName* }+
      uncompress -cv { *fileName* }+

compress replaces a file by its compressed version, appending a ''.Z'' suffix. The **-c** option sends the compressed version to standard output rather than overwriting the original file. The **-v** option displays the amount of compression that takes place.
      uncompress reverses the effect of **compress,** re-creating the original file from its compressed version.

---

compress is useful for reducing your disk space and packing more files into an archive file. Here's an example:

```
$ ls -l palindrome.c reverse.c            ...examine the originals.
-rw-r--r--  1 glass          224 Jan 10 13:05 palindrome.c
-rw-r--r--  1 glass          266 Jan 10 13:05 reverse.c
$ compress -v palindrome.c reverse.c      ...compress them.
palindrome.c: Compression: 20.08% -- replaced with palindrome.c.Z
reverse.c: Compression: 22.93%    -- replaced with reverse.c.Z
$ ls -l palindrome.c.Z reverse.c.Z        ...the compressed files.
-rw-r--r--  1 glass          179 Jan 10 13:05 palindrome.c.Z
-rw-r--r--  1 glass          205 Jan 10 13:05 reverse.c.Z
$ uncompress -v *.Z                        ...restore the originals.
palindrome.c.Z:  -- replaced with palindrome.c
reverse.c.Z:     -- replaced with reverse.c
```

```
$ ls -l palindrome.c reverse.c                  ...confirm.
-rw-r--r--  1 glass          224 Jan 10 13:05 palindrome.c
-rw-r--r--  1 glass          266 Jan 10 13:05 reverse.c
$ _
```

File Encryption: crypt

The **crypt** utility creates a key-encoded version of a text file. The only way to retrieve the original text from the encoded file is by executing **crypt** with the same key that was used to encode the file. Here's how it works:

Utility: **crypt** [*key*]

crypt performs one of two duties:

- If the standard input is regular text, an encoded version of the text is sent to standard output using *key* as the encoding key.
- If the standard input is encoded text, a decoded version of the text is sent to standard output using *key* as the decoding key.

If *key* is not specified, **crypt** prompts you for a key that you must enter from your terminal. The key that you enter is not echoed. If you supply *key* on the command line, beware; a **ps** listing will show the value of *key*.

   crypt uses a coding algorithm similar to the one that was used in the German "Enigma" machine.

Here's an example of **crypt:**

```
$ cat sample.txt                               ...list original.
Here's a file that will be encrypted.
$ crypt agatha < sample.txt > sample.crypt     ...agatha is the key.
$ rm sample.txt                                ...remove original.
$ crypt agatha < sample.crypt > sample.txt     ...decode.
$ cat sample.txt                               ...list original.
Here's a file that will be encrypted.
$ _
```

Stream Editing: sed

The **sed** utility scans one or more files and performs an editing action on all of the lines that match a particular condition. The actions and conditions may be stored in a **sed** script. **sed** is useful for performing simple repetitive editing tasks.

sed is a fairly comprehensive utility. Because of this, I've only attempted to describe the main features and options of **sed;** however, I think that the material that I describe in this section will allow you to write a good number of useful **sed** scripts.

Here's a synopsis of **sed:**

Utility: **sed** [-e *script*] [-f *scriptfile*] { *fileName* }*

sed is a utility that edits an input stream according to a script that contains editing commands. Each editing command is separated by a newline, and describes an action and a line or range of lines to perform the action upon. A **sed** script may be stored in a file and executed by using the **-f** option. If a script is placed directly on the command line, it should be surrounded by single quotes. If no files are specified, **sed** reads from standard input. The format of **sed** scripts is described in the following sections.

---

sed Commands

A **sed** script is a list of one or more of the following commands, separated by newlines:

Command syntax	Meaning
address **a** text	Append *text* after the line specified by *address*.
addressRange **c** *text*	Replace the text specified by *addressRange* with *text*.
addressRange **d**	Delete the text specified by *addressRange*.
address **i** *text*	Insert *text* after the line specified by *address*.
address **r** *name*	Append the contents of the file *name* after the line specified by *address*.
addressRange **s**/*expr*/*str*/	Substitute the first occurrence of the regular expression *expr* by the string *str*.
addressRange **a**/*expr*/*str*/**g**	Substitute every occurrence of the regular expression *expr* by the string *str*.

The following rules apply:

- *address* must be either a line number or a regular expression. A regular expression selects all of the lines that match the expression. You may use $ to select the last line.
- *addressRange* can be a single address or a couple of addresses separated by commas. If two addresses are specified, then all of the lines between the first line that matches the first address and the first line that matches the second address are selected.
- If no address is specified, then the command is applied to all of the lines.

Substituting text

In the following example, I supplied the **sed** script on the command line. The script inserted a couple of spaces at the start of every line.

```
$ cat arms                               ...look at the original file.
People just like me,
Are all around the world,
Waiting for the loved ones that they need.
And with my heart,
I make a simple wish,
Plain enough for anyone to see.
$ sed 's/^/  /' arms > arms.indent       ...indent the file.
$ cat arms.indent                        ...look at the result.
  People just like me,
  Are all around the world,
  Waiting for the loved ones that they need.
  And with my heart,
  I make a simple wish,
  Plain enough for anyone to see.
$ _
```

To remove all of the leading spaces from a file, use the substitute operator in the reverse fashion:

```
$ sed 's/^ *//' arms.indent              ...remove leading spaces.
People just like me,
Are all around the world,
Waiting for the loved ones that they need.
And with my heart,
I make a simple wish,
Plain enough for anyone to see.
$ _
```

Deleting text

The next example illustrates a script that deleted all of the lines that contained the regular expression 'a':

```
$ sed '/a/d' arms          ...remove all lines containing an 'a'.
People just like me,
$ _
```

To delete only those lines that contain the *word* 'a', I surrounded the regular expression by escaped angled brackets (\< and \>):

```
$ sed '/\<a\>/d' arms          ...remove lines containing the word 'a'.
People just like me,
Are all around the world,
Waiting for the loved ones that they need.
And with my heart,
Plain enough for anyone to see.
$ _
```

Inserting text

In the next example, I inserted a copyright notice at the top of the file by using the insert command. Notice that I stored the **sed** script in a file and executed it by using the **-f** option.

```
$ cat sed5                    ...look at the sed script.
1i\
Copyright 1992 by Graham Glass\
All rights reserved\

$ sed -f sed5 arms            ...insert a copyright notice.
Copyright 1992 by Graham Glass
All rights reserved

People just like me,
Are all around the world,
Waiting for the loved ones that they need.
And with my heart,
I make a simple wish,
Plain enough for anyone to see.
$ _
```

Replacing text

To replace lines, use the change function. In the following example, I replaced the group of lines 1..3 with a censored message:

```
$ cat sed6                      ...list the sed script.
1,3c\
Lines 1-3 are censored.
$ sed -f sed6 arms              ...execute the script.
Lines 1-3 are censored.
And with my heart,
I make a simple wish,
Plain enough for anyone to see.
$ _
```

To replace individual lines with a message rather than an entire group, supply a separate command for each line:

```
$ cat sed7                      ...list the sed script.
1c\
Line 1 is censored.
2c\
Line 2 is censored.
3c\
Line 3 is censored.
$ sed -f sed7 arms              ...execute the script.
Line 1 is censored.
Line 2 is censored.
Line 3 is censored.
And with my heart,
I make a simple wish,
Plain enough for anyone to see.
$ _
```

Inserting files

In the following example, I inserted a message after the last line of the file:

```
$ cat insert                    ...list the file to be inserted.

The End
$ sed '$r insert' arms          ...execute the script.
People just like me,
Are all around the world,
Waiting for the loved ones that they need.
And with my heart,
I make a simple wish,
Plain enough for anyone to see.

The End
$ _
```

Multiple sed commands

This last example illustrates the use of multiple **sed** commands. I inserted a '<<' sequence at the start of each line, and appended a '>>' sequence to the end of each line:

```
$ sed -e 's/^/<< /' -e 's/$/ >>/' arms     ...multiple sed commands.
<< People just like me, >>
<< Are all around the world, >>
<< Waiting for the loved ones that they need. >>
<< And with my heart, >>
<< I make a simple wish, >>
<< Plain enough for anyone to see. >>
$ _
```

Translating Characters: tr

The **tr** utility maps the characters in a file from one character set to another, and works like this:

Utility: **tr** -cds *string1 string2*

tr maps all of the characters in its standard input from the character set *string1* to the character set *string2*. If the length of *string2* is less than the length of *string1*, it's padded by repeating its last character; in other words, the command '*tr abc de*' is equivalent to '*tr abc dee*'.

A character set may be specified using the [ ] notation of shell filename substitution:

- To specify the character set a, d, and f, simply write them as a single string: *adf*.
- To specify the character set a thru z, separate the start and end characters by a dash: *a-z*.

By default, **tr** replaces every character of standard input in *string1* by its corresponding character in *string2*.

The **-c** option causes *string1* to be complemented before the mapping is performed. *Complementing* a string means that it is replaced by a string that contains every ASCII character except those in the original string. The net effect of this is that every character of standard input that *does not* occur in *string1* is replaced.

The **-d** option causes every character in *string1* to be deleted from standard input.

The **-s** option causes every repeated output character to be condensed into a single instance.

Here are some examples of **tr** in action:

```
$ cat go.cart                ...list the sample input file.
go cart

racing
$ tr a-z A-Z < go.cart       ...translate all lowercase to uppercase.
GO CART

RACING
$ tr a-c D-E < go.cart       ...replace abc by DEE.
go EDrt

rDEing
$ tr -c a X < go.cart        ...replace every non-a character by an X.
XXXXaXXXXXaXXXXX$            ...even the last newline is replaced.
$ tr -c a-z '\012' < go.cart ...replace non-alphas by ASCII 12
(newline).
go
cart

racing
$ tr -cs a-z '\012' < go.cart ...repeat, but condense repeated newlines.
go
cart
racing
$ tr -d a-c < go.cart        ...delete all a-c characters.
go rt

ring
$ _
```

Converting Underline Sequences: ul

The **ul** utility transforms a file that contains underlining characters so that it appears correctly on a particular terminal type, and works like this:

Utility: **ul** *-tterminal* { *filename* }*

ul is a utility that transforms underline characters in its input so that they will display correctly on the specified terminal. If no terminal is specified, the one in the $TERM environment variable is assumed. The "/etc/termcap" file is used by **ul** to determine the correct underline sequence.

For example, let's say that you want to use the **man** utility to produce a document that you wish to print on a simple ASCII-only printer. The **man** utility generates underline characters for your current terminal, so to filter the output so that it's suitable for a dumb printer, pipe the output of **man** through **ul** with the ''dumb'' terminal setting. Here's an example:

```
$ man who | ul -tdumb > man.txt      ...prepare for a dumb terminal.
$ head man.txt                       ...look at the first 10 lines.
WHO(1)                    USER COMMANDS                    WHO(1)


NAME
     who - who is logged in on the system

SYNOPSIS
     who [ who-file ] [ am i ]
$ _
```

LOOKING AT RAW FILE CONTENTS: od

The octal dump utility, **od,** allows you to see the contents of a non-text file in a variety of formats, and works as follows:

Utility: **od** -acbcdfhilox *fileName* [*offset*[.][b]]

od displays the contents of *fileName* in a form specified by one of several options:

OPTION	MEANING
-a	Interpret bytes as characters, and print as ASCII names (i.e., 0 = nul).
-b	Interpret bytes as unsigned octal.
-c	Interpret bytes as characters, and print in C notation (i.e., 0 = \0).
-d	Interpret two-byte pairs as unsigned decimal.
-f	Interpret four-byte pairs as floating point.
-h	Interpret two-byte pairs as unsigned hex.
-i	Interpret two-byte pairs as signed decimal.
-l	Interpret four-byte pairs as signed decimal.
-o	Interpret two-byte pairs as unsigned octal.
-s[*n*]	Look for strings of minimum length *n* (default 3), terminated by null characters.
-x	Interpret two-byte pairs as hex.

> By default, the contents are displayed as a series of octal numbers. *offset* specifies where the listing should begin. If the offset ends in **b,** then it is interpreted as a number of blocks; otherwise, it is interpreted as an octal number. To specify a hex number, precede it by **x.** To specify a decimal number, end it with a period.

In the following example, I displayed the contents of the ''/bin/od'' executable as octal numbers, and then as characters starting from location 1000 (octal):

```
$ od /bin/od                ...dump the "/bin/od" file in octal.
0000000  100002 000410 000000 017250 000000 003630 000000 006320
0000020  000000 000000 000000 020000 000000 000000 000000 000000
0000040  046770 000000 022027 043757 000004 021002 162601 044763
0000060  014004 021714 000002 000410 045271 000000 020746 063400
0000100  000006 060400 000052 044124 044123 027402 047271 000000
0000120  021170 047271 000000 021200 157374 000014 027400 047271
0000140  000002 000150 054217 027400 047271 000002 000160 047126
...
$ od -c /bin/od 1000    ...dump the "/bin/od" file as characters.
0001000   H   x  \0 001   N   @  \0 002  \0  \0   /   u   s   r   /   l
0001020   i   b   /   l   d   .   s   o  \0   /   d   e   v   /   z   e
0001040   r   o  \0  \0  \0  \0  \0 030   c   r   t  \0   :       n   o
0001060       /   u   s   r   /   l   i   b   /   l   d   .   s   ,o  \n
0001100  \0  \0  \0   %   c   r   t  \0   :       /   u   s   r   /   l
0001120   i   b   /   l   d   .   s   o       m   a   p   p   i   n   g
0001140       f   a   i   l   u   r   e  \n  \0  \0  \0  \0 023   c   r
0001160   t  \0   :       n   o       /   d   e   v   /   z   e   r   o
0001200  \n  \0 200  \0  \0 002 200  \0  \0 022  \0  \0  \0 007  \0  \0
...
$ _
```

You may search for strings of a minumum length by using the **-s** option. Any series of characters followed by an ASCII null is considered to be a string.

```
$ od -s7 /bin/od            ...search file for strings of 7 chars or more.
0000665 \fN^Nu o
0001012 /usr/lib/ld.so
0001031 /dev/zero
0001050 crt0: no /usr/lib/ld.so\n
0001103 %crt0: /usr/lib/ld.so mapping failure\n
...
$ _
```

MOUNTING FILE SYSTEMS: mount/umount

A super-user may extend the file system by using the **mount** utility, which works as follows:

Utility: **mount** -o*options* [*deviceName directory*]
　　　　umount *deviceName*

mount is a utility that allows you to "splice" a device's file system into the root hierarchy. When used without any arguments, **mount** displays a list of the currently mounted devices. To specify special options, follow **-o** by a list of valid codes. These codes include **rw**, which mounts a file system for read/write, and **ro**, which mounts a file system for read-only. The **umount** utility unmounts a previously mounted file system.

In the following example, I spliced the file system contained on the "/dev/dsk2" device onto the "/usr" directory. Notice that before I performed the mount, the "/usr" directory was empty; after the mount, the files stored on the "/dev/dsk2" device appeared inside this directory.

```
$ mount                 ...list the currently mounted devices.
/dev/dsk1 on /  (rw)
$ ls /usr               .../usr is currently empty.
$ mount /dev/dsk2 /usr ...mount the /dev/dsk2 device.
$ mount                 ...list the currently mounted devices.
/dev/dsk1 on / (rw)
/dev/dsk2 on /usr (rw)
$ ls /usr               ...list the contents of the mounted device.
bin/        etc/        include/    lost+found/ src/        ucb/
demo/       games/      lib/        pub/        sys/        ucblib/
dict/       hosts/      local/      spool/      tmp/
$ _
```

To unmount a device, use the **umount** utility. In the following example, I unmounted the "/dev/dsk2" device and then listed the "/usr" directory. The files were no longer accessible.

```
$ umount /dev/dsk2  ...unmount the device.
$ mount             ...list the currently mounted devices.
/dev/dsk1 on / (rw)
$ ls /usr           ...note that /usr is empty again.
$ _
```

IDENTIFYING SHELLS: whoami

Let's say that you come across a vacated terminal and there's a shell prompt on the screen. Obviously someone was working on the UNIX system and forgot to log off. You wonder curiously who that person was. To solve the mystery, you can use the **whoami** utility, which displays the owner of a shell:

Utility: **whoami**

Displays the owner of a shell.

For example, when I executed **whoami** at my terminal, I saw this:

```
$ whoami
glass
$ _
```

IDENTIFYING TERMINALS: tty

The **tty** utility identifies the name of your terminal, and works as follows:

Utility: **tty**

tty displays the pathname of your terminal. It returns zero if its standard input is a terminal; otherwise, it returns 1.

In the following example, my login terminal was the special file "/dev/ttyp0":

```
$ tty                    ...display the pathname of my terminal.
/dev/ttyp0
$ _
```

TEXT FORMATTING: nroff/troff/style/spell

One of the first uses of UNIX was to support the text-processing facilities at Bell labs. Several utilities including **nroff, troff, style,** and **spell** were created for text formatting. Although these utilities were reasonable in their time, they have been made virtually obselete by far more sophisticated WYSIWYG (what you see is what you get) tools. For example, **nroff** requires you to manually place special commands such as ".pa" inside a text document in order for it to format correctly, whereas modern tools allow you to do this graphically.

For more information about these old-style text-processing utilities, see [1,159].

CHAPTER REVIEW

Checklist

In this chapter, I described utilities that:

- filter files
- sort files
- compare files
- archive files
- find files
- schedule commands
- support programmable text processing
- create hard and soft links
- substitute users
- check for mail
- transform files
- look at raw file contents
- mount file systems
- prepare documents

Quiz

1. Under what circumstances would you archive files using **tar**?
2. How would you convert a file to uppercase?
3. Describe what it means to "mount" a file system.
4. Which process serves the **crontab** system?
5. What additional functionality does an *extended* regular expression have?
6. What are the main differences between **sed** and **awk**?
7. How did **awk** get its name?

8. Under what circumstances would you use a symbolic link instead of a hard link?

9. What are the drawbacks of using a symbolic link?

10. What is meant by an *incremental* backup, and how would you perform one?

Exercises

1. After you've read chapter 4, design a script that periodically finds all of your files in the file system that haven't been accessed for a specified time and archives them in a compressed format. The archived files should be stored in a subdirectory for easy retrieval. [level: *medium*]

2. Perform some timing tests on **grep** and **fgrep** to determine the advantage of using **fgrep**'s speed. [level: *easy*]

3. Ask the system administrator to demonstrate the use of **tar** to produce a backup tape of your files. [level: *easy*]

4. Use **crontab** to schedule a script that removes your old core files at the start of each day. [level: *medium*]

5. Write a script called **squirrel** that takes two arguments; a filename and a key string. **squirrel** should compress the specified file and then encrypt the compressed version using the key. Write a companion script called **dig** that also takes two arguments; a filename and a key string. **dig** should decrypt the file using the key and then uncompress it. [level: *easy*]

Project

1. After you've read chapter 4, design a script that periodically finds all of your files in the file system that haven't been accessed for a specified time and archives them in a compressed format. The archived files should be stored in a subdirectory for easy retrieval. [level: *medium*]

Chapter 8

Networking

Motivation

One of the most significant advantages of UNIX over other competing operating systems is that it taps into the large Internet network that spans the globe. Tens of thousands of users and programs share information on this network for a myriad of reasons, from distributing large computational tasks to exchanging a good recipe for lasagna. In order to make use of the network resources, you must understand the utilities that manage the exchange of information. This chapter describes the most useful network utilities.

Prerequisites

In order to understand this chapter, you should have already read chapters 1 and 2. It also helps if you have access to a UNIX system so that you can try out the various utilities that I discuss.

Objectives

In this chapter, I'll show you how to find out what's on the network, how to talk to other users, how to copy files across a network, and how to execute processes on other computers on the network.

Presentation

This chapter begins with an overview of network concepts and terminology, and then describes the UNIX network utilities.

Commands

This section introduces the following utilities, listed in alphabetical order:

finger	rsh	w
ftp	rusers	wall
hostname	rwho	who
mesg	talk	whois
rcp	telnet	write
rlogin	users	

INTRODUCTION

A network is an interconnected system of cooperating computers. Through a network, you can share resources with other users and communicate via electronic mail systems.

There will be a huge explosion of UNIX network use in the 1990s. For example, the client-server paradigm described in chapter 1 is being adopted by all of the major computer corporations, and relies heavily on the operating system's network capabilities to distribute the workload between the server and its clients.

In order to prepare yourself for the advent of widespread networking, it's important to know the following items:

- common network terminology
- how networks are built
- how to talk to other people on the network
- how to use other computers on the network

This chapter covers all of these issues and more.

BUILDING A NETWORK

One of the best ways to understand how modern networks work is to look at how they evolved. Imagine that two people in an office want to hook their computers together so that they can share data. The easiest way to do this is to connect a cable between their serial ports. This is the simplest form of *local area network* (LAN), and requires virtually no special software or hardware. When one computer wants to send information to the other, it simply sends it out of its serial port:

Figure 8.1 The simplest LAN

Ethernets

To make things a little more interesting, let's assume that another person wants to tie into the other two guys' existing network. With three computers in the network, we need an addressing scheme so that the computers can be differentiated. We would also like to keep the number of connections down to a minimum. The most common implementation of this kind of LAN is called an *Ethernet*, and works like this:

• Each computer contains an Ethernet card, which is a special piece of hardware that has a unique Ethernet address.
• Every computer's Ethernet card is connected to the same single piece of wire.
• When a computer wishes to send a message to another computer with a particular Ethernet address, it broadcasts the message onto the Ethernet together with Ethernet header and trailer information that contain the Ethernet destination address. Only the Ethernet card whose address matches the broadcasted destination address accepts the message.
• If two computers try to broadcast to the Ethernet at the same time it is known as a *collision*. When a collision occurs, they both wait a random period of time and then try again.

Here's a diagram:

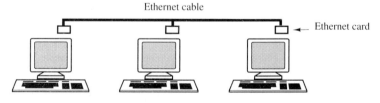

Figure 8.2 An Ethernet

Ethernets can transmit data in the order of megabytes per second, so they're pretty good for handling small networks of computers like the one shown above.

Bridges

Let's assume that the Ethernet in the office works so well that the people in the office next door build themselves an Ethernet too. How does one computer on one Ethernet talk to another computer on another Ethernet? The solution is to connect a special bit of hardware called a *bridge* between the Ethernets. A bridge passes an Ethernet message between the Ethernets whenever necessary.

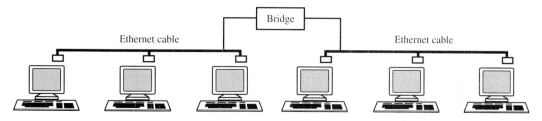

Figure 8.3 A bridge

Routers

The use of bridges facilitates the construction of small serial linked sections of Ethernet, but it's a pretty inefficient way to link together large numbers of networks. For example, assume that a corporation has four LANs that it wishes to interconnect in an efficient way. To do this, it needs to use a *router*, which is a device that hooks together two or more networks and automatically routes incoming messages to the correct network.

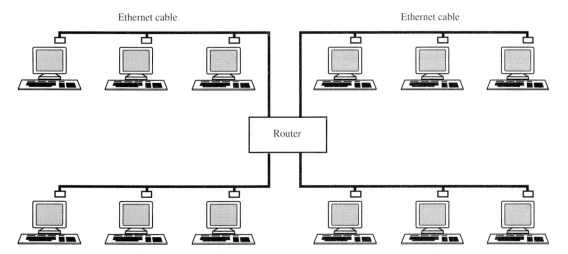

Figure 8.4 A router

Gateways

The final stage in network evolution occurs when many corporations wish to connect their local area networks together into a single, large wide area network (WAN). To do this, several high-capacity routers called *gateways* are placed throughout the country, and each corporation ties its LAN into the nearest gateway.

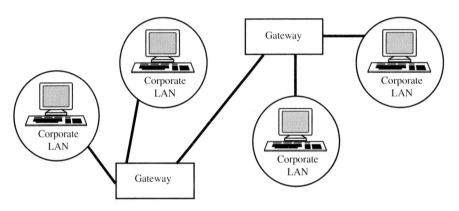

Figure 8.5 Gateways

THE INTERNET

In order for a collection of LANs and WANs to be able route information amongst themselves, they must agree upon a network-wide addressing and routing scheme. The largest collection of cooperating networks uses a communications protocol called TCP/IP, and is called the *Internet*. The IP part of TCP/IP stands for *Internet Protocol*, and refers to the addressing scheme that is used. The TCP part stands for *Transport Control Protocol*, and refers to the way that large messages are sent as several smaller messages and then reconstructed at the destination. More on IP and TCP later.

Universities, large corporations, government offices, and military sites have all got computers that are part of the Internet which are generally linked together by high-speed data links. The largest of these computer systems are joined together to form what is known as the *backbone* of the Internet. Other smaller establishments link their LANs to the backbone.

The Internet is administered by the Network Information Center (NIC) at the Stanford Research Institute (SRI), which is in charge of allocating unique Internet addresses to LANs on the Internet and keeping track of who's who.

Later on in this chapter, I'll show you how to connect to their Internet database and query it. SRI-NIC cares only about how corporations connect their LANs to the Internet backbone, and doesn't concern itself with how they arrange and administer their LANs internally.

Internet Addresses

Not all computers on the Internet are connected by Ethernet. For example, some LANs use the IBM token ring system, and others use the Cambridge ring. The IP addressing system therefore uses a hardware-independent labelling scheme; the bridges, routers and gateways transmit messages based purely on their destination IP address. The IP address is mapped to a physical hardware address only when the message reaches the destination host's LAN.

When an organization is setting up a LAN that it wishes to be part of the Internet, it requests a unique Internet address from the SRI-NIC. The number that is allocated depends on the size of the organization:

- A huge organization, such as a country or massive corporation, is allocated an A-class address. An A-class address is a number that is the first 8 bits of a 32-bit IP address. The organization is then free to use the remaining 24 bits for labelling its local hosts. The SRI-NIC rarely allocates these A-class numbers, as each one uses up a lot of the total 32-bit number space.
- A medium-sized organization, such as a mid-size corporation, is allocated a B-class address. A B-class address is a number that is the first 16 bits of a 32-bit IP address. The organization can then use the remaining 16 bits to label its local hosts.
- A small organization is allocated a C-class address, which is the first 24 bits of a 32-bit IP address.

For example, the University of Texas at Dallas is classified as a medium-sized organization, and its LAN was allocated the 16-bit number 33134. IP addresses are written as a series of four 8-bit numbers, with the most significant byte written first. All computers on the UT Dallas LAN therefore have an IP address of the form 129.110.XXX.YYY,[1] where XXX and YYY are numbers between 0 and 255.

Symbolic Addresses

SRI-NIC also associates every IP address that it allocates with a unique symbolic name of the form *host.org*, where *host* denotes the name of the organization and

---

[1] 129 * 256 + 110 = 33134.

org denotes the category of organization according to the following table:

Name	Category
com	commerical
edu	educational
gov	governmental
org	non-profit organization
mil	military
XX	two-letter country code

For example, the UT Dallas LAN was allocated the symbolic name "utdallas.edu". Other examples of symbolic names include "standford.edu" and "ddn-.mil". Once an organization has obtained its unique IP and symbolic address, it may use the rest of the IP number to label the hosts on the LAN. My own two computers at UT Dallas are labeled as follows:

- one is called "vanguard" and was allocated the IP address 129.110.43.128
- one is called "csservr2" and was allocated the IP address 129.110.42.1

To symbolically address a local host anywhere on the Internet, follow its local name by the name of the LAN itself. For example, the Internet address of my "vanguard" computer is "vanguard.utdallas.edu".

The UNIX **mail** utility uses the Internet for its operation, and allows mail to be sent to individual users using a similar addressing scheme. To send mail to a particular user on a named LAN, send mail using an address of the form *userId*@LAN. For example, to send mail to me at UT Dallas, use the address "glass@utdallas.edu".

Naming

The mapping of IP addresses to local host names is kept by the LAN's system administrator in a file called "/etc/hosts". To show you what this looks like, here's a small section of the file from UT Dallas:

```
IP Address            Symbolic Address            Host Name

129.110.41.1          manmax03.utdallas.edu       manmax03
129.110.42.1          csservr2.utdallas.edu       csservr2
129.110.43.2          ncube01.utdallas.edu        ncube01
```

```
129.110.43.128      vanguard.utdallas.edu      vanguard
129.110.43.129      jupiter.utdallas.edu       jupiter
129.110.66.8        neocortex.utdallas.edu     neocortex
129.110.102.10      corvette.utdallas.edu      corvette
```

Routing

The Internet software performs two kinds of routing - static and dynamic. Static routing information is kept in the file ''/etc/route'', and is of the form: ''You may get to the destination DEST via the gateway GATE with X hops.'' When a router has to forward a message, it can use the information in this file to determine the best route. Dynamic routing information is shared between hosts via the ''/etc/routed'' or ''/etc/gated'' daemons.[2] These programs constantly update their local routing tables based on information gleaned from Internet traffic, and periodically share their information with other neighboring daemons.

Packet Switching

When one node on the Internet sends a message to another node, the message is split up into small packets, each of which can be routed independently through the network. The packets contain special Transport Control Protocol (TCP) information that allow them to be recombined at the destination. They also contain Internet Protocol (IP) information for routing purposes, including the Internet address of the source and destination nodes. The combined set of protocols is called the TCP/IP protocol suite. The BSD socket interprocess communication system uses TCP/IP to allow UNIX processes on different machines to talk to each other.

Security

Several of the UNIX networking utilities that I discuss later in this chapter allow a user with accounts on several machines to execute a command on one of these machines from another. For example, I have an account on both the ''csservr2'' and ''vanguard'' machines at UT Dallas. To execute the **date** command on the vanguard machine from the csservr2 machine I can use the **rsh** utility as follows:

```
$ rsh vanguard date   ...execute date on the vanguard host.
```

The interesting thing about **rsh** and a few other utilities is that they are able to obtain a shell on the remote host *without requiring a password*. They can do this

---

[2] A daemon is a fancy term for a constantly running background process that is normally started when the system is booted.

because of a UNIX facility called *machine equivalence*. If you create a file called
".rhosts" in your home directory that contains a list of host names, then any user
with the same user id as your own may log into your account from these hosts
without supplying a password. Both my "csservr2" and "vanguard" home directories contain a file ".rhosts" that contains the following lines:

```
csservr2.utdallas.edu
vanguard.utdallas.edu
```

This allows me to execute remote commands from either computer without any
hassle. UNIX also allows a system administrator to list globally equivalent machines in the file "/etc/hosts.equiv". Global equivalence means that *any* user on
the listed machines can log into the local host without a password. For example,
if the "vanguard" "/etc/hosts.equiv" file contained the lines:

```
csservr2.utdallas.edu
vanguard.utdallas.edu
```

then any user on "csservr2" could log into the "vanguard" or execute a remote
command on it without a password. Global equivalence should be used with great
care (if ever).

Ports And Common Services

When one Internet host talks to another, it does so via a set of numbered ports.
Every Internet host supports some standard ports for common uses and allows
application programs to create other ports for transient communication. The file
"/etc/services" contains a list of the standard ports. Here's a snippet from the UT
Dallas file:

```
Port            Number/Protocol   Use
echo            7/tcp
discard         9/tcp             sink null
systat          11/tcp            users
daytime         13/tcp
ftp-data        20/tcp
ftp             21/tcp
telnet          23/tcp
smtp            25/tcp            mail
time            37/tcp            timserver
rlp             39/udp            resource
whois           43/tcp            nicname       # usually to sri-nic
finger          79/tcp
sunrpc          111/tcp
exec            512/tcp
login           513/tcp
```

The description of the **telnet** utility later in this chapter contains some examples where I connected to some of these standard ports.

Programming For The Internet

The BSD socket system allows you to communicate with other programs at a known IP address and port. This facility is described near the end of chapter 10, together with the full source code for an "Internet shell" which can pipe and redirect to other Internet shells on different hosts.

USERS

UNIX networking is all about moving around the Internet and talking to other people. Therefore, one of the most basic things to learn is how to find out who's on a particular host. There are several utilities that do this, each with its own strengths:

- **users**, which lists all of the users on your local host
- **rusers**, which lists all of the users on your local network
- **who**, which is like **users** except that it gives you more information
- **rwho**, which is like **rusers** except that it gives you more information
- **w**, which is like **who** except that it gives you *even more* information
- **whois**, which allows you to obtain information about major Internet sites
- **hostname**, which displays your local host's name.

The next few subsections describe each of these utilities in turn.

Listing Users: users/rusers

The **users** and **rusers** utilities simply list the current users of your local host and local network, respectively:

Utility: **users**

users displays a simple, terse list of the users on your local host.

Utility: **rusers** -a { *host* }*

rusers displays a list of the users on your local network. By default, all of the machines on the local network are interrogated, although you may override this default by supplying a list of host names. It works by broadcasting a request for information to all of the hosts and then displays the responses as they arrive. In order for a host to respond, it must be running the **rusersd** daemon (see chapter 12 for more information about daemons).

Here's an example of **users** and **rusers** in action:

```
$ users              ...display the users on the local host (csservr2).
glass posey
$ rusers -al         ...display the users on the local network.
csservr4.utd posey
vanguard.utd huynh posey datta venky
csservr2.utd posey glass
$ _
```

More User Listings: who/rwho/w

The **who** and **rwho** utilities supply a little more information than the **users** and **rusers** utilities:

Utility: **who** [*whoFile*] [am i]

By default, **who** displays a list of every user on your local host. If you supply the arguments "am i", **who** only describes yourself.
    Whenever a user logs in or out, the file "/var/adm/wtmp" is updated with information about their login session. You may give the name of this file as the *whoFile* argument (or a file in the same format), in which case **who** decodes this information and presents it in the typical **who** format.

Utility: **rwho**

rwho is just like **who**, except that it displays a list of the users logged onto all of the remote hosts on your local network.

Here's an example of **who**:

```
$ who                    ... list all users currently on local host.
posey     ttyp0    May 15 16:31 (blackfoot.utdall)
glass     ttyp2    May 17 17:00 (bridge05.utdalla)
$ who am i               ...list myself.
csservr2!glass    ttyp2    May 17 17:00    (bridge05.utdalla)
$ who /var/adm/wtmp      ...examine the who file.
lcui      ttyp2    May 17 12:48 (bridge05.utdalla)
juang     ttyp3    May 17 12:49 (annex.utdallas.e)
          ttyp3    May 17 12:52
          ttyp2    May 17 12:57
weidman   ttyp2    May 17 16:25 (annex.utdallas.e)
          ttyp2    May 17 16:33
glass     ttyp2    May 17 17:00 (bridge05.utdalla)
$ _
```

The **w** utility is just as easy to use:

Utility: **w** { *userId* }*

w displays a list that describes what each specified user is doing. In other
words, it's almost the same as **who**.

Here's an example:

```
$ w           ...obtain more detailed information than who.
  5:27pm  up 11 days, 11 mins,  3 users,  load average: 0.08, 0.03, 0.01
User      tty          login@  idle   JCPU   PCPU  what
posey     ttyp0    Fri 4pm 2days      1            -csh
glass     ttyp2    5:00pm   1         13     1     w
$ w glass    ...examine just myself.
  5:27pm  up 11 days, 11 mins,  3 users,  load average: 0.08, 0.03, 0.01
User      tty          login@  idle   JCPU   PCPU  what
glass     ttyp2    5:00pm             13     1     w glass
$ _
```

Internet Information: whois

The **whois** utility allows you to obtain information about major Internet sites:

Utility: **whois** [-h *hostName*] *id*

whois contacts *hostName* to ask it for information about the Internet identi-
fier *id*. *hostName* must be running a **whois** server. If no named host is
supplied, the system supplies a default name (which is sometimes out of
date). The current up-to-date host name to use is the symbolic Internet
address "nic.ddn.mil".

In the following example, I asked for information about "utdallas":

```
$ whois -h nic.ddn.mil utdallas         ...locate information about UTD.
(UTDALLAS)          UTDALLAS.EDU                     129.110.10.1
University of Texas at Dallas (NET-UTDALLAS) UTDALLAS 129.110.0.0

To single out one record, look it up with "!xxx", where xxx is the
handle, shown in parenthesis following the name, which comes first.
$ _
```

In the next example, I asked for information about the particular IP address that
was listed as the main one for utdallas:

```
$ whois -h nic.ddn.mil 129.110.10.1 ...inquire about specific IP address
(UTDALLAS)

  Hostname: UTDALLAS.EDU
  Address: 129.110.10.1
  System: SUN running UNIX

  Coordinator:
     Lippke, David L.   (DLL32)   lippke@UTDALLAS.EDU
     (214)690-2632

  domain server

  Record last updated on 01-May-89.


To see this host record with registered users, repeat the command with
a star ('*') before the name; or, use '%' to show JUST the registered
users.
$ _
```

For more examples of interaction with "nic.ddn.mil", see the discussion of **telnet**
later in this chapter.

Your Own Host Name: hostname

To find out the name of your local host, use **hostname**:

Utility: **hostname** [*hostName*]

When used with no parameters, **hostname** displays the name of your local host. A super-user may change this name by supplying the the new host name as an argument, which is usually done automatically in the "/etc/ rc.local" file. For more information about this file, see chapter 12.

Here's an example:

```
$ hostname          ...display my host's name.
csservr2
$ _
```

Personal Data: finger

Once you've obtained a list of the people on your system, it's handy to be able to learn a little bit more about them. The **finger** utility allows you to do this:

Utility: **finger** {*userId* }*

finger displays information about a list of users that is gleaned from several sources:

- The user's home directory, startup shell, and full name are read from the password file "/etc/passwd".
- If the user supplies a file called ".plan" in his/her home directory, its contents are displayed as the user's "plan".
- If the user supplies a file called ".project" in his/her home directory, its contents are displayed as the user's "project".

If no user ids are listed, **finger** displays information about every user that is currently logged on. You may finger a user on a remote host by using the "@" protocol, in which case the remote host's finger daemon is used to reply to the local finger's request.

I recommend that you create your own ".plan" and ".project" files in your home directory so that people can "finger" *you* back. Have fun!

In the following example, I fingered everyone on the system and then fingered myself:

```
$ finger                          ...finger everyone on the system.
Login        Name                 TTY Idle    When      Where
posey     John Posey              p0   2d Fri 16:31  blackfoot.utdall
glass     Graham Glass            p2      Sun 17:00  bridge05.utdalla
$ finger glass                    ...finger myself.
Login name: glass                 In real life: Graham Glass
Directory: /usr/glass             Shell: /bin/ksh
On since May 17 17:00:47 on ttyp2 from bridge05.utdalla
No unread mail
Project: To earn an enjoyable, honest living.
Plan: To work hard and have fun and not notice the difference.
$ _
```

In the next example, I listed the three sources of **finger**'s information about me:

```
$ cat .plan                ...list the ".plan" file.
To work hard and have fun and not notice any difference.
$ cat .project             ...list the ".project" file.
To earn an enjoyable, honest living.
$ grep glass /etc/passwd      ...look at the password file.
glass:##glass:496:62:Graham Glass:/home/csservr2/glass:/bin/ksh
$ _
```

In this final example, I used **rusers** to get a listing of the remote users and then performed a remote **finger** to learn all about Susan:

```
$ rusers                     ...look at remote users.
csservr4.utd posey
vanguard.utd huynh posey datta venky
centaur.utda susan
csservr2.utd posey posey lcui glass
$ finger susan@centaur        ...do a remote finger.
[centaur.utdallas.edu]
Login name: susan                  In real life: Susan Marsh
Directory: /home/csservr2/susan       Shell: /bin/csh
On since May 11 11:00:55 on console    1 day 23 hours Idle Time
New mail received Fri May 15 19:24:01 1992;
  unread since Fri May 15 16:40:28 1992
No Plan.
$ _
```

COMMUNICATING WITH USERS

There are several utilities that allow you to communicate with a user:

- **write**, which allows you to send individual lines to a user, one at a time
- **talk**, which allows you to have an interactive split-screen two-way conversation
- **wall**, which allows you to send a message to everyone on the local host
- **mail**, which allows you to send mail messages

The **mail** utility was described in chapter 2, and supports the full standard Internet addressing scheme. The rest of these utilities are described in this section, together with a simple utility called **mesg** that allows you to shield yourself from other people's messages.

Shielding Yourself From Communication: mesg

The **write, talk,** and **wall** utilities communicate with other users by writing directly to their terminals. You may disable the ability of other users to write to your terminal by using the **mesg** utility:

Utility: **mesg** [n | y]

mesg allows you to prevent other users from writing to your terminal. It works by modifying the write permission of your tty device. The **n** and **y** arguments disable and enable writes, respectively. If no arguments are supplied, your current status is displayed.

In the following example, **mesg** prevented me from receiving a **write** message:

```
$ mesg n                         ...protect terminal.
$ write glass                    ...try to write to myself.
write: You have write permission turned off
$ _
```

Sending A Line At A Time: write

write is a simple utility that allows you to send one line at a time to a named user:

Utility: **write** *userId* [*tty*]

write copies its standard input, one line at a time, to the terminal associated with *userId*. If the user is logged onto more than one terminal, you may specify the particular tty as an optional argument.

The first line of input that you send to a user via **write** is preceded by the message:

Message from yourHost!yourId on yourTty

so that the receiver may initiate a **write** command to talk back to you. To exit **write**, type a *Control-D* on a line of its own. You may disable writes to your terminal by using **mesg**.

In the following example, I received a **write** message from my friend Tim and then initiated my own **write** command to respond. We used the -o- (over) and -oo- (over and out) conventions for synchronization:

```
$
Message from tim@csservr2 on ttyp2 at 18:04 ...   ...message from tim.
hi Graham -o-                                      ...from tim.
$ write tim                                        ...initiate a reply.
hi Tim -o-                                         ...from me.
don't forget the movie later -oo-                  ...from tim.
OK -oo-                                            ...from me.
^D                                                 ...end of my input.
$ _
```

Although you can have a two-way conversation using **write**, it's awfully clumsy. A better way is to use the **talk** utility, which is described next.

Interactive Conversations: talk

The **talk** utility allows you to have a two-way conversation across the Internet:

Utility: **talk** *userId* [*tty*]

talk allows you to talk to a user on the Internet via a split-screen interface. If the user is logged onto more than one terminal, you may choose a particular terminal by supplying a specific tty name.

To talk to someone, type the following at your terminal:

```
$ talk theirUserId@theirHost
```

This causes the following message to appear on their screen:

```
Message from TalkDaemon@theirHost...
talk: connection requested by yourUserId@yourHost
talk: respond with: talk yourUserId@yourHost
```

If they agree to your invitation, they'll type the following at their shell prompt:

```
$ talk yourUserId@yourHost
```

At this point, your screen divides into two portions, one containing your keyboard input, and the other containing the other guy's. Everything that you type is echoed at the other guy's terminal, and vice versa. To redraw the screen if it ever gets messed up, type *Control-L*. To quit from **talk**, press *Control-C*.

To prevent other people from talking to you, use the **mesg** utility.

talk is a really fun utility that is worth exploring with a friend.

Messages To Everyone: wall

If you've ever got something really important to say to the world (or at least to everyone on your local host), **wall** is the way to say it. **wall** stands for write-all, and allows you to broadcast a message like this:

Utility: **wall** [*fileName*]

wall copies its standard input (or the contents of *fileName* if supplied) to the terminals of every user on the local host, preceding it with the message ''Broadcast Message ...''. If a user has disabled terminal communication by using **mesg**, the message will not be received unless the user of **wall** is a super-user.

In the following example, I sent a one-liner to everyone on the local host (including myself):

```
$ wall                                        ...write to everyone.
this is a test of the broadcast system
^D                                            ...end of input.

Broadcast Message from glass@csservr2 (ttyp2) at 18:04 ...

this is a test of the broadcast system
$ _
```

DISTRIBUTING DATA

A very basic kind of remote operation is the transmission of files, and once again UNIX has several utilities for doing this:

- **rcp** (remote copy) allows you to copy files between your local UNIX host and another remote UNIX host.
- **ftp** (file transfer protocol) allows you to copy files between your local UNIX host and any other host (possibly non-UNIX) that supports the **ftp** protocol. **ftp** is thus more powerful than **rcp**.
- **uucp** (unix-to-unix copy) is similar to **rcp**, and allows you to copy files between any two UNIX hosts.

The next couple of sections describe **rcp** and **ftp**.

Copying Files Between Two UNIX Hosts: rcp

rcp allows you to copy files between UNIX hosts:

Utility: **rcp** -p *originalFile newFile*
        rcp -pr { *fileName* }+ *directory*

rcp allows you to copy files between UNIX hosts. Both your local host and the remote host must be registered as equivalent machines (see earlier in this chapter for more information). To specify a remote file on *host*, use the syntax:

        host:pathName

    If *pathName* is relative, it's interpreted as being relative to your home directory on *host*. The **-p** option tries to preserve the last modification time, last access time, and permission flags during the copy. The **-r** option causes any file that is a directory to be recursively copied.

In the following example, I copied the file ''original.txt'' from the remote ''vanguard'' host to a file called ''new.txt'' on my local ''csservr2'' host. I then copied the file ''original2.txt'' from my local host to the file ''new2.txt'' on the remote host.

```
$ rcp vanguard:original.txt new.txt      ...copy from remote to local.
$ rcp original2.txt vanguard:new2.txt    ...copy from local to remote.
$ _
```

Copying Files Using The File Transfer Protocol: ftp

The file transfer protocol is a generic protocol for the transmission of files, and is supported by many machines. You can therefore use it to transfer files from your local UNIX host to any other kind of remote host as long as you know the Internet address of the remote host's ftp server. VMS users often use **ftp** for transferring files between UNIX and VMS. Here's a brief description of **ftp**:

Utility: **ftp** -n [*hostName*]

ftp allows you to manipulate files and directories on both your local host and a remote host. If you supply a remote host name, **ftp** searches the ''.netrc'' file to see if the remote host has a password-less anonymous **ftp** account. If it does, it uses it to log you into the remote host. If it doesn't have an anonymous account, it assumes that you have an account on the remote host and prompts you for its user id and password. If the login is successful, **ftp** enters its command mode and displays the prompt ''ftp>''. If you don't supply a remote host name, **ftp** enters its command mode immediately and you must use the open command to connect to a remote host.

The **-n** option prevents **ftp** from attempting the initial automatic login sequence.

ftp's command mode supports many commands for file manipulation. The most common of these commands are described on the following page. You may abort file transfers without quitting **ftp** by pressing *Control-C*.

Here's a list of the most useful **ftp** commands that are available from its command mode:

Command	Meaning
!command	Executes *command* on local host.
append *localFile remoteFile*	Appends the local file *localFile* to the remote file *remoteFile*.

Command	Meaning
bell	Causes a beep to be sounded after every file transfer.
bye	Shuts down the current remote host connection and then quits **ftp**.
cd *remoteDirectory*	Changes your current remote working directory to be *remoteDirectory*.
close	Shuts down the current remote host connection.
delete *remoteFile*	Deletes *remoteFile* from the remote host.
get *remoteFile* [*localFile*]	Copies the remote file *remoteFile* to the local file *localFile*. If *localFile* is omitted, it is given the same name as the remote file.
help [*command*]	Displays help about *command*. If *command* is omitted, a list of all **ftp** commands is displayed.
lcd *localDirectory*	Changes your current local working directory to be *localDirectory*.
ls *remoteDirectory*	Lists the contents of your current remote working directory.
mkdir *remoteDirectory*	Creates *remoteDirectory* on the remote host.
open *hostName* [*port*]	Attempts a connection to the host with name *hostName*. If you specify an optional port number, **ftp** assumes that this port is an **ftp** server.
put *localFile* [*remoteFile*]	Copies the local file *localFile* to the remote file *remoteFile*. If *remoteFile* is omitted, it is given the same name as the local file.
pwd	Displays your current remote working directory.
quit	Same as **bye**.
rename *remoteFrom remoteTo*	Renames a remote file from *remoteFrom* to *remoteTo*.
rmdir *remoteDirectory*	Deletes the remote directory *remoteDirectory*.

In the following example, I copied "writer.c" from the remote host "vanguard" to my local host, and then copied "who.c" from my local host to the remote host:

```
$ ftp vanguard                    ...build ftp connection to "vanguard".
Connected to vanguard.utdallas.edu.
vanguard FTP server (SunOS 4.1) ready.
Name (vanguard:glass): glass  ...login
Password required for glass.
Password: ...secret!
User glass logged in.
ftp> ls                           ...obtain directory of remote host.
PORT command successful.
ASCII data connection for /bin/ls (129.110.42.1,4919) (0 bytes).
...                               ...lots of files were listed here.
uniq
upgrade
who.c
writer.c
ASCII Transfer complete.
1469 bytes received in 0.53 seconds (2.7 Kbytes/s)
ftp> get writer.c                 ...copy from remote host.
PORT command successful.
ASCII data connection for writer.c (129.110.42.1,4920) (1276 bytes).
ASCII Transfer complete.
local: writer.c remote: writer.c
1300 bytes received in 0.012 seconds (1e+02 Kbytes/s)
ftp> !ls                          ...obtain directory of local host.
reader.c    who.c       writer.c
ftp> put who.c                    ...copy file to remote host.
PORT command successful.
ASCII data connection for who.c (129.110.42.1,4922).
ASCII Transfer complete.
ftp> quit                         ...disconnect.
Goodbye.
$ _
```

DISTRIBUTING PROCESSING

The power of distributed systems becomes clearer when you start moving around the Internet and logging into different hosts. Some hosts supply limited password-less accounts with user ids like ''guest'' so that explorers can roam the Internet without causing any harm. Three utilities for using distributed processing are:

- **rlogin**, which allows you to log in to a remote UNIX host
- **rsh**, which allows you to execute a command on a remote UNIX host

- **telnet**, which allows you to execute commands on any remote host that has a telnet server

telnet is the most flexible utility, as there are other systems in addition to UNIX that support telnet servers. These three utilities are described in the following sections.

Remote Logins: rlogin

To log into a remote host, use **rlogin**:

Utility: **rlogin** -ec [-l *userId*] *hostName*

rlogin attempts to log you into the remote host *hostName*. If you don't supply a user id by using the **-l** option, your local user id is used during the login process.

If the remote host isn't set as an equivalent of your local host in your "$HOME/.rhost" file, you are asked for your password on the remote host.

Once connected, your local shell goes to sleep and the remote shell starts to execute. When you're finished with the remote login shell, terminate it in the normal fashion (usually with a *Control-D*) and your local shell will then awaken.

There are a few special "escape commands" that you may type that have a special meaning; each is preceded by the escape character, which is a tilde (˜) by default. You may change this escape character by following the **-e** option with the preferred escape character. Here is a list of the escape commands:

SEQUENCE	MEANING
˜.	Disconnect immediately from remote host.
˜susp	Suspend remote login session. Restart remote login using using **fg**.
˜dsusp	Suspend input half of remote login session, but still echo output from login session to your local terminal. Restart remote login using **fg**.

In the following example, I logged into the remote host "vanguard" from my local host "csservr2", executed the **date** utility, and then disconnected:

```
$ rlogin vanguard                          ...remote login.
Last login: Tue May 19 17:23:51 from csservr2.utdallas
SunOS Release 4.1.1

vanguard% date                             ...execute a command on vanguard.
Wed May 20 18:50:47 CDT 1992
vanguard% ^D                               ...terminate the remote login shell.
Connection closed.
$ _                                        ...back home again at csservr2!
```

Executing Remote Commands: rsh

If you want to execute just a single command on a remote host, **rsh** is much handier than **rlogin**. Here's how it works:

Utility: **rsh** [-l *userId*] *hostName* [*command*]

rsh attempts to create a remote shell on the host *hostName* to execute *command*. **rsh** copies its standard input to *command* and copies the standard output and errors from *command* to its own standard output and error channels. Interrupt, quit, and terminate signals are forwarded to *command* so you may *Control-C* a remote command. **rsh** terminates immediately after *command* terminates.

If you do not supply a user id by using the **-l** option, your local user id is used during the connection. If no command is specified, **rsh** gives you a remote shell by invoking **rlogin**.

Quoted metacharacters are processed by the remote host; all others are processed by the local shell.

In the following example, I executed the **hostname** utility on my local "csservr2" host and the remote "vanguard" host:

```
$ hostname                      ...execute on my local host.
csservr2
$ rsh vanguard hostname         ...execute on the remote host.
vanguard
$ _
```

Remote Connections: telnet

telnet allows you to communicate with any remote host on the Internet that has a **telnet** server. Here's how it works:

Utility: **telnet** [*host* [*port*]]

telnet establishes a two-way connection with a remote port. If you supply a host name but not a port specifier, you are automatically connected to a **telnet** server on the specified host, which typically allows you to log into the remote machine. If you don't even supply a host name, **telnet** goes directly into command mode (in the same fashion as **ftp**).

What happens after the connection is complete depends on the functionality of the port you're connected to. For example, port 13 of any Internet machine will send you the time of day and then disconnect, whereas port 7 will echo ("ping") back to you anything that you enter from the keyboard.

To enter command mode after you've established a connection, press the sequence *Control-]*, which is the **telnet** escape sequence. This causes the command mode prompt to be displayed, which accepts commands including the following:

COMMAND	MEANING
close	Close current connection.
open *host* [*port*]	Connect to *host* with optional *port* specifier.
quit	Exit **telnet**.
z	Suspend **telnet**.
?	Print summary of **telnet** commands.

Therefore, to terminate a **telnet** connection, press *Control-]* followed by the command **quit**.

In the following example, I used **telnet** to emulate the **rlogin** functionality by omitting an explicit port number with the **open** command:

```
$ telnet                          ...start telnet.
telnet> ?                         ...get help.
Commands may be abbreviated.  Commands are:

close        close current connection
display      display operating parameters
mode         try to enter line-by-line or character-at-a-time mode
open         connect to a site
quit         exit telnet
send         transmit special characters ('send ?' for more)
set          set operating parameters ('set ?' for more)
status       print status information
toggle       toggle operating parameters ('toggle ?' for more)
```

```
z               suspend telnet
?               print help information
telnet> open vanguard          ...get a login shell from vanguard.
Trying 129.110.43.128 ...
Connected to vanguard.utdallas.edu.
Escape character is '^]'.


SunOS UNIX (vanguard)

login: glass                   ...enter my user id.
Password:                      ...secret!
Last login: Tue May 19 17:22:45 from csservr2.utdalla
SunOS Release 4.1.1 (GENERIC) #1: Sat Oct 13 06:05:48 PDT 1990


*** For assistance, send mail to UNIXINFO.

Tue May 19 17:23:21 CDT 1992
Erase is Backspace
vanguard% date                 ...execute a command.
Tue May 19 17:23:24 CDT 1992
vanguard% ^D                   ...disconnect from remote host.
Connection closed by foreign host.
$ _                            ...telnet terminates.
```

You may specify the host name directly on the command line if you like:

```
$ telnet vanguard              ...specify host name on command line.
Trying 129.110.43.128 ...
Connected to vanguard.utdallas.edu.
Escape character is '^]'.


SunOS UNIX (vanguard)

login: glass                   ...enter user id, etc...
```

You may use **telnet** to try out some of the standard port services that I described earlier in this chapter. For example, port 13 outputs the day and time on the remote host and then immediately disconnects:

```
$ telnet vanguard 13                      ...what's the remote time & day?
Trying 129.110.43.128 ...
Connected to vanguard.utdallas.edu.
Escape character is '^]'.
Tue May 19 17:26:32 1992
Connection closed by foreign host  ....telnet terminates.
$ _
```

Similarly, port 79 allows you to enter the name of a remote user and obtain finger information:

```
$ telnet vanguard 79                    ...manually perform a remote finger.
Trying 129.110.43.128 ...
Connected to vanguard.utdallas.edu.
Escape character is '^]'.
glass                                   ...enter the user id.
Login name: glass                       In real life: Graham Glass
Directory: /home/csservr2/glass            Shell: /bin/csh
Last login Tue May 19 17:23 on ttyp3 from csservr2.utdalla
No unread mail
No Plan.
Connection closed by foreign host.   ...telnet terminates.
$ _
```

When system administrators are testing a network, they often use port 7 to check host connections. Port 7 echoes everything that you type back to your terminal, and is sometimes known as a "ping-port":

```
$ telnet vanguard 7                  ...try a ping.
Trying 129.110.43.128 ...
Connected to vanguard.utdallas.edu.
Escape character is '^]'.
hi                                   ...my line.
hi                                   ...the echo.
there
there
^]                                   ...escape to command mode.
telnet> quit                         ...terminate connection.
Connection closed.
$ _
```

telnet accepts numeric Internet addresses as well as symbolic names:

```
$ telnet 129.110.43.128 7   ...ping using vanguard's numeric address.
Trying 129.110.43.128 ...
Connected to 129.110.43.128.
Escape character is '^]'.
hi                     ...my line.
hi                     ...the echo.
^]                     ...escape to command mode.
telnet> quit           ...disconnect.
Connection closed.
$ _
```

The Internet address of the NIC center where Internet information is accessible
online is "nic.ddn.mil". Here's a sample session where I connected to the center
and browsed through its menu system - it looked very interesting to me....

```
$ telnet nic.ddn.mil                          ...connect to NIC.
Trying 192.112.36.5 ...
Connected to nic.ddn.mil.
Escape character is '^]'.


SunOS UNIX (nic.ddn.mil) (ttyp2)

*
* For TAC news, type:                TACNEWS <return>
* For user and host information, type: WHOIS <return>
* For NIC information, type:         NIC <return>
*
* For user assistance call (800) 365-3642 or (800) 365-DNIC or (703)
802-4535
* Please report system problems to ACTION@NIC.DDN.MIL

NIC, SunOS Release 4.1.1 (NIC) #1:
Cmdinter Ver 1.2 Tue May 19 18:53:34 1992 EST
@ ?                              ...obtain a list of commands.
Command, one of the following
 BLANK          DAYTIME        FINGER         HELP          HOST
 KERMIT         LOGIN          LOGOUT         NIC           QUERY
 SYSTAT         TACNEWS        WHOIS
@ DAYTIME                         ...try one out for grins.
Tue May 19 18:53:54 EDT 1992
@ HOST                            ...get host database server.
Connecting to id Database . . . . . .
Connected to id Database
NIC WHOIS Version: 2.7 Tue, 19 May 92 18:53:59

  Enter a handle, name, hostname, address, or other field, "?" for a
  short options list, "HELP" for full help, "WHOIS xxx" for WHOIS-type
  output, or hit RETURN to exit.
Host: utdallas                   ...what does NIC know about my host?
UTDALLAS.EDU
   A SUN running UNIX.
   129.110.10.1 (UTDALLAS)
   Connect Type:
   Protocols: UDP/DOMAIN
Host: quit                       ...I'm done for now.
@ QUERY                          ...perform some queries.
NIC/Query Version: 1.4 Tue, 19 May 92 18:54:38
```

```
Stop output every 24 lines? ([Y]/N/# of lines) y
ROOT

Use NIC/Query to access a hierarchy of information about the
Defense Data Network (DDN) and the Network Information Center (NIC)
using simple menus. Bugs to BUG-SERVICE@NIC.DDN.MIL.

    1) HELP -- Introduction, changes, detailed help, help summary.
    2) WHOIS -- Directory of DDN users.
    3) HOSTS -- Describes DDN hosts.
    4) PROTOCOLS -- Describes DDN protocols.
    5) RFCS -- Requests For Comments technical notes.
    6) NIC DOCUMENTS -- Documents available from the NIC.
    7. TACNEWS -- TACnews program.

ROOT: Enter a menu# (1 - 7), or a command ('?' to list).
NIC/Query: quit               ...time to go, dinner's ready.
@ quit                        ...quit from the remote host.

Tue May 19 18:54:52 1992 EST
Connection closed by foreign host.
$ _                           ...back on the local host.
```

NETWORK SERVICES

There are several Internet services that contain an amazing amount of information about subjects ranging from raising chickens to "deviant" sexual behavior. USENET is the largest Internet user service, and deserves a book of its own. For more information about USENET, see [12, 137].

NETWORK FILE SYSTEM: NFS

In order to make good use of the UNIX network capabilities, Sun Microsystems introduced a public domain specification for a network file system (NFS). NFS supports the following useful features:

- It allows several local file systems to be mounted into a single network file hierarchy that may be transparently accessed from any host. To support this, NFS includes a remote mounting facility.
- RPC: remote procedure call. Under NFS, one machine may make a procedure call to another machine, thereby encouraging distributed computation.

- XDR: external data representation. NFS supports a host-neutral data representation scheme that allows programmers to create data structures that may be shared by hosts that have different byte-ordering and word lengths.
- YP: yellow pages. NFS includes a network database management system for managing password and group information. This information is stored in a single database and then distributed through the network to local YP servers that service programs such as **login**.

NFS is very popular and is used on most machines that run BSD UNIX. See [16, 280] for more details on NFS.

FOR MORE INFORMATION...

If you've enjoyed this overview of UNIX networking and you wish to find out more, then I recommend that you read *UNIX Network Programming* [13], *UNIX Communications* [12], and the network section of *UNIX System Administration Handbook* [16, 218].

CHAPTER REVIEW

Checklist

In this chapter, I described:

- the main Internet concepts and terminology
- utilities for listing users and communicating with them
- utilities for manipulating remote files
- utilities for obtaining remote login shells and executing remote commands

Quiz

1. What's the difference between a bridge, a router, and a gateway?
2. Why does the SRI-NIC allocate very few class-A addresses?
3. What's a good way for a system administrator to tell people about important events?
4. Why is **ftp** more powerful than **rcp**?
5. Describe some uses of common ports.
6. What does *machine equivalence* mean and how can you make use of it?

Exercises

1. Write a shell script that operates in the background on two machines that ensures that the contents of a named directory on one machine is always a mirror image of another named directory on the other machine. [level: *hard*]

2. If you have accounts on different machines, write a "worm" program that moves between these accounts and performs some kind of benign operation. If you're the owner of the system, you can make the worm do some fun stuff, such as replicating and mutating now and again. [level: *hard*]

3. Try out **rcp** and **rsh** as follows:
   • copy a single file from your local host to a remote host by using **rcp**
   • obtain a shell on the remote host using **rsh** and edit the file that you just copied
   • exit the remote shell using *exit*
   • copy the file from the remote host back to the local host using **rcp**
   [level: *easy*]

4. Use **telnet** to obtain the time of day at several remote host sites. Are the times accurate relative to each other? [level: *medium*]

Project

1. Connect to the "nic.ddn.mil" address using **telnet** and then explore the system as deeply as you can. This sounds easy, but isn't, due to a fairly poor online user guide. [level: *medium*]

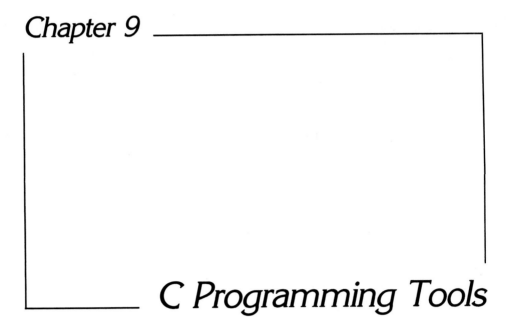

Chapter 9

C Programming Tools

Motivation

The most commonly used programming language on UNIX systems is C. This isn't surprising, since UNIX was written in C and has always come with a standard C compiler. Most (or possibly all) UNIX utilities are written in C, and most commerical products such as the X windows library, the Motif graphical user interface, and the Oracle database are written in C. It's therefore likely that you will find knowledge about writing, compiling, and running C programs very useful. Of course, UNIX supports most other popular programming languages such as C++, Smalltalk, assembly language, COBOL, FORTRAN, Pascal, and Ada, but this section applies primarily to the C language and its supporting tools.

Prerequisites

This chapter assumes that you already know the C language and have compiled programs on at least one platform. For example, many readers will probably have used the Borland or Microsoft C compilers.

Objectives

In this chapter, I describe the tools that support the various different stages of program development - compilation, debugging, maintaining libraries, profiling, and source code control.

Presentation

The C programming environment is introduced in a natural fashion, with plenty of examples and small programs.

Utilities

This section introduces the following utilities, listed in alphabetical order:

admin	ld	sact
ar	lint	strip
cc	lorder	touch
comb	make	tsort
dbx	prof	unget
get	prs	
help	ranlib	

THE C LANGUAGE

Before we get into any source code, I'd like to make an important point: *the source code in this book does not use all of features of ANSI C.* This is unfortunate, because ANSI C contains several nice syntactic and type-checking facilities that encourage maintainable and readable programs. The only reason that I did not use these features is because several major corporations and universities that I know of first hand only support K&R C, which is not as powerful or modern as ANSI C. In order to make my source code as portable and useful as possible, I tailored the code to the most reasonable lowest common denominator. I didn't enjoy doing this, as I'm a professional software developer as well as an author, and it really goes against my grain. In fact, I'd rather have written all of the code in C++, but that's another story.

SINGLE-MODULE PROGRAMS

Let's examine a C program that performs a simple task: reversing a string. To begin with, I'll show you how to write, compile, link, and execute a program that solves the problem using a single source file. Then I'll explain why it's better to split the program up into several independent modules, and show you how to do this. Here's a source code listing of the first version of the reverse program:

```
1   /* REVERSE.C */
2
3   #include <stdio.h>
4
5   /* Function Prototype */
6   reverse ();
7
8   /****************************************************************/
9
10  main ()
11
12  {
13    char str [100]; /* Buffer to hold reversed string */
14
15    reverse ("cat", str); /* Reverse the string "cat" */
16    printf ("reverse ("cat") = %s\n", str); /* Display result */
17    reverse ("noon", str); /* Reverse the string "noon" */
18    printf ("reverse ("noon") = %s\n", str); /* Display Result */
19  }
20
21  /****************************************************************/
22
23  reverse (before, after)
24
25  char *before; /* A pointer to the source string */
26  char *after; /* A pointer to the reversed string */
27
28  {
29    int i;
30    int j;
31    int len;
32
33    len = strlen (before);
34
35    for (j = len - 1; i = 0; j >= 0; j--; i++) /* Reverse loop */
36      after[i] = before[j];
37
38    after[len] = NULL; /* NULL terminate reversed string */
39  }
```

Compiling A C Program

To create and run the "reverse" program, I first created a subdirectory called "reverse" inside my home directory and then created the file "reverse.c" using the UNIX **emacs** editor. I then compiled the C program using the **cc** utility.

To prepare an executable version of a single, self-contained program, follow **cc** by the name of the source code file, which must end in a ".c" suffix. **cc** doesn't produce any output when the compilation is successful. By default, **cc** creates an executable file called "a.out" in the current directory. To run the program, type "a.out". Any errors that are encountered are sent to the standard error channel, which is connected by default to your terminal's screen.

Here's what happened:

```
$ mkdir reverse            ...create subdirectory for source code.
$ cd reverse
$ ... I created the file reverse.c at this point using emacs.
$ cc reverse.c            ...compile source.
"reverse.c", line 16: syntax error at or near variable name "cat"
"reverse.c", line 18: syntax error at or near variable name "noon"
"reverse.c", line 35: syntax error at or near symbol ;
"reverse.c", line 35: syntax error at or near symbol )
$ _
```

As you can see, **cc** found a number of compile-time errors:

- The errors on lines 16 and 18 were due to inappropriate use of double quotes within double quotes.
- The errors on line 35 were due to an illegal use of ;.

Since these errors were pretty easy to correct, I copied the error-laden "reverse.c" file to a file called "reverse.old1.c" and then removed the compile-time errors using **emacs**. I left the original file in the directory so that I could see the evolution of my programming attempts.

A Listing Of The Corrected Reverse Program

Here is the second, corrected version of the reverse program. The lines containing the errors that I corrected are in italics:

```
1   /* REVERSE.C */
2
3   #include <stdio.h>
4
5   /* Function Prototype */
6   reverse ();
7
8   /************************************************************/
```

```
 9
10   main ()
11
12   {
13     char str [100]; /* Buffer to hold reversed string */
14
15     reverse ("cat", str); /* Reverse the string "cat" */
16     printf ("reverse (\"cat\") = %s\n", str); /* Display */
17     reverse ("noon", str); /* Reverse the string "noon" */
18     printf ("reverse (\"noon\") = %s\n", str); /* Display */
19   }
20
21   /******************************************************************/
22
23   reverse (before, after)
24
25   char *before; /* A pointer to the source string */
26   char *after; /* A pointer to the reversed string */
27
28   {
29     int i;
30     int j;
31     int len;
32
33     len = strlen (before);
34
35     for (j = len - 1, i = 0; j >= 0; j--, i++) /* Reverse loop */
36       after[i] = before[j];
37
38     after[len] = NULL; /* NULL terminate reversed string */
39   }
```

Running A C Program

After compiling the second version of "reverse.c", I ran it by typing the name of the executable file, "a.out". As you can see, the answers were correct:

```
$ cc reverse.c                    ...compile source.
$ ls -l reverse.c a.out           ...list file information.
-rwxr-xr-x  1 glass        24576 Jan5 16:16 a.out*
-rw-r--r--  1 glass          439 Jan5 16:15 reverse.c
$ a.out                           ...run program.
reverse ("cat") = tac
reverse ("noon") = noon
$ _
```

Overriding The Default Executable Name

The name of the default executable, "a.out", is rather cryptic, and an "a.out" file produced by a subsequent compilation would overwrite the one that I just produced. To avoid both problems, it's best to use the **-o** option with **cc**, which allows you to specify the name of the executable file that you wish to create:

```
$ cc reverse.c -o reverse      ...call the executable "reverse".
$ ls -l reverse
-rwxr-xr-x  1 glass        24576 Jan  5 16:19 reverse*
$ reverse                      ...run the executable "reverse".
reverse ("cat") = tac
reverse ("noon") = noon
$ _
```

MULTI-MODULE PROGRAMS

The trouble with the way that I built the reverse program is that the reverse function cannot easily be used in other programs. For example, let's say that I wanted to write a function that returns 1 if a string is a palindrome, and 0 otherwise. A palindrome is a string that reads the same forward and backward; for example, "noon" is a palindrome, and "noone" is not. I could use the reverse function to implement my palindrome function. One way to do this is to cut and paste reverse () into the palindrome program, but this is a poor technique for at least three reasons:

- Performing a cut-and-paste operation is slow.
- If we came up with a better piece of code for performing a reverse operation, we'd have to replace every copy of the old version with the new version, which is a maintenance nightmare.
- Each copy of reverse () soaks up disk space.

As I'm sure you realize, there's a better way to share functions.

Reusable Functions

A better strategy for sharing reverse () is to remove reverse () from the reverse program, compile it separately, and then link the resultant object module into whichever programs wish to use it. This technique therefore avoids all three of the problems listed in the previous section, and allows the function to be used in many different programs. Functions with this property are termed *reusable* functions.

Preparing A Reusable Function

To prepare a reusable function, create a source code module that contains the source code of the function, together with a header file that contains the function's prototype. Then compile it into an object module by using the **-c** option of **cc**. An object module contains machine code together with symbol table information that allows it to be combined with other object modules when an executable file is being created. Here are the listings of the new ''reverse.c'' and ''reverse.h'' files:

Reverse.h

```
1   /* REVERSE.H */
2
3   reverse (); /* Declare but do not define this function */
```

Reverse.c

```
1    /* REVERSE.C */
2
3    #include <stdio.h>
4    #include "reverse.h"
5
6    /****************************************************************/
7
8    reverse (before, after)
9
10   char *before; /* A pointer to the original string */
11   char *after; /* A pointer to the reversed string */
12
13   {
14      int i;
15      int j;
16      int len;
17
18      len = strlen (before);
19
20      for (j = len - 1, i = 0; j >= 0; j--, i++) /* Reverse loop */
21        after[i] = before[j];
22
23      after[len] = NULL; /* NULL terminate reversed string */
24   }
```

Here's a listing of a main program that uses reverse ():

Main1.c

```
1   /* MAIN1.C */
2
3   #include <stdio.h>
4   #include "reverse.h" /* Contains the prototype of reverse () */
5
6   /******************************************************************/
7
8   main ()
9
10  {
11    char str [100];
12
13    reverse ("cat", str); /* Invoke external function */
14    printf ("reverse (\"cat\") = %s\n", str);
15    reverse ("noon", str); /* Invoke external function */
16    printf ("reverse (\"noon\") = %s\n", str);
17  }
```

Separately Compiling And Linking Modules

To compile each source code file separately, use the **-c** option of **cc**. This creates a separate object module for each source code file, each with a ".o" suffix:

```
$ cc -c reverse.c              ...compile reverse.c to reverse.o.
$ cc -c main1.c                ...compile main1.c to main1.o.
$ ls -l reverse.o main1.o
-rw-r--r-- 1 glass            311 Jan  5 18:24 main1.o
-rw-r--r-- 1 glass            181 Jan  5 18:08 reverse.o
$ _
```

Alternatively, you can place all of the source code files on one line:

```
$ cc -c reverse.c main1.c      ...compile each .c file to .o file.
$ _
```

To link them all together into an executable called "main1", list the names of all the object modules after the **cc** command:

```
$ cc reverse.o main1.o -o main1    ...link the object modules.
$ ls -l main1                      ...examine the executable.
```

```
$ cc -c palindrome.c          ...compile palindrome.c to palindrome.o.
$ cc -c main2.c               ...compile main2.c to main2.o.
$ cc reverse.o palindrome.o main2.o -o main2    ...link them all.
$ ls -l reverse.o palindrome.o main2.o main2
-rwxr-xr-x  1 glass        24576 Jan  5 19:09 main2*
-rw-r--r--  1 glass          306 Jan  5 19:00 main2.o
-rw-r--r--  1 glass          189 Jan  5 18:59 palindrome.o
-rw-r--r--  1 glass          181 Jan  5 18:08 reverse.o
$ main2                       ...run the program.
palindrome ("cat") = 0
palindrome ("noon") = 1
$ _
```

Maintaining Multi-module Programs

There are several different issues that must be considered when maintaining multi-module systems:

Q1. What ensures that object modules and executables are kept up to date?
Q2. What stores the object modules?
Q3. What tracks each version of source and header files?

Fortunately, there are UNIX utilities that address each problem. Here are some solutions to each question:

A1. make, the UNIX file dependency system
A2. ar, the UNIX archive system
A3. sccs, the UNIX source code control system

The next few subsections discuss each utility in turn.

THE UNIX FILE DEPENDENCY SYSTEM: MAKE

You've now seen how several independent object modules may be linked into a single executable. You've also seen that the same object module may be linked into several different executables. Although multi-module programs are efficient in terms of reusability and disk space, they must also be carefully maintained. For example, let's assume that we change the source code of ''reverse.c'' to use pointers instead of array subscripts. This would result in a faster reverse function. In order to update the two main program executables ''main1'' and ''main2'' manually, we'd have to perform the following steps, in order:

Appending A File

To append a file to a named archive, use the **ar** utility with the **q** option as follows:

> **ar q** *archiveName* { *fileName* }+

This option appends all of the specified files to the archive file *archiveName*, regardless of whether they already exist. If the archive file doesn't exist, it is automatically created. This option is handy if you know that the file isn't already present, as it allows **ar** to avoid searching through the archive.

Obtaining A Table Of Contents

To obtain a table of contents of an archive, use the **ar** utility with the **t** option as follows:

> **ar t** *archiveName*

Deleting A File

To delete a list of files from an archive, use the **ar** utility with the **d** option as follows:

> **ar d** *archiveName* { *fileName* }+

Extracting A File

To copy a list of files from an archive to the current directory, use the **ar** utility with the **x** option. If you don't specify a list of files, then all of the files in the archive are copied.

> **ar x** *archiveName* { *fileName* }+

Maintaining An Archive From The Command Line

Here is an example that illustrates how an archive may be built and manipulated from the command line, using the object modules built earlier in this chapter. Later in this section I'll show how a library can be maintained automatically from a make file.

First, I built an archive file called "string.a" to hold all of my string-related object modules. Next, I added each module in turn using the **r** option. Finally, I demonstrated the various different **ar** options:

```
$ cc -c reverse.c palindrome.c main2.c      ...create object modules.
$ ls *.o                                     ...confirm.
main2.o     palindrome.o      reverse.o
$ ar r string.a reverse.o palindrome.o       ...add them to an archive.
ar: creating string.a
$ ar t string.a                              ...obtain a table of contents.
reverse.o
palindrome.o
$ cc main2.o string.a -o main2               ...link the object modules.
$ main2                                       ...execute the program.
palindrome ("cat") = 0
palindrome ("noon") = 1
$ ar d string.a reverse.o                     ...delete a module.
$ ar t string.a                              ...confirm deletion.
palindrome.o
$ ar r string.a reverse.o                     ...put it back again.
$ ar t string.a                              ...confirm addition.
palindrome.o
reverse.o
$ rm palindrome.o reverse.o                   ...delete originals.
$ ls *.o                                      ...confirm.
main2.o
$ ar x string.a reverse.o                     ...copy them back again.
$ ls *.o                                      ...confirm.
main2.oreverse.o
$ _
```

Maintaining An Archive Using The Make System

Although an archive can be built and maintained from the command line, it's much better to use the make system. To refer to an object file inside an archive, place the name of the object file inside parentheses, preceded by the name of the archive. The make system has built-in rules that take care of the archive operations automatically. Here is the updated "main2.make" file that uses archives instead of plain object files:

```
main2:                main2.o string.a(reverse.o) string.a(palindrome.o)
                      cc main2.o string.a -o main2

main2.o:              palindrome.h

string.a(reverse.o):     reverse.h

string.a(palindrome.o): palindrome.h reverse.h
```

Here is the output from a make performed using this file:

```
$ rm *.o                    ...remove all object modules.
$ make -f main2.make        ...perform a make.
cc -c main2.c
cc -c reverse.c
ar rv string.a reverse.o    ...object module is automatically saved.
a - reverse.o
ar: creating string.a
rm -f reverse.o             ...original is removed automatically.
cc -c palindrome.c
ar rv string.a palindrome.o
a - palindrome.o
rm -f palindrome.o
cc main2.o string.a -o main2 ...archived object modules are accessed.
$ _
```

Notice that the built-in make rules automatically removed the original object file once it had been copied into the archive.

Ordering Archives

The built-in make rules do not maintain any particular order in an archive file. On most systems, this is fine, as the **cc** and **ld** utilities are able to extract object modules and resolve external references regardless of order. However, on some older systems this is unfortunately not the case. Instead, if an object module A contains a function that calls a function in an object module B, then B must come before A in the link sequence. If A and B are in the same library, then B must appear before A in the library. If your system is one of these older types, then you'll probably get the following error at the end of the make shown in the last example:

```
ld: Undefined symbol
   _reverse
*** Error code 2
make: Fatal error: Command failed for target `main2'
```

This cryptic error occurs because "reverse.o" contains a call to palindrome ( ) in "palindrome.o", which means that "reverse.o" should be *after* "palindrome.o" in the archive, but isn't. To resolve this error, you must either reorder the modules in the archive using the **lorder** and **tsort** utilities, or use **ranlib** as described in the next section. In the following example, I created a new ordered version of the old archive and then renamed it to replace the original. The make file then worked correctly.

```
$ ar cr string2.a `lorder string.a | tsort`    ...order archive.
$ ar t string.a                                 ...old order.
reverse.o
palindrome.o
$ ar t string2.a                                ...new order.
palindrome.o
reverse.o
$ mv string2.a string.a                         ...replace old archive.
$ make -f main2d.make                           ...try make again.
cc main2.o string.a -o main2
$ _
```

For more information on **lorder** and **tsort**, please use the **man** facility.

Creating A Table Of Contents: ranlib

You can help the linker to resolve out-of-order object modules by adding a table of contents to each archive using the **ranlib** utility:

> *Utility:* **ranlib** { *archive* }+
>
> **ranlib** adds a table of contents to each specified archive (it does this by inserting an entry called ___.SYMDEF into the archive).

In the following example, the unresolved reference error was due to an out-of-order sequence of object modules in the "string.a" archive. **cc** reminded me that I should add a table of contents, so I followed its recommendation. As you can see, the next link was successful.

```
$ ar r string.a reverse.o palindrome.o      ...this order causes problems.
ar: creating string.a
$ cc main2.o string.a -o main2              ...compile fails.
ld: string.a: warning: archive has no table of contents; add one using
ranlib(1)
ld: Undefined symbol
   _reverse
```

```
$ ranlib string.a                    ...add table of contents.
$ cc main2.o string.a -o main2       ...no problem.
$ main2                              ...program runs fine.
palindrome ("cat") = 0
palindrome ("noon") = 1
$ _
```

THE UNIX SOURCE CODE CONTROL SYSTEM: SCCS

To maintain a large project properly, it's important to be able to store, access, and protect all of the versions of source code files. For example, if I decided to change reverse () to use pointers for efficiency reasons, it would be nice if I could easily go back and see how the source file looked *before* the changes were made. Similarly, it's important to be able to "lock out" other users from altering a file while you're actively modifying it. Here is an outline of how the UNIX source code control system works:

- When you create the original version of a function, you convert it into a special "sccs" format file using the **admin** utility. An sccs format file is stored specially, and may not be edited or compiled in the usual manner.
- Whenever you wish to edit an sccs format file, you must first "check out" the latest version of the file using the **get** utility. This creates a standard format text file that you may edit and compile. The **get** utility also allows you to obtain a previous version of a file.
- When the new version of the file is complete, you must return it to the sccs file using the **delta** utility, which optimizes the storage of the sccs file by only saving the differences between the old version and the new version. The **get** utility does not allow anyone else to check out the file until you return it.
- The **sact** utility allows you to see the current editing activity on a particular sccs file.

The source code control system also contains several other utilities; namely, **help**, **prs**, **comb**, **what**, and **unget**. Before we investigate the more advanced sccs options, let's take a look at a sample sccs session.

Warning: Some systems vary in the way that **sccs** works; I suggest that you consult **man** to see if the **sccs** examples in this book tally with your own system's version of **sccs**.

Creating An sccs File

To create an sccs file, use the **admin** utility, which works as follows:

Utility: **admin** -i*name* -fl*list* -dl*list* -e*name* -a*name sccsfile*

admin is an sccs utility that allows you to create and manipulate an sccs format file. The **-i** option creates an sccs format file called *sccsfile* from the file *name*. *sccsfile* should have a ".s" prefix. The **-fl** and **-dl** options allow you to lock and unlock a set of listed releases, respectively. The **-a** and **-e** options allow you to add and subtract named users from the list of users that are able to obtain an editable version of the sccs file. Once the sccs file has been created, you may delete the original. If you get an error from any sccs-related utility, invoke the sccs **help** utility with the code of the message as its argument.

In the following example, I created an sccs version of the "reverse.c" source file:

```
$ ls -l reverse.c                   ...look at the original.
-rw-r--r--   1 gglass        266 Jan  7 16:37 reverse.c
$ admin -ireverse.c s.reverse.c     ...create an sccs file.
No id keywords (cm7)
$ help cm7                          ...get help on "cm7".
cm7: "No id keywords"
No SCCS identification keywords were substituted for. You may not
have any keywords in the file, in which case you can ignore this
warning. If this message came from delta then you just made a delta
without any keywords. If this message came from get then the last
time you made a delta you changed the lines on which they appeared.
It's a little late to be telling you that you messed up the last
time you made a delta, but this is the best we can do for now, and
it's better than nothing.
This isn't an error, only a warning.
$ ls -l s.reverse.c                 ...look at the sccs file.
-r--r--r--   1 gglass        411 Jan  7 17:39 s.reverse.c
$ rm reverse.c                      ...remove the original.
$ _
```

Here's a synopsis of the **help** utility:

Utility: **help** { *message* }+

help is an sccs utility that displays an explanation of the named key messages. Key messages are generated by other sccs utilities in the case of warning or fatal error situations.

Checking Out A File

To make a read-only copy of an sccs file, use the **get** utility:

Utility: **get** -e -p -r*revision sccsfile*

get is an sccs utility that checks out a revision of a file from its sccs counter-part. If no version number is supplied, the latest version is checked out. If the **-e** option is used, the file is modifiable and should be returned to the sccs file using **delta**; otherwise, it is read-only and should not be returned. The **-p** option causes a read-only copy of the file to be displayed to standard output; no file is created.

In the following example, I checked out a read-only copy of the latest version of the "reverse.c" file:

```
$ get s.reverse.c        ...check out a read-only copy.
1.1                      ...version number.
29 lines                 ...number of lines in file.
No id keywords (cm7)
$ ls -l reverse.c        ...look at the copy.
-r--r--r--   1 gglass       266 Jan  7 18:04 reverse.c
$ _
```

The **get** command displays the version number of the file that is being copied out; in this case, it's the default, version 1.1. A version number is of the form:

---

release.delta

Every time a change is saved to an sccs file, the delta number is incremented automatically. The release number is changed only when explicitly done so using the **get** utility. I'll show you how to create a new release later in this section.

When you obtain a read-only version of a file, it may not be edited, and does not prevent anyone else from accessing the sccs file. To check out an editable version of an sccs file, use the **-e** option. This creates a writeable file and prevents multiple "gets":

```
$ get -e s.reverse.c        ...check out a writeable version.
1.1
new delta 1.2               ...editable version is 1.2.
29 lines
```

```
$ ls -l reverse.c                    ...look at it.
-rw-r-xr-x    1 gglass          266 Jan  7 18:05 reverse.c
$ get -e s.reverse.c                 ...version is locked.
ERROR [s.reverse.c]: writable `reverse.c' exists (ge4)
$ _
```

Monitoring sccs Activity

The **sact** utility displays a list of the current activity related to a named file, and works like this:

Utility: **sact** {*sccsfile* }+

sact is an sccs utility that displays the current editing activity on the named sccs files. The output contains the version of the existing delta, the version of the new delta, the user that checked out the file using **get -e**, and the date and time that the **get -e** was executed.

Here's the output of **sact** after the previous example:

```
$ sact s.reverse.c                   ...monitor activity on "reverse.c".
1.1 1.2 gglass 92/01/07 18:05:11
$ _
```

Undoing A Check Out/Returning A File

If you perform a **get** and then wish that you hadn't, you may undo the **get** by using the **unget** utility, which works like this:

Utility: **unget** -r*revision* -n { *sccsfile* }+

unget is an sccs utility that reverses the effect of a previous **get**. It restores the sccs file to its previous state, deletes the non-sccs version of the file, and unlocks the file for other people to use. If there are several revisions that are current being edited, use the **-r** option to specify which revision you which to unget. By default, **unget** moves the file back into the sccs file. The **-n** option causes unget to *copy* the file instead, leaving the checked out version in place.

In the following example, assume that I had just performed a **get** on "reverse.c", and then changed my mind:

```
$ ls -l reverse.c              ...look at checked out file.
-rw-r-xr-x    1 gglass        266 Jan  7 18:05 reverse.c
$ unget s.reverse.c            ...return it.
1.2                            ...version of returned file.
$ ls -l reverse.c              ...original is gone.
reverse.c not found
$ sacts.reverse.c              ...original activity is gone.
No outstanding deltas for: s.reverse.c
$ _
```

Creating A New Delta

Let's say that you check out an editable version of "reverse.c" and change it so that it uses pointers instead of array subscripts. Here is a listing of the new version:

```
 1   /* REVERSE.C */
 2
 3   #include <stdio.h>
 4   #include "reverse.h"
 5
 6
 7   reverse (before, after)
 8
 9   char *before;
10   char *after;
11
12   {
13      char* p;
14
15      p = before + strlen (before);
16
17      while (p-- != before)
18         *after++ = *p;
19
20      *after = NULL;
21   }
```

When the new version of the file is saved, you must return it to the sccs file using the **delta** command, which works like this:

Utility: **delta** -r*revision* -n { *sccsfile* }+

delta is an sccs utility that returns a checked out file back to the specified
sccs file. The new version's delta number is equal to the old delta number
plus one. As a bonus, **delta** describes the changes that you made to the file.
delta prompts you for a comment before returning the file. If the same user
has two outstanding versions and wishes to return one of them, the **-r** option
must be used to specify the revision number. By default, a file is removed
after it is returned. The **-n** option prevents this.

Here's an example:

```
$ delta s.reverse.c             ...return the modified checked out version.
comments? converted the function to use pointers     ...comment.
No id keywords (cm7)
1.2                             ...new version number.
5 inserted                      ...description of modifications.
7 deleted
16 unchanged
$ ls -l reverse.c               ...the original was removed.
reverse.c not found
$ _
```

Obtaining A File's History

To get a listing of an sccs file's modification history, use the **prs** utility, which
works like this:

Utility: **prs** -r*revision* { *sccsfile* }+

prs is an sccs utility that displays the history associated with the named sccs
files. By default, all of a file's history is displayed. You may limit the output
to a particular version by using the **-r** option. The numbers in the right-hand
column of the output refer to the number of lines inserted, deleted, and
unchanged, respectively.

Here's an example:

```
$ prs s.reverse.c          ...display the history.
s.reverse.c:
```

```
D 1.2 92/01/07 18:45:47 gglass 2 1        00005/00007/00016
MRs:
COMMENTS:
converted the function to use pointers

D 1.1 92/01/07 18:28:53 gglass 1 0        00023/00000/00000
MRs:
COMMENTS:
date and time created 92/01/07 18:28:53 by gglass

$ _
```

sccs Identification Keywords

There are several special character sequences that you can place in a source file that are processed specially by **get** when read-only copies of a version are obtained. Here are a few of the most common sequences:

Sequence	Replaced with
%M%	the name of the source code file
%I%	the release.delta.branch.sequence number
%D%	the current date
%H%	the current hour
%T%	the current time

It's handy to place these sequences in a comment at the top of a source file. The comment won't affect your source code program, and will be easily visible when the file is read. The next section contains an example of how these sequences are used.

Creating A New Release

To create a new release of an sccs file, specify the new release number using the **-r** option of **get**. The new release number is based on the most recent version of the previous release. In the following example, I created release 2 of the "reverse.c" file, and inserted the SCCS identification keywords described in the previous section. Note that they were replaced when I obtained a read-only copy of version 2 later in the example.

```
$ get -e -r2 s.reverse.c        ...check out version 2.
1.2                             ...previous version number.
new delta 2.1                   ...new version number.
21 lines
$ vi reverse.c                  ...edit the writeable copy.
... I added the following lines at the top of the program:
/*
   Module: %M%
   SCCS Id: %I%
      Time: %D% %H% %T%
*/
... and then saved the file.
$ delta s.reverse.c             ...return the new version.
comments? added SCCS identification keywords
2.1
6 inserted
0 deleted
21 unchanged
$ get -p s.reverse.c            ...display the file to standard output.
2.1
/* REVERSE.H */

/*
   Module: reverse.c
   SCCS Id: 2.1
      Time: 92/01/07 1/7/92 22:32:38
*/
... rest of file
$ _
```

Checking Out Read-Only Copies Of Previous Versions

To check out a version other than the latest, use the **-r** option of **get** to specify the version number. For example, let's say that I wanted to obtain a read-only copy of version 1.1 of "reverse.c". Here's how it's done:

```
$ get -r1.1 s.reverse.c         ...check out version 1.1.
1.1
23 lines
$ _
```

Checking Out Editable Copies Of Previous Versions

If you want to obtain an editable copy of a previous version, use the **-e** or **-r** option of **get**. Let's say that I wanted to obtain an editable copy of version 1.1 of "reverse.c". The version of the editable copy cannot be 1.2, since that version already

exists. Instead, **get** creates a new "branch" off the 1.1 version numbered
1.1.1.1. Deltas added to this branch are numbered 1.1.1.2, 1.1.1.3, etc.

```
1.1 ─────► 1.2
   \
    \ Branch
     \
1.1.1.1 ─────► 1.1.1.2    Figure 9.4   Delta branching
```

Here's an example:

```
$ get -e -r1.1 s.reverse.c    ...get a branch off version 1.1.
1.1
new delta 1.1.1.1
23 lines
$ _
```

Editing Multiple Versions

You may edit multiple revisions of a file at one time. If you do this, you must
specify the revision number of the file that you're returning when you perform the
delta. You must also rename the name of the copy when obtaining another copy,
since all copies are given the same name. In the following example, I obtained a
copy of version 1.1 and version 2.1 for editing, and then saved them both.

```
$ get -e -r1.1 s.reverse.c       ...edit a new version based on 1.1.
1.1
new delta 1.1.1.1
23 lines
$ mv reverse.c reverse2.c        ...rename version 1.1.1.1.
$ get -e -r2.1 s.reverse.c       ...edit a new version based on 2.1.
2.1
new delta 2.2
27 lines
$ sact s.reverse.c               ...view sccs activity.
1.1 1.1.1.1 gglass 92/01/07 22:42:26
2.1 2.2 gglass 92/01/07 22:42:49
$ delta s.reverse.c              ...ambiguous return.
comments? try it
ERROR [s.reverse.c]: missing -r argument (de1)
$ delta -r2.1 s.reverse.c        ...return modified version 2.1.
comments? try again
2.2
0 inserted
```

```
0 deleted
27 unchanged
$ mv reverse2.c reverse.c        ...rename other version.
$ delta s.reverse.c              ...unambiguous return.
comments? save it
No id keywords (cm7)
1.1.1.1
0 inserted
0 deleted
23 unchanged
$ sact s.reverse.c
No outstanding deltas for: s.reverse.c
$ _
```

Deleting Versions

You may remove a delta from an sccs file as long as it's a leaf node on the sccs version tree. To do this, use the **rmdel** utility, which works as follows:

Utility: **rmdel** -r*revision sccsfile*

rmdel removes the specified version from an sccc file as long as it's a leaf node.

In the following example, I wasn't allowed to delete version 1.1, as it's not a leaf node, but I was allowed to delete version 1.1.1.1:

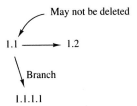

Figure 9.5   Only leaf nodes may be deleted

Here's an example:

```
$ rmdel -r1.1 s.reverse.c        ...try removing non-leaf node 1.1.
ERROR [s.reverse.c]: not a 'leaf' delta (rc5)
$ rmdel -r1.1.1.1 s.reverse.c ...remove leaf node 1.1.1.1.
$ _
```

Compressing sccs Files

You may compress an sccs file and remove any unnecessary deltas by using the **comb** utility, which works like this:

> *Utility:* **comb** { *sccsfile* }+
>
> **comb** compresses an sccs file so that it contains only the latest version of the source. Only the latest delta and the deltas that have branches remain. It works by generating a Bourne shell script that must then be run to perform the actual compression. The script is sent to standard output, so it must be saved and then executed.

In the following example, assume that "s.reverse.c" contained several different versions. I compressed it into a smaller file containing just the latest version.

```
$ comb s.reverse.c > comb.out          ...generate compression script.
$ cat comb.out                         ...look at the script.
trap "rm -f COMB$$ comb$$ s.COMB$$; exit 2" 1 2 3 15
get -s -k -r2.3 -p s.reverse.c > COMB$$
...other lines go here.
rm comb$$
rm -f s.reverse.c
mv s.COMB$$ s.reverse.c
admin -dv s.reverse.c
$ chmod +x comb.out                    ...make the script executable.
$ comb.out                             ...execute the script.
$ prs s.reverse.c                      ...look at the history.
s.reverse.c:

D 2.3 92/01/08 15:35:53 gglass 1 0   00028/00000/00000
MRs:
COMMENTS:
This was COMBined
$ _
```

Restricting Access To sccs Files

By default, a file may be checked out of an sccs file by anyone. However, you may restrict access to one or more users and/or groups by using the **-a** and **-e** options to **admin**. The **-a** option may be followed by a couple of values:

- a user name, in which case the user is added to the list of users that may check out
- a group number, in which case any user in the group may check out

If the value is preceded by an !, then the specified user/group is *denied* check out rights. If you're using the C shell, be sure to escape the ! to prevent accidental reference to the history list. To remove a user from the list, use the **-e** option instead. Multiple **-a** and **-e** options may occur on a single command line. In the following example, I denied my own access rights and then restored them:

```
$ admin -a\!glass s.reverse.c          ...remove rights of user "glass".
$ get -e s.reverse.c                   ...try to access.
2.3
ERROR [s.reverse.c]: not authorized to make deltas (co14)
$ admin -aglass s.reverse.c            ...restore access.
$ get -e s.reverse.c                   ...no problem.
2.3
new delta 2.4
28 lines
$ unget s.reverse.c                    ...return file.
2.4
$ admin -atim s.reverse.c              ...add tim to user list.
$ admin -eglass s.reverse.c            ...deny "glass" access rights.
$ get -e s.reverse.c                   ...try to access.
2.3
ERROR [s.reverse.c]: not authorized to make deltas (co14)
$ admin -aglass s.reverse.c            ...restore rights to "glass".
$ admin -a182 s.reverse.c              ...give access to group 182.
$ _
```

Locking Releases

You may prevent either a single release or all releases from being edited by using **admin** with the **-fl** and **-dl** options. To lock a particular release, follow **-fl** with the number of the release. To lock all releases, follow **-fl** with the letter "a". To release a lock, use the same rules with the **-dl** option. Here's an example:

```
$ admin -fla s.reverse.c               ...lock all releases.
$ get -e -r2.1 s.reverse.c             ...try to access.
2.1
ERROR [s.reverse.c]: SCCS file locked against editing
(co23)
$ admin -dla s.reverse.c               ...release all locks.
$ get -e -r1.1 s.reverse.c             ...no problem.
1.1
new delta 1.1.1.1
21 lines
$ _
```

THE UNIX PROFILER: PROF

It's often handy to be able to see where a program is spending its time. For example, if a greater-than-expected amount of time is being spent in a particular function, it might be worth optimizing the function by hand for better performance. The **prof** utility allows you to obtain a program's profile, and works like this:

Utility: **prof** -ln [*executableFile* [*profileFile*]]

prof is the standard UNIX profiler. It generates a table of time and repetitions of each function in the executable *executableFile* based on the performance trace stored in the file *profileFile*. If *profileFile* is omitted, "mon.out" is assumed. If *executableFile* is omitted, "a.out" is assumed. The executable file must have been compiled using the **-p** option of **cc**, which instructs the compiler to generate special code that writes a "mon.out" file when the program runs. The **prof** utility then looks at this output file after the program has terminated and displays the information contained therein. For information on how to make a file using the **-p** option, refer to the "make" section of this chapter. By default, the profile information is listed in descending order of time. The **-l** option orders the information by name, and the **-n** option orders the information by cumulative time.

Here's an example of **prof** in action:

```
$ main2                   ...execute the program.
palindrome ("cat") = 0    ...program output.
palindrome ("noon") = 1
$ ls -l mon.out           ...list the monitor output.
-rw-r-xr-x   1 gglass         1472 Jan  8 17:19 mon.out
$ prof main2 mon.out      ...profile the program.
 %Time Seconds Cumsecs #Calls   msec/call  Name
  42.9   0.05    0.05                      rdpcs
  42.9   0.05    0.10    2002    0.025      reverse
  14.3   0.02    0.12    2002    0.008      palindrome
   0.0   0.00    0.12       1    0.         main
$ prof -l main2           ...order by name
 %Time Seconds Cumsecs #Calls   msec/call  Name
   0.0   0.00    0.05       1    0.         main
  14.3   0.02    0.07    2002    0.008      palindrome
  42.9   0.05    0.05                      rdpcs
  42.9   0.05    0.12    2002    0.025      reverse
$ _
```

After a profile has been viewed, you may decide to do some hand-tuning and then obtain another profile.

DOUBLE-CHECKING PROGRAMS: LINT

There's a handy utility called **lint** that checks your program more thoroughly than **cc**:

Utility: **lint** { *fileName* }*

lint scans the specified source files and displays any potential errors that it finds.

If you're building a program out of several source modules, it's a good idea to specify them all on the same command line so that **lint** can check module interactions. Here's an example that demonstrates the difference between single-module checking and multi-module checking:

```
$ lint reverse.c                       ...check "reverse.c".
reverse defined( reverse.c(12) ), but never used
$ lint palindrome.c                    ...check "palindrome.c".
palindrome defined( palindrome.c(12) ), but never used
reverse used( palindrome.c(14) ), but not defined
$ lint main2.c                         ...check "main2.c".
main2.c(11): warning: main() returns random value to invocation
environment
printf returns value which is always ignored
palindrome used( main2.c(9) ), but not defined
$ lint main2.c reverse.c palindrome.c  ...check all modules together.
main2.c:
main2.c(11): warning: main() returns random value to invocation
environment
reverse.c:
palindrome.c:
Lint pass2:
printf returns value which is always ignored
$ _
```

THE UNIX DEBUGGER: DBX

The UNIX debugger **dbx** allows you to symbolically debug a program. Although it's not as good as most professional debuggers on the market, it comes as a handy standard utility. **dbx** includes the following facilities:

- single stepping
- breakpoints
- editing from within the debugger
- accessing and modifying variables
- searching for functions
- tracing

Here's a synopsis of **dbx**:

Utility: **dbx** *executableFilename*

dbx is a standard UNIX debugger. The named executable file is loaded into the debugger and a user prompt is displayed. To obtain information on the various **dbx** commands, enter **help** at the prompt.

To demonstrate **dbx**, let's debug the following recursive version of palindrome ( ):

```
1   /* PALINDROME.C */
2
3   #include "palindrome.h"
4   #include <string.h>
5
6
7   enum { FALSE, TRUE };
8
9
10  int palindrome (str)
11
12  char *str;
13
14  {
15     return (palinAux (str, 1, strlen (str)));
16  }
17
18  /*******************************************************************/
19
20  int palinAux (str, start, stop)
```

```
21
22   char *str;
23   int start;
24   int stop;
25
26   {
27     if (start >= stop)
28       return (TRUE);
29     else if (str[start] != str[stop])
30       return (FALSE);
31     else
32       return (palinAux (str, start + 1, stop - 1));
33   }
```

Preparing A Program For Debugging

To debug a program, it must have been compiled using the **-g** option to **cc**, which places debugging information into the object module.

Entering The Debugger

Once a program has been compiled correctly, invoke **dbx** with the name of the executable as the first argument. **dbx** presents you with a prompt. I recommend that you enter **help** at the prompt to see a list of all the **dbx** commands:

```
$ dbx main2        ...enter the debugger.
dbx version sr10.3(4) of 7/6/90 17:52
reading symbolic information ...
Type 'help' for help.
(dbx) help         ...obtain help.
run [args]                   - begin execution of the program
stop at <line>               - suspend execution at the line
stop in <func>               - suspend execution when <func> is called
stop if <cond>               - suspend execution when <cond> is true
trace <line#>                - trace execution of the line
trace <func>                 - trace calls to the function
trace <var>                  - trace changes to the variable
trace <exp> at <line#>       - print <exp> when <line> is reached
status                  - print numbered list of traces and stops in effect
delete <#> [<#> ...]         - cancel trace or stop of each number given
cont                         - continue execution from where it stopped
step                    - execute one source line, stepping into functions
next                    - execute one source line, skipping over calls
return                       - continue until the current function returns
call <func>(<params>)        - execute the given function call
```

```
print <exp> [, <exp> ...]   - print the values of the expressions
where                       - print currently active procedures
whatis <name>               - print the declaration of the name
assign <var> = <exp> - assign the program variable the value of <exp>
dump <func>                 - print all variables in the active function
list [<line#> [, <line#>]] - list source lines
use <directory-list>        - set the search path for source files
sh <command-line>           - pass the command line to the shell
quit                        - exit dbx
(dbx) _
```

Running A Program

To run your program, enter the **run** command. This runs the program to completion.

```
(dbx) run                 ...run the program.
palindrome ("cat") = 0
palindrome ("noon") = 0
program exited
(dbx) _
```

Oops! The string ''noon'' is a palindrome, but my function thinks that it isn't. Time to delve into **dbx**...

Tracing A Program

To obtain a line-by-line **trace**, use the trace command. When any kind of trace is requested, **dbx** returns you an index number that can be used by the **delete** command to turn off the trace. In this continuing example, I restarted the program from the beginning by using the **rerun** command:

```
(dbx) trace         ...request a trace.
[1] trace           ...request is #1.
(dbx) rerun         ...run the program from the start.
trace:      9       printf ("palindrome (\"cat\") = %d\n", palindrome
("cat"));
trace:     10    int palindrome (str)
trace:     15       return (palinAux (str, 1, strlen (str)));
trace:     20    int palinAux (str, start, stop)
trace:     27       if (start >= stop)
trace:     29       else if (str[start] != str[stop])
trace:     30          return (FALSE);
trace:     33    }
trace:     33    }
```

```
trace:      16    }
palindrome ("cat") = 0
trace:      10      printf ("palindrome (\"noon\") = %d\n", palindrome
("noon"));
trace:      10    int palindrome (str)
trace:      15      return (palinAux (str, 1, strlen (str)));
trace:      20    int palinAux (str, start, stop)
trace:      27      if (start >= stop)
trace:      29      else if (str[start] != str[stop])
trace:      30        return (FALSE);
trace:      33    }
trace:      33    }
trace:      16    }
palindrome ("noon") = 0
trace:      11    }
trace:      11    }
program exited
(dbx) _
```

Tracing Variables And Function Calls

A trace may be placed on a variable's value or a call to a particular function by
adding parameters to the **trace** command. To trace a variable, the syntax is:

> **trace** *variable* **in** *function*

and to trace a call to a named function, use the syntax:

> **trace** *function*

Here's the output from **dbx** when three new traces were added and then the
program was restarted.

```
(dbx) trace start in palinAux     ...trace the variable called "start".
[2] trace start in palinAux
(dbx) trace stop in palinAux      ...trace the variable called "stop".
[3] trace stop in palinAux
(dbx) trace palinAux              ...trace the function "palinAux".
[4] trace palinAux
(dbx) rerun                       ...run the program from the start.
trace:      9     printf ("palindrome (\"cat\") = %d\n", palindrome
("cat"));
trace:      10    int palindrome (str)
```

```
trace:      15      return (palinAux (str, 1, strlen (str)));
trace:      20   int palinAux (str, start, stop)
calling palinAux(str = "cat", start = 1, stop = 3) from function
palindrome.palindrome
trace:      27      if (start >= stop)
initially (at line 27 in "/usr/glass/reverse/palindrome.c"): start = 1
initially (at line 27 in "/usr/glass/reverse/palindrome.c"): stop = 3
trace:      29      else if (str[start] != str[stop])
trace:      30         return (FALSE);
trace:      33   }
trace:      33   }
trace:      16   }
palindrome ("cat") = 0
trace:      10      printf ("palindrome (\"noon\") = %d\n", palindrome
("noon"));
trace:      10   int palindrome (str)
trace:      15      return (palinAux (str, 1, strlen (str)));
trace:      20   int palinAux (str, start, stop)
after line 20 in "/usr/glass/reverse/palindrome.c": stop = 4
calling palinAux(str = "noon", start = 1, stop = 4) from function
palindrome.palindrome
trace:      27      if (start >= stop)
trace:      29      else if (str[start] != str[stop])
trace:      30         return (FALSE);
trace:      33   }
trace:      33   }
trace:      16   }
palindrome ("noon") = 0
trace:      11   }
trace:      11   }
program exited
(dbx) _
```

The Bug

By now, the bug is fairly clear; the values of *start* and *stop* are incorrect, each being one greater than they should be. It's a very common error to forget that C array indices begin at zero rather than one. You may call up the editor specified by the $EDITOR environment variable by using the **edit** command. This is handy for correcting errors on the fly, although you must remember to recompile the program before debugging it again.

Here is the correct version of the palindrome ( ) function:

```
int palindrome (str)

char *str;
```

```
{
    return (palinAux (str, 0, strlen (str) - 1));
}
```

I'll end this section with a brief discussion of some useful miscellaneous **dbx** commands for setting breakpoints, single stepping, accessing variables, and listing portions of the program.

Breakpoints

To make **dbx** stop when it encounters a particular function, use the **stop** command. This allows you to run a program at full speed until the function that you wish to examine more closely is executed:

```
(dbx) stop in palinAux          ...set breakpoint.
[7] stop in palinAux
(dbx) rerun                     ...run the program from the start.
trace:       9      printf ("palindrome (\"cat\") = %d\n", palindrome
("cat"));
trace:      10    int palindrome (str)
trace:      15      return (palinAux (str, 1, strlen (str)));
trace:      20    int palinAux (str, start, stop)
calling palinAux(str = "cat", start = 1, stop = 3) from function
palindrome.palindrome
[7] stopped in palinAux at line 27 in file
"/usr/glass/reverse/palindrome.c"
    27        if (start >= stop)
(dbx) _
```

Single Stepping

To step through a program one line at a time, use the **step** command. This command causes **dbx** to redisplay its prompt immediately the next line of program has been executed, and is useful for high-resolution interrogation of a function. In the following example, I entered **step** after my program stopped at line 27.

```
(dbx) step        ...execute line after #27 and then stop.
trace:      29      else if (str[start] != str[stop])
initially (at line 29 in "/usr/glass/reverse/palindrome.c"):
start = 1
initially (at line 29 in "/usr/glass/reverse/palindrome.c"):
stop = 3
stopped in palinAux at line 29 in file "/usr/glass/reverse/palindrome.c"
    29      else if (str[start] != str[stop])
(dbx) _
```

Accessing Variables

To print the value of a particular variable at any time, use the **print** command. The **whatis** command displays a variable's declaration, and the **which** command tells you where the variable is declared. The **where** command displays a complete stack trace, and the **whereis** command tells you where a particular function is located:

```
(dbx) print start        ...display current value of start.
1
(dbx) whatis start       ...get type information.
int start;
(dbx) which start        ...find its location.
palindrome.palinAux.start
(dbx) where              ...obtain stack trace.
palinAux(str = "cat", start = 1, stop = 3), line 29 in
"/usr/glass/reverse/palindrome.c"
palindrome.palindrome(str = "cat"), line 15 in
"/usr/glass/reverse/palindrome.c"
main(), line 9 in "/usr/glass/reverse/main2.c"
unix_$main() at 0x3b4e7a14
_start(), line 137 in "//garcon/unix_src/lang/sgs/src/crt0/crt0.c"
(dbx) whereis palinAux   ...locate a function.
palindrome.palinAux
(dbx) whereis start      ...locate a variable.
palindrome.palinAux.start
(dbx) _
```

Listing A Program

The **list** command allows you to list the first few lines of a function and the / and **?** commands allows you to search forward and backward through text, respectively:

```
(dbx) list palindrome          ...list ten lines.
    5
    6
    7    enum { FALSE, TRUE };
    8
    9
   10    int palindrome (str)
   11
   12    char* str;
   13
   14    {
   15        return (palinAux (str, 1, strlen (str)));
```

```
(dbx) list 10,20          ...list lines 10 thru 20.
   10    int palindrome (str)
   11
   12    char* str;
   13
   14    {
   15       return (palinAux (str, 1, strlen (str)));
   16    }
   17
   18    /**************************************************************/
   19
   20    int palinAux (str, start, stop)
   21
(dbx) ?palinAux           ...search backward for string "palinAux".
   20    int palinAux (str, start, stop)
(dbx) /palinAux           ...search forward for string "palinAux".
   32       return (palinAux (str, start + 1, stop - 1));
(dbx) _
```

Leaving The Debugger

To quit out of **dbx**, use the **quit** command. This exits you back to your shell:

```
(dbx) quit                ...leave the debugger.
$ _
```

Summary

I've presented a smattering of the commonly used **dbx** commands. Used wisely, they can provide useful hints about the errors in your program. In my own opinion, **dbx** is actually a pretty poor debugger compared with some of the popular PC debuggers such as Borland's Turbo Debugger, and advanced UNIX systems like ObjectWorks\C++. On the positive side, at least it's available on most UNIX machines, which makes a rudimentary understanding of its operation fairly handy.

WHEN YOU'RE DONE: STRIP

The debugger and profile utilities both require you to compile a program using special options, each of which adds code to the executable file. To remove this extra code after debugging and profiling are done with, use the **strip** utility, which works as follows:

> *Synopsis:* **strip** { *fileName* }+
>
> **strip** removes all of the symbol table, relocation, debugging, and profiling information from the named files.

Here's an example of how much space you can save:

```
$ ls -l main2            ...look at original file.
-rwxr-xr-x   1 gglass      5904 Jan  8 22:18 main2*
$ strip main2            ...strip out spurious information.
$ ls -l main2            ...look at stripped version.
-rwxr-xr-x   1 gglass      3373 Jan  8 23:17 main2*
$ _
```

CHAPTER REVIEW

Checklist

In this chapter, I described utilities that:

- compile C programs
- manage the compilation of multi-module programs
- maintain archives
- maintain multiple versions of source code
- profile executable files
- debug executable files

Quiz

1. What's the definition of a leaf node on an sccs delta tree?
2. What's the benefit of the **-q** option of **ar**?
3. Can the **make** system use object modules stored in an archive file?
4. What does the term "reusable function" mean?
5. Why would you profile an executable file?
6. Describe briefly what the **strip** utility does.

Exercises

1. Compile "reverse.c" and "palindrome.c" and place them into an archive called "string.a". Write a main program in "prompt.c" that prompts the user for a string and then outputs 1 if the string is a palindrome, and 0 otherwise. Create a makefile for the program that links "prompt.o" with the reverse () and palindrome () functions stored in "string.a". Use **dbx** to debug your code if any bugs exist. [level: *medium*]

2. Replace the original version of palindrome () stored in "palindrome" with a pointer-based version. Use SCCS to manage the source code changes, and **ar** to replace the old version in "string.a". [level: *medium*].

3. Try a modern debugger such as the Borland C++ source level debugger. How does it compare against **dbx**? [level: *medium*].

Project

1. Write a paper that describes how you would use the utilities in this section to help manage a 10-person computing team. [level: *medium*]

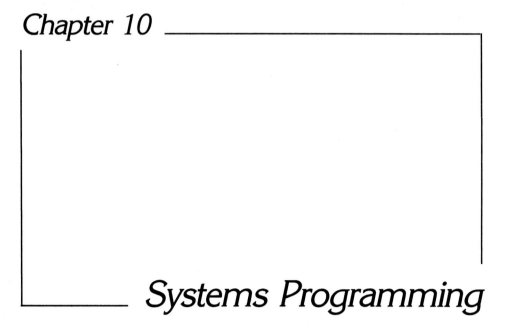

Chapter 10

Systems Programming

Motivation

If you're a C programmer and you wish to take advantage of the UNIX multitasking and interprocess communication facilities, it's essential that you have a good knowledge of the UNIX system calls.

Prerequisites

In order to understand this chapter, you should have a good working knowledge of C. For the Internet section of this chapter, it helps if you have read chapter 8.

Objectives

In this chapter, I'll explain and demonstrate a majority of the UNIX system calls, including those that support I/O, process management, and interprocess communication.

Presentation

The information in this section is presented in the form of several sample programs, including a shell designed for the Internet.

System calls

This section contains the following system calls, listed in alphabetical order:

accept	gethostbyname	pause
alarm	gethostname	perror
bind	getpgrp	pipe
chdir	getpid	read
chmod	getppid	setgid
chown	htonl	setpgrp
close	htons	setuid
connect	inet_addr	signal
dup	inet_ntoa	socket
dup2	ioctl	stat
exec..	kill	sync
exit	link	truncate
fchmod	listen	unlink
fchown	lseek	wait
fctnl	mknod	write
fork	nice	
fstat	open	
ftruncate		
getdents		

INTRODUCTION

In order to make use of services such as file creation, process duplication, and interprocess communication, application programs must talk to the operating system. They can do this via a collection of routines called *system calls*, which are the programmer's functional interface to the UNIX kernel. They're just like library routines except that they perform a subroutine call directly into the heart of UNIX.

The UNIX system calls can be loosely grouped into three main categories:

- file management
- process management
- error handling

Interprocess communication (IPC) is in fact a subset of file management, since UNIX treats IPC mechanisms as special files. Here's a diagram that illustrates the file management system call hierarchy:

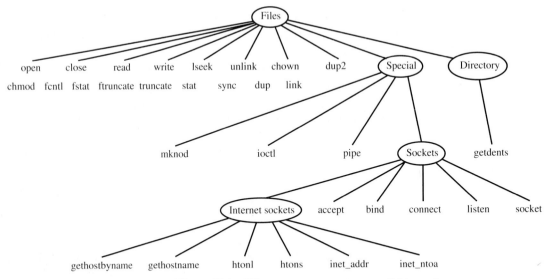

Figure 10.1   File management system call hierarchy

The process management system call hierarchy includes routines for duplicating, differentiating, and terminating processes, and looks like this:

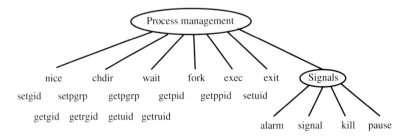

Figure 10.2   Process management system call hierarchy

The only system call that supports error handling is perror ( ), which I'll put it in a hierarchy just to be consistent:

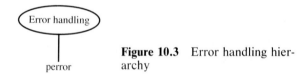

Figure 10.3   Error handling hier-archy

This chapter covers the system calls shown in these hierarchy diagrams in the following order:

- **Error handling**. I start the chapter with a description of perror ( ).
- **Regular file management**. This includes information on how to create, open, close, read, and write regular files.
- **Process management**. This explains how to duplicate, differentiate, suspend, and terminate processes.
- **Signals**. Although the signal facility could come under the heading of either process management or interprocess communication, it's a significant enough topic to warrant a section of its own.
- **Pipes**. This section describes interprocess communication via pipes, covering both unnamed pipes and named pipes.
- **Sockets**. This section describes interprocess communication via sockets, including information about Internet sockets.

This chapter ends with a source code listing and discussion of a complete Internet shell, which is a shell that supports piping and redirection to other Internet shells on remote hosts. The Internet shell program uses most of the facilities that are described in this chapter.

ERROR HANDLING: PERROR ( )

Most system calls are capable of failing in some way. For example, the open ( ) system call will fail if you try to open a non-existent file for reading. By convention, all system calls return -1 if an error occurs. However, this doesn't tell you much about *why* the error occurred; the open ( ) system call can fail for one of several different reasons. If you want to deal with system call errors in a systematic way, you must know about two things:

- **errno**, a global variable that holds the numeric code of the last system call error
- perror ( ), a subroutine that describes system call errors

Every process contains a global variable called **errno**, which is originally set to zero when the process is created. When a system call error occurs, **errno** is set to the numeric code associated with the cause of the error. For example, if you try to open a file that doesn't exist for reading, **errno** is set to 2. The file "/usr/include/sys/errno.h" contains a list of the predefined error codes. Here's a snippet of the file:

```
#define     EPERM       1       /* Not owner */
#define     ENOENT      2       /* No such file or directory */
#define     ESRCH       3       /* No such process */
#define     EINTR       4       /* Interrupted system call */
#define     EIO         5       /* I/O error */
```

A successful system call never affects the current value of **errno**, and an unsuccessful system call always overwrites the current value of **errno**. To access **errno** from your program, include <errno.h>. The perror () subroutine converts the current value of **errno** into an English description, and works like this:

Library Routine: void **perror** (char* *str*)

perror () displays the string *str*, followed by a colon, followed by a description of the last system call error. If there is no error to report, it displays the string "Error 0." Actually, perror () isn't a system call—it's a standard C library routine.

Your program should check system calls for a return value of -1 and then deal with the situation immediately. One of the first things to do in these situations, especially during debugging, is to call perror () for a description of the error.

In the following example, I forced a couple of system call errors to demonstrate perror (), and then demonstrated that **errno** retained the last system call error code even after a successful call was made. The only way to reset **errno** is to manually assign it to zero. Don't worry about how open () works; I'll describe it later in this chapter.

```
#include <stdio.h>
#include <sys/file.h>
#include <errno.h>

main ()

{
  int fd;

  /* Open a non-existent file to cause an error */
  fd = open ("nonexist.txt", O_RDONLY);
  if (fd == -1) /* fd == -1 => an error occurred */
    {
      printf ("errno = %d\n", errno);
      perror ("main");
    }
```

```
fd = open ("/", O_WRONLY); /* Force a different error */
if (fd == -1)
   {
   printf ("errno = %d\n", errno);
   perror ("main");
   }
/* Execute a successful system call */
fd = open ("nonexist.txt", O_RDONLY | O_CREAT, 0644);
printf ("errno = %d\n", errno); /* Display after successful call */
perror ("main");
errno = 0; /* Manually reset error variable */
perror ("main");
}
```

Here's the output from the program shown above:

```
$ showErrno                    ...run the program.
errno = 2
main: No such file or directory
errno = 21
main: Is a directory
errno = 21
main: Is a directory
main: Error 0
$ _
```

REGULAR FILE MANAGEMENT

My description of file management system calls is split up into four main subsections:

- A primer that describes the main concepts behind UNIX files and file descriptors.
- A description of the basic file management system calls, using a sample program called "reverse" that reverses the lines of a file.
- An explanation of a few advanced system calls, using a sample program called "monitor," which periodically scans directories and displays the names of files within them that have changed since the last scan.
- A description of the remaining file management system calls using some miscellaneous snippets of source code.

A File Management Primer

The file management system calls allow you to manipulate the full collection of regular, directory, and special files, including:

- disk-based files
- terminals
- printers
- interprocess communication facilities, such as pipes and sockets

In most cases, open ( ) is used to initially access or create a file. If the system call succeeds, it returns a small integer called a *file descriptor* that is used in subsequent I/O operations on that file. If open ( ) fails, it returns -1. Here's a snippet of code that illustrates a typical sequence of events:

```
int fd; /* File descriptor */
...
fd = open (fileName, ...); /* Open file, return file descriptor */
if (fd == -1) { /* deal with error condition */ }
...
fcntl (fd, ...); /* Set some I/O flags if necessary */
...
read (fd, ...); /* Read from file */
...
write (fd, ...); /* Write to file */
...
lseek (fd, ...); /* Seek within file*/
...
close (fd); /* Close the file, freeing file descriptor */
```

When a process no longer needs to access an open file, it should close it using the close ( ) system call. All of a process's open files are automatically closed when the process terminates. Although this means that you may often omit an explicit call to close ( ), it's better programming practice to explicitly close your files.

File descriptors are numbered sequentially, starting from zero. Every process may have up to 20 (the usual system limit) open files at any one time, with the file descriptor values thus ranging between 0 and 19. By convention, the first three file descriptor values have a special meaning:

Value	Meaning
0	standard input
1	standard output
2	standard error

For example, the printf () library function always sends its output using file descriptor 1, and scanf () always reads its input using file descriptor 0. When a reference to a file is closed, the file descriptor is freed and may be reassigned by a subsequent open (). Most I/O system calls require a file descriptor as their first argument so that they know which file to operate on.

A single file may be opened several times and thus have several file descriptors associated with it:

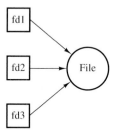

Figure 10.4 Many file descriptors, one file

Each file descriptor has its own private set of properties that have nothing to do with the file that it is associated with, including:

- A file pointer that records the offset in the file where it is reading/writing. When a file descriptor is created, its file pointer is positioned at offset 0 in the file (the first character) by default. As the process reads and/or writes, the file pointer is updated accordingly. For example, if a process opened a file and then read 10 bytes from the file, the file pointer would end up positioned at offset 10. If the process then wrote 20 bytes, the bytes at offset 10..29 in the file would be overwritten and the file pointer would end up positioned at offset 30.
- A flag that indicates whether the descriptor should be automatically closed if the process execs. exec () is described in the ''Process Management'' section of this chapter.
- A flag that indicates whether all of the output to the file should be appended to the end of the file.

In addition to these values, there are some other values that are meaningful only if the file is a special file such as a pipe or a socket:

- A flag that indicates whether a process should block on input from the file if the file doesn't currently contain any input.
- A number that indicates a process id or process group that should be sent a SIGIO signal if input becomes available on the file. Signals and process groups are discussed later in this chapter.

The system calls open () and fcntl () allow you to manipulate these flags, and are described later in this section.

First Example: reverse

In this first section, I'll describe the most basic I/O system calls. Here's a list of them, together with a brief description of their function:

Name	Function
open	opens/creates a file
read	reads bytes from a file into a buffer
write	writes bytes from a buffer to a file
lseek	moves to a particular offset in a file
close	closes a file
unlink	removes a file

To illustrate the use of these system calls, I'll use a small utility program called "reverse.c". As well as being a good vehicle for my presentation, it also doubles as a nice example of how to write a UNIX utility. Here's a description of **reverse**:

Utility: **reverse** -c [*fileName*]

reverse reverses the lines of its input and displays them to standard output. If no file name is specified, **reverse** reverses its standard input. When the **-c** option is used, **reverse** also reverses the characters in each line.

Here's an example of **reverse** in action:

```
$ cc reverse.c -o reverse      ...compile the program.
$ cat test                     ...list the test file.
Christmas is coming,
The days that grow shorter,
Remind me of seasons I knew in the past.
$ reverse test                 ...reverse the file.
Remind me of seasons I knew in the past.
The days that grow shorter,
Christmas is coming,
```

```
$ reverse -c test              ...reverse the lines too.
.tsap eht ni wenk I snosaes fo em dnimeR
,retrohs worg taht syad ehT
,gnimoc si samtsirhC
$ cat test | reverse           ...pipe output to "reverse".
Remind me of seasons I knew in the past.
The days that grow shorter,
Christmas is coming,
$ _
```

How reverse Works

The **reverse** utility works by performing two passes over its input. During the first pass, it notes the starting offset of each line in the file and stores this information in an array. During the second pass, it jumps to the start of each line in reverse order, copying it from the original input file to its standard output.

If no filename is specified on the command line, **reverse** reads from its standard input during the first pass and copies it into a temporary file for the second pass. When the program is finished, the temporary file is removed.

Here's an overview of the program flow, together with a list of the functions that are associated with each action, and a list of the system calls used by each step:

Step	Action	Functions	System calls
1	Parse command line.	parseCommandLine, processOptions	open
2	If reading from standard input, create temporary file to store input; otherwise open input file for reading.	pass1	open
3	Read from file in chunks, storing the starting offset of each line in an array. If reading from standard input, copy each chunk to the temporary file.	pass1, trackLines	read, write
4	Read the input file again, backward, copying each line to standard output. Reverse the line if the -c option was chosen.	pass2, processLine, reverseLine	lseek
5	Close file, removing it if it was a temporary file.	pass2	close

The next few pages contain a complete listing of "reverse.c," the source code of **reverse**. I suggest that you skim through it and then read the description of the system calls that follow.

reverse.c: Listing

```
1    #include <sys/file.h> /* For file mode definitions */
2    #include <stdio.h>
3    #include <stdlib.h>
4
5
6    /* Enumerator */
7    enum { FALSE, TRUE }; /* Standard false and true values */
8    enum { STDIN, STDOUT, STDERR }; /* Standard I/O channel indices */
9
10
11   /* #define Statements */
12   #define BUFFER_SIZE     4096 /* Size of copy buffer */
13   #define NAME_SIZE       10
14   #define MAX_LINES       100000 /* Max lines in file */
15
16
17   /* Globals */
18   char *fileName = NULL; /* Points to file name */
19   char tmpName [NAME_SIZE];
20   int charOption = FALSE; /* Set to true if -c option is used */
21   int standardInput = FALSE; /* Set to true if reading stdin */
22   int lineCount = 0; /* Total number of lines in input */
23   int lineStart [MAX_LINES]; /* Store offsets of each line */
24   int fileOffset = 0; /* Current position in input */
25   int fd; /* File descriptor of input */
26
27   /*****************************************************************/
28
29   main (argc, argv)
30
31   int argc;
32   char* argv [];
33
34   {
35     parseCommandLine (argc,argv); /* Parse command line */
36     pass1 (); /* Perform first pass through input */
37     pass2 (); /* Perform second pass through input */
38     return (/* EXIT_SUCCESS */ 0); /* Done */
39   }
40
41   /*****************************************************************/
42
43   parseCommandLine (argc, argv)
44
45   int argc;
```

```
46   char* argv [];
47
48   /* Parse command line arguments */
49
50   {
51     int i;
52
53     for (i= 1; i < argc; i++)
54       {
55         if(argv[i][0] == '-')
56           processOptions (argv[i]);
57         else if (fileName == NULL)
58           fileName= argv[i];
59         else
60           usageError (); /* An error occurred */
61       }
62
63     standardInput = (fileName == NULL);
64   }
65
66   /****************************************************************/
67
68   processOptions (str)
69
70   char* str;
71
72   /* Parse options */
73
74   {
75     int j;
76
77     for (j= 1; str[j] != NULL; j++)
78       {
79         switch(str[j]) /* Switch on command line flag */
80           {
81             case'c':
82               charOption = TRUE;
83               break;
84
85             default:
86               usageError ();
87               break;
88           }
89       }
90   }
91
92   /****************************************************************/
93
```

```
94   usageError ()
95
96   {
97     fprintf (stderr, "Usage: reverse -c [filename]\n");
98     exit (/* EXIT_FAILURE */ 1);
99   }
100
101  /*****************************************************************/
102
103  pass1 ()
104
105  /* Perform first scan through file */
106
107  {
108    int tmpfd, charsRead, charsWritten;
109    char buffer [BUFFER_SIZE];
110
111    if (standardInput) /* Read from standard input */
112       {
113         fd = STDIN;
114         sprintf (tmpName, ".rev.%d",getpid ()); /* Random name */
115         /* Create temporary file to store copy of input */
116         tmpfd = open (tmpName, O_CREAT | O_RDWR, 0600);
117         if (tmpfd == -1) fatalError ();
118       }
119    else /* Open named file for reading */
120       {
121         fd = open (fileName, O_RDONLY);
122         if (fd == -1) fatalError ();
123       }
124
125    lineStart[0] = 0; /* Offset of first line */
126
127    while (TRUE) /* Read all input */
128       {
129         /* Fill buffer */
130         charsRead = read (fd, buffer, BUFFER_SIZE);
131         if (charsRead == 0) break; /* EOF */
132         if (charsRead == -1) fatalError (); /* Error */
133         trackLines (buffer, charsRead); /* Process line */
134         /* Copy line to temporary file if reading from stdin */
135         if (standardInput)
136            {
137              charsWritten = write (tmpfd, buffer, charsRead);
138              if(charsWritten != charsRead) fatalError ();
139            }
140       }
141
```

```
142        /* Store offset of trailing line, if present */
143        lineStart[lineCount + 1] = fileOffset;
144
145        /* If reading from standard input, prepare fd for pass2 */
146        if (standardInput) fd = tmpfd;
147    }
148
149    /********************************************************************/
150
151    trackLines (buffer, charsRead)
152
153    char* buffer;
154    int charsRead;
155
156    /* Store offsets of each line start in buffer */
157
158    {
159        int i;
160
161        for (i = 0; i < charsRead; i++)
162          {
163             ++fileOffset; /* Update current file position */
164             if (buffer[i] == '\n') lineStart[++lineCount] = fileOffset;
165          }
166    }
167
168    /********************************************************************/
169
170    int pass2 ()
171
172    /* Scan input file again, displaying lines in reverse order */
173
174    {
175        int i;
176
177        for (i = lineCount - 1; i >= 0; i--)
178          processLine (i);
179
180        close (fd); /* Close input file */
181        if (standardInput) unlink (tmpName); /* Remove temp file */
182    }
183
184    /********************************************************************/
185
186    processLine (i)
187
188    int i;
189
```

```
190   /* Read a line and display it */
191
192   {
193     int charsRead;
194     char buffer [BUFFER_SIZE];
195
196     lseek (fd, lineStart[i], L_SET); /* Find the line and read it */
197     charsRead = read (fd, buffer, lineStart[i+1] - lineStart[i]);
198     /* Reverse line if -c option was selected */
199     if (charOption) reverseLine (buffer, charsRead);
200     write (1, buffer, charsRead); /* Write it to standard output */
201   }
202
203   /*********************************************************************/
204
205   reverseLine (buffer, size)
206
207   char* buffer;
208   int size;
209
210   /* Reverse all the characters in the buffer */
211
212   {
213     int start = 0, end = size - 1;
214     char tmp;
215
216     if (buffer[end] == '\n') --end; /* Leave trailing newline */
217
218     /* Swap characters in a pairwise fashion */
219     while (start < end)
220       {
221         tmp = buffer[start];
222         buffer[start] = buffer[end];
223         buffer[end] = tmp;
224         ++start; /* Increment start index */
225         --end; /* Decrement end index */
226       }
227   }
228
229   /*********************************************************************/
230
231   fatalError ()
232
233   {
234     perror ("reverse: "); /* Describe error */
235     exit (1);
236   }
```

Opening A File: open ( )

The **reverse** utility begins by executing parseCommandLine ( ) [43] which sets various flags depending on which options are chosen. If a filename is specified, the variable **fileName** is set to point to the name and **standardInput** is set to FALSE; otherwise, **fileName** is set to NULL and **standardInput** is set to TRUE. Next, pass1 ( ) [103] is executed, which performs one of the following actions:

- If **reverse** is reading from standard input, a temporary file is created. The file is created with read and write permissions for the owner, and no permissions for anyone else (octal mode 600). It is opened in read/write mode, and is used to store a copy of the standard input for use during pass 2. During pass 1, the input is taken from standard input, and so the file descriptor **fd** is set to STDIN, defined to be 0 at the top of the program. Recall that standard input is always file descriptor zero.
- If **reverse** is reading from a named file, the file is opened in read-only mode so that its contents may be read during pass 1 using the file descriptor **fd**.

Each action uses the open ( ) system call; the first action uses it to create a file, and the second action uses it to access an existing file.

System Call: int **open** (char* *fileName*, int *mode* [, int *permissions*])

open ( ) allows you to open or create a file for reading and/or writing. *fileName* is an absolute or relative pathname and *mode* is a bitwise or'ing of a read/write flag together with zero or more miscellaneous flags. *permissions* is a number that encodes the value of the file's permission flags, and should only be supplied when a file is being created. It is usually written using the octal encoding scheme described in chapter 2. The *permissions* value is affected by the process's umask value, described in chapter 3. The values of the predefined read/write and miscellaneous flags are stored in "/usr/include/sys/file.h". The read/write flags are as follows:

FLAG	MEANING
O_RDONLY	Open for read-only.
O_WRONLY	Open for write-only.
O_RDWR	Open for read and write.

The miscellaneous flags are as follows:

FLAG	MEANING
O_APPEND	Position the file pointer at the end of the file before each write ().
O_CREAT	If the file doesn't exist, create the file, set the owner ID to the process's effective UID, and set the group id to the group id of the directory in which the file is created. The umask value is used when determining the initial permission flag settings.
O_EXCL	If O_CREAT is set and the file exists, then open () fails.
O_NONBLOCK	(Called O_NDELAY on some systems.) This setting works only for named pipes. If set, an open for read-only will return immediately, regardless of whether the write end is open, and an open for write-only will fail if the read end isn't open. If clear, an open for read-only or write-only will block until the other end is also open.
O_TRUNC	If the file exists, it is truncated to length zero.

open () returns a non-negative file descriptor if successful; otherwise, it returns -1.

Creating a file

To create a file, use the O_CREAT flag as part of the mode flags, and supply the initial file permission flag settings as an octal value. For example, lines 114..117 create a temporary file with read and write permission for the owner, and then open it for reading and writing:

```
114     sprintf (tmpName, ".rev.%d", getpid ()); /* Random name *
115     /* Create temporary file to store copy of input */
116     tmpfd = open (tmpName, O_CREAT | O_RDWR, 0600);
117     if (tmpfd == -1) fatalError ();
```

The getpid () function is a system call that returns the process's id number (PID), which is guaranteed to be unique. This is a handy way to generate unique temporary file names. For more details on this system call, see the ''Process Management'' section of this chapter. Note that I chose the name of the temporary file to begin with a period so that it doesn't show up in an **ls** listing. Files that begin with a period are sometimes known as *hidden* files.

Opening an existing file

To open an existing file, specify the mode flags only. Lines 121..122 open a named file for read-only:

```
121     fd = open (fileName, O_RDONLY);
122     if (fd == -1) fatalError ();
```

Other open flags

The other more complicated flag settings for open (), such as O_NONBLOCK, are intended for use with the pipes and sockets that are described later in this chapter. Right now, the O_CREAT flag is probably the only miscellaneous flag that you'll need.

Reading From A File: read ()

Once **reverse** has initialized the file descriptor **fd** for input, it reads chunks of input and processes them until the end of the file is reached. To read bytes from a file, it uses the read () system call, which works as follows:

System Call: int **read** (int *fd*, char* *buf*, int *count*)

Note: this synopsis describes how read () operates when reading a regular file. For information on reading from special files, please refer to later sections of this chapter.
        read () copies *count* bytes from the file referenced by the file descriptor *fd* into the buffer *buf*. The bytes are read from the current file position, which is then updated accordingly.
        read () copies as many bytes from the file as it can, up to the number specified by *count*, and returns the number of bytes actually copied. If a read () is attempted after the last byte has already been read, it returns 0, which indicates end-of-file.
        If successful, read () returns the number of bytes that it read; otherwise, it returns -1.

The read () system call performs low-level input, and has none of the formatting capabilities of scanf (). The benefit of read () is that it bypasses the additional layer of buffering supplied by the C library functions, and is therefore very fast. Although I could have read one character of input at a time, this would have resulted in a large number of system calls, thus slowing down the execution of my program considerably. Instead, I used read () to read up to BUFFER_SIZE characters at a time. BUFFER_SIZE was chosen to be a multiple of the disk block size, for efficient copying. Lines 130..132 perform the read and test the return result:

```
130     charsRead = read (fd, buffer, BUFFER_SIZE);
131     if (charsRead == 0) break; /* EOF */
132     if (charsRead == -1) fatalError (); /* Error */
```

As each chunk of input is read, it is passed to the trackLines () function. This function scans the input buffer for newlines and stores the offset of the first character in each line in the **lineStart** array. The variable **fileOffset** is used to maintain the current file offset. The contents of **lineStart** are used during the second pass.

Writing To A File: write ( )

When **reverse** is reading from standard input, it creates a copy of the input for use during pass two. To do this, it sets the file descriptor **tmpfd** to refer to a temporary file, and then writes each chunk of input to the file during the read loop. To write bytes to a file, it uses the write () system call, which works as follows:

System Call: int **write** (int *fd*, char* *buf*, int *count*)

Note: this synopsis describes how write ( ) operates when writing to a regular file. For information on writing to special files, please refer to later sections of this chapter.

write () copies *count* bytes from a buffer *buf* to the file referenced by the file descriptor *fd*. The bytes are written at the current file position, which is then updated accordingly. If the O_APPEND flag was set for *fd*, the file position is set to the end of the file before each write.

write () copies as many bytes from the buffer as it can, up to the number specified by *count*, and returns the number of bytes actually copied. Your process should always check the return value. If the return value isn't *count*, then the disk probably filled up and no space was left.

If successful, write () returns the number of bytes that were written; otherwise, it returns -1.

The write () system call performs low-level output, and has none of the formatting capabilities of printf (). The benefit of write () is that it bypasses the additional

layer of buffering supplied by the C library functions, and is **therefore** every fast.
Lines 134..139 perform the write operation:

```
134     /* Copy line to temporary file if reading standard input */
135     if (standardInput)
136        {
137         charsWritten = write (tmpfd, buffer, charsRead);
138         if (charsWritten != charsRead) fatalError ();
139        }
```

Moving In A File: lseek ()

Once the first pass has completed, the array **lineStart** contains the offsets of the
first character of each line of the input file. During pass two, the lines are read in
reverse order and displayed to standard output. In order to read the lines out of
sequence, the program makes use of lseek ( ), which is a system call that allows a
descriptor's file pointer to be changed. Here's a descripton of lseek ( ):

System Call: long **lseek** (int *fd*, long *offset*, int *mode*)

lseek ( ) allows you to change a descriptor's current file position. *fd* is the file
descriptor, *offset* is a long integer, and *mode* describes how *offset* should be
interpreted. The three possible values of modeare defined in "/usr/include/
sys/file.h", and have the following meaning:

VALUE	MEANING
L_SET	*offset* is relative to the start of the file.
L_CUR	*offset* is relative to the current file position.
L_END	*offset* is relative to the end of the file.

lseek ( ) fails if you try to move before the start of the file.
If successful, lseek ( ) returns the current file position; otherwise, it
returns -1.

Lines 196..197 seek to the start of a line and then read in all of its characters. Note
that the number of characters to read is calculated by subtracting the start offset of
the next line from the start offset of the current line.

```
196     lseek (fd, lineStart[i], L_SET); /* Find line and read it */
197     charsRead = read (fd, buffer, lineStart[i+1] - lineStart[i]);
```

If you want to find out your current location without moving, use an offset value of zero relative to the current position:

```
currentOffset = lseek (fd, 0, L_CUR);
```

If you move past the end of the file and then perform a write (), the kernel automatically extends the size of the file and treats the intermediate file area as if it were filled with NULL (ASCII 0) characters. Interestingly enough, it doesn't allocate disk space for the intermediate area, which is confirmed by the following example:

```
$ cat sparse.c                        ...list the test file.
#include <sys/file.h>
#include <stdio.h>
#include <stdlib.h>

/***************************************************************/

main ()

{
  int i, fd;

  /* Create a sparse file */
  fd = open ("sparse.txt", O_CREAT | O_RDWR, 0600);
  write (fd, "sparse", 6);
  lseek (fd, 60006, L_SET);
  write (fd, "file", 4);
  close (fd);

  /* Create a normal file */
  fd = open ("normal.txt", O_CREAT | O_RDWR, 0600);
  write (fd, "normal", 6);
  for (i = 1; i <= 60000; i++)
    write (fd, "/0", 1);
  write (fd, "file", 4);
  close (fd);
}
$ sparse                              ...execute the file.
$ ls -l *.txt                         ...look at the files.
-rw-r--r--   1 glass       60010 Feb 14 15:06 normal.txt
-rw-r--r--   1 glass       60010 Feb 14 15:06 sparse.txt
$ ls -s *.txt                         ...list their block usage.
  60 normal.txt*                      ...uses a full 60 blocks.
   8 sparse.txt*                      ...only uses 8 blocks.
$ _
```

Files that contain "gaps" like this are termed "sparse" files. For details on how they are actually stored, consult chapter 11.

Closing A File: Close ()

When pass two is over, **reverse** uses the close () system call to free the input file descriptor. Here's a description of close ():

System Call: int **close** (int *fd*)

close () frees the file descriptor *fd*. If *fd* is the last file descriptor associated with a particular open file, the kernel resources associated with the file are deallocated. When a process terminates, all of its file descriptors are automatically closed, but it's better programming practice to close a file when you're done with it. If you close a file descriptor that's already closed, an error occurs.

   If successful, close () returns zero; otherwise, it returns -1.

Line 180 contains the call to close ():

```
180    close (fd); /* Close input file */
```

When a file is closed, it does not guarantee that the file's buffers are immediately flushed to disk. For more information on file buffering, consult chapter 11.

Deleting A File: unlink ()

If **reverse** reads from standard input, it stores a copy of the input in a temporary file. At the end of pass two, it removes this file using the unlink () system call, which works like this:

System Call: int **unlink** (char* *fileName*)

unlink () removes the hard link from the name *fileName* to its file. If *fileName* is the last link to the file, the file's resources are deallocated. In this case, if any process's file descriptors are currently associated with the file, the directory entry is removed immediately but the file is only deallocated after all of the file descriptors are closed. This means that an executable file can unlink itself during execution and still continue to completion.

   If successful, unlink () returns zero; otherwise, it returns -1.

Line 181 contains the call to unlink ( ):

```
181      if (standardInput) unlink (tmpName); /* Remove temp file */
```

For more information about hard links, consult chapter 11.

Second Example: monitor

This section contains a description of some more advanced system calls:

Name	Function
stat	obtains status information about a file
fstat	works just like stat
getdents	obtains directory entries

These calls are demonstrated in the context of a program called "monitor," which allows a user to monitor a series of named files and obtain information whenever any of them are modified. Here's a description of **monitor**:

Utility: **monitor** [-t *delay*] [-l *count*]{ *fileName* }+

monitor scans all of the specified files every *delay* seconds and displays information about any of the specified files that were modified since the last scan. If *fileName* is a directory, all of the files inside that directory are scanned. File modification is indicated in one of three ways:

LABEL	MEANING
ADDED	Indicates that the file was created since the last scan. Every file in the file list is given this label during the first scan.
CHANGED	Indicates that the file was modified since the last scan.
DELETED	Indicates that the file was deleted since the last scan.

By default, **monitor** will scan forever, although you can specify the total number of scans by using the **-c** option. The default delay time is 10 seconds between scans, although this may be overridden by using the **-t** option.

In the following example, I monitored an individual file and a directory, storing the output of monitor into a temporary file. Notice how the contents of the "monitor.out" file reflected the additions, modifications, and deletions of the monitored file and directory:

```
$ ls                                   ...look at home directory.
monitor.c    monitor      tmp/
$ ls tmp                               ...look at "tmp" directory.
b
$ monitor tmp myFile.txt >& monitor.out & ...start monitor.
[1] 12841
$ cat > tmp/a                          ...create a file in "~/tmp".
hi there
^D
$ cat > myFile.txt                     ...create "myFile.txt".
hi there
^D
$ cat >> myFile.txt                    ...change "myFile.txt".
hi again
^D
$ rm tmp/a                             ...delete "tmp/a".
$ jobs                                 ...look at jobs.
[1]  + Running              monitor tmp myFile.txt >& monitor.out
$ kill %1                              ...kill monitor job.
[1]    Terminated           monitor tmp myFile.txt >& monitor.out
$ cat monitor.out                      ...look at output.
ADDED tmp/b size 9 bytes, mod. time = Sat Jan 18 00:38:55 1992
ADDED tmp/a size 9 bytes, mod. time = Fri Feb 14 18:51:09 1992
ADDED myFile.txt size 9 bytes, mod. time = Fri Feb 14 18:51:21 1992
CHANGED myFile.txt size 18 bytes, mod. time = Fri Feb 14 18:51:49 1992
DELETED tmp/a
$ _
```

How monitor Works

The **monitor** utility continually scans the specified files and directories for modifications. It uses the stat () system call to obtain status information about named files, including their type and last modification time, and uses the getdents () system call to scan directories. It maintains a status table called **stats**, which holds the following information about each file that it finds:

- the name of the file
- the status information obtained by the stat ()
- a record of whether the file was present during the present scan and the previous scan

During a scan, **monitor** processes each file as follows:

- If the file isn't currently in the scan table, it's added and the message "ADDED" is displayed.
- If the file is already in the scan table and has been modified since the last scan, the message "CHANGED" is displayed.

At the end of a scan, all entries that were present during the previous scan but not during the current scan are removed from the table and the message "DE-LETED" is displayed.

Following is a complete listing of "monitor.c", the source code of **monitor**. I suggest that you skim through it and then read the description of the system calls that follow.

monitor.c: Listing

```
1    #include <stdio.h>              /* For printf, fprintf */
2    #include <string.h>             /* For strcmp */
3    #include <ctype.h>              /* For isdigit */
4    #include <sys/file.h>           /* For O_RDONLY, L_SET */
5    #include <sys/dir.h>            /* For getdents */
6    #include <sys/stat.h>           /* For IS_ macros */
7    #include <sys/types.h>          /* For mode_t */
8    #include <time.h>               /* For localtime, asctime */
9
10
11   /* #define Statements */
12   #define MAX_FILES             100
13   #define MAX_FILENAME          50
14   #define NOT_FOUND             -1
15   #define FOREVER               -1
16   #define DEFAULT_DELAY_TIME    10
17   #define DEFAULT_LOOP_COUNT    FOREVER
18
19
20   /* Booleans */
21   enum { FALSE, TRUE };
22
23
24   /* Status structure, one per file. */
25   struct statStruct
26     {
27       char fileName [MAX_FILENAME]; /* File name */
28       int lastCycle, thisCycle; /* To detect changes */
29       struct statstatus; /* Information from stat () */
30     };
```

```
31
32
33   /* Globals */
34   char* fileNames [MAX_FILES]; /* One per file on command line */
35   int fileCount; /* Count of files on command line */
36   struct statStruct stats [MAX_FILES]; /* One per matching file */
37   int loopCount = DEFAULT_LOOP_COUNT; /* Number of times to loop */
38   int delayTime = DEFAULT_DELAY_TIME; /* Seconds between loops */
39
40   /*****************************************************************/
41
42   main (argc, argv)
43
44   int argc;
45   char* argv [];
46
47   {
48     parseCommandLine (argc, argv); /* Parse command line */
49     monitorLoop (); /* Execute main monitor loop */
50     return (/* EXIT_SUCCESS */ 0);
51   }
52
53   /*****************************************************************/
54
55   parseCommandLine (argc, argv)
56
57   int argc;
58   char* argv [];
59
60   /* Parse command line arguments */
61
62   {
63     int i;
64
65     for (i = 1; i < argc; i++)
66       {
67         if (argv[i][0] ==  '-')
68           processOptions (argv[i]);
69         else
70           fileNames[fileCount++] = argv[i];
71       }
72
73     if (fileCount == 0) usageError ();
74   }
75
76   /*****************************************************************/
77
78   processOptions (str)
```

```
79
80   char* str;
81
82   /* Parse options */
83
84   {
85     int j;
86
87     for (j = 1; str[j] != NULL; j++)
88        {
89          switch(str[j]) /* Switch on option letter */
90             {
91               case 't':
92                 delayTime = getNumber (str, &j);
93                 break;
94
95               case 'l':
96                 loopCount = getNumber (str, &j);
97                 break;
98             }
99        }
100  }
101
102  /******************************************************************/
103
104  getNumber (str, i)
105
106  char* str;
107  int* i;
108
109  /* Convert a numeric ASCII option to a number */
110
111  {
112    int number = 0;
113    int digits = 0; /* Count the digits in the number */
114
115    while (isdigit (str[(*i) + 1])) /* Convert chars to ints */
116       {
117         number = number * 10 + str[++(*i)] - '0';
118         ++digits;
119       }
120
121    if (digits == 0) usageError (); /* There must be a number */
122    return (number);
123  }
124
125  /******************************************************************/
126
```

```
127  usageError ()
128
129  {
130     fprintf (stderr, "Usage: monitor -t<seconds> -l<loops>
{filename}+\n");
131     exit (/* EXIT_FAILURE */ 1);
132  }
133
134  /*******************************************************************/
135
136  monitorLoop ()
137
138  /* The main monitor loop */
139
140  {
141    do
142      {
143        monitorFiles (); /* Scan all files */
144        fflush (stdout); /* Flush standard output */
145        fflush (stderr); /* Flush standard error */
146        sleep (delayTime); /* Wait until next loop */
147      }
148    while (loopCount == FOREVER || --loopCount > 0);
149  }
150
151  /*******************************************************************/
152
153  monitorFiles ()
154
155  /* Process all files */
156
157  {
158    int i;
159
160    for (i = 0; i < fileCount; i++)
161      monitorFile (fileNames[i]);
162
163    for (i = 0; i< MAX_FILES; i++) /* Update stat array */
164      {
165        if (stats[i].lastCycle && !stats[i].thisCycle)
166          printf ("DELETED %s\n", stats[i].fileName);
167
168        stats[i].lastCycle = stats[i].thisCycle;
169        stats[i].thisCycle = FALSE;
170      }
171  }
172
173  /*******************************************************************/
```

```
174
175   monitorFile (fileName)
176
177   char* fileName;
178
179   /* Process a single file/directory*/
180
181   {
182     struct stat statBuf;
183     mode_t mode;
184     int result;
185
186     result = stat (fileName, &statBuf); /* Obtain file status */
187
188     if (result == -1) /* Status was not available */
189       {
190         fprintf (stderr, "Cannot stat %s\n", fileName);
191         return;
192       }
193
194     mode = statBuf.st_mode; /* Mode of file */
195
196     if(S_ISDIR (mode)) /* Directory */
197       processDirectory (fileName);
198     else if (S_ISREG (mode) || S_ISCHR (mode) || S_ISBLK (mode))
199       updateStat (fileName, &statBuf); /* Regular file */
200   }
201
202   /********************************************************************/
203
204   processDirectory (dirName)
205
206   char* dirName;
207
208   /* Process all files in the named directory */
209
210   {
211     int fd, charsRead;
212     struct direct dirEntry;
213     char fileName {MAX_FILENAME};
214
215     fd = open (dirName, O_RDONLY); /* Open for reading */
216     if (fd == -1) fatalError ();
217
218     while (TRUE) /* Read all directory entries */
219       {
220         charsRead = getdents(fd, &dirEntry, sizeof (struct direct));
221         if (charsRead == -1) fatalError ();
```

```
222          if (charsRead == 0) break; /* EOF */
223          if (strcmp (dirEntry.d_name, ".") != 0&&
224             strcmp (dirEntry.d_name, "..") != 0) /* Skip . and .. */
225            {
226             sprintf (fileName, "%s/%s", dirName, dirEntry.d_name);
227             monitorFile (fileName); /* Call recursively */
228            }
229
230          lseek (fd, dirEntry.d_off, L_SET); /* Find next entry */
231        }
232
233    close (fd); /* Close directory */
234  }
235
236  /*********************************************************************/
237
238  updateStat (fileName, statBuf)
239
240  char* fileName;
241  struct stat* statBuf;
242
243  /* Add a status entry if necessary */
244
245  {
246    int entryIndex;
247
248    entryIndex = findEntry (fileName); /* Find existing entry */
249
250    if (entryIndex == NOT_FOUND)
251      entryIndex = addEntry (fileName, statBuf); /* Add new entry */
252    else
253      updateEntry (entryIndex, statBuf); /* Update existing entry */
254
255    if (entryIndex != NOT_FOUND)
256      stats{entryIndex}.thisCycle = TRUE; /* Update status array */
257  }
258
259  /*********************************************************************/
260
261  findEntry (fileName)
262
263  char* fileName;
264
265  /* Locate the index of a named filein the status array */
266
267  {
268    int i;
269
```

```
270    for (i = 0; i < MAX_FILES; i++)
271      if (stats{i}.lastCycle &&
272          strcmp (stats{i}.fileName, fileName) == 0) return (i);
273
274    return (NOT_FOUND);
275  }
276
277  /*****************************************************************/
278
279  addEntry (fileName, statBuf)
280
281  char* fileName;
282  struct stat* statBuf;
283
284  /* Add a new entry into the status array */
285
286  {
287    int index;
288
289    index = nextFree (); /* Find the next free entry */
290    if (index == NOT_FOUND) return (NOT_FOUND); /* None left */
291    strcpy (stats{index}.fileName, fileName); /* Add filename */
292    stats{index}.status = *statBuf; /* Add status information */
293    printf ("ADDED "); /* Notify standard output */
294    printEntry (index); /* Display status information */
295    return (index);
296  }
297
298  /*****************************************************************/
299
300  nextFree ()
301
302  /* Return the nextfree index in the status array */
303
304  {
305    int i;
306
307    for (i = 0; i < MAX_FILES; i++)
308      if (!stats{i}.lastCycle && !stats{i}.thisCycle) return (i);
309
310    return (NOT_FOUND);
311  }
312
313  /*****************************************************************/
314
315  updateEntry (index, statBuf)
316
317  int index;
```

```
318   struct stat* statBuf;
319
320   /*Display information if the file has been modified */
321
322   {
323     if (stats{index}.status.st_mtime != statBuf->st_mtime)
324       {
325         stats{index}.status = *statBuf; /* Store stat information */
326         printf ("CHANGED "); /* Notify standard output */
327         printEntry (index);
328       }
329   }
330
331   /*****************************************************************/
332
333   printEntry (index)
334
335   int index;
336
337   /* Display an entry of the status array */
338
339   {
340     printf ("%s ", stats{index}.fileName);
341     printStat (&stats{index}.status);
342   }
343
344   /*****************************************************************/
345
346   printStat (statBuf)
347
348   struct stat* statBuf;
349
350   /* Display a status buffer */
351
352   {
353     printf ("size %lu bytes, mod. time = %s",  statBuf->st_size,
354             asctime (localtime (&statBuf->st_mtime)));
355   }
356
357   /*****************************************************************/
358
359   fatalError ()
360
361   {
362     perror ("monitor: ");
363     exit (/* EXIT_FAILURE */ 1);
364   }
```

Obtaining File Information: stat ( )

monitor obtains its file information by calling stat ( ), which works as follows:

System Call: int **stat** (char* *name*, struct stat* *buf*)
                        int **fstat** (int *fd*, struct stat* *buf*)

stat ( ) fills the buffer *buf* with information about the file *name*. The **stat** structure is defined in ''/usr/include/sys/stat.h''. fstat ( ) performs the same function as stat ( ), except that it takes the file descriptor of the file to be stat'ed as its first parameter. The **stat** structure contains the following members:

NAME	MEANING
st_dev	the device number
st_ino	the inode number
st_mode	the permission flags
st_nlink	the hard link count
st_uid	the user id
st_gid	the group id
st_size	the file size
st_atime	the last access time
st_mtime	the last modification time
st_ctime	the last status change time

There are some predefined macros defined in ''/usr/include/sys/stat.h'' that take **st_mode** as their argument and return true (1) for the following file types:

MACRO	RETURNS TRUE FOR FILE TYPE
S_ISDIR	directory
S_ISCHR	character special device
S_ISBLK	block special device
S_ISREG	file regular file
S_ISFIFO	pipe

The time fields may be decoded using the standard C library asctime ( ) and localtime ( ) subroutines.
            stat ( ) and fstat ( ) return 0 if successful and -1 otherwise.

The **monitor** utility invokes stat () from monitorFile () [175] on line 186:

```
186        result = stat (fileName, &statBuf); /* Obtain file status */
```

It examines the mode of the file using the S_ISDIR, S_ISREG, S_ISCHR, and S_ISBLK macros, processing directory files and other files as follows:

- If the file is a directory file, it calls processDirectory () [204], which applies monitorFile () recursively to each of its directory entries.
- If the file is a regular file, character special file, or block special file, it calls updateStat () [238], which either adds or updates the file's status entry. If the status changes in any way, updateEntry () [315] is called to display the file's new status. The decoding of the time fields is performed by the localtime () and asctime () routines in printStat () [346].

Reading Directory Information: getdents ()

processDirectory () [204] opens a directory file for reading and then uses getdents () to obtain every entry in the directory, as follows:

System Call: int **getdents** (int *fd*, struct direct* *buf*, int *structSize*)

getdents () reads the directory file with descriptor *fd* from its current position and fills the structure pointed to by *buf* with the next entry. The structure **direct** is defined in ''/usr/include/sys/dir.h'', and contains the following fields:

NAME	MEANING
d_off	the offset of the next directory entry
d_fileno	the inode number
d_reclen	the length of the directory entry structure
d_namlen	the length of the filename
d_name	the name of the file

getdents () returns the length of the directory entry when successful, 0 when the last directory entry has already been read, and -1 in the case of an error.

---

processDirectory () is careful not to trace into the ''.'' and ''..'' directories, and uses lseek () to jump from one directory entry to the next. When the directory has been completely searched, it is closed.

Miscellaneous File Management System Calls

There now follows a brief description of the following miscellaneous file management system calls:

Name	Function
chown	changes a file's owner and/or group
chmod	changes a file's permission settings
dup	duplicates a file descriptor
dup2	similar to dup
fchown	works just like chown
fchmod	works just like chmod
fctnl	gives access to miscellaneous file characteristics
ftruncate	works just like truncate
ioctl	controls a device
link	creates a hard link
mknod	creates a special file
sync	schedules all file buffers to be flushed to disk
truncate	truncates a file

Changing A File's Owner And/Or Group: chown ( )/fchown ( )

chown ( ) and fchown ( ) change the owner and/or group of a file, and work like this:

System Call: int **chown** (char* *fileName*, int *ownerId*, int *groupId*)
              int **fchown** (int *fd*, int *ownerId*, int *groupId*)

chown ( ) causes the owner and group ids of *fileName* to be changed to *ownerId* and *groupId*, respectively. A value of -1 in a particular field means that its associated value should remain unchanged.

Only a super-user can change the ownership of a file, and a user may change the group only to another group that he/she is a member of. If *fileName* is a symbolic link, the owner and group of the link is changed instead of the file that the link is referencing.

fchown () is just like chown () except that it takes an open descriptor as an argument instead of a filename.

They both return -1 if unsuccessful, and 0 otherwise.

In the following example, I changed the group of the file "test.txt" from "music" to "cs," which has group id number 62. For more information about group ids and how to locate them, consult chapter 12.

```
$ cat chown.c                    ...list the file.
main ()

{
  int flag;
  flag = chown ("test.txt", -1, 62); /* Leave user id unchanged */
  if (flag == -1) perror("chown.c");
}
$ ls -lg test.txt                ...examine file before.
-rw-r--r--  1 glass      music       3 May 25 11:42 test.txt
$ chown.exe                      ...run program.
$ ls -lg test.txt                ...examine file after.
-rw-r--r--  1 glass      cs          3 May 25 11:42 test.txt
$ _
```

Changing A File's Permissions: chmod ( )/fchmod ( )

chmod () and fchmod () change a file's permission flags, and work like this:

System Call: int **chmod** (char* *fileName*, int *mode*)
int **fchmod** (int *fd*, int *mode*);

chmod () changes the mode of *fileName* to *mode*, where *mode* is usually supplied as an octal number as described in chapter 2. The set-user-id and set-group-id flags have the octal values 4000 and 2000, respectively. To change a file's mode, you must either own it or be a super-user.

fchmod () works just like chmod () except that it takes an open file descriptor as an argument instead of a filename.

They both return -1 if unsuccessful, and 0 otherwise.

In the following example, I changed the permission flags of the file "test.txt" to 600 octal, which corresponds to read and write permission for the owner only:

```
$ cat chmod.c                    ...list the file.
main ()

{
  int flag;
  flag = chmod ("test.txt", 0600); /* Use an octal encoding */
  if (flag == -1) perror ("chmod.c");
}
$ ls -l test.txt                 ...examine file before.
-rw-r--r--  1 glass       3 May 25 11:42 test.txt
$ chmod.exe                      ...run the program.
$ ls -l test.txt                 ...examine file after.
-rw-------  1 glass       3 May 25 11:42 test.txt
$ _
```

Duplicating A File Descriptor: dup ( )/dup2 ( )

dup ( ) and dup2 ( ) allow you to duplicate file descriptors, and work like this:

System Call: int **dup** (int *oldFd*)
                int **dup2** (int *oldFd*, int *newFd*)

dup ( ) finds the smallest free file descriptor entry and points it to the same file as *oldFd*. dup2 ( ) closes *newFd* if it's currently active and then points it to the same file as *oldFd*. In both cases, the original and copied file descriptors share the same file pointer and access mode.

They both return the index of the new file descriptor if successful, and -1 otherwise.

The shells use dup2 ( ) to perform redirection and piping. For examples that show how this is done, read the "Process Management" section of this chapter and study the Internet shell at the end of this chapter.

In the following example, I created a file called "test.txt" and wrote to it via four different file descriptors:

- The first file descriptor was the original descriptor.
- The second descriptor was a copy of the first, allocated in slot 4.
- The third descriptor was a copy of the first, allocated in slot 0 that was freed by the close (0) statement (the standard input channel).
- The fourth descriptor was a copy of descriptor 3, copied over the existing descriptor in slot 2 (the standard error channel).

```
$ cat dup.c                          ...list the file.
#include <stdio.h>
#include <sys/file.h>


main ()

{
  int fd1, fd2, fd3;

  fd1 = open ("test.txt", O_RDWR | O_TRUNC);
  printf ("fd1 = %d\n", fd1);
  write (fd1, "what's", 6);

  fd2 = dup (fd1); /* Make a copy of fd1 */
  printf ("fd2 = %d\n", fd2);
  write (fd2, " up", 3);

  close (0); /* Close standard input */
  fd3 = dup (fd1); /* Make another copy of fd1 */
  printf ("fd3 = %d\n", fd3);
  write (0, " doc", 4);

  dup2 (3, 2); /* Duplicate channel 3 to channel 2 */
  write (2, "?\n", 2);
}
$ dup.exe                    ...run the program.
fd1 = 3
fd2 = 4
fd3 = 0
$ cat test.txt               ...list the output file.
what's up doc?
$ _
```

File Descriptor Operations: fcntl ()

fcntl () directly controls the settings of the flags associated with a file descriptor, and works as follows:

System Call: int **fcntl** (int *fd*, int *cmd*, int *arg*)

fcntl () performs the operation encoded by *cmd* on the file associated with the file descriptor *fd*. *arg* is an optional argument for *cmd*. Here are the most common values of *cmd*:

VALUE	OPERATION
F_SETFD	Set the close-on-exec flag to the lowest bit of *arg* (0 or 1).
F_GETFD	Return a number whose lowest bit is 1 if the close-on-exec flag is set, and 0 otherwise.
F_GETFL	Return a number corresponding to the current descriptor status flags.
F_SETFL	Set the current descriptor status flags to *arg*. The legal values of the flags are usually stored in the file ''/usr/include/sys/fcntlcom.h''
F_GETOWN	Return the process id or process group that is currently set to receive SIGIO/SIGURG signals. If the returned value is positive, it refers to a process id. If it's negative, its absolute value refers to a process group.
F_SETOWN	Set the process id or process group that should receive SIGIO/SIGURG signals to *arg*. The encoding scheme is as described for F_GETOWN.

fcntl () returns -1 if unsuccessful.

In the following example, I opened an existing file for writing and overwrote the initial few letters with the phrase ''hi there.'' I then used fcntl () to set the file descriptor's APPEND flag, which instructed it to append all further writes. This caused ''guys'' to be placed at the end of the file, even though I moved the file position pointer back to the start with lseek ():

```
$ cat fcntl.c                      ...list the program.
#include <sys/file.h>

main ()

{
  int fd;

  fd = open ("test.txt", O_WRONLY); /* Open file for writing */
  write (fd, "hi there\n", 9);
  lseek (fd, 0, L_SET); /* Seek to beginning of file */
  fcntl (fd, F_SETFL, O_WRONLY | O_APPEND); /* Set APPEND flag */
  write (fd, " guys\n", 6);
  close (fd);
}
```

```
$ cat test.txt                     ...list the original file.
here are the contents of
the original file.
$ fcntl.exe                        ...run the program.
$ cat test.txt                     ...list the new contents.
hi there
the contents of
the original file.
 guys                              ...note that "guys" is at the end.
$ _
```

Controlling Devices: ioctl ( )

> *System Call:* int **ioctl** (int *fd*, int *cmd*, int *arg*)
>
> ioctl ( ) performs the operation encoded by *cmd* on the file associated with the file descriptor *fd*. *arg* is an optional argument for *cmd*. The valid values of *cmd* depend on the device that *fd* refers to, and are typically documented in the manufacturer's operating instructions. I therefore supply no examples for this system call.
> ioctl ( ) returns -1 if unsuccessful.

Creating Hard Links: link ( )

link ( ) creates a hard link to an existing file, and works as follows:

> *System Call:* int **link** (char* *oldPath*, char* *newPath*)
>
> link ( ) creates a new label *newPath* and links it to the same file as the label *oldPath*. The hard link count of the associated file is incremented by one. If *oldPath* and *newPath* reside on different physical devices, a hard link may not be made and link ( ) fails. Only a super-user may form a link to a directory. For more information about hard links, consult the description of **ln** in chapter 7.
> link ( ) returns -1 if unsuccessful, and 0 otherwise.

In the following example, I created the filename "another.txt" and linked it to the file referenced by the existing name "original.txt". I then demonstrated that both labels were linked to the same file.

```
$ cat link.c                         ...list the program.
main ()


{
  link ("original.txt", "another.txt");
}
$ cat original.txt                   ...list original file.
this is a file.
$ ls -l original.txt another.txt     ...examine files before.
another.txt not found
-rw-r--r--  1 glass           16 May 25 12:18 original.txt
$ link.exe                           ...run the program.
$ ls -l original.txt another.txt     ...examine files after.
-rw-r--r--  2 glass           16 May 25 12:18 another.txt
-rw-r--r--  2 glass           16 May 25 12:18 original.txt
$ cat >> another.txt                 ...alter "another.txt".
 hi
^D
$ ls -l original.txt another.txt     ...both labels reflect the change.
-rw-r--r--  2 glass           20 May 25 12:19 another.txt
-rw-r--r--  2 glass           20 May 25 12:19 original.txt
$ rm original.txt                    ...remove original label.
$ ls -l original.txt another.txt     ...examine labels.
original.txt not found
-rw-r--r--  1 glass           20 May 25 12:19 another.txt
$ cat another.txt                    ...list contents via other label.
this is a file.
 hi
$ _
```

Creating Special Files: mknod ()

mknod () allows you to create a special file, and works like this:

System Call: int **mknod** (char* *fileName*, int *type*, int *device*)

mknod () creates a new regular, directory, or special file called *fileName* whose *type* can be one of the following:

VALUE	MEANING
S_IFDIR	directory
S_IFCHR	character-oriented file
S_IFBLK	block-oriented file
S_IFREG	regular file
S_IFIFO	named pipe

If the file is a character- or block-oriented file, then the low-order byte of *device* should specify the minor device number, and the high-order byte should specify the major device number. In other cases, the value of *device* is ignored. For more information on special files, consult chapter 11.

Only a super-user can use mknod () to create directories, character-oriented files, or block-oriented special files. If you're not a super-user and you wish to create a directory, use the standard library routine system () to call the **mkdir** utility.

mknod () returns -1 if unsuccessful, and 0 otherwise.

For an example of mknod (), consult the section on named pipes later in this chapter.

Flushing The File System Buffer: sync ()

sync () flushes the file system buffers, and works as follows:

System Call: int **sync** ()

sync () schedules all of the file system buffers to be written to disk. For more information on the buffer system, consult chapter 11. sync () should be performed by any programs that bypass the file system buffers and examine the raw file system.

sync () always succeeds.

Truncating A File: truncate ( )/ftruncate ( )

truncate () and ftruncate () set the length of a file, and work like this:

System Call: int **truncate** (char* *fileName*, long *length*)
            int **ftruncate** (int *fd*, long *length*)

truncate () sets the length of the file *fileName* to be *length* bytes. If the file is longer than *length*, it is truncated. If it is shorter than *length*, it is padded with ASCII nulls.

ftruncate () works just like truncate () except that it takes an open file descriptor as an argument instead of a filename.

They both return -1 if unsuccessful, and 0 otherwise.

In the following example, I set the length of two files to 10 bytes; one of the files was originally shorter than that, and the other was longer:

```
$ cat truncate.c                    ...list the program.
main ()

{
  truncate ("file1.txt", 10);
  truncate ("file2.txt", 10);
}
$ cat file1.txt                     ...list "file1.txt".
short
$ cat file2.txt                     ...list "file2.txt".
long file with lots of letters

$ ls -l file*.txt                   ...examine both files.
-rw-r--r--  1 glass           6 May 25 12:16 file1.txt
-rw-r--r--  1 glass          32 May 25 12:17 file2.txt
$ truncate.exe                      ...run the program.
$ ls -l file*.txt                   ...examine both files again.
-rw-r--r--  1 glass          10 May 25 12:16 file1.txt
-rw-r--r--  1 glass          10 May 25 12:17 file2.txt
$ cat file1.txt                     ..."file1.txt" is longer.
short
$ cat file2.txt                     ..."file2.txt" is shorter.
long file $ _
```

PROCESS MANAGEMENT

Every process in a UNIX system has the following attributes:

- some code
- some data
- a stack
- a unique process id number (PID)

When UNIX is first started, there's only one visible process in the system. This process is called "init," and is PID 1. The only way to create a new process in UNIX is to duplicate an existing process, so "init" is the ancestor of all subsequent processes. When a process duplicates, the parent and child processes are identical in every way except their PIDs; the child's code, data, and stack are a copy of the parent's, and they even continue to execute the same code. A child process may, however, replace its code with that of another executable file, thereby differentiating itself from its parent. For example, when "init" starts executing, it quickly duplicates several times. Each of the duplicate child processes then replaces its code from the executable file called "getty," which is responsible for handling user logins. The process hierarchy therefore looks like this:

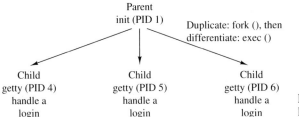

Figure 10.5 The initial process hierarchy

When a child process terminates, its death is communicated to its parent so that the parent may take some appropriate action.

It's very common for a parent process to suspend until one of its children terminates. For example, when a shell executes a utility in the foreground, it duplicates into two shell processes; the child shell process replaces its code with that of the utility, whereas the parent shell waits for the child process to terminate. When the child terminates, the original parent process awakens and presents the user with the next shell prompt.

Here's an illustration of the way that a shell executes a utility; I've indicated the system calls that are responsible for each phase of the execution:

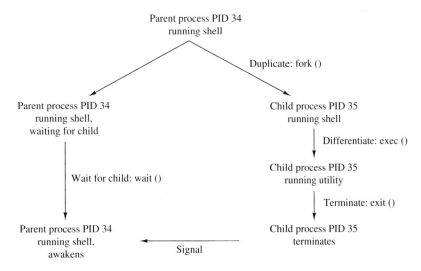

Figure 10.6 How a shell runs a utility

The Internet shell that I present later in this chapter has the basic process management facilities of the classic UNIX shells, and is a good place to look for some in-depth coding examples that utilize process-oriented system calls. In the meantime, let's look at some simple programs that introduce the system calls one by one. The next few subsections describe the following system calls:

Name	Function
fork	duplicates a process
getpid	obtains a process's id number
getppid	obtains a parent process's id number
exit	terminates a process
wait	waits for a child process
exec..	replaces the code, data, and stack of a process

Creating A New Process: fork ( )

A process may duplicate itself by using fork ( ), which works like this:

System Call: int **fork** ( )

fork ( ) causes a process to duplicate. The child process is an almost-exact duplicate of the original parent process; it inherits a copy of its parent's code, data, stack, open file descriptors, and signal table. However, the parent and child have different process id numbers and parent process id numbers.

   If fork ( ) succeeds, it returns the PID of the child to the parent process, and returns 0 to the child process. If it fails, it returns -1 to the parent process and no child is created.

---

fork ( ) is a strange system call, because one process (the original) calls it, but two processes (the original and its child) return from it. Both processes continue to run the same code concurrently, but have completely separate stack and data spaces.

   It reminds me of a great sci-fi story I read once, about a man who comes across a fascinating booth at a circus. The vendor at the booth tells the man that the booth is a matter-replicator; anyone who walks through the booth is duplicated. The original person walks out of the booth unharmed, but the duplicate person walks out onto the surface of Mars as a slave of the Martian construction crews. The vendor then tells the man that he'll be given a million dollars if he allows himself to be replicated, and he agrees. He happily walks through the machine, looking forward to collecting the million dollars... and walks out onto the surface of Mars. Meanwhile, back on Earth, his duplicate is walking off with a stash of cash. The question is this: If you came across the booth, what would you do?

A process may obtain its own process id and parent process id numbers by using the getpid () and getppid () system calls, respectively. Here's a synopsis of these system calls:

System Call: int **getpid** ()
            int **getppid** ()

getpid () and getppid () return a process's id and parent process's id numbers, respectively. They always succeed. The parent process id number of PID 1 is 1.

To illustrate the operation of fork (), here's a small program that duplicates and then branches based on the return value of fork ():

```
$ cat fork.c                      ...list the program.
#include <stdio.h>

main ()

{
  int pid;
  printf ("I'm the original process with PID %d and PPID %d.\n",
          getpid (), getppid ());
  pid = fork (); /* Duplicate. Child and parent continue from here */
  if (pid != 0) /* pid is non-zero, so I must be the parent */
     {
       printf ("I'm the parent process with PID %d and PPID %d.\n",
               getpid (), getppid ());
       printf ("My child's PID is %d\n", pid);
     }
  else /* pid is zero, so I must be the child */
     {
       printf ("I'm the child process with PID %d and PPID %d.\n",
               getpid (), getppid ());
     }
  printf ("PID %d terminates.\n"); /* Both processes execute this */
}
```

```
$ fork.exe                    ...run the program.
I'm the original process with PID 13292 and PPID 13273.
I'm the parent process with PID 13292 and PPID 13273.
My child's PID is 13293.
I'm the child process with PID 13293 and PPID 13292.
PID 13293 terminates.        ...child terminates.
PID 13292 terminates.        ...parent terminates.
$ _
```

The PPID of the parent refers to the PID of the shell that executed the "fork.exe" program.

WARNING: As you will soon see, it is dangerous for a parent to terminate without waiting for the death of its child. The only reason that the parent doesn't wait for its child in this example is because I haven't yet described the wait () system call!

Orphan Processes

If a parent dies before its child, the child is automatically adopted by the original "init" process, PID 1. To illustrate this, I modified the previous program by inserting a sleep statement into the child's code. This ensured that the parent process terminated before the child.

Here's the program and the resultant output:

```
$ cat orphan.c                    ...list the program.
#include <stdio.h>

main ()

{
  int pid;

  printf ("I'm the original process with PID %d and PPID %d.\n",
          getpid (), getppid ());
  pid = fork (); /* Duplicate. Child and parent continue from here */
  if (pid != 0) /* Branch based on return value from fork () */
    {
      /* pid is non-zero, so I must be the parent */
      printf ("I'm the parent process with PID %d and PPID %d.\n",
              getpid (), getppid ());
      printf ("My child's PID is %d\n", pid);
    }
  else
    {
      /* pid is zero, so I must be the child */
```

```
     sleep (5); /* Make sure that the parent terminates first */
     printf ("I'm the child process with PID %d and PPID %d.\n",
             getpid (), getppid ());
  }

  printf ("PID %d terminates.\n"); /* Both processes execute this */
}
$ orphan.exe                    ...run the program.
I'm the original process with PID 13364 and PPID 13346.
I'm the parent process with PID 13364 and PPID 13346.
PID 13364 terminates.
I'm the child process with PID 13365 and PPID 1.            ...orphaned!
PID 13365 terminates.
$ _
```

Here's an illustration of the orphaning effect:

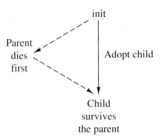

Figure 10.7   Adoption

Terminating A Process: exit ( )

A process may terminate at any time by executing exit ( ), which works as follows:

System Call: int **exit** (int *status*)

exit ( ) closes all of a process's file descriptors, deallocates its code, data, and stack, and then terminates the process. When a child process terminates, it sends its parent a SIGCHLD signal and waits for its termination code *status* to be accepted. A process that is waiting for its parent to accept its return code is called a *zombie* process. A parent accepts a child's termination code by executing wait ( ), which is described shortly.

The kernel ensures that all of a terminating process's children are orphaned and adopted by "init" by setting their PPID to 1. The "init" process always accepts its children's termination codes.

exit ( ) never returns.

The termination code of a child process may be used for a variety of purposes by the parent process. Shells may access the termination code of their last child process via one of their special variables. For example, the C shell stores the termination code of the last command in the variable $status:

```
% cat exit.c                 ...list the program.
#include <stdio.h>

main ()

{
  printf ("I'm going to exit with return code 42\n");
  exit (42);
}

% exit.exe                   ...run the program.
I'm going to exit with return code 42
% echo $status               ...display the termination code.
42
% _
```

Zombie Processes

A process that terminates cannot leave the system until its parent accepts its return code. If its parent process is already dead, it'll already have been adopted by the "init" process, which always accepts its children's return codes. However, if a process's parent is alive but never executes a wait (), the process's return code will never be accepted and the process will remain a zombie. A zombie process doesn't have any code, data, or stack, so it doesn't use up many system resources, but it does continue to inhabit the system's fixed-size process table. Too many zombie processes can require the system administrator to intervene; see chapter 12 for more details.

The following program created a zombie process, which was indicated in the output from the **ps** utility. When I killed the parent process, the child was adopted by "init" and allowed to rest in peace.

```
$ cat zombie.c               ...list the program.
#include <stdio.h>

main ()

{
  int pid;

  pid = fork (); /* Duplicate */
```

```
if (pid != 0) /* Branch based on return value from fork () */
  {
    while (1)  /* Never terminate, and never execute a wait () */
      sleep (1000);
  }
else
  {
    exit (42); /* Exit with a silly number */
  }
}
$ zombie.exe &                    ...execute the program in the background.
[1] 13545
$ ps                              ...obtain process status.
  PID TT STAT   TIME COMMAND
13535 p2 S     0:00 -ksh (ksh)...the shell.
13545 p2 S     0:00 zombie.exe...the parent process.
13546 p2 Z     0:00 <defunct> ...the zombie child process.
13547 p2 R     0:00 ps
$ kill 13545                      ...kill the parent process.
[1]     Terminated          zombie.exe
$ ps                              ...notice the zombie is gone now.
  PID TT STAT   TIME COMMAND
13535 p2 S     0:00 -csh (csh)
13548 p2 R     0:00 ps
$ _
```

Waiting For A Child: wait ()

A parent process may wait for one of its children to terminate and then accept its child's termination code by executing wait ():

System Call: int **wait** (int* *status*)

wait () causes a process to suspend until one of its children terminates. A successful call to wait () returns the pid of the child that terminated and places a status code into *status* that is encoded as follows:

- If the rightmost byte of status is zero, the leftmost byte contains the low eight bits of the value returned by the child's exit ()/return ().
- If the rightmost byte is non-zero, the rightmost seven bits are equal to the number of the signal that caused the child to terminate, and the remaining bit of the rightmost byte is set to 1 if the child produced a core dump.

> If a process executes a wait () and has no children, wait () returns immediately with -1. If a process executes a wait () and one or more of its children are already zombies, wait () returns immediately with the status of one of the zombies.

In the following example, the child process terminated before the end of the program by executing an exit () with return code 42. Meanwhile, the parent process executed a wait () and suspended until it received its child's termination code. At this point, the parent displayed information about its child's demise and executed the rest of the program:

```
$ cat wait.c                           ...list the program.
#include <stdio.h>

main ()

{
  int pid, status, childPid;

  printf ("I'm the parent process and my PID is %d\n", getpid ());
  pid = fork (); /* Duplicate */
  if (pid != 0) /* Branch based on return value from fork () */
    {
      printf ("I'm the parent process with PID %d and PPID %d\n",
              getpid (), getppid ());
      childPid = wait (&status); /* Wait for a child to terminate. */
      printf ("A child with PID %d terminated with exit code %d\n",
              childPid, status >> 8);
    }
  else
    {
      printf ("I'm the child process with PID %d and PPID %d\n",
              getpid (), getppid ());
      exit (42); /* Exit with a silly number */
    }

  printf ("PID %d terminates\n");
}
$ wait.exe                      ...run the program.
I'm the parent process and my PID is 13464
I'm the child process with PID 13465 and PPID 13464
I'm the parent process with PID 13464 and PPID 13409
A child with PID 13465 terminated with exit code 42
PID 13465 terminates
$ _
```

seteuid () (setegid ()) sets the calling process's effective user (group) id.
setruid () (setrgid ()) set the calling process's real user (group) id. setuid ()
(setgid ()) sets the calling process's effective and real user (group) ids to the
specified value.

These calls succeed only if executed by a super-user, or if *id* is the real
or effective user (group) id of the calling process. They return 0 if successful; otherwise, they return -1.

Sample Program: Background Processing

Here's a sample program that makes use of fork () and exec () to execute a
program in the background. The original process creates a child to "exec" the
specified executable and then terminates. The orphaned child is automatically
adopted by "init." Notice how I craftily passed the argument list from main () to
execvp () by passing &argv[1] as the second argument to execvp (). Note also
that I used execvp () instead of execv () so that the program could use $PATH to
find the executable file:

```
$ cat background.c            ...list the program.
#include <stdio.h>

main (argc, argv)

int argc;
char* argv [];

  {
   if (fork () == 0) /* Child */
     {
       execvp (argv[1], &argv[1]); /* Execute other program */
       fprintf (stderr, "Could not execute %s\n", argv[1]);
     }
  }
$ background.exe cc wait.c     ...run the program.
$ ps                          ...confirm that "cc" is in
background.
  PID TT STAT   TIME COMMAND
13664 p0 S      0:00 -csh (csh)
13716 p0 R      0:00 ps
13717 p0 D      0:00 cc wait.c
$ _
```

Sample Program: Disk Usage

The next programming example uses a novel technique for counting the number of
non-directory files in a hierarchy. When the program is started, its first argument
must be the name of the directory to search. It searches through each entry in the
directory, spawning off a new process for each entry. Each child process either
exits with 1 if its associated file is a non-directory file, or repeats the process,
summing up the exit codes of its children and exiting with the total count. This
technique is interesting but silly. Not only does it create a large number of processes, which is not particularly efficient, but since it uses the termination code to
return the file count, it's limited to an 8-bit total count.

```
$ cat count.c                        ...list the program.
#include <stdio.h>
#include <sys/file.h>
#include <sys/dir.h>
#include <sys/stat.h>

long processFile ();
long processDirectory ();

main (argc, argv)

int argc;
char* argv []

{
  long count;

  count = processFile (argv[1]);
  printf ("Total number of non-directory files is %ld\n", count);
  return (/* EXIT_SUCCESS */ 0);
}


long processFile (name)

char* name;

{
  struct stat statBuf; /* To hold the return data from stat () */
  mode_t mode;
  int result;

  result = stat (name, &statBuf); /* Stat the specified file */
  if (result == -1) return (0); /* Error */
```

```
    mode = statBuf.st_mode; /* Look at the file's mode */
    if (S_ISDIR (mode)) /* Directory */
      return (processDirectory (name));
    else
      return (1); /* A non-directory file was processed */
}


long processDirectory (dirName)

char* dirName;

{
    int fd, children, i, charsRead, childPid, status;
    long count, totalCount;
    char fileName [100];
    struct direct dirEntry;

    fd = open (dirName, O_RDONLY); /* Open directory for reading */
    children = 0; /* Initialize child process count */

    while (1) /* Scan directory */
      {
        charsRead = getdents (fd, &dirEntry, sizeof (struct direct));
        if (charsRead == 0) break; /* End of directory */
        if (strcmp (dirEntry.d_name, ".") != 0 &&
            strcmp (dirEntry.d_name, "..") != 0)
          {
            if (fork () == 0) /* Create a child to process dir. entry */
              {
                sprintf (fileName, "%s/%s", dirName, dirEntry.d_name);
                count = processFile (fileName);
                exit (count);
              }
            else
              ++children; /* Increment count of child processes */
          }
        lseek (fd, dirEntry.d_off, L_SET); /* Jump to next dir.entry */
      }
    close (fd); /* Close directory */
    totalCount = 0; /* Initialize file count */
    for (i = 1; i <= children; i++) /* Wait for children to terminate */
      {
        childPid = wait (&status); /* Accept child's termination code */
        totalCount += (status >> 8); /* Update file count */
      }

    return (totalCount); /* Return number of files in directory */
}
```

```
$ ls -F                   ...list current directory.
a.out*            disk.c            fork       tmp/        zombie.exe*
background        exec.c            fork.c     wait.c
background.c      exit.c            orphan.c   wait.exe*
count*            exit.exe*         orphan.exe* zombie.c
$ ls tmp                  ...list only subdirectory.
a.out*            disk.c            exit.c            orphan.c
background.c      exec.c            fork.c            wait.c
zombie.c
$ count .                 ...count regular files from ".".
Total number of non-directory files is 25
$ _
```

Redirection

When a process forks, the child inherits a copy of its parent's file descriptors. When a process execs, all non-close-on-exec file descriptors remain unaffected, including the standard input, output, and error channels. The UNIX shells use these two pieces of information to implement redirection. For example, say you type the following command at a terminal:

```
ls > ls.out
```

To perform the redirection, the shell performs the following series of actions:

- The parent shell forks and then waits for the child shell to terminate.
- The child shell opens the file "ls.out," creating it or truncating it as necessary.
- The child shell then duplicates the file descriptor of "ls.out" to the standard output file descriptor, number 1, and then closes the original descriptor of "ls.out". All standard output is therefore redirected to "ls.out".
- The child shell then exec's the **ls** utility. Since the file descriptors are inherited during an exec ( ), all of the standard output of **ls** goes to "ls.out".
- When the child shell terminates, the parent resumes. The parent's file descriptors are unaffected by the child's actions, as each process maintains its own private descriptor table.

To redirect the standard error channel in addition to standard output, the shell would simply have to duplicate the "ls.out" descriptor twice; once to descriptor 1 and once to descriptor 2.

Here's a small program that does approximately the same kind of redirection as a UNIX shell. When invoked with the name of a file as the first parameter and a command sequence as the remaining parameters, the program "redirect.exe" redirects the standard output of the command to the named file.

```
$ cat redirect.c                ...list the program.
#include <stdio.h>
#include <sys/file.h>


main (argc, argv)

int argc;
char* argv [];

{
  int fd;

  /* Open file for redirection */
  fd = open (argv[1], O_CREAT | O_TRUNC | O_WRONLY, 0600);
  dup2 (fd, 1); /* Duplicate descriptor to standard output */
  close (fd); /* Close original descriptor to save descriptor space */
  execvp (argv[2], &argv[2]); /* Invoke program; will inherit stdout */
  perror ("main"); /* Should never execute */
}
$ redirect.exe ls.out ls -l    ...redirect "ls -l" to "ls.out".
$ cat ls.out                   ...list the output file.
total 5
-rw-r-xr-x    1 gglass          0 Feb 15 10:35 ls.out
-rw-r-xr-x    1 gglass        449 Feb 15 10:35 redirect.c
-rwxr-xr-x    1 gglass       3697 Feb 15 10:33 redirect.exe
$ _
```

The Internet shell described at the end of this chapter has better redirection facilities than the standard UNIX shells; it can redirect output to another Internet shell on a remote host.

SIGNALS

Programs must sometimes deal with unexpected or unpredictable events, such as:

- a floating point error
- a power failure
- an alarm clock "ring" (discussed soon)
- the death of a child process
- a termination request from a user (i.e., a *Control-C*)
- a suspend request from a user (i.e., a *Control-Z*)

These kind of events are sometimes called *interrupts*, as they must interrupt the regular flow of a program in order to be processed. When UNIX recognizes that such an event has occurred, it sends the corresponding process a *signal*. There is a unique, numbered signal for each possible event, ranging from 1 to 31 in BSD UNIX. For example, if a process causes a floating point error, the kernel sends the offending process signal number 8:

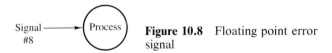

Figure 10.8   Floating point error signal

The kernel isn't the only one that can send a signal; any process can send any other process a signal, as long as it has permission. The rules regarding permissions are discussed shortly.

A programmer may arrange for a particular signal to be ignored or to be processed by a special piece of code called a *signal handler*. In the latter case, the process that receives the signal suspends its current flow of control, executes the signal handler, and then resumes the original flow of control when the signal handler finishes.

By learning about signals, you can "protect" your programs from *Control-C*, arrange for an alarm clock signal to terminate your program if it takes too long to perform a task, and learn how UNIX uses signals during everyday operations.

The Predefined Signals

There are 31 different signals defined in "/usr/include/signal.h". A programmer may choose for a particular signal to trigger a user-supplied signal handler, trigger the default kernel-suppied handler, or be ignored. The default handler usually performs one of the following actions:

- terminates the process and generates a core file (*dump*)
- terminates the process without generating a core image file (*quit*)
- ignores and discards the signal (*ignore*)
- suspends the process (*suspend*)
- resumes the process

Following is a list of all the predefined signals, together with their macro definition, numeric value, default action, and a brief description.

A List Of Signals

Here's a list of the BSD prefined signals:

Macro	#	Default	Description
SIGHUP	1	quit	hangup
SIGINT	2	quit	interrupt
SIGQUIT	3	dump	quit
SIGILL	4	dump	illegal instruction
SIGTRAP	5	dump	trace trap (used by debuggers)
SIGIOT	6	dump	I/O trap instruction
SIGEMT	7	dump	emulator trap instruction
SIGFPE	8	dump	floating point exception
SIGKILL	9	quit	kill (cannot be caught, blocked, or ignored)
SIGBUS	10	dump	bus error (bad format address)
SIGSEGV	11	dump	segmentation violation (out of range address)
SIGSYS	12	dump	bad argument to system call
SIGPIPE	13	quit	write on a pipe or other socket with no one to read it
SIGALRM	14	quit	alarm clock
SIGTERM	15	quit	software termination signal (default signal sent by kill)
SIGURG	16	ignore	urgent condition present on socket
SIGSTOP	17	suspend	stop (can't catch, block, or ignored)
SIGTSTP	18	suspend	stop signal generated from keyboard
SIGCONT	19	ignore	continue after stop
SIGCHLD	20	ignore	child status has changed
SIGTTIN	21	suspend	background read attempted from control terminal
SIGTTOU	22	suspend	background write attempted to control terminal
SIGIO	23	ignore	I/O is possible on a descriptor

Macro	#	Default	Description
SIGXCPU	24	quit	CPU time limit exceeded
SIGXFSZ	25	quit	file size limit exceeded
SIGVTALRM	26	quit	virtual time alarm
SIGPROF	27	quit	profiling timer alarm
SIGWINCH	28	ignore	window size change
SIGLOST	29	quit	resource lost
SIGUSR1	30	quit	user-defined signal 1
SIGUSR2	31	quit	user-defined signal 2

Terminal Signals

The easiest way to send a signal to a foreground process is by pressing *Control-C* or *Control-Z* from the keyboard. When the terminal driver (the piece of software that supports the terminal) recognizes a *Control-C*, it sends a SIGINT signal to all of the processes in the current foreground job. Similarly, *Control-Z* causes it to send a SIGTSTP signal to all of the processes in the current foreground job. By default, SIGINT terminates a process and SIGTSTP suspends a process. Later on in this section, I'll show you how to perform similar actions from a C program.

Requesting An Alarm Signal: alarm ()

One of the simplest ways to see a signal in action is to arrange for a process to receive an alarm clock signal, SIGALRM, by using alarm (). The default handler for this signal displays the message "Alarm clock" and terminates the process. Here's how alarm () works:

Library Routine: unsigned int **alarm** (unsigned int *count*)

alarm () instructs the kernel to send the SIGALRM signal to the calling process after *count* seconds. If an alarm had already been scheduled, it is overwritten. If *count* is 0, any pending alarm requests are cancelled.

  alarm () returns the number of seconds that remain until the alarm signal is sent.

Here's a small program that uses alarm (), together with its output:

```
$ cat alarm.c                  ...list the program.
#include <stdio.h>


main ()

{
  alarm (3); /* Schedule an alarm signal in three seconds */
  printf ("Looping forever...\n");
  while (1);
  printf ("This line should never be executed\n");
}
$ alarm.exe                    ...run the program.
Looping forever...
Alarm clock                    ...occurs three seconds later.
$ _
```

The next section shows you how you override a default signal handler and make your program respond specially to a particular signal.

Handling Signals: signal ( )

The last example program reacted to the alarm signal SIGALRM in the default manner. The signal ( ) system call may be used to override the default action, and works as follows:

System Call: void (***signal** (int *sigCode*, void (**func*)( ))) ( )

signal ( ) allows a process to specify the action that it will take when a particular signal is received. The parameter *sigCode* specifies the number of the signal that is to be reprogrammed, and *func* may be one of several values:

- SIG_IGN, which indicates that the specified signal should be ignored and discarded.
- SIG_DFL, which indicates that the kernel's default handler should be used.
- an address of a user-defined function, which indicates that the function should be executed when the specified signal arrives.

The valid signal numbers are stored in "/usr/include/signal.h". The signals SIGKILL and SIGSTP may not be reprogrammed. A child process inherits the signal settings from its parent during a fork (). When a process performs an exec (), previously ignored signals remain ignored but installed handlers are set back to the default handler.

With the exception of SIGCHLD, signals are not stacked. This means that if a process is sleeping and three identical signals are sent to it, only one of the signals is actually processed.

signal () returns the previous *func* value associated with *sigCode* if successful; otherwise it returns -1.

I made a couple of changes to the previous program so that it caught and processed the SIGALRM signal efficiently:

- I installed my own signal handler, alarmHandler (), by using signal ().
- I made the while loop less draining on the timesharing system by making use of a system call called pause (). The old version of the while loop had an empty code body which caused it to loop very fast and soak up CPU resources. The new version of the while loop suspends each time through the loop until a signal is received.

Before I show you the updated program, here's a description of pause ():

System Call: int **pause** ()

pause () suspends the calling process and returns when the calling process receives a signal. It is most often used to wait efficiently for an alarm signal. pause () doesn't return anything useful.

Here's the updated version:

```
$ cat handler.c                    ...list the program.
#include <stdio.h>
#include <signal.h>

int alarmFlag = 0; /* Global alarm flag */
alarmHandler (); /* Forward declaration of alarm handler */

/*******************************************************************/

main ()

{
  signal (SIGALRM, alarmHandler); /* Install signal handler */
  alarm (3); /* Schedule an alarm signal in three seconds */
  printf ("Looping...\n");
  while (!alarmFlag) /* Loop until flag set */
```

```
  {
    pause (); /* Wait for a signal */
  }
  printf ("Loop ends due to alarm signal\n");
}

/**************************************************************/

alamrHandler ()

{
  printf ("An alarm clock signal was received\n");
  alarmFlag = 1;
}
$ handler.exe                        ...run the program.
Looping...
An alarm clock signal was received  ...occurs three seconds later.
Loop ends due to alarm signal
$ _
```

Protecting Critical Code And Chaining Interrupt Handlers

The same techniques that I just described may be used to protect critical pieces of code against *Control-C* attacks and other such signals. In these cases, it's common to save the previous value of the handler so that it can be restored after the critical code has executed. Here's the source code of a program that protects itself against SIGINT signals:

```
$ cat critical.c                     ...list the program.
#include <stdio.h>
#include <signal.h>


main ()

{
    int (*oldHandler) (); /* To hold old handler value */

    printf ("I can be Control-C'ed\n");
    sleep (3);
    oldHandler = signal (SIGINT, SIG_IGN); /* Ignore Control-C */
    printf ("I'm protected from Control-C now\n");
    sleep (3);
    signal (SIGINT, oldHandler); /* Restore old handler */
    printf ("I can be Control-C'ed again\n");
    sleep (3);
    printf ("Bye!\n");
}
```

```
$ critical.exe                        ...run the program.
I can be Control-C'ed
^C                                    ...Control-C works here.
$ critical.exe                        ...run the program again.
I can be Control-C'ed
I'm protected from Control-C now
^C                                    ...Control-C is ignored.
I can be Control-C'ed again
Bye!
$ _
```

Sending Signals: kill ()

A process may send a signal to another process by using the kill () system call. kill () is a misnomer, since many of the signals that it can send do not terminate a process. It's called kill () because of historical reasons; the only use of signals when UNIX was first designed was to terminate processes. kill () works like this:

System Call: int **kill** (int *pid*, int *sigCode*)

kill () sends the signal with value *sigCode* to the process with PID *pid*. kill () succeeds and the signal is sent as long as at least one of the following conditions is satisfied:

- The sending process and the receiving process have the same owner.
- The sending process is owned by a super-user.

   There are a few variations on the way that kill () works:

- If *pid* is 0, the signal is sent to all of the processes in the sender's process group.
- If *pid* is -1 and the sender is owned by a super-user, the signal is sent to all processes, including the sender.
- If *pid* is -1 and the sender is not a super-user, the signal is sent to all of the processes owned by the same owner as the sender, excluding the sending process.
- If the *pid* is negative and not -1, the signal is sent to all of the processes in the process group whose id is the absolute value of *pid*.

   Process groups are discussed later in this chapter. If kill () manages to send at least one signal successfully, it returns 0; otherwise, it returns -1.

Death Of Children

When a parent's child terminates, the child process sends its parent a SIGCHLD signal. A parent process often installs a handler to deal with this signal, which typically executes a wait ( ) to accept the child's termination code and let the child de-zombify.[1]

Alternatively, the parent can choose to ignore SIGCHLD signals, in which case the child de-zombifies automatically. One of the socket programs that follows later in this chapter makes use of this feature.

The next example illustrates a SIGCHLD handler, and allows a user to limit the amount of time that a command takes to execute. The first parameter of "limit.exe" is the maximum number of seconds that is allowed for execution, and the remaining parameters are the command itself. The program works by performing the following steps:

1. The parent process installs a SIGCHLD handler that is executed when its child process terminates.
2. The parent process forks a child process to execute the command.
3. The parent process sleeps for the specified number of seconds. When it wakes up, it sends its child process a SIGINT signal to kill it.
4. If the child terminates before its parent finishes sleeping, the parent's SIGCHLD handler is executed, causing the parent to terminate immediately.

Here's the source code and sample output from the program:

```
$ cat limit.c                    ...list the program.
#include <stdio.h>
#include <signal.h>

int delay;
childHandler ();

/********************************************************************/

main (argc, argv)

int argc;
char* argv[];

  {
    int pid;
    signal (SIGCHLD, childHandler); /* Install death-of-child handler */
```

---

[1] This means that the child is completely laid to rest and is no longer a zombie.

```
  pid = fork (); /* Duplicate */
  if (pid == 0) /* Child */
    {
       execvp (argv[2[, &argv[2]); /* Execute command */
       perror ("limit"); /* Should never execute */
    }
  else /* Parent */
    {
       sscanf (argv[1], "%d", &delay); /* Read delay from command line */
       sleep (delay); /* Sleep for the specified number of seconds */
       printf ("Child %d exceeded limit and is being killed\n", pid);
       kill (pid, SIGINT); /* Kill the child */
    }
}


/****************************************************************************/

childHandler () /* Executed if the child dies before the parent */

{
  int childPid, childStatus;
  childPid = wait (&childStatus); /* Accept child's termination code */
  printf ("Child %d terminated within %d seconds\n", childPid, delay);
  exit (\* EXIT_SUCCESS */ 0);
}
$ limit.exe 5 ls                 ...run the program; command finishes OK.
a.out          alarm.exe     critical.exe   handler.exe    limit.exe
alarm.c        critical.c    handler.c      limit.c
Child 4030 terminated within 5 seconds
$ limit.exe 4 sleep 100          ...run it again; command takes too long.
Child 4032 exceeded limit and is being killed
$ _
```

Suspending And Resuming Processes

The SIGSTOP and SIGCONT signals suspend and resume a process, respectively. They are used by the UNIX shells to implement built-in commands like *stop*, *fg*, and *bg*.

In the following example, the main program created two children which both entered an infinite loop and displayed a message every second. The main program waited for three seconds and then suspended the first child. The second child continued to execute as usual. After another three seconds, the parent restarted the first child, waited a little while longer, and then terminated both children.

```
$ cat pulse.c            ...list the program.
#include <signal.h>
#include <stdio.h>
```

```
main ()

{
  int pid1;
  int pid2;

  pid1 = fork ();
  if (pid1 == 0) /* First child */
    {
      while (1) /* Infinite loop */
        {
          printf ("pid1 is alive\n");
          sleep (1);
        }
    }
  pid2 = fork (); /* Second child */
  if (pid2 == 0)
    {
      while (1) /* Infinite loop */
        {
          printf ("pid2 is alive\n");
          sleep (1);
        }
    }
  sleep (3);
  kill (pid1, SIGSTOP); /* Suspend first child */
  sleep (3);
  kill (pid1, SIGCONT); /* Resume first child */
  sleep (3);
  kill (pid1, SIGINT); /* Kill first child */
  kill (pid2, SIGINT); /* Kill second child */
}
```

```
$ pulse                    ...run the program.
pid1 is alive              ...both run in first three seconds.
pid2 is alive
pid1 is alive
pid2 is alive
pid1 is alive
pid2 is alive
pid2 is alive              ...just the second child runs now.
pid2 is alive
pid2 is alive
pid1 is alive              ...the first child is resumed.
pid2 is alive
pid1 is alive
pid2 is alive
pid1 is alive
pid2 is alive
$ _
```

Process Groups And Control Terminals

When you're in a shell and you execute a program that creates several children, a single *Control-C* from the keyboard will normally terminate the program and its children and then return you to the shell. In order to support this kind of behavior, UNIX introduced a few new concepts:

- In addition to having a unique process id number, every process is also a member of a *process group*. Several processes can be members of the same process group. When a process forks, the child inherits its process group from its parent. A process may change its process group to a new value by using setpgrp (). When a process execs, its process group remains the same.
- Every process can have an associated *control terminal*. When a process forks, the child inherits its control terminal from its parent. When a process execs, its control terminal stays the same.
- Every terminal can be associated with a single *control* process. When a metacharacter such as a *Control-C* is detected, the terminal sends the appropriate signal to all of the processes in the process group of its control process.
- If a process attempts to read from its control terminal and is not a member of the same process group as the terminal's control process, the process is sent a SIGTTIN signal, which normally suspends the process.

Here's how a shell uses these features:

- When an interactive shell begins, it is the control process of a terminal and has that terminal as its control terminal. How this occurs is beyond the scope of this book.
- When a shell executes a foreground process, the child shell places itself in a different process group before exec'ing the command, and takes control of the terminal. Any signals generated from the terminal thus go to the foreground command rather than the original parent shell. When the foreground command terminates, the original parent shell takes back control of the terminal.
- When a shell executes a background process, the child shell places itself in a different process group before exec'ing, but does not take control of the terminal. Any signals generated from the terminal continue to go to the shell. If the background process tries to read from its control terminal, it is suspended by a SIGTTIN signal.

The following diagram illustrates a typical setup. Assume that process 145 and process 230 are the process leaders of background jobs, and that process 171 is the process leader of the foreground job.

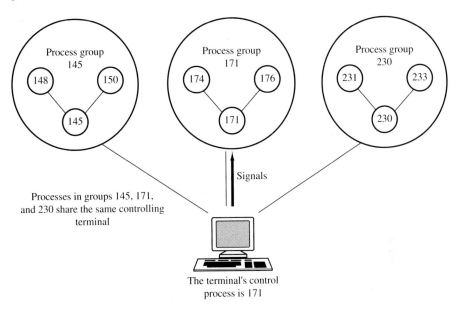

Processes in groups 145, 171,
and 230 share the same controlling
terminal

Signals

The terminal's control
process is 171

Figure 10.9   Control terminals and process groups

setpgrp () changes a process's group, and works as follows:

System Call: int **setpgrp** (int *pid*, int *pgrpId*)

setpgrp () sets the process group id of the process with PID *pid* to *pgrpId*. If *pid* is zero, the caller's process group id is set to *pgrpId*. In order for setpgrp () to succeed and set the process group id, at least one of the following conditions must be met:

- The caller and the specified process must have the same owner.
- The caller must be owned by a super-user.

When a process wants to start its own unique process group, it typically passes its own process id number as the second parameter to setpgrp ().
   If setpgrp () fails, it returns −1.

A process may find out its current process group id by using getpgrp (), which works like this:

System Call: int **getpgrp** (int *pid*)

getpgrp ( ) returns the process group id of the process with PID pid. If *pid* is
zero, the process group id of the caller is returned.

The following example illustrates the fact that a terminal distributes signals to all
of the processes in its control process's process group. Since the child inherited
its process group from its parent, both the parent and child caught the SIGINT
signal:

```
$ cat pgrp1.c                 ...list program.
#include <signal.h>
#include<stdio.h>

sigintHandler ();

main ()

{
   signal (SIGINT, sigintHandler); /* Handle Control-C */
   if (fork () == 0)
     printf ("Child PID %d PGRP %d waits\n", getpid (),getpgrp (0));
   else
     printf ("Parent PID %d PGRP %dwaits\n", getpid (), getpgrp (0));
   pause (); /* Wait for asignal */
}



sigintHandler ()

{
   printf ("Process %d got a SIGINT\n",getpid ());
}
$ pgrp1                    ...run the program.
Parent PID 24583 PGRP 24583 waits
Child PID 24584PGRP 24583 waits
^C                         ...press Control-C.
Process 24584 got a SIGINT
Process 24583 got a SIGINT
$ _
```

If a process places itself into a different process group, it is no longer associated
with the terminal's control process, and does not receive signals from the terminal. In the following example, the child process was not affected by a *Control-C*:

```
$ cat pgrp2.c                      ...list the program.
#include <signal.h>
#include <stdio.h>

sigintHandler ();

main()

{
  int i;

  signal (SIGINT, sigintHandler); /* Install signal handler */
  if (fork () == 0)
    setpgrp (0, getpid ()); /* Place child in its own process group */
  printf ("Process PID %dPGRP %d is waits\n", getpid (), getpgrp (0));
  for (i = 1; i <= 3; i++) /* Loop three times */
    {
      printf ("Process %d is alive\n", getpid ());
      sleep(1);
    }
}


sigintHandler ()

{
  printf ("Process %d got a SIGINT\n", getpid ());
  exit (1);
}
$ pgrp2                            ...run the program.
Process PID 24591 PGRP 24591 waits
Process PID 24592 PGRP 24592 waits
^C                                 ...Control-C
Process 24591 got a SIGINT    ...parent receives signal.
Process 24592 is alive        ...child carries on.
Process 24592 is alive
Process 24592 is alive
$ _
```

If a process attempts to read from its control terminal after it disassociates itself with the terminal's control process, it is sent a SIGTTIN signal, which suspends the receiver by default. In the following example, I trapped SIGTTIN with my own handler to make the effect a little clearer:

```
$ cat pgrp3.c                      ...list the program.
#include <signal.h>
#include <stdio.h>
```

```
#include <sys/termio.h>
#include <sys/file.h>

sigttinHandler ();

main ()

{
  int status;
  char str {100};

  if (fork () == 0) /* Child */
    {
      signal (SIGTTIN, sigttinHandler); /* Install handler */
      setpgrp (0, getpid ()); /* Place myself in a new process group */
      printf ("Enter a string: ");
      scanf ("%s", str); /* Try to read from control terminal */
      printf ("You entered %s\n", str);
    }
  else /* Parent */
    {
      wait (&status); /* Wait for child to terminate */
    }
}


sigttinHandler ()

{
  printf ("Attempted inappropriate read from control terminal\n");
  exit (1);
}
$ pgrp3                                  ...run the program.
Enter a string: Attempted inappropriate read from control terminal
$ _
```

PIPES

Pipes are an interprocess communication mechanism that allow two or more processes to send information to each other. They are commonly used from within shells to connect the standard output of one utility to the standard input of another. For example, here's a simple shell command that determines how many users there are on the system:

```
$ who | wc -l
```

The **who** utility generates one line of output per user. This output is then "piped" into the **wc** utility, which, when invoked with the **−1** option, outputs the total number of lines in its input. Thus, the pipelined command craftily calculates the total number of users by counting the number of lines that **who** generates. Here's a diagram of the pipeline:

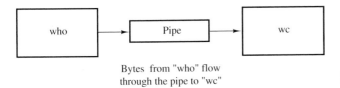

Bytes from "who" flow
through the pipe to "wc"   **Figure 10.10**   A simple pipe

It's important to realize that both the writer process and the reader process of a pipeline execute concurrently; a pipe automatically buffers the output of the writer and suspends the writer if the pipe gets too full. Similarly, if a pipe empties, the reader is suspended until some more output becomes available.

All versions of UNIX support *unnamed* pipes, which are the kind of pipes that shells use. System V also supports a more powerful kind of pipe called a *named pipe*. In this section, I'll show you how to program each kind of pipe, starting with unnamed pipes.

Unnamed Pipes: pipe ()

An unnamed pipe is a unidirectional communications link that automatically buffers its input up to a maximum of 4K (BSD) or 40K (System V), and may be created using the pipe () system call. Each end of a pipe has an associated file descriptor. The "write" end of the pipe may be written to using write (), and the "read" end may be read from using read (). When a process has finished with a pipe's file descriptor, it should close it using close (). Here's how pipe () works:

System Call: int **pipe** (int *fd* [ ])

pipe () creates an unnamed pipe and returns two file descriptors; the descriptor associated with the "read" end of the pipe is stored in *fd*[0], and the descriptor associated with the "write" end of the pipe is stored in *fd*[1].
     The following rules apply to processes that read from a pipe:

- If a process reads from a pipe whose write end has been closed, the read () returns a 0, indicating end-of-input.
- If a process reads from an empty pipe whose write end is still open, it sleeps until some input becomes available.

- If a process tries to read more bytes from a pipe than are present, all of the current contents are returned and read () returns the number of bytes actually read.

The following rules apply to processes that write to a pipe:

- If a process writes to a pipe whose read end has been closed, the write fails and the writer is sent a SIGPIPE signal. The default action of this signal is to terminate the receiver.
- If a process writes fewer bytes to a pipe than the pipe can hold, the write () is guaranteed to be atomic; that is, the writer process will complete its system call without being preempted by another process. If a process writes more bytes to a pipe than the pipe can hold, no similar guarantees of atomicity apply.

Since access to an unnamed pipe is via the file descriptor mechanism, only the process that creates a pipe and its descendants may use the pipe. lseek () has no meaning when applied to a pipe.

If the kernel cannot allocate enough space for a new pipe, pipe () returns −1; otherwise, it returns 0.

If the following code was executed:

```
int fd [2];
pipe (fd);
```

then the data structures shown in this diagram would be created:

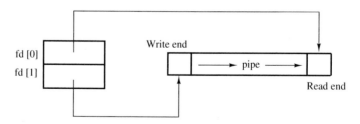

Figure 10.11   An unnamed pipe

Unnamed pipes are usually used for communication between a parent process and its child, with one process writing and the other process reading. The typical sequence of events is as follows:

1. The parent process creates an unnamed pipe using pipe ().
2. The parent process forks.
3. The writer closes its read end of the pipe, and the designated reader closes its write end of the pipe.
4. The processes communicate by using write () and read () calls.
5. Each process closes its active pipe descriptor when it's finished with it.

Bidirectional communication is only possible by using two pipes.

Here's a small program that uses a pipe to allow the parent to read a message from its child:

```
$ cat talk.c                      ...list the program.
#include <stdio.h>

#define READ   0      /* The index of the read end of the pipe */
#define WRITE  1      /* The index of the write end of the pipe */

char* phrase = "Stuff this in your pipe and smoke it";

main ()

{
  int fd [2], bytesRead;
  char message [100]; /* Parent process' message buffer */

  pipe (fd); /*Create an unnamed pipe */
  if (fork () == 0) /* Child, writer */
    {
      close(fd[READ]); /* Close unused end */
      write (fd[WRITE],phrase, strlen (phrase) + 1); /* include NULL*/
      close (fd[WRITE]); /* Close used end*/
    }
  else /* Parent, reader*/
    {
      close (fd[WRITE]); /* Close unusedend */
      bytesRead = read (fd[READ], message, 100);
      printf ("Read %d bytes: %s\n", bytesRead, message); /* Send */
      close (fd[READ]); /* Close usedend */
    }
}
$ talk.exe                        ...run the program.
Read 37 bytes: Stuff this in your pipe and smoke it
$ _
```

Notice that the child included the phrase's NULL terminator as part of the message so that the parent could easily display it. When a writer process sends more than one variable-length message into a pipe, it must use a protocol to indicate to the reader an end-of-message. Methods for doing this include:

- sending the length of a message (in bytes) before sending the message itself
- ending a message with a special character such as a newline or a NULL

The UNIX shells use unnamed pipes to build pipelines. They use a trick similar to the redirection mechanism described in the ''Process Management'' section to connect the standard output of one process to the standard input of another. To illustrate this approach, here's the source code of a program that executes two named programs, connecting the standard output of the first to the standard input of the second. It assumes that neither programs are invoked with options, and that the names of the programs are listed on the command line.

```
$ cat connect.c                    ...list the program.
#include <stdio.h>

#define READ   0
#define WRITE  1

main (argc, argv)

int argc;
char* argv [];

{
  int fd [2];

  pipe (fd); /* Create an unamed pipe */

  if (fork () ! = 0) /* Parent, writer */
    {
      close (fd[READ]); /* Close unused end */
      dup2 (fd[WRITE], 1); /* Duplicate used end to stdout */
      close (fd[WRITE]); /* Close original used end */
      execlp (argv[1], argv[1], NULL); /* Execute writer program */
      perror ("connect");  /* Should never execute */
    }
  else /* Child, reader */
    {
      close (fd]WRITE]); /* Close unused end */
      dup2 (fd[READ], 0); /* Duplicate used end to stdin */
      close (fd[READ]); /* Close original used end */
      execlp (argv[2], argv[2], NULL); /* Execute reader program */
      perror ("connect"); /* Should never execute */
    }
}
```

```
$ who                                ...execute "who" by itself.
gglass                    ttyp0        Feb 15 18:45   (xyplex_3)
$ connect who wc                     ...pipe "who" through "wc".
        1         6       57        ...1 line, 6 words, 57 chars.
$ _
```

For a more sophisticated example of unnamed pipes, refer to the Internet shell that is described later in this chapter. Note also that the chapter review contains an interesting exercise that involves building a ring of pipes.

Named Pipes

Named pipes (often referred to as FIFOs- first in, first out) are less restricted than unnamed pipes, and offer the following advantages:

- They have a name that exists in the file system.
- They may be used by unrelated processes.
- They exist until explicitly deleted.

Unfortunately, they are only supported by System V. All of the pipe rules that I mentioned in the ''Unnamed Pipes'' section apply to named pipes, except that named pipes have a larger buffer capacity, typically about 40K.

Named pipes exist as special files in the file system, and may be created in one of two ways:

- by using the UNIX **mknod** utility
- by using the mknod ( ) system call

To create a named pipe using **mknod**, use the **p** option. For more information about **mknod**, see chapter 12. The mode of the named pipe may be set using **chmod**, allowing others to access the pipe that you create. Here's an example of this procedure, executed from a Korn shell:

```
$ mknod myPipe p                     ...create pipe.
$ chmod ug+rw myPipe                 ...update permissions.
$ ls -lg myPipe                      ...examine attributes.
  prw-rw----   1 glass        cs             0 Feb 27 12:38 myPipe
$ _
```

Note that the type of the named pipe is ''p''in the **ls** listing.

To create a named pipe using mknod ( ), specify S_IFIFO as the file mode. The mode of the pipe can then be changed using chmod ( ). Here's a snippet of C code that creates a named pipe with read and write permission for the owner and group:

```
mknod ("myPipe", S_IFIFO, 0); /* Create a named pipe */
chmod ("myPipe", 0660); /* Modify its permission flags */
```

Regardless of how you go about creating a named pipe, the end result is the same: a special file is added into the file system. Once a named pipe is opened using open (), write () adds data at the start of the FIFO queue, and read () removes data from the end of the FIFO queue. When a process has finished using a named pipe, it should close it using close (), and when a named pipe is no longer needed, it should be removed from the file system using unlink ().

Like an unnamed pipe, a named pipe is only intended for use as a unidirectional link. Writer processes should open a named pipe for write-only, and reader processes should open for read-only. Although a process could open a named pipe for both reading and writing, this doesn't have much practical application. Before I show you an example program that uses named pipes, here are a couple of special rules concerning their use:

- If a process tries to open a named pipe for read-only and no process currently has it open for writing, the reader will wait until a process opens it for writing, unless O_NDELAY is set, in which case open () succeeds immediately.
- If a process tries to open a named pipe for write-only and no process currently has it open for reading, the writer will wait until a process opens it for reading, unless O_NDELAY is set, in which case open () fails immediately.
- Named pipes will not work across a network.

The following example uses two programs, "reader" and "writer", and works like this:

- A single reader process is executed, which creates a named pipe called "aPipe". It then reads and displays NULL-terminated lines from the pipe until the pipe is closed by all of the writing processes.
- One or more writer processes are executed, each of which opens the named pipe called "aPipe" and sends three messages to it. If the pipe does not exist when a writer tries to open it, the writer retries every second until it succeeds. When all of a writer's messages are sent, the writer closes the pipe and exits.

Following are the source code for each file and some sample output.

Sample output

```
$ reader & writer & writer &   ...start 1 reader, 2 writers.
[1] 4698      ...reader process.
[2] 4699      ...first writer process.
[3] 4700      ...second writer process.
Hello from PID 4699
Hello from PID 4700
Hello from PID 4699
Hello from PID 4700
Hello from PID 4699
Hello from PID 4700
[2]    Done              writer     ...first writer exits.
[3]    Done              writer     ...second writer exits.
[1]    Done              reader     ...reader exits.
$_
```

Reader program

```c
#include <stdio.h>
#include <sys/types.h>
#include <sys/stat.h>            /* For S_IFIFO */
#include <sys/file.h>

/*********************************************************************/

main ()

{
  int fd;
  char str[100];

  unlink("aPipe"); /* Remove named pipe if it already exists */
  mknod ("aPipe", S_IFIFO, 0); /* Create named pipe */
  chmod ("aPipe", 0660); /* Change its permissions */
  fd = open ("aPipe", O_RDONLY); /* Open it for reading */

  while (readLine (fd, str)) /* Display received messages */
    printf ("%s\n", str);

  close (fd); /* Close pipe */
}

/*********************************************************************/

readLine (fd, str)

int fd;
char* str;
```

```
/* Read a single NULL-terminated line into str from fd */
/* Return 0 when the end-of-input is reached and 1 otherwise */

{
  int n;

  do /* Read characters until NULL or end-of-input */
    {
      n = read (fd, str, 1); /* Read one character */
    }
  while (n > 0 && *str++ != NULL);
  return (n > 0); /* Return false if end-of-input */
}
```

Writer program

```
#include <stdio.h>
#include <sysfile.h>

/**************************************************************************/

main ()

{
  int fd, messageLen, i;
  char message [100];

  /* Prepare message */
  sprintf (message, "Hello from PID %d", getpid ());
  messageLen = strlen (message) + 1;

  do /* Keep trying to open the file until successful */
    {
      fd = open ("aPipe", O_WRONLY); /* Open named pipe for writing */
      if (fd == -1) sleep (1); /* Try again in 1 second */
    }
  while (fd == -1);

  for (i = 1; i <= 3; i++) /* Send three messages */
    {
      write (fd, message, messageLen); /* Write message down pipe */
      sleep (3); /* Pause a while */
    }

  close (fd); /* Close pipe descriptor */
}
```

SOCKETS

Sockets are an interprocess communication mechanism that allows processes to talk to each other, even if they're on different machines. It is this across-network capability that makes them so useful. For example, the **rlogin** utility, which allows a user on one machine to log into a remote host, is implemented using sockets. Other common uses of sockets include:

- printing a file on one machine from another machine
- transferring files from one machine to another machine

Process communication via sockets is based on the client-server model. One process, known as a server process, creates a socket whose name is known by other client processes. These client processes can talk to the server process via a connection to its named socket. To do this, a client process first creates an unnamed socket and then requests that it be connected to the server's named socket. A successful connection returns one file descriptor to the client and one to the server, both of which may be used for reading and writing. Note that unlike pipes, socket connections are bidirectional. Here's an illustration of the process:

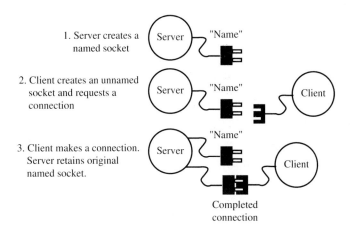

1. Server creates a named socket

2. Client creates an unnamed socket and requests a connection

3. Client makes a connection. Server retains original named socket.

Completed connection

Figure 10.12   The socket connection

Once a socket connection is made, it's quite common for the server process to fork a child process to converse with the client, while the original parent process continues to accept other client connections. A typical example of this is a remote print server: the server process accepts a client that wishes to send a file for printing, and then forks a child to perform the file transfer. The parent process meanwhile waits for more client print requests.

In the coming sections, we'll take a look at the following topics:

- the different kinds of sockets
- how a server creates a named socket and waits for connections
- how a client creates an unnamed socket and requests a connection from a server
- how a server and client communicate after a socket connection is made
- how a socket connection is closed.
- how a server can create a child process to converse with the client

The Different Kinds Of Sockets

The various kinds of sockets may be classified according to three attributes:

- the *domain*
- the *type*
- the *protocol*

Domains

The domain of a socket indicates where the server and client sockets may reside; the domains that are currently supported include:

- AF_UNIX (the clients and server must be in the same machine)
- AF_INET (the clients and server may be anywhere on the Internet)
- AF_NS (the clients and server may be on a XEROX network system)

AF stands for "Address Family." There is a similar set of constants that begin with PF, which stands for "Protocol Family" (i.e., PF_UNIX, PF_INET, etc.). Either set may be used, as they are equivalent. This book contains information about AF_UNIX and AF_INET sockets, but not AF_NS sockets.

Types

The type of a socket determines the type of communication that can exist between the client and server; the two main types that are currently supported are:

- SOCK_STREAM: sequenced, reliable, two-way connection based, variable length streams of bytes
- SOCK_DGRAM: like telegrams; connectionless, unreliable, fixed-length messages

Other types that are either in the planning stages or only implemented in some domains include:

- SOCK_SEQPACKET: sequenced, reliable, two-way connection based, fixed-length packets of bytes
- SOCK_RAW: provides access to internal network protocols and interfaces

This book contains information only on how to use SOCK_STREAM sockets, which are the most common. They are both intuitive and easy to use.

Protocols

The protocol value specifies the low-level means by which the socket type is implemented. System calls that expect a protocol parameter accept 0 as meaning "the correct protocol"; in other words, the protocol value is something that you generally won't have to worry about. Most systems only support protocols other than 0 as an optional extra, so I'll use the default protocol in all the examples.

Writing Socket Programs

Any program that uses sockets must include "/usr/include/sys/types.h" and "/usr/include/sys/socket.h". Additional header files must be included based on the socket domain that you wish to use:

Domain	Additional header files
AF_UNIX	/usr/include/sys/un.h
AF_INET	/usr/include/netinet/in.h /usr/include/arpa/inet.h /urs/include/netdb.h

To illustrate clearly the way that a program that uses sockets is written, I'll build my description of the socket-oriented system calls around a small client/server example that uses AF_UNIX sockets. Once I've done this, I'll show you another example that uses AF_INET sockets. The AF_UNIX example is comprised of two programs:

- "chef," the server, which creates a named socket called "recipe" and writes the recipe to any clients who request it. The recipe is a collection of variable-length NULL-terminated strings.
- "cook," the client, which connects to the named socket called "recipe" and reads the recipe from the server. It displays the recipe to standard output as it reads it, and then terminates.

The chef server process runs in the background. Any client cook processes that connect to the server cause the server to fork a duplicate server to handle the recipe transfer, allowing the original server to accept other incoming connections. Here's some sample output from the chef/cook example:

```
$ chef &                         ...run the server in the background.
[1] 5684
$ cook                           ...run a client-display the recipe.
spam, spam, spam, spam,
spam, and spam.
$ cook                           ...run another client-display the recipe
spam, spam, spam, spam,
spam, and spam.
$ kill %1                        ...kill the server.
[1]    Terminated         chef
$ _
```

Chef/Cook Listing

This section contains the complete listing of the chef and cook programs. I suggest that you quickly skim through the code and then read the sections that follow for details on how they both work. I have purposely left out a great deal of error checking in the interests of space.

Chef Server

```
1   #include <stdio.h>
2   #include <signal.h>
3   #include <sys/types.h>
4   #include <sys/socket.h>
5   #include <sys/un.h>                    /* For AF_UNIX sockets */
6
7   #define DEFAULT_PROTOCOL    0
8
9   /*****************************************************************/
10
11  main ()
12
13  {
14    int serverFd, clientFd, serverLen, clientLen;
15    struct sockaddr_un serverUNIXAddress;/* Server address */
16    struct sockaddr_un clientUNIXAddress; /* Client address */
17    struct sockaddr* serverSockAddrPtr; /* Ptr to server address */
18    struct sockaddr* clientSockAddrPtr; /* Ptr to client address */
```

```
19
20    /* Ignore death-of-child signals to prevent zombies */
21    signal (SIGCHLD, SIG_IGN);
22
23    serverSockAddrPtr = (structsockaddr*) &serverUNIXAddress;
24    serverLen = sizeof (serverUNIXAddress);
25
26    clientSockAddrPtr = (struct sockaddr*) &clientUNIXAddress;
27    clientLen = sizeof (clientUNIXAddress);
28
29    /* Create a UNIX socket, bidirectional, default protocol */
30    serverFd = socket (AF_UNIX, SOCK_STREAM, DEFAULT_PROTOCOL);
31    serverUNIXAddress.sun_family = AF_UNIX; /* Set domain type */
32    strcpy (serverUNIXAddress.sun_path, "recipe"); /* Set name */
33    unlink ("recipe"); /* Remove file if it already exists */
34    bind (serverFd, serverSockAddrPtr, serverLen); /* Create file */
35    listen (serverFd, 5); /* Maximum pending connection length */
36
37    while (1) /* Loop forever */
38      {
39        /* Accept a client connection */
40        clientFd = accept (serverFd, clientSockAddrPtr, &clientLen);
41
42        if (fork () == 0) /* Create child to send receipe */
43          {
44            writeRecipe (clientFd); /* Send the recipe */
45            close (clientFd); /* Close the socket */
46            exit (/* EXIT_SUCCESS */ 0); /* Terminate */
47          }
48        else
49          close (clientFd); /* Close the client descriptor */
50      }
51  }
52
53  /******************************************************************/
54
55  writeRecipe (fd)
56
57  int fd;
58
59  {
60    static char* line1 = "spam, spam, spam, spam,";
61    static char* line2 = "spam, and spam.";
62    write (fd, line1, strlen (line1) + 1); /* Write first line */
63    write (fd, line2, strlen (line2) + 1); /* Write second line */
64  }
```

Cook Client

```
1   #include <stdio.h>
2   #include <signal.h>
3   #include <sys/types.h>
4   #include <sys/socket.h>
5   #include <sys/un.h>                        /* For AF_UNIX sockets */
6
7   #define DEFAULT_PROTOCOL     0
8
9   /*****************************************************************/
10
11  main ()
12
13  {
14    int clientFd, serverLen, result;
15    struct sockaddr_un serverUNIXAddress;
16    struct sockaddr* serverSockAddrPtr;
17
18    serverSockAddrPtr = (struct sockaddr*) &serverUNIXAddress;
19    serverLen = sizeof (serverUNIXAddress);
20
21    /* Create a UNIX socket, bidirectional, default protocol */
22    clientFd = socket (AF_UNIX, SOCK_STREAM, DEFAULT_PROTOCOL);
23    serverUNIXAddress.sun_family = AF_UNIX; /* Server domain */
24    strcpy (serverUNIXAddress.sun_path, "recipe"); /* Server name */
25
26    do /* Loop until a connection is made with the server */
27      {
28        result = connect (clientFd, serverSockAddrPtr, serverLen);
29        if (result == -1) sleep (1); /* Wait and then try again */
30      }
31    while (result == -1);
32
33    readRecipe (clientFd); /* Read the recipe */
34    close (clientFd); /* Close the socket */
35    exit (/* EXIT_SUCCESS */ 0); /* Done */
36  }
37
38  /*****************************************************************/
39
40  readRecipe (fd)
41
42  int fd;
43
44  {
```

```
45     char str[200];
46
47     while (readLine (fd, str)) /* Read lines until end-of-input */
48         printf ("%s\n", str); /* Echo line from socket */
49   }
50
51   /***************************************************************/
52
53   readLine (fd, str)
54
55   int fd;
56   char* str;
57
58   /* Read a single NULL-terminated line */
59
60   {
61     int n;
62
63     do /* Read characters until NULL or end-of-input */
64         {
65             n = read (fd,str, 1); /* Read one character */
66         }
67     while (n > 0 && *str++ != NULL);
68     return (n > 0); /* Return false if end-of-input */
69   }
```

Analyzing The Source Code

Now that you've glanced at the program, it's time to go back and analyze it. The next few subsections cover the following topics:

- an overview of a server
- creating a server socket
- naming a server socket
- specifying the maximum number of pending connections to a server socket
- accepting connections on a server socket
- serving a client
- an overview of a client
- creating a client socket
- connecting a client socket to the server socket
- communicating via sockets

The Server

A server is the process that's responsible for creating a named socket and accepting connections to it. To accomplish this, it must use the following system calls in their presented order:

Name	Meaning
socket	creates an unnamed socket
bind	gives the socket a name
listen	specifies the maximum number of pending connections
accept	accepts a socket connection from a client

The next few subsections describe each of these system calls.

Creating A Socket: socket ( )

A process may create a socket by using socket ( ), which works like this:

> *System Call:* int **socket** (int *domain*, int *type*, int *protocol*)
>
> socket ( ) creates an unnamed socket of the specified domain, type, and protocol. The legal values of these parameters were described earlier in this section.
>   If socket ( ) is successful, it returns a file descriptor associated with the newly created socket; otherwise, it returns -1.

The chef server creates its unnamed socket on line 30:

```
30    serverFd = socket (AF_UNIX, SOCK_STREAM, DEFAULT_PROTOCOL);
```

Naming A Socket: bind ( )

Once the server has created an unnamed socket, it must bind it to a name by using bind ( ), which works like this:

System Call: int **bind** (int *fd,* struct sockaddr* *address,*int *addressLen*)

bind () associates the unnamed socket with file descriptor *fd* with the socket address stored in *address. addressLen* must contain the length of the address structure. The type and value of the incoming address depend on the socket domain.

    If the socket is in the AF_UNIX domain, a pointer to a **sockaddr_un** structure must be cast to a (**sockaddr***) and passed in as *address.* This structure has two fields that should be set as follows:

FIELD	ASSIGN THE VALUE
sun_family	AF_UNIX
sun_path	the full UNIX pathname of the socket (absolute or relative), up to 108 characters long

    If the named AF_UNIX socket already exists, an error occurs, so it's a good idea to unlink () a name before attempting to bind to it.

    If the socket is in the AF_INET domain, a pointer to a **sockaddr_in** structure must be cast to a (**sockaddr***) and passed in as *address.* This structure has four fields that should be set as follows:

FIELD	ASSIGN THE VALUE
sin_family	AF_INET
sin_port	the port number of the Internet socket
sin_addr	a structure of type **in_addr** that holds the Internet address
sin_zero	leave empty

    For more information about Internet ports and addresses, please consult the Internet-specific part of this section.

    If bind () succeeds, it returns a 0; otherwise, it returns −1.

The chef server assigns the **sockaddr_un** fields and performs a bind () on lines 31..34:

```
31   serverUNIXAddress.sun_family = AF_UNIX; /* Set domain type */
32   strcpy (serverUNIXAddress.sun_path, "recipe"); /* Set name */
33   unlink ("recipe"); /* Remove file if it already exists */
34   bind (serverFd, serverSockAddrPtr, serverLen); /* Create file */
```

Creating A Socket Queue: listen ( )

When a server process is servicing a client connection, it's always possible that another client will also attempt a connection. The listen ( ) system call allows a process to specify the number of pending connections that may be queued, and works like this:

System Call: int **listen** (int *fd,* int *queueLength*)

listen ( ) allows you to specify the maximum number of pending connections on a socket. Right now, the maximum queue length is 5. If a client attempts a connection to a socket whose queue is full, it is denied.

The chef server listens to its named socket on line 35:

```
35    listen (serverFd, 5); /* Maximum pending connection length */
```

Accepting A Client: accept ( )

Once a socket has been created, named, and its queue size has been specified, the final step is to accept client connection requests. To do this, the server must use accept ( ), which works as follows:

System Call: int **accept** (int *fd,* struct sockaddr* *address,* int* *addressLen*)

accept ( ) listens to the named server socket referenced by *fd* and waits until a client connection request is received. When this occurs, accept ( ) creates an unnamed socket with the same attributes as the original named server socket, connects it to the client's socket, and returns a new file descriptor that may be used for communication with the client. The original named server socket may be used to accept more connections.

The *address* structure is filled with the address of the client, and is normally only used in conjunction with Internet connections. The *ad-dressLen* field should be initially set to point to an integer containing the size of the structure pointed to by *address.* When a connection is made, the integer that it points to is set to the actual size, in bytes, of the resulting *address.*

If accept ( ) succeeds, it returns a new file descriptor that may be used to talk with the client; otherwise, it returns −1.

The chef server accepts a connection on line 40:

```
40        clientFd = accept (serverFd, clientSockAddrPtr, &clientLen),
```

Serving A Client

When a client connection succeeds, the most common sequence of events is this:

- The server process forks.
- The parent process closes the newly formed client file descriptor and loops back to accept (), ready to service new client connection requests.
- The child process talks to the client using read () and write (). When the conversation is complete, the child process closes the client file descriptor and exits.

The chef server process follows this series of actions on lines 37..50:

```
37     while (1) /* Loop forever */
38        {
39           /* Accept a client connection */
40           clientFd = accept (serverFd, clientSockAddrPtr, &clientLen);
41
42           if (fork () == 0) /* Create child to send receipe */
43              {
44                 writeRecipe (clientFd); /* Send the recipe */
45                 close (clientFd); /* Close the socket */
46                 exit (/*EXIT_SUCCESS */ 0); /* Terminate */
47              }
48           else
49              close (clientFd); /* Close the client descriptor */
50        }
```

Note that the server chose to ignore SIGCHLD signals on line 21 so that its children can die immediately without requiring the parent to accept their return codes. If the server had not done this, it would had to have installed a SIGCHLD handler, which would have been more tedious.

The Client

Now that you've seen how a server program is written, let's take a look at the construction of a client program. A client is a process that's responsible for creating an unnamed socket and then attaching it to a named server socket. To accomplish this, it must use the following system calls in their presented order:

Name	Meaning
socket	creates an unnamed socket
connect	attaches an unnamed client socket to a named server socket

The way that a client uses socket ( ) to create an unnamed socket is the same as the way that the server uses it. The domain, type, and protocol of the client socket must match those of the targeted server socket. The cook client process creates its unnamed socket on line 22:

```
22    clientFd = socket (AF_UNIX, SOCK_STREAM, DEFAULT_PROTOCOL);
```

Making The Connection: connect ( )

To connect to a server's socket, a client process must fill a structure with the address of the server's socket and then use connect ( ), which works like this:

System Call: int **connect** (int *fd*, struct sockaddr* *address*, int *addressLen*)

connect ( ) attempts to connect to a server socket whose address is contained within a structure pointed to by *address*. If successful, *fd* may be used to communicate with the server's socket. The type of structure that *address* points to must follow the same rules as those stated in the description of bind ( ):

- If the socket is in the AF_UNIX domain, a pointer to a **sockaddr_un** structure must be cast to a (**sockaddr***) and passed in as *address*.
- If the socket is in the AF_INET domain, a pointer to a **sockaddr_in** structure must be cast to a (**sockaddr***) and passed in as *address*.

addressLen must be equal to the size of the address structure. For examples of Internet clients, see the next socket example and the Internet shell program at the end of this chapter.

If the connection is made, connect ( ) returns 0. If the server socket doesn't exist or its pending queue is currently filled, connect ( ) returns −1.

The cook client process calls connect () until a successful connection is made in lines 26..31:

```
26   do /* Loop until a connection is made with the server */
27     {
28        result = connect (clientFd, serverSockAddrPtr, serverLen);
29        if (result == -1) sleep (1); /* Wait and then try again */
30     }
31   while (result == -1);
```

Communicating Via Sockets

Once the server socket and client socket have connected, their file descriptors may be used by write () and read (). In the example program, the server uses write () in lines 55..64:

```
55   writeRecipe (fd)
56
57   int fd;
58
59   {
60     static char* line1 = "spam, spam, spam, spam,";
61     static char* line2 = "spam, and spam.";
62     write (fd, line1, strlen (line1) + 1); /* Write first line */
63     write (fd, line2, strlen (line2) + 1); /* Write second line*/
64   }
```

and the client uses read () in lines 53..69:

```
53   readLine (fd, str)
54
55   int fd;
56   char* str;
57
58   /* Read a single NULL-terminated line */
59
60   {
61     int n;
62
63     do /* Read characters until NULL or end-of-input */
64        {
65           n = read (fd, str, 1); /* Read one character */
66        }
67     while (n > 0 &&*str++ != NULL);
68     return (n > 0); /* Return false if end-of-input */
69   }
```

The server and client should be careful to close their socket file descriptors when they are no longer needed.

Internet Sockets

The AF_UNIX sockets that you've seen so far are OK for learning about sockets, but they aren't where the action is. Most of the useful stuff involves communicating between machines on the Internet, and so the rest of this chapter is dedicated to AF_INET sockets. If you haven't already read about the Internet in chapter 8, now's a good time to do so.

An Internet socket is specified by two values: a 32-bit IP address, which specifies a single unique Internet host, and a 16-bit port number, which specifies a particular port on the host. This means that an Internet client must know not only the IP address of the server, but also the server's port number.

As I mentioned in chapter 8, there are several standard port numbers that are reserved for system use. For example, port 13 is always served by a process that echos the host's time of day to any client that's interested. The first Internet socket example allows you to connect to port 13 of any Internet host in the world and find out the "remote" time of day. It allows three kinds of Internet address:

- If you enter "s", it automatically means the local host.
- If you enter something that starts with a digit, it's assumed to be an A.B.C.D format IP address, and is converted into a 32-bit IP address by software.
- If you enter a string, it's assumed to be a symbolic host name, and is converted into a 32-bit IP address by software.

Here's some sample output from the "Internet time" program. The third address that I entered is the IP address of "ddn.nic.mil," the national Internet database server. Notice the one-hour time difference between my local host's time and the database server host's time.

Sample Output

```
$ inettime                               ...run the program.
Host name (q= quit, s = self): s         ...what's my time?
Self host name is csservr2
Internet Address= 129.110.42.1
The time on the target port is Wed May 27 17:03:50 1992

Host name (q = quit, s= self): wotan      ...what's the time on "wotan"?
Internet Address = 129.110.2.1
The time on the target port is Wed May 27 17:03:55 1992
```

```
Host name (q = quit, s = self): 192.112.36.5     ...try ddn.nic.mil.
The time on the target port is Wed May 27 18:02:02 1992

Host name (q = quit, s = self): q               ...quit program.
$ _
```

Internet Time Listing

This section contains the complete listing of the Internet time client program. I suggest that you quickly skim through the code and then read the sections that follow for details on how it works.

```
1    #include <stdio.h>
2    #include <signal.h>
3    #include <ctype.h>
4    #include <sys/types.h>
5    #include <sys/socket.h>
6    #include <netinet/in.h>                  /* For AF_INET sockets */
7    #include <arpa/inet.h>
8    #include <netdb.h>
9
10   #define DAYTIME_PORT          13         /* Standard port # */
11   #define DEFAULT_PROTOCOL      0
12
13   unsigned long promptForINETAddress ();
14   unsigned long nameToAddr ();
15
16   /****************************************************************/
17
18   main ()
19
20   {
21      int clientFd; /* Client socket file descriptor */
22      int serverLen; /* Length of server address structure */
23      int result; /* From connect () call */
24      struct sockaddr_in serverINETAddress; /* Server address */
25      struct sockaddr* serverSockAddrPtr; /* Pointer to address */
26      unsigned long inetAddress; /* 32-bit IP address */
27
28      /* Set the two server variables */
29      serverSockAddrPtr = (struct sockaddr*) &serverINETAddress;
30      serverLen = sizeof (serverINETAddress); /* Length of address */
31
32      while (1) /* Loop until break */
33        {
34           inetAddress = promptForINETAddress (); /* Get 32-bit IP */
```

```
35          if (inetAddress == 0) break; /* Done */
36          /* Start by zeroing out the entire address structure */
37          bzero ((char*)&serverINETAddress,sizeof(serverINETAddress));
38          serverINETAddress.sin_family = AF_INET; /* Use Internet */
39          serverINETAddress.sin_addr.s_addr = inetAddress; /* IP */
40          serverINETAddress.sin_port = htons (DAYTIME_PORT);
41          /* Now create the client socket */
42          clientFd = socket (AF_INET, SOCK_STREAM, DEFAULT_PROTOCOL);
43          do /* Loop until a connection is made with the server */
44            {
45              result = connect (clientFd,serverSockAddrPtr,serverLen);
46              if (result == -1) sleep (1); /* Try again in 1 second */
47            }
48          while (result == -1);
49
50          readTime (clientFd); /* Read the time from the server */
51          close (clientFd); /* Close the socket */
52        }
53
54    exit (/* EXIT_SUCCESS */ 0);
55  }
56
57  /****************************************************************/
58
59  unsigned long promptForINETAddress ()
60
61  {
62    char hostName [100]; /* Name from user: numeric or symbolic */
63    unsigned long inetAddress; /* 32-bit IP format */
64
65    /* Loop until quit or a legal name is entered */
66    /* If quit, return 0 else return host's IP address */
67    do
68      {
69        printf ("Host name (q = quit, s = self): ");
70        scanf ("%s", hostName); /* Get name from keyboard */
71        if (strcmp (hostName, "q") == 0) return (0); /* Quit */
72        inetAddress = nameToAddr (hostName); /* Convert to IP */
73        if (inetAddress == 0) printf ("Host name not found\n");
74      }
75    while (inetAddress == 0);
76  }
77
78  /****************************************************************/
79
80  unsigned long nameToAddr (name)
81
82  char* name;
83
```

```
 84   {
 85      char hostName [100];
 86      struct hostent* hostStruct;
 87      struct in_addr* hostNode;
 88
 89      /* Convert name into a 32-bit IP address */
 90
 91      /* If name begins with a digit, assume it's a valid numeric */
 92      /* Internet address of the form A.B.C.D and convert directly */
 93      if (isdigit (name[0])) return (inet_addr (name));
 94
 95      if (strcmp (name, "s") == 0) /* Get host name from database */
 96         {
 97            gethostname (hostName,100);
 98            printf ("Self host name is %s\n", hostName);
 99         }
100      else /* Assume name is a valid symbolic host name */
101         strcpy (hostName, name);
102
103      /* Now obtain address information from database */
104      hostStruct = gethostbyname (hostName);
105      if (hostStruct == NULL) return (0); /* Not Found */
106      /* Extract the IP Address from the hostent structure */
107      hostNode = (struct in_addr*) hostStruct->h_addr;
108      /* Display a readable version for fun */
109      printf ("Internet Address = %s\n", inet_ntoa (*hostNode));
110      return (hostNode->s_addr); /* Return IP address */
111   }
112
113   /*******************************************************************/
114
115   readTime (fd)
116
117   int fd;
118
119   {
120      char str [200]; /* Line buffer */
121
122      printf ("The time on the target port is ");
123      while (readLine (fd, str)) /* Read lines until end-of-input */
124         printf ("%s\n", str); /* Echo line from server to user */
125   }
126
127   /*******************************************************************/
128
129   readLine (fd, str)
130
131   int fd;
132   char* str;
```

```
133
134  /* Read a single NEWLINE-terminated line */
135
136  {
137    int n;
138
139    do /* Read characters until NULL or end-of-input */
140      {
141        n = read (fd, str, 1); /* Read one character */
142      }
143    while (n > 0 && *str++ != '\n');
144    return (n > 0); /* Return false if end-of-input */
145  }
```

Analyzing The Source Code

Now that you've had a brief look through the Internet socket source code, it's time to examine the interesting bits. This program focuses mostly on the client side of an Internet connection, so I'll describe that portion first.

Internet Clients

The procedure for creating an Internet client is the same as that of an AF_UNIX client, except for the initialization of the socket address. I mentioned earlier in this section during the discussion of bind () that an Internet socket address structure is of type **struct sockaddr_in**, and has four fields:

- **sin_family**, the domain of the socket, which should be set to AF_INET
- **sin_port**, the port number, which in this case is 13
- **sin_addr**, the 32-bit IP number of the client/server
- **sin_zero**, which is padding and is not set

When creating the client socket, the only tricky bit is determining the server's 32-bit IP address. promptForINETAddress () [59] gets the host's name from the user and then invokes nameToAddr () [80] to convert it into an IP address. If the user enters a string starting with a digit, inet_addr () is invoked to perform the conversion. Here's how it works:

Library Call: unsigned long **inet_addr** (char* *string)*

inet_addr () returns the 32-bit IP address that corresponds to the A.B.C.D format *string*. The IP address is in network-byte order.

"Network-byte" order is a host-neutral ordering of bytes in the IP address. This is necessary, since regular byte-ordering can differ from machine to machine, which would make IP addresses non-portable.

If the string doesn't start with a digit, the next step is to see if it's "s," which means the local host. The name of the local host is obtained by gethostname () [97], which works as follows:

System Call: int **gethostname** (char* *name*, int *nameLen*)

gethostname () sets the character array pointed to by *name* of length *nameLen* to a null-terminated string equal to the local host's name.

Once the symbolic name of the host is determined, the next stage is to look it up in the network host file, "/etc/hosts." This is performed by gethostbyname () [104], which works like this:

Library Call: struct hostent* **gethostbyname** (char* *name*)

gethostbyname () searches the "/etc/hosts" file and returns a pointer to a **hostent** structure that describes the file entry associated with the string *name*.

If *name* is not found in the "/etc/hosts" file, NULL is returned.

The **hostent** structure has several fields, but the only one we're interested in is a field of type (**struct in_addr***) called **h_addr**. This field contains the host's associated IP number in a subfield called **s_addr**. Before returning this IP number, the program displays a string description of the IP address by calling inet_ntoa () [109]:

Library Call: char* **inet_ntoa** (struct in_addr *address*)

inet_ntoa () takes a structure of type *in_addr* as its argument and returns a pointer to a string that describes the address in the format A.B.C.D.

The final 32-bit address is then returned by line 110. Once the IP address **inetAddress** has been determined, the client's socket address fields are filled by lines 37..40.

```
37      bzero ((char*)&serverINETAddress,sizeof(serverINETAddress));
38      serverINETAddress.sin_family = AF_INET; /* Use Internet */
39      serverINETAddress.sin_addr.s_addr = inetAddress; /* IP */
40      serverINETAddress.sin_port = htons (DAYTIME_PORT);
```

bzero () clears the socket address structure's contents before its fields are assigned:

Library Call: void **bzero** (char* *buffer*, int *length*)

bzero () fills the array *buffer* of size *length* with zeroes (ASCII NULL).

Like the IP address, the port number is also converted to a network-byte ordering by htons (), which works like this:

Library Call: unsigned long **htonl** (unsigned long *hostLong*)
                unsigned short **htons** (unsigned short *hostShort*)
                unsigned long **ntohl** (unsigned long *networkLong*)
                unsigned short **ntohs** (unsigned short *networkShort*)

Each of these functions performs a conversion between a host-format number and a network-format number. For example, htonl () returns the network-format equivalent of the host-format unsigned long *hostLong*, and ntohs () returns the host-format equivalent of the network-format unsigned short *networkShort*.

The final step is to create the client socket and attempt the connection. The code for this is almost the same as for AF_UNIX sockets:

```
42    clientFd = socket (AF_INET, SOCK_STREAM, DEFAULT_PROTOCOL);
43    do /* Loop until a connection is made with the server */
44      {
45        result = connect (clientFd,serverSockAddrPtr,serverLen);
46        if (result == -1) sleep (1); /* Try again in 1 second */
47      }
48    while (result == -1);
```

The rest of the program contains nothing new. Now it's time to look at how an Internet server is built.

Internet Servers

Constructing an Internet server is actually pretty easy. The **sin_family**, **sin_port**, and **sin_zero** fields of the socket address structure should be filled in as they were in the client example. The only difference is that the **s_addr** field should be set to the network-byte ordered value of the constant INADDR_ANY, which means "accept any incoming client requests." The following example of how to create a server socket address is a slightly modified version of some code taken from the Internet shell program that ends this chapter:

```
int serverFd; /* Server socket
struct sockaddr_in serverINETAddress; /* Server Internet address */
struct sockaddr* serverSockAddrPtr; /* Pointer to server address */
struct sockaddr_in clientINETAddress; /* Client Internet address */
struct sockaddr* clientSockAddrPtr; /* Pointer to client address */
int port = 13; /* Set to the port that you wish to serve */
int serverLen; /* Length of address structure */

serverFd = socket (AF_INET, SOCK_STREAM, DEFAULT_PROTOCOL); /* Create */
serverLen = sizeof (serverINETAddress); /* Length of structure */

bzero ((char*) &serverINETAddress, serverLen); /* Clear structure */
serverINETAddress.sin_family = AF_INET; /* Internet domain */
serverINETAddress.sin_addr.s_addr = htonl (INADDR_ANY); /* Accept all */
serverINETAddress.sin_port = htons (port); /* Server port number */
```

When the address is created, the socket is bound to the address, and its queue size is specified in the usual way:

```
serverSockAddrPtr = (struct sockaddr*) &serverINETAddress;
bind (serverFd, serverSockAddrPtr, serverLen);
listen (serverFd, 5);
```

The final step is to accept client connections. When a successful connection is made, the client socket address is filled with the client's IP address and a new file descriptor is returned:

```
clientLen = sizeof (clientINETAddress);
clientSockAddrPtr = (struct sockaddr*) clientINETAddress;
clientFd = accept (serverFd, clientSockAddrPtr, &clientLen);
```

As you can see, an Internet server's code is very similar to that of an AF_UNIX server. The final example in this chapter is the Internet shell.

THE INTERNET SHELL

Have you ever wondered what the inside of a shell looks like? Well, here's a great opportunity to learn how they work and to obtain some source code that could help you to create your own shell. I designed the Internet shell to be a lot like the standard UNIX shells in the sense that it provides piping and background processing facilities, but I also added some Internet-specific abilities that the other shells lack.

Restrictions

In order to pack the functionality of the Internet shell into a reasonable size, there are a few restrictions:

- All tokens must be separated by whitespace (tabs or spaces). This means that instead of writing **ls; date** you must write **ls ; date**. This makes the lexical analyzer very simple.
- Filename substitution (globbing) is not supported. This means that the standard *, ?, and [ ] metacharacters are not understood.

These features are nice to have in an everyday shell, but their implementation wouldn't have taught you anything significant about how shells work.

Command Syntax

The syntax of an Internet shell command is very similar to that of the standard UNIX shells, and is formally described below using BNF notation. Note that the redirection symbols < and > are escaped by a \ to prevent ambiguity. See the appendix for a discussion of BNF.

```
<internetShellcommand> = <sequence> [ & ]
<sequence> = <pipeline> { ; <pipeline> }*
<pipeline> = <simple> { | <simple> }
<simple> = { <token> }* { <redirection>}*
<redirection> = <fileRedirection> | <socketRedirection>
<fileRedirection> = \> <file> | >> <file> | \< <file>
<socketRedirection> = <clientRedirection> | <serverRedirection>
<clientRedirection> = @\>c <socket> | @\<c <socket>
<serverDirection> = @\>s <socket> | @\<s <socket>
<token> = a string of characters
<file> = a valid UNIX pathname
<socket> = either a UNIX pathname (UNIX domain socket) or
           an Internet socket name of the form hostname.port#
```

Starting The Internet Shell

I named the Internet shell executable **ish**. The Internet shell prompt is a question mark.

When **ish** is started, it inherits the $PATH environment variable from the shell that invokes it. The value of $PATH may be changed by using the **setenv** built-in command that is described shortly.

To exit the Internet shell, press a *Control-D* on a line of its own.

Built-in Commands

The Internet shell executes most commands by creating a child shell that exec's the specified utility while the parent shell waits for the child. However, some

commands are built into the shell and are executed directly. Here is a list of the
built-ins:

Built-in	Function
echo {<token>}*	echoes tokens to the terminal
cd *path*	changes the shell's working directory to *path*
getenv *name*	displays the value of the environment variable *name*
setenv *name value*	sets the value of the environment variable *name* to *value*

Built-in commands may be redirected. Before I describe the construction and
operation of the Internet shell, let's take a look at a few examples of both regular
commands and Internet-specific commands.

Some Regular Examples

Here are some examples that illustrate the sequencing, redirection, and piping
capabilities of the Internet shell:

```
$ ish                               ...start shell.
Internet Shell.
? ls                                ...simple command.
ish.c       ish.cs            ish.van          who.socket   who.sort
? ls | wc                           ...pipe.
        5        5       41
? who | sort > who.sort &           ...pipe + redirect + background.
[4356]                              ...PID of background process.
? cat who.sort                      ...show redirection worked.
glass     ttyp2    May 28 18:33 (bridge05.utdalla)
posey     ttyp0    May 22 10:19 (blackfoot.utdall)
posey     ttyp1    May 22 10:19 (blackfoot.utdall)
? date ; whoami                     ...sequence of commands.
Thu May 28 18:36:24 CDT 1992
glass
? echo hi there                     ...execute a built-in.
hi there
? getenv PATH                       ...look at PATH env variable.
.:.:/usr/local/bin:/usr/ucb:/usr/bin:/bin:/usr/etc
? mail glass < who.sort             ...input redirection works too.
? ^D                                ...exit shell.
$ _
```

Some Internet Examples

The Internet shell becomes pretty interesting when you examine its socket features. Here's an example that uses a UNIX domain socket to communicate information:

```
$ ish                    ...start the Internet shell.
Internet Shell.
? who @>s who.sck &      ...server sends output to socket "who.sck".
[2678]
? ls                     ...execute a command for fun.
ish.c      ish.van          who.sock    who.sort
ish.cs     who.sck          who.socket
? sort @<c who.sck       ...client reads input from socket "who.sck".
glass      ttyp2    May 28 18:33 (bridge05.utdalla)
posey      ttyp0    May 22 10:19 (blackfoot.utdall)
posey      ttyp1    May 22 10:19 (blackfoot.utdall)
veerasam ttyp3     May 28 18:39 (129.110.70.139)
? ^D                     ...quit shell.
$ _
```

The really fun stuff happens when you introduce Internet sockets. The first shell
in the next example was run on a host called "csservr2," and the second shell was
run on a host called "vanguard":

```
$ ish                    ...run Internet shell on csservr2.
Internet Shell.
? who @>s 5000 &         ...background server sends output to port 5000.
[7221]
? ^D                     ...quit shell.
$ rlogin vanguard        ...login to vanguard host.
% ish                    ...run Internet shell on vanguard.
Internet Shell.
? sort @<c csservr2.5000      ...client reads input from csservr2.
                              ...port 5000.
IP address = 129.110.42.1     ...echoed by Internet shell.
glass      ttyp2    May 28 18:42 (bridge05.utdalla)      ...output from
posey      ttyp0    May 22 10:19 (blackfoot.utdall)      ...who on
posey      ttyp1    May 22 10:19 (blackfoot.utdall)      ...csservr2!
veerasam ttyp3     May 28 18:39 (129.110.70.139)
? ^D                     ...quit shell.
% ^D                     ...logout from vanguard.
logout
$ _                      ...back to csservr2
```

Here's an illustration of the socket connection:

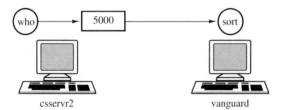

Figure 10.13 Internet shell redirection

The next example is even more interesting. The first shell uses one socket to talk to the second shell, and the second shell uses another socket to talk to the third:

```
$ ish                      ...start shell on csservr2.
Internet Shell.
? who @>s 5001 &           ...background server sends output to port 5001.
[2001]
? ^D                       ...quit shell.
$ rlogin vanguard          ...login to vanguard.
% ish                      ...start shell onvanguard.
Internet Shell.
? sort @<c csservr2.5001 @>s 5002 &      ...background process reads
[3756]                                   ...input from port 5001 on
                                         ...csservr2 and sends it to
                                         ...local port 5002.
IP address = 129.110.42.1                ...echoed by shell.
? ^D                       ...quit shell.
% ^D                       ...logout of vanguard.
logout
$ ish                      ...start another shell on csservr2.
Internet Shell.
? cat @<c vanguard.5002 ...read input from port 5002 on vanguard.
IP address = 129.110.43.128       ...echoed by the shell.
glass    ttyp2    May 28 18:42 (bridge05.utdalla)
posey    ttyp0    May 22 10:19 (blackfoot.utdall)
posey    ttyp1    May 22 10:19 (blackfoot.utdall)
veerasam ttyp3    May 28 18:39 (129.110.70.139)
? ^D                       ...quit shell.
$ _
```

Here's an illustration of the two socket connections:

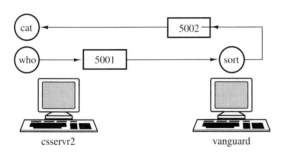

Figure 10.14 More Internet shell redirection

How It Works

The operation of the Internet shell can be broken down into several main sections:

- the main command loop
- parsing
- executing built-in commands
- executing pipelines
- executing sequences
- background processing
- dealing with signals
- performing file redirection
- performing socket redirection

Each operation will now be described, together with code fragments and diagrams when necessary. Before you continue, I suggest that you glance through the source code listing at the end of this chapter to familiarize yourself with its overall layout.

The Main Command Loop

When the shell starts, it initializes a signal handler to catch keyboard interrupts and resets an error flag. It then enters commandLoop ( ) [167], which prompts the user for a line of input, parses it, and then executes the command. This function loops until the user enters a *Control-D*, at which point the shell terminates. The next few subsections describe the parsing and execution process.

Parsing

In order to easily check the command line for errors, the line is first broken down into separate tokens by tokenize ( ) [321], which is located in the lexical analyzer section of the source code. tokenize ( ) is called by the commandLoop ( ) [167] routine, and fills the global **tokens** array with pointers to each individual token. For example, if the input line was ''ls -l,'' **tokens**[0] would point to the string ''ls,'' and **tokens**[1] would point to the string ''-l''. Once the line is parsed, the global token pointer **tIndex** is set to zero [350] in preparation for the parsing process.

The parsing is performed in a top-down fashion. The main parser, parseSequence ( ) [194], is called from the commandLoop ( ) function. This function parses each pipeline in the sequence by invoking parsePipeline ( ), and records the information that parsePipeline ( ) returns. Finally, it checks to see whether the sequence is to be executed in the background.

Similarly, parsePipeline ( ) [222] parses each simple command in the pipeline by calling parseSimple ( ), and records the information that parseSimple ( ) returns.

parseSimple ( ) [242] records the tokens in the simple command and then processes any trailing metacharacters such as >, >>, and @>s.

The information that each of these parsing functions gathers is stored in structures for later use by the execution routines. A **struct sequence** [75] can hold the details of up to 5 (MAX_PIPES) pipelines, together with a flag indicating whether or not the sequence is to be executed in the background. Each pipeline is recorded in a **struct pipeline** [67], which can record the details of up to 5 (MAX_SIMPLE) simple commands. Finally, a **struct simple** [52] can the hold up to 100 (MAX_TOKENS) tokens together with several fields that record information related to I/O redirection.

If a command is parsed with no errors, the local variable **sequence** [182] is equal to a **struct sequence**, which holds the analyzed version of the command.

Please note that although I could have used pointers to return structures more efficiently, I chose to keep the program as simple as I could in order to focus on the UNIX-specific aspects.

Executing A Command Sequence

The main command loop executes a successfully parsed command by invoking executeSequence ( ) [444]. This routine does one of two things:

- If the command is to be executed in the background, it creates a child process to execute the pipelines in sequence; the original parent shell does not wait for the child. Before executing the pipeline, the child restores its original interrupt handler and places itself into a new process group to make it immune from hangups and other signals. This ensures that a background process will continue to execute even when the shell is terminated and the user logs out.
- If the command is to be executed in the foreground, the parent shell executes the pipelines in sequence.

In both cases, executePipeline ( ) [472] is used to execute each pipeline component of the command sequence.

Executing Pipelines

executePipeline ( ) [472] performs one of two actions:

- If the pipeline is a simple built-in command, it executes the simple command directly, without creating a child process. This is very important. For example, the built-in command **cd** executes chdir ( ) to change the shell's current working directory. If a child shell was created to execute this built-in command, the original parent shell's working directory would be unaffected, which would be incorrect.

• If the pipeline is more than a simple built-in command, it creates a child shell to execute the pipeline; the original parent shell waits for the child to complete. Notice that the parent waits for a specific PID by calling waitForPid ( ) [503]. This is because the parent shell might have created some previous children to execute background processes, and it would be incorrect for the parent to resume when one of these background processes terminated. If the pipeline contains only one simple command, then no pipes need to be created, and executeSimple ( ) [569] is invoked. Otherwise, executePipes ( ) [516] is invoked, which connects each command by its own pipe.

executePipes ( ) is a fairly complicated routine. If the pipeline contains **n** simple commands, then executePipes ( ) creates **n** child processes, one for each command, and **n-1** pipes to connect the children. Each child reconnects its standard input and/or output channels to the appropriate pipe, and then closes all of the original pipe file descriptors. Each child then executes its associated simple command. Meanwhile, the original process that invoked executePipes ( ) waits for all of its children to terminate.

Executing A Simple Command

executeSimple ( ) [569] redirects the standard input and/or output channels as necessary and then executes either executeBuiltIn ( ) [635] or executePrimitive ( ) [596], depending on the category of the command. builtIn ( ) [624] returns true if a token is the name of a built-in command.

If the command is a built-in, it's possible that the command is being executed directly by the shell. To prevent the shell's I/O channels being altered by redirection, the original standard input and output channels are recorded and restored later.

executePrimitive ( ) [596] simply execs the command using execvp ( ). Fortunately (but not coincidentally), **p->token** is already in the form required by execvp ( ). Built-in functions are executed by executeBuiltIn ( ) [635] using a simple switch statement.

Redirection

redirect ( ) [761] performs all of the preprocessing necessary for both file and socket redirection. The basic technique for redirecting the standard I/O channels is the same as I described earlier in this chapter.

If file redirection is required, dupFd ( ) [806] is invoked to create the file with the appropriate mode and to duplicate the standard file descriptor.

If socket redirection is required, either server ( ) [950] or client ( ) [879] is invoked to create the appropriate type of socket connection. These functions manipulate both UNIX domain and Internet domain sockets in the same way as the earlier socket examples.

Extensions

I think that it could be a lot of fun and fairly educational to add some new features to the Internet shell. If you're interested, please see the project section at the end of this chapter for some suggestions.

Internet Source Code Listing

```
1   #include <stdio.h>
2   #include <stdlib.h>
3   #include <string.h>
4   #include <signal.h>
5   #include <ctype.h>
6   #include <sys/types.h>
7   #include <sys/file.h>
8   #include <sys/ioctl.h>
9   #include <sys/socket.h>
10  #include <sys/un.h>
11  #include <netinet/in.h>
12  #include <arpa/inet.h>
13  #include <netdb.h>
14
15
16  /* Macros */
17  #define MAX_STRING_LENGTH       200
18  #define MAX_TOKENS              100
19  #define MAX_TOKEN_LENGTH        30
20  #define MAX_SIMPLE              5
21  #define MAX_PIPES               5
22  #define NOT_FOUND               -1
23  #define REGULAR                 -1
24  #define DEFAULT_PERMISSION      0660
25  #define DEFAULT_PROTOCOL        0
26  #define DEFAULT_QUEUE_LENGTH    5
27  #define SOCKET_SLEEP            1
28
29
30  /* Enumerators */
31  enum { FALSE, TRUE };
```

```
32   enum metacharacterEnum
33     {
34       SEMICOLON, BACKGROUND, END_OF_LINE, REDIRECT_OUTPUT,
35       REDIRECT_INPUT, APPEND_OUTPUT, PIPE,
36       REDIRECT_OUTPUT_SERVER, REDIRECT_OUTPUT_CLIENT,
37       REDIRECT_INPUT_SERVER, REDIRECT_INPUT_CLIENT
38     };
39   enum builtInEnum { ECHO_BUILTIN, SETENV, GETENV, CD };
40   enum descriptorEnum { STDIN, STDOUT, STDERR };
41   enum pipeEnum { READ, WRITE };
42   enum IOEnum
43     {
44       NO_REDIRECT, FILE_REDIRECT,
45       SERVER_REDIRECT, CLIENT_REDIRECT
46     };
47   enum socketEnum { CLIENT, SERVER };
48   enum { TWO_WAY_SOCKET, INPUT_SOCKET, OUTPUT_SOCKET };
49
50
51   /* Every simple command has one of these associated with it */
52   struct simple
53     {
54       char* token [MAX_TOKENS]; /* The tokens of the command */
55       int count; /* The number of tokens */
56       int outputRedirect; /* Set to an IOEnum */
57       int inputRedirect; /* Set to an IOEnum */
58       int append; /* Set to true for append mode */
59       char *outputFile; /* Name of output file or NULL if none */
60       char *inputFile; /* Name of input file or NULL if none */
61       char *outputSocket; /* Output socket name or NULL if none */
62       char *inputSocket; /* Name of input socket or NULL if none */
63     };
64
65
66   /* Every pipeline has one of these associated with it */
67   struct pipeline
68     {
69       struct simple simple [MAX_SIMPLE]; /* Commands in pipe */
70       int count; /* The number of simple commands */
71     };
72
73
74   /* Every command sequence has one of these associated with it */
75   struct sequence
76     {
77       struct pipeline pipeline [MAX_PIPES]; /* Pipes in sequence */
78       int count; /* The number of pipes */
79       int background; /* True if this is a background sequence */
```

```
80    };
81
82
83    /* Prototypes */
84    struct sequence parseSequence ();
85    struct pipeline parsePipeline ();
86    struct simple parseSimple ();
87    char *nextToken ();
88    char *peekToken ();
89    char *lastToken ();
90    char* getToken ();
91
92
93    /* Globals */
94    char* metacharacters [] = { ";", "&", "\n", ">", "<", ">>",
95       "|", "@>s", "@>c", "@<s", "@<c", "" };
96    char* builtIns [] = { "echo", "setenv", "getenv", "cd", "" };
97    char line [MAX_STRING_LENGTH]; /* The current line */
98    char tokens [MAX_TOKENS][MAX_TOKEN_LENGTH]; /* Tokens in line */
99    int tokenCount; /* The number of tokens in the current line */
100   int tIndex; /* Index into line: used by lexical analyzer */
101   int errorFlag; /* Set to true when an error occurs */
102
103
104   /* Some forward declarations */
105   void (*originalQuitHandler) ();
106   int quitHandler ();
107
108
109   /* Externals */
110   char **environ; /* Pointer to the environment */
111
112   /******************************************************************/
113
114   main (argc, argv)
115
116   int argc;
117   char* argv [];
118
119   {
120     initialize (); /* Initialize some globals */
121     commandLoop (); /* Accept and process commands */
122     return (/* EXIT_SUCCESS */ 0);
123   }
124
125   /******************************************************************/
126
127   initialize ()
```

```
128
129   {
130     printf ("Internet Shell.\n"); /* Introduction */
131     /* Set the Control-C handler to catch keyboard interrupts */
132     originalQuitHandler = signal (SIGINT, quitHandler);
133   }
134
135   /*****************************************************************/
136
137   quitHandler ()
138
139   {
140     /* Control-C handler */
141     printf ("\n");
142     displayPrompt ();
143   }
144
145   /*****************************************************************/
146
147   error (str)
148
149   char* str;
150
151   {
152     /* Display str as an error to the standard error channel */
153     fprintf (stderr, "%s", str);
154     errorFlag = TRUE; /* Set error flag */
155   }
156
157   /*****************************************************************/
158
159   displayPrompt ()
160
161   {
162     printf ("? ");
163   }
164
165   /*****************************************************************/
166
167   commandLoop ()
168
169   {
170     struct sequence sequence;
171
172     /* Accept and process commands until a Control-D occurs */
173     while (TRUE)
174       {
175         displayPrompt ();
```

```
176            if (gets (line) == NULL) break; /* Get a line of input */
177            tokenize (); /* Break the input line into tokens */
178            errorFlag = FALSE; /* Reset the error flag */
179
180            if (tokenCount > 1) /* Process any non-empty line */
181               {
182                  sequence = parseSequence (); /* Parse the line */
183                  /* If no errors occurred during the parsing, */
184                  /* execute the command */
185                  if (!errorFlag) executeSequence (&sequence);
186               }
187          }
188    }
189
190    /********************************************************************/
191    /*                      PARSER ROUTINES                             */
192    /********************************************************************/
193
194    struct sequence parseSequence ()
195
196    {
197       struct sequence q;
198
199       /* Parse a command sequence and return structure description */
200       q.count = 0; /* Number of pipes in the sequence */
201       q.background = FALSE; /* Default is not in background */
202
203       while (TRUE) /* Loop until no semicolon delimiter is found */
204          {
205             q.pipeline[q.count++] = parsePipeline (); /* Parse */
206             if (peekCode () != SEMICOLON) break;
207             nextToken (); /* Flush semicolon delimiter */
208          }
209
210       if (peekCode () == BACKGROUND) /* Sequence is in background */
211          {
212             q.background = TRUE;
213             nextToken (); /* Flush ampersand */
214          }
215
216       getToken (END_OF_LINE); /* Check end-of-line is reached */
217       return (q);
218    }
219
220    /********************************************************************/
221
222    struct pipeline parsePipeline ()
223
```

```
224   {
225      struct pipeline p;
226
227      /* Parse a pipeline and return a structure description of it */
228      p.count = 0; /* The number of simple commands in the pipeline */
229
230      while (TRUE) /* Loop until no pipe delimiter is found */
231         {
232            p.simple[p.count++] = parseSimple (); /* Parse command */
233            if (peekCode () != PIPE) break;
234            nextToken (); /* Flush pipe delimiter */
235         }
236
237      return (p);
238   }
239
240   /******************************************************************/
241
242   struct simple parseSimple ()
243
244   {
245      struct simple s;
246      int code;
247      int done;
248
249      /* Parse a simple command and return a structure description */
250      s.count = 0; /* The number of tokens in the simple command */
251      s.outputFile = s.inputFile = NULL;
252      s.inputSocket = s.outputSocket = NULL;
253      s.outputRedirect = s.inputRedirect = NO_REDIRECT; /* Defaults */
254      s.append = FALSE;
255
256      while (peekCode () == REGULAR) /* Store all regular tokens */
257         s.token[s.count++] = nextToken ();
258
259      s.token[s.count] = NULL; /* NULL-terminate token list */
260      done = FALSE;
261
262      /* Parse special metacharacters that follow, like > and >> */
263      do
264         {
265            code = peekCode ();/* Peek at next token */
266
267            switch (code)
268               {
269                  case REDIRECT_INPUT: /* < */
270                     nextToken ();
271                     s.inputFile = getToken (REGULAR);
```

```
272                    s.inputRedirect = FILE_REDIRECT;
273                    break;
274
275                case REDIRECT_OUTPUT: /* > */
276                case APPEND_OUTPUT: /* >> */
277                    nextToken ();
278                    s.outputFile = getToken (REGULAR);
279                    s.outputRedirect = FILE_REDIRECT;
280                    s.append = (code == APPEND_OUTPUT);
281                    break;
282
283                case REDIRECT_OUTPUT_SERVER: /* @>s */
284                    nextToken ();
285                    s.outputSocket = getToken (REGULAR);
286                    s.outputRedirect = SERVER_REDIRECT;
287                    break;
288
289                case REDIRECT_OUTPUT_CLIENT: /* @>c */
290                    nextToken ();
291                    s.outputSocket = getToken (REGULAR);
292                    s.outputRedirect = CLIENT_REDIRECT;
293                    break;
294
295                case REDIRECT_INPUT_SERVER: /* @<s */
296                    nextToken ();
297                    s.inputSocket = getToken (REGULAR);
298                    s.inputRedirect = SERVER_REDIRECT;
299                    break;
300
301                case REDIRECT_INPUT_CLIENT: /* @<c */
302                    nextToken ();
303                    s.inputSocket = getToken (REGULAR);
304                    s.inputRedirect = CLIENT_REDIRECT;
305                    break;
306
307            default:
308                done = TRUE;
309                break;
310            }
311        }
312    while (!done);
313
314    return (s);
315 }
316
317 /********************************************************************/
318 /*                  LEXICAL ANALYZER ROUTINES                       */
319 /********************************************************************/
```

```
320
321  tokenize ()
322
323  {
324    char* ptr = line; /* Point to the input buffer */
325    char token [MAX_TOKEN_LENGTH]; /* Holds the current token */
326    char* tptr; /* Pointer to current character */
327
328    tIndex = 0; /* Global: points to the current token */
329
330    /* Break the current line of input into tokens */
331    while (TRUE)
332      {
333        tptr = token;
334        while (*ptr == ' ') ++ptr; /* Skip leading spaces */
335        if (*ptr == NULL) break; /* End of line */
336
337        do
338          {
339            *tptr++ = *ptr++;
340            }
341        while (*ptr != ' ' && *ptr != NULL);
342
343        *tptr = NULL;
344        strcpy (tokens[tIndex++], token); /* Store the token */
345      }
346
347    /* Place an end-of-line token at the end of the token list */
348    strcpy (tokens[tIndex++], "\n");
349    tokenCount = tIndex; /* Remember total token count */
350    tIndex = 0; /* Reset token index to start of token list */
351  }
352
353  /****************************************************************/
354
355  char* nextToken ()
356
357  {
358    return (tokens[tIndex++]); /* Return next token in list */
359  }
360
361  /****************************************************************/
362
363  char *lastToken ()
364
365  {
366    return (tokens[tIndex - 1]); /* Return previous token in list */
367  }
```

```
368
369     /******************************************************************/
370
371     peekCode ()
372
373     {
374        /* Return a peek at code of the next token in the list */
375        return (tokenCode (peekToken ()));
376     }
377
378     /******************************************************************/
379
380     char* peekToken ()
381
382     {
383        /* Return a peek at the next token in the list */
384        return (tokens[tIndex]);
385     }
386
387     /******************************************************************/
388
389     char *getToken (code)
390
391     int code;
392
393     {
394        char str [MAX_STRING_LENGTH];
395
396        /* Generate error if the code of the next token is not code */
397        /* Otherwise return the token */
398        if (peekCode () != code)
399           {
400              sprintf (str, "Expected %s\n", metacharacters[code]);
401              error (str);
402              return (NULL);
403           }
404        else
405           return (nextToken ());
406     }
407
408     /******************************************************************/
409
410     tokenCode (token)
411
412     char* token;
413
414     {
```

```
415     /* Return the index of token in the metacharacter array */
416     return (findString (metacharacters, token));
417   }
418
419   /*****************************************************************/
420
421   findString (strs, str)
422
423   char* strs [];
424   char* str;
425
426   {
427     int i = 0;
428
429     /* Return the index of str in the string array strs */
430     /* or NOT_FOUND if it isn't there */
431     while (strcmp (strs[i], "") != 0)
432       if (strcmp (strs[i], str) == 0)
433         return (i);
434       else
435         ++i;
436
437     return (NOT_FOUND); /* Not found */
438   }
439
440   /*****************************************************************/
441   /*                  COMMAND EXECUTION ROUTINES                   */
442   /*****************************************************************/
443
444   executeSequence (p)
445
446   struct sequence* p;
447
448   {
449     int i, result;
450
451     /* Execute a sequence of statments (possibly just one) */
452     if (p->background) /* Execute in background */
453       {
454         if (fork () == 0)
455           {
456             printf ("[%d]\n", getpid ()); /* Display child PID */
457           /* Child process */
458             signal (SIGQUIT, originalQuitHandler); /* Oldhandler */
459             setpgrp (0, getpid ()); /* Change process group */
460             for (i = 0; i < p->count; i++) /* Execute pipelines */
461               executePipeline (&p->pipeline[i]);
462             exit (/* EXIT_SUCCESS */ 0);
```

```
463                  }
464          }
465      else /* Execute in foreground */
466          for (i = 0; i < p->count; i++) /* Execute each pipeline */
467              executePipeline (&p->pipeline[i]);
468  }
469
470  /******************************************************************/
471
472  executePipeline (p)
473
474  struct pipeline *p;
475
476  {
477      int pid, processGroup, result;
478
479      /* Execute every simple command in pipeline (possibly one) */
480      if (p->count == 1 && builtIn (p->simple[0].token[0]))
481          executeSimple (&p->simple[0]); /* Execute it directly */
482      else
483          {
484              if ((pid = fork ()) == 0)
485                  {
486                      /* Child shell executes the simple commands */
487                      if (p->count == 1)
488                          executeSimple (&p->simple[0]); /* Execute command */
489                      else
490                          executePipes (p); /* Execute more than one command */
491                      exit ( /* EXIT_SUCCESS */ 0);
492                  }
493              else
494                  {
495                      /* Parent shell waits for child to complete */
496                      waitForPID (pid);
497                  }
498          }
499  }
500
501  /******************************************************************/
502
503  waitForPID (pid)
504
505  int pid;
506
507  {
508      int status;
509
510      /* Return when the child process with PID pid terminates */
```

```
511      while (wait (&status) != pid);
512    }
513
514    /**************************************************************/
515
516    executePipes (p)
517
518    struct pipeline *p;
519
520    {
521      int pipes, status, i;
522      int pipefd [MAX_PIPES][2];
523
524      /* Execute two or more simple commands connected by pipes */
525      pipes = p->count - 1; /* Number of pipes to build */
526      for (i = 0; i < pipes; i++) /* Build the pipes */
527        pipe (pipefd[i]);
528      for (i = 0; i < p->count; i++) /* Build one process per pipe */
529        {
530          if (fork () != 0) continue;
531          /* Child shell */
532          /* First, connect stdin to pipe if not the first command */
533          if (i != 0) dup2 (pipefd[i-1][READ], STDIN);
534          /* Second, connect stdout to pipe if not the last command */
535          if (i != p->count - 1) dup2 (pipefd[i][WRITE], STDOUT);
536          /* Third, close all of the pipes' file descriptors */
537          closeAllPipes (pipefd, pipes);
538          /* Last, execute the simple command */
539          executeSimple (&p->simple[i]);
540          exit (/* EXIT_SUCCESS */0);
541        }
542
543      /* The parent shell comes here after forking the children */
544      closeAllPipes (pipefd, pipes);
545      for (i = 0; i < p->count; i++) /* Wait for children to finish */
546        wait (&status);
547    }
548
549    /**************************************************************/
550
551    closeAllPipes (pipefd, pipes)
552
553    int pipefd [][2];
554    int pipes;
555
556    {
557      int i;
558
```

```
559      /* Close every pipe's file descriptors */
560      for (i = 0; i < pipes; i++)
561        {
562          close (pipefd[i][READ]);
563          close (pipefd[i][WRITE]);
564        }
565  }
566
567  /******************************************************************/
568
569  executeSimple (p)
570
571  struct simple* p;
572
573  {
574    int copyStdin, copyStdout;
575
576    /* Execute a simple command */
577    if (builtIn (p->token[0])) /* Built-in */
578      {
579        /* The parent shell is executing this, so remember */
580        /* stdin and stdout in case of built-in redirection */
581        copyStdin = dup (STDIN);
582        copyStdout = dup (STDOUT);
583        if (redirect (p)) executeBuiltIn (p); /* Execute built-in */
584        /* Restore stdin and stdout */
585        dup2 (copyStdin, STDIN);
586        dup2 (copyStdout, STDOUT);
587        close (copyStdin);
588        close (copyStdout);
589      }
590    else if (redirect (p)) /* Redirect if necessary */
591      executePrimitive (p); /* Execute primitive command */
592  }
593
594  /******************************************************************/
595
596  executePrimitive (p)
597
598  struct simple* p;
599
600  {
601    /* Execute a command by exec'ing */
602    if (execvp (p->token[0], p->token) == -1)
603      {
604        perror ("ish");
605        exit (/* EXIT_FAILURE */ 1);
606      }
```

```
607  }
608
609  /*******************************************************************/
610  /*                    BUILT-IN COMMANDS                            */
611  /*******************************************************************/
612
613  builtInCode (token)
614
615  char* token;
616
617  {
618    /* Return the index of token in the builtIns array */
619    return (findString (builtIns, token));
620  }
621
622  /*******************************************************************/
623
624  builtIn (token)
625
626  char* token;
627
628  {
629    /* Return true if token is a built-in */
630    return (builtInCode (token) != NOT_FOUND);
631  }
632
633  /*******************************************************************/
634
635  executeBuiltIn (p)
636
637  struct simple* p;
638
639  {
640    /* Execute a single built-in command */
641    switch (builtInCode (p->token[0]))
642      {
643        case CD:
644          executeCd (p);
645          break;
646
647        case ECHO_BUILTIN:
648          executeEcho (p);
649          break;
650
651        case GETENV:
652          executeGetenv (p);
653          break;
654
```

```
655              case SETENV:
656                 executeSetenv (p);
657                 break;
658          }
659  }
660
661  /******************************************************************/
662
663  executeEcho (p)
664
665  struct simple* p;
666
667  {
668     int i;
669
670     /* Echo the tokens in this command */
671     for (i = 1; i < p->count; i++)
672       printf ("%s ", p->token[i]);
673
674     printf ("\n");
675  }
676
677  /******************************************************************/
678
679  executeGetenv (p)
680
681  struct simple* p;
682
683  {
684     char* value;
685
686     /* Echo the value of an environment variable */
687     if (p->count != 2)
688       {
689          error ("Usage: getenv variable\n");
690          return;
691       }
692
693     value = getenv (p->token[1]);
694
695     if (value == NULL)
696       printf ("Environment variable is not currently set\n");
697     else
698       printf ("%s\n", value);
699  }
700
701  /******************************************************************/
702
```

```
703   executeSetenv (p)
704
705   struct simple* p;
706
707   {
708     /* Set the value of an environment variable */
709     if (p->count != 3)
710       error ("Usage: setenv variable value\n");
711     else
712       setenv (p->token[1], p->token[2]);
713   }
714
715   /****************************************************************/
716
717   setenv (envName, newValue)
718
719   char* envName;
720   char* newValue;
721
722   {
723     int i = 0;
724     char newStr [MAX_STRING_LENGTH];
725     int len;
726
727     /* Set the environment variable envName to newValue */
728     sprintf (newStr, "%s=%s", envName, newValue);
729     len = strlen (envName) + 1;
730
731     while (environ[i] != NULL)
732       {
733         if (strncmp (environ[i], newStr, len) == 0) break;
734         ++i;
735       }
736
737     if (environ[i] == NULL) environ[i+1] = NULL;
738
739     environ[i] = (char*) malloc (strlen (newStr) + 1);
740     strcpy (environ[i], newStr);
741   }
742
743   /****************************************************************/
744
745   executeCd (p)
746
747   struct simple* p;
748
749   {
750     /* Change directory */
```

```
751    if (p->count != 2)
752      error ("Usage: cd path\n");
753    else if (chdir (p->token[1]) == -1)
754      perror ("ish");
755  }
756
757  /******************************************************************/
758  /*                         REDIRECTION                          */
759  /******************************************************************/
760
761  redirect (p)
762
763  struct simple *p;
764
765  {
766    int mask;
767
768    /* Perform input redirection */
769    switch (p->inputRedirect)
770       {
771         case FILE_REDIRECT: /* Redirect from a file */
772            if (!dupFd (p->inputFile, O_RDONLY, STDIN)) return(FALSE);
773            break;
774
775         case SERVER_REDIRECT: /* Redirect from a server socket */
776            if (!server (p->inputSocket, INPUT_SOCKET)) return(FALSE);
777            break;
778
779         case CLIENT_REDIRECT: /* Redirect from a client socket */
780            if (!client (p->inputSocket, INPUT_SOCKET)) return(FALSE);
781            break;
782       }
783
784    /* Perform output redirection */
785    switch (p->outputRedirect)
786       {
787         case FILE_REDIRECT: /* Redirect to a file */
788            mask = O_CREAT | O_WRONLY | (p->append?O_APPEND:O_TRUNC);
789            if (!dupFd (p->outputFile, mask, STDOUT)) return (FALSE);
790            break;
791
792         case SERVER_REDIRECT: /* Redirect to a server socket */
793            if (!server(p->outputSocket,OUTPUT_SOCKET)) return(FALSE);
794         break;
795
796         case CLIENT_REDIRECT: /* Redirect to a client socket */
797            if (!client(p->outputSocket,OUTPUT_SOCKET)) return(FALSE);
798            break;
```

```
799        }
800
801     return (TRUE); /* If I got here, then everything went OK */
802    }
803
804    /****************************************************************/
805
806    dupFd (name, mask, stdFd)
807
808    char* name;
809    int mask, stdFd;
810
811    {
812      int fd;
813
814      /* Duplicate a new file descriptor over stdin/stdout */
815      fd = open (name, mask, DEFAULT_PERMISSION);
816
817      if (fd == -1)
818        {
819          error ("Cannot redirect\n");
820          return (FALSE);
821        }
822
823      dup2 (fd, stdFd); /* Copy over standard file descriptor */
824      close (fd); /* Close other one */
825      return (TRUE);
826    }
827
828    /****************************************************************/
829    /*                   SOCKET MANAGEMENT                          */
830    /****************************************************************/
831
832    internetAddress (name)
833
834    char* name;
835
836    {
837      /* If name contains a digit, assume it's an internet address */
838      return (strpbrk (name, "01234567890") != NULL);
839    }
840
841    /****************************************************************/
842
843    socketRedirect (type)
844
845    int type;
846
```

```
847  {
848     return (type == SERVER_REDIRECT || type == CLIENT_REDIRECT);
849  }
850
851  /*****************************************************************/
852
853  getHostAndPort (str, name, port)
854
855  char *str, *name;
856  int* port;
857
858  {
859     char *tok1, *tok2;
860
861     /* Decode name and port number from input string of the form */
862     /* NAME.PORT */
863     tok1 = strtok (str, ".");
864     tok2 = strtok (NULL, ".");
865     if (tok2 == NULL) /* Name missing, so assume local host */
866        {
867           strcpy (name, "");
868           sscanf (tok1, "%d", port);
869        }
870     else
871        {
872           strcpy (name, tok1);
873           sscanf (tok2, "%d", port);
874        }
875  }
876
877  /*****************************************************************/
878
879  client (name, type)
880
881  char* name;
882  int type;
883
884  {
885     int clientFd, result, internet, domain, serverLen, port;
886     char hostName [100];
887     struct sockaddr_un serverUNIXAddress;
888     struct sockaddr_in serverINETAddress;
889     struct sockaddr* serverSockAddrPtr;
890     struct hostent* hostStruct;
891     struct in_addr* hostNode;
892
893     /* Open a client socket with specified name and type */
894     internet = internetAddress (name); /* Internet socket? */
```

```
895     domain = internet ? AF_INET : AF_UNIX; /* Pick domain */
896     /* Create client socket */
897     clientFd = socket (domain, SOCK_STREAM, DEFAULT_PROTOCOL);
898
899     if (clientFd == -1)
900        {
901          perror ("ish");
902          return (FALSE);
903        }
904
905     if (internet) /* Internet socket */
906        {
907          getHostAndPort (name, hostName, &port); /* Get name, port */
908          if (hostName[0] == NULL) gethostname (hostName, 100);
909          serverINETAddress.sin_family = AF_INET; /* Internet */
910          hostStruct = gethostbyname (hostName); /* Find host */
911
912          if (hostStruct == NULL)
913             {
914               perror ("ish");
915               return (FALSE);
916             }
917
918          hostNode = (struct in_addr*) hostStruct->h_addr;
919          printf ("IP address = %s\n", inet_ntoa (*hostNode));
920          serverINETAddress.sin_addr = *hostNode; /* Set IP address */
921          serverINETAddress.sin_port = port; /* Set port */
922          serverSockAddrPtr = (struct sockaddr*) &serverINETAddress;
923          serverLen = sizeof (serverINETAddress);
924        }
925     else /* UNIX domain socket */
926        {
927          serverUNIXAddress.sun_family = AF_UNIX; /* Domain */
928          strcpy (serverUNIXAddress.sun_path, name); /* File name */
929          serverSockAddrPtr = (struct sockaddr*) &serverUNIXAddress;
930          serverLen = sizeof (serverUNIXAddress);
931        }
932
933     do /* Connect to server */
934        {
935          result = connect (clientFd, serverSockAddrPtr, serverLen);
936          if (result == -1) sleep (SOCKET_SLEEP); /* Try again soon */
937        }
938     while (result == -1);
939
940     /* Perform redirection */
941     if (type == OUTPUT_SOCKET) dup2 (clientFd, STDOUT);
942     if (type == INPUT_SOCKET) dup2 (clientFd, STDIN);
943     close (clientFd); /* Close original client file descriptor */
```

```
944
945      return (TRUE);
946    }
947
948    /*******************************************************************/
949
950    server (name, type)
951
952    char* name;
953    int type;
954
955    {
956      int serverFd, clientFd, serverLen, clientLen;
957      int domain, internet, port;
958      struct sockaddr_un serverUNIXAddress;
959      struct sockaddr_un clientUNIXAddress;
960      struct sockaddr_in serverINETAddress;
961      struct sockaddr_in clientINETAddress;
962      struct sockaddr* serverSockAddrPtr;
963      struct sockaddr* clientSockAddrPtr;
964
965      /* Prepare a server socket */
966      internet = internetAddress (name); /* Internet? */
967      domain = internet ? AF_INET : AF_UNIX; /* Pick domain */
968      /* Create the server socket*/
969      serverFd = socket (domain, SOCK_STREAM, DEFAULT_PROTOCOL);
970
971      if (serverFd == -1)
972        {
973          perror ("ish");
974          return (FALSE);
975        }
976
977      if (internet) /* Internet socket */
978        {
979          sscanf (name, "%d", &port); /* Get port number */
980          /* Fill in server socket address fields */
981          serverLen = sizeof (serverINETAddress);
982          bzero ((char*) &serverINETAddress, serverLen);
983          serverINETAddress.sin_family = AF_INET; /* Domain */
984          serverINETAddress.sin_addr.s_addr = htonl (INADDR_ANY);
985          serverINETAddress.sin_port = htons (port); /* Port */
986          serverSockAddrPtr = (struct sockaddr*) &serverINETAddress;
987        }
988      else /* UNIX domain socket */
989        {
990          serverUNIXAddress.sun_family = AF_UNIX; /* Domain */
991          strcpy (serverUNIXAddress.sun_path,name); /* Filename */
992          serverSockAddrPtr = (struct sockaddr*) &serverUNIXAddress;
```

```
993            serverLen = sizeof (serverUNIXAddress);
994            unlink (name); /* Delete socket if it already exists */
995          }
996
997      /* Bind to socket address */
998      if (bind (serverFd, serverSockAddrPtr, serverLen) == -1)
999          {
1000           perror ("ish");
1001           return (FALSE);
1002         }
1003
1004     /* Set max pending connection queue length */
1005     if (listen (serverFd, DEFAULT_QUEUE_LENGTH) == -1)
1006         {
1007           perror ("ish");
1008           return (FALSE);
1009         }
1010
1011     if (internet) /* Internet socket */
1012         {
1013           clientLen = sizeof (clientINETAddress);
1014           clientSockAddrPtr = (struct sockaddr*) &clientINETAddress;
1015         }
1016     else /* UNIX domain socket */
1017         {
1018           clientLen = sizeof (clientUNIXAddress);
1019           clientSockAddrPtr = (struct sockaddr*) &clientUNIXAddress;
1020         }
1021
1022     /* Accept a connection */
1023     clientFd = accept (serverFd, clientSockAddrPtr, &clientLen);
1024
1025     close (serverFd); /* Close original server socket */
1026
1027     if (clientFd == -1)
1028         {
1029           perror ("ish");
1030           return (FALSE);
1031         }
1032
1033     /* Perform redirection */
1034     if (type == OUTPUT_SOCKET) dup2 (clientFd, STDOUT);
1035     if (type == INPUT_SOCKET) dup2 (clientFd, STDIN);
1036     close (clientFd); /* Close original client socket */
1037
1038     return (TRUE);
1039 }
1040
```

CHAPTER REVIEW

Checklist

In this chapter, I described:

- all of the common file management system calls
- the system calls for duplicating, terminating, and differentiating processes
- how a parent may wait for its children
- the terms *orphan* and *zombie*
- how signals may be trapped and ignored
- the way to kill processes
- how processes may be suspended and resumed
- unnamed pipes and named pipes
- the client/server paradigm
- UNIX domain and Internet domain sockets
- the design and operation of an Internet shell

Quiz

1. How can you tell when you've reached the end of a file?
2. What is a file descriptor?
3. What's the quickest way to move to the end of a file?
4. Describe the way that shells implement I/O redirection.
5. What is an orphaned process?
6. Underwhat circumstances do zombies accumulate?
7. How can a parent find out how its children died?
8. What's the difference between execv () and execvp ()?
9. Why is the name of the system call kill () a misnomer?
10. How can you protect critical code?
11. What is the purpose of process groups?
12. What happens when a writer tries to overflow a pipe?
13. How can you create a named pipe?
14. Describethe client/server paradigm.
15. Describe the stages that a client and a server go through to establish a connection.

Exercises

---

1. Process trees

Write a program that takes a single integer argument n from the command line and creates a binary tree of processes of depth n. When the tree is created, each process should display the phrase "I am process x" and then terminate. The nodes of the process tree should be numbered according to a breadth-first traversal. For example, if the user enters this:

```
$ tree 4                        ...build a tree of depth 4.
```

then the process tree would look like this:

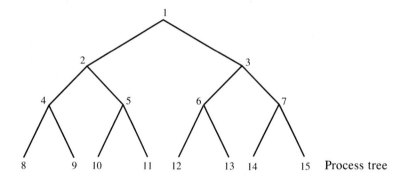

Process tree

and the output would be:

```
I am process 1
I am process 2
...
I am process 15
```

Make sure that the original parent process does not terminate until all of its children have died. This is so that you can terminate the parent and its children from your terminal with a *Control-C*. [level: *medium*]

2. Circular pipes

Write a program that creates a ring of three processes connected by pipes. The first process should prompt the user for a string and then send it to the second process. The second process should reverse the string and send it to the third process. The third process should convert the string to uppercase and send it back to the first process. When the first process gets the processed string, it should display it to the terminal. When this is done, all three processes should terminate. Here's an illustration of the process ring:

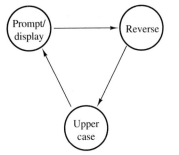

Process ring

Here's an example of the program in action:

```
$ ring                          ...run the program.
Please enter a string: ole
Processed string is: ELO
$ _
```

[level: *medium*]

3. Rewrite the "ghoul" exercise of chapter 4 using the C language. [level: *medium*]

4. Write a program that uses setuid ( ) to achieve the same kind of special "file ownership" as demonstrated by **rogue**. In other words, a user may use the program to access a file that he/she could not normally access. [level: *medium*]

Projects

Rock, paper, scissors: part 1

Write a suite of programs that run in parallel and interact to play the "Paper, Scissors, Rock" game. In this game, two players secretly choose either paper, scissors, or rock. They then reveal their choice. A referee decides who wins as follows:

- Paper beats rock (by covering it).
- Rock beats scissors (by blunting it).
- Scissors beats paper (by cutting it).
- Matching choices draw.

The winning player gets a point. In a draw, no points are awarded. Your program should simulate such a game, allowing the user to choose how many iterations are performed, observe the game, and see the final score. Here's an example of a game:

```
$ play 3                     ...play three iterations.

Paper, Scissors, Rock: 3 iterations

Player 1: ready
Player 2: ready

Go Players [1]
   Player 1: Scissors
   Player 2: Rock
Player 2 wins

Go Players [2]
   Player 1: Paper
   Player 2: Rock
Player 1 wins

Go Players [3]
   Player 1: Paper
   Player 2: Paper
Players draw.

Final score:
   Player 1: 1
   Player 2: 1
Players Draw
$ _
```

You should write three programs, which operate as follows:

1. One program is the main program, which fork/execs one referee process and two player processes. It then waits until all three terminate. It should check that the command line parameter that specifies the number of turns is legal and pass it to the referee process as a parameter to exec ().
2. One program is a referee program, which plays the role of the server. This program should prepare a socket and then listen for both players to send the string "READY", which means that they're ready to make a choice. It should then tell each player to make a choice by sending them both the string "GO". Their responses are then read, and their scores are calculated and updated. This process should be repeated until all of the turns have been taken, at which point the referee should send both players the string "STOP", which causes them to terminate.

3. One program is a player program, which plays the role of the client. This program is executed twice by the main program, and should start by connecting to the referee's socket. It should then send the "READY" message. When it receives the "GO" message back from the referee, it should make a choice and send it as a string to the referee. When it receives the string "STOP", it should kill itself.

These programs will almost certainly share some functions. To do a good job, create a makefile that separately compiles these common functions and links them into the executables that use them. Don't avoid sending strings by encoding them as one-byte numbers - that's part of the problem. [level: *medium*]

Rock, paper, scissors: part 2

Rewrite part 1 using unnamed pipes instead of sockets. Which do you think was easier to write? Which is easier to understand? [level: *medium*]

Rock, paper, scissors: part 3

Rewrite part 1 to allow the players to reside on different Internet machines. Each component of the game should be able to start separately. [level: *hard*]

```
...execute this command on vanguard.
$ referee 5000              ...use local port 5000.
...execute this command on csservr2.
$ player vanguard.5000      ...player is on a remote port.
...execute this command on wotan.
$ player vanguard.5000      ...player is on a remote port.
```

Internet shell enhancements

The Internet shell is ripe for enhancements. Here is a list of features that would be challenging to add:

- The ability to supply an Internet address of the form A.B.C.D. This would be easy to add, as my first Internet example can already do this. [level: *easy*]
- Job control features like fg, bg, and jobs. [level: *medium*]
- Filename substitution using *, ?, and [ ]. [level: *hard*]
- A two-way socket feature that connects the standard input and output channels of either the keyboard or a specified process to an Internet socket. This would allow you to connect to standard services without the aid of **telnet**. [level: *hard*]
- A simple built-in programming language. [level: *medium*]
- The ability to refer to any Internet address symbolically. For example, it would be nice to be able to redirect to "vanguard.utdallas.3000." [level: *medium*]

Chapter 11

UNIX Internals

Motivation

The UNIX operating system was one of the most cleanly designed operating systems of its time. I use the past tense here because several research establishments are currently developing operating systems that I believe to be superior in both concept and philosophy (see chapter 13 for more information). However, a lot of the basic underlying operating system concepts embedded in UNIX will continue to be used in some form or fashion for a long time to come. For example, the way that UNIX shares CPUs between competing processes is used in many other operating systems such as OS/2 and Microsoft Windows NT. Knowledge of *how* the system works can aid in designing high-performance UNIX applications. For example, knowledge of the internals of the virtual memory system can help you arrange data structures so that the amount of information transfer between main and secondary memory is minimized. In summary, knowledge of UNIX internals is useful for two reasons: as a source of reusable information that may help you in designing other similar systems, and to help you design high-performance UNIX applications.

Prerequisites

You should already have read chapter 10. It also helps to have a good knowledge of data structures, pointers, and linked lists.

Objectives

In this chapter, I describe the mechanisms that UNIX uses to support processes, memory management, input/output, and the file system. I also explain the main kernel data structures and algorithms.

Presentation

The information in this section is presented in the form of several subsections, each of which describes a portion of the UNIX system.

INTRODUCTION

The UNIX system is a fairly complex thing, and it's getting more complex as time goes by. In order to understand it well, it's necessary to break the system down into manageable portions and to tackle each portion in a layered fashion. Here's a description of each section of this chapter:

- *Kernel Basics*, which discusses system calls and interrupts.
- *The File System*, which describes how the directory hierarchy, regular files, peripherals, and multiple file systems are managed.
- *Process Management*, which explains how processes share the CPU and memory. It also describes the implementation of signals.
- *Input/Output*, which describes how processes access files. Special attention is given to terminal I/O.
- *Interprocess Communication* (IPC), which explains the mechanisms that allow processes to communicate with each other, even if they're on different machines.

There are some differences between the way that the BSD and System V designers implemented portions of these subsystems. Any major differences in approach are pointed out at the appropriate time.

KERNEL BASICS

The UNIX kernel is the part of the UNIX operating system that contains the code for:

- sharing the CPU and RAM between competing processes
- processing all system calls
- handling peripherals

The kernel is a program that is loaded from disk into RAM when the computer is first turned on. It always stays in RAM, and runs until the system is turned off or crashes. Although it's mostly written in C, some parts of the kernel were written in assembly language for efficiency reasons. User programs make use of the kernel via the system call interface.

Kernel Subsystems

The kernel facilities may be divided into several subsystems:

- memory management
- process management
- interprocess communication (IPC)
- input/output
- file management

These subsystems interact in a fairly hierarchical way. Here's an illustration of the layering:

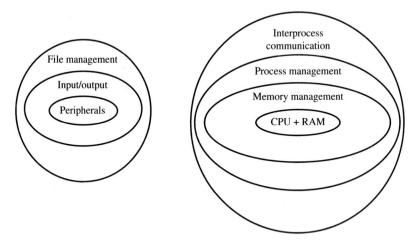

Figure 11.1 UNIX subsystems

Processes And Files

The UNIX kernel supports the concepts of processes and files. Processes are the "life-forms" that live in the computer and make decisions. Files are containers of information that processes read and write. In addition, processes may talk to each other via several different kinds of interprocess communication mechanisms, including signals, pipes, and sockets. Here's an illustration of what I mean:

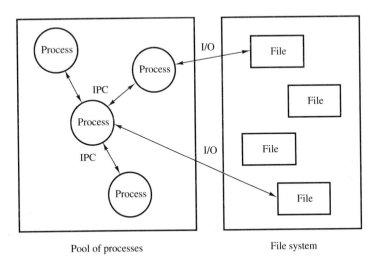

Figure 11.2   UNIX supports processes and files

Talking To The Kernel

Processes access kernel facilities via the system call interface, and peripherals (special files) communicate with the kernel via hardware interrupts. System calls and hardware interrupts are the only ways that the outside world can talk to the kernel, as illustrated by the following diagram:

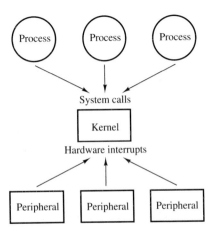

Figure 11.3   Talking to the kernel

Since systems calls and interrupts are obviously very important, I'll begin the discussion of UNIX internals with a description of each mechanism.

System Calls

System calls are the programmer's functional interface to the kernel. They are subroutines that reside inside the UNIX kernel, and support basic system functions such as the ones listed in the table below:

Function	System call
open a file	open
close a file	close
perform I/O	read/write
send a signal	kill
create a pipe	pipe
create a socket	socket
duplicate a process	fork
overlay a process	exec
terminate a process	exit

System calls may be loosely grouped into three main categories, as illustrated in the following diagram:

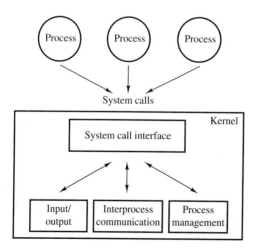

Figure 11.4   Major system call subsystems

User Mode And Kernel Mode

The kernel contains several data structures that are essential to the functioning of the system. Examples include:

- the *process table*, which contains one entry for every process in the system
- the *open file table*, which contains one entry for every open file in the system

These data structures reside in the kernel's memory space, which is protected from user processes by a memory management system that I'll describe to you later. User processes cannot therefore accidentally corrupt these important kernel data structures. System call routines are different from regular functions because they *can* directly manipulate kernel data structures, albeit in a carefully controlled manner.

When a user process is running, it operates in a special machine mode called *user mode*. This mode prevents a process from executing certain privileged machine instructions, including those that would allow it to access the kernel data structures. The other machine mode is called *kernel mode*. A kernel mode process may execute any machine instruction.

The only way for a user process to enter kernel mode is to execute a system call. Every system call is allocated a code number, starting from 1. For example, the open () system call might be allocated code number 1, and close () might be allocated code number 2. When a process invokes a system call, the C runtime library version of the system call places the system call parameters and the system call code number into some machine registers, and then executes a *trap* machine instruction. The trap instruction flips the machine into kernel mode and uses the system call code number as an index into a *system call vector table* located in low kernel memory. The system call vector table is an array of pointers to the kernel code for each system call. The code corresponding to the indexed function executes in kernel mode, modifying kernel data structures as necessary, and then performs a *return* instruction. This instruction flips the machine back into user mode and returns to the user process's code.

When I was first learning about UNIX, I didn't understand why this approach was taken. Why not just use a client/server model with a kernel server process that services system requests from client user processes? This avoids the need of user processes to ever directly execute kernel code. The reason is pure and simple - speed. In current architectures, the overhead of swapping between processes is too great to make the client/server approach practical. However, it's interesting to note that some of the modern micro kernel systems are taking the latter approach.

From a programmer's standpoint, using a system call is easy; you call the C function with the correct parameters, and the function returns when complete. If an error occurs, the function returns −1 and the global variable **errno** is set to indicate the cause of the error. Here's a diagram that illustrates the flow of control during a system call:

User process

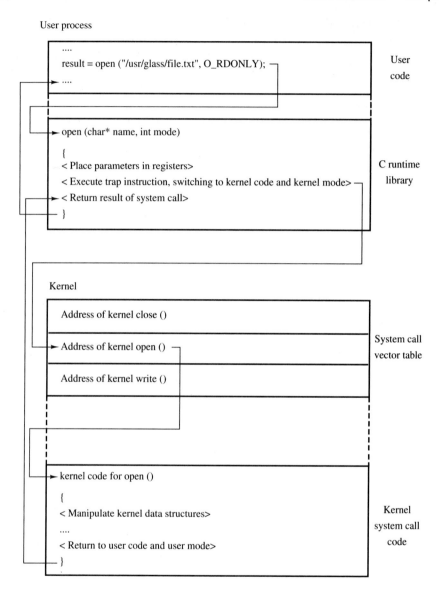

Figure 11.5   User mode and kernel mode

Synchronous Versus Asynchronous Processing

When a process performs a system call, it cannot usually be preempted. This means that the scheduler will not assign the CPU to another process during the operation of a system call. However, some system calls request I/O operations from a device, which can take a while to complete. To avoid leaving the CPU idle during the wait for I/O completion, the kernel sends the waiting process to sleep and only wakes it up again when a hardware interrupt signaling I/O completion is received. The scheduler does not allocate a sleeping process any CPU time, and so allocates the CPU to other processes while the hardware device is servicing the I/O request.

An interesting consequence of the way that UNIX handles read () and write () is that user processes experience synchronous execution of system calls, whereas the kernel experiences asynchronous behavior.

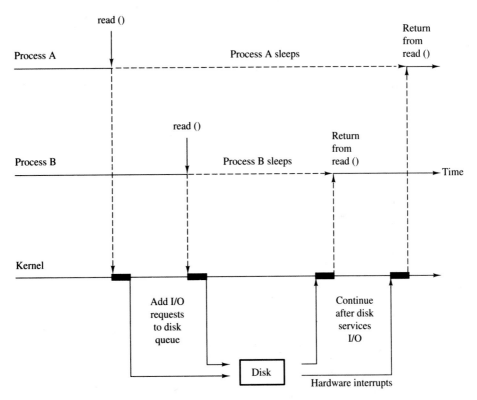

Figure 11.6   Synchronous and asynchronous events

Interrupts

Interrupts are the way that hardware devices notify the kernel that they would like some attention. In the same way that processes compete for CPU time, hardware devices compete for interrupt processing. Devices are allocated an interrupt priority based on their relative importance. For example, interrupts from the system clock have a higher priority than those from the keyboard.

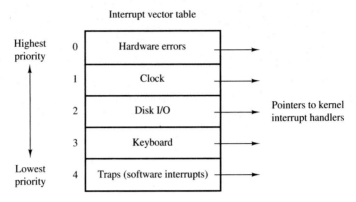

Figure 11.7   Interrupts have priorities

When an interrupt occurs, the current process is suspended and the kernel determines the source of the interrupt. It then examines its interrupt vector table, located in low kernel memory, to find the location of the code that processes the interrupt. This "interrupt handler" code is then executed. When the interrupt handler completes, the current process is resumed.

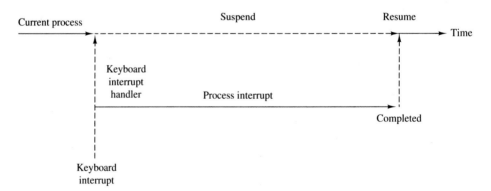

Figure 11.8   Interrupt processing

Interrupting Interrupts

Interrupt processing may itself be interrupted! If an interrupt of a higher priority than the current interrupt arrives, a similar sequence of events occurs, and the lower-priority interrupt handler is suspended until the higher-priority interrupt completes.

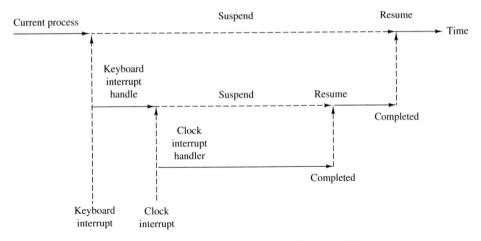

Figure 11.9 Interrupts may be interrupted

If an interrupt is being processed and another interrupt of an equal or lower priority occurs, the incoming interrupt is ignored and discarded. Interrupt handlers are therefore designed to be very fast, as the quicker they execute, the less likely it is that other interrupts will be lost.

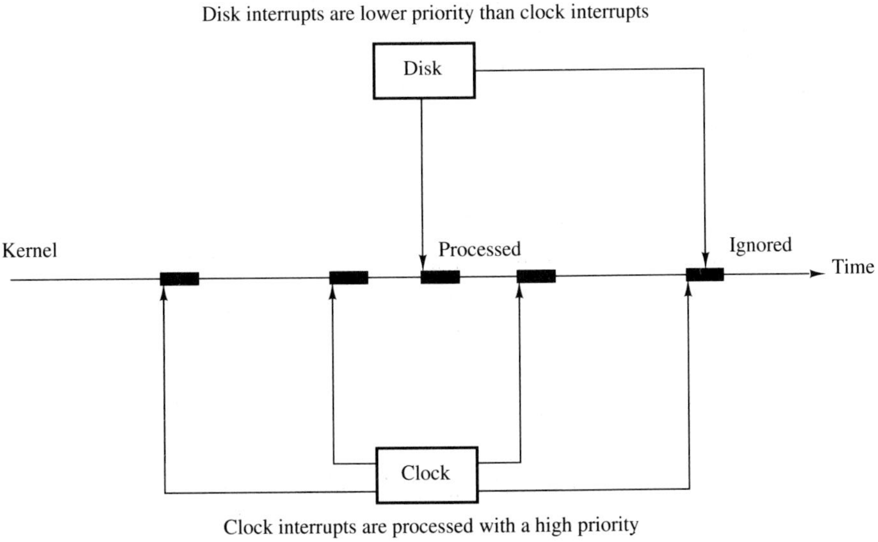

Disk interrupts are lower priority than clock interrupts

Clock interrupts are processed with a high priority

Figure 11.10 Interrupts may be ignored

Most machines have instructions that allow a program to ignore all interrupts below a certain priority level. Critical sections of kernel code protect themselves from interrupts by temporarily invoking such instructions. Here's some pseudo-code that does just that:

```
...
<disable all but highest priority interrupts>
<enter critical section of code>
...
...
<leave critical section of code>
<re-enable all interrupts>
...
```

The "Input/Output" section later on in this chapter describes the way that peripherals use the kernel interrupt facilities to perform efficient I/O.

THE FILE SYSTEM

UNIX uses files for long-term storage, and RAM for short-term storage. Programs, data, and text are all stored in files. Files are usually stored on hard disks, but can also be stored on other media such as tape and floppy disks. UNIX files are organized by a hierarchy of labels, commonly known as a *directory structure*. The files referenced by these labels may be of three kinds:

- *Regular files*, which contain a sequence of bytes that generally corresponds to code or data. They may be referenced via the standard I/O system calls.
- *Directory files*, which are stored on disk in a special format and form the backbone of the file system. They may only be referenced via directory-specific system calls.
- *Special files*, which correspond to peripherals such as printers and disks, or interprocess communication mechanisms such as pipes and sockets. They may be referenced via the standard I/O system calls.

Conceptually, a UNIX file is a linear sequence of bytes. The UNIX kernel does not support any higher order of file structure, such as records and/or fields. This is evident if you consider the lseek () system call, which allows you to position the file pointer only in terms of a byte offset. Older operating systems tended to support record structures, so UNIX was fairly unusual in this regard.

Let's begin our study of the UNIX file system by looking at the hardware architecture of the most common file media: a disk.

Disk Architecture

Here's a diagram of a typical disk architecture:

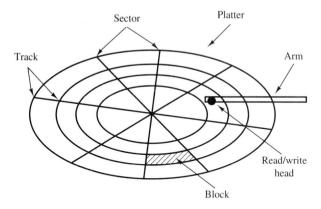

Figure 11.11   Disk architecture

A disk is split up in two ways: it's sliced up like a pizza into areas called *sectors*, and further subdivided into concentric rings called *tracks*. The individual areas bounded by the intersection of sectors and tracks are called *blocks*, and form the basic unit of disk storage. A typical disk block can hold 4K bytes. A single read/write head travels up and down a stationary arm, accessing information as the disk rotates and its surface passes underneath. A special chip called a *disk controller* moves the read/write head in response to instructions from the disk device driver, which is a special piece of software located in the UNIX kernel.

There are several variations of this simple disk architecture. Many disk drives actually contain several platters, stacked one upon the other. In these systems, the collection of tracks with the same index number is called a *cylinder*. In most multi-platter systems, the disk arms are connected to each other so that the read/write heads all move synchronously, rather like a comb moving through hair. The read/write heads of such disk systems therefore move through cylinders of media. Some sophisticated disk drives have separately controllable read/write heads.

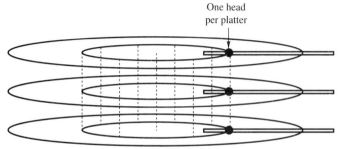

Figure 11.12   A multi-platter architecture

Notice that the blocks on the outside track are larger than the blocks on the inside track, due to the way that a disk is partitioned. If a disk always rotates at the same speed, it means that the density of data on outer blocks is less than it could be, thus wasting potential storage. Some of the latest disk drive designs attempt to keep the data density constant throughout the disk surface by increasing the number of blocks on the outer tracks and then either slowing down the disk rotation or increasing the data transfer rate as the head moves toward the outside of the disk.

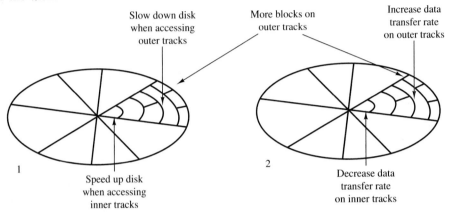

Figure 11.13   Disk storage techniques

Interleaving

When a sequence of contiguously numbered blocks is read, there's a latency delay between each block due to the overhead of the communication between the disk controller and the device driver. Logically contiguous blocks are therefore spaced apart on the surface of the disk so that by the time the latency delay is over, the head is positioned over the correct area. The spacing between blocks due to this delay effect is called the *interleave factor*. Here are a couple of pictures that illustrate two different interleave factors:

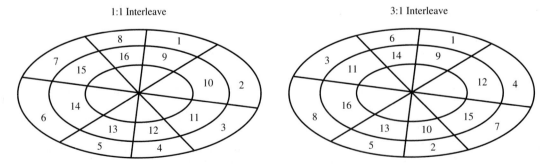

Figure 11.14   Disk interleaving

Storing A File

Assuming a 4K block size, a single 9K UNIX file requires 3 blocks of storage - one to hold the first 4K, one to hold the next 4K, and the last to hold the remaining 1K. The loss of storage due to the under-use of the last 4K block is called *fragmentation*. A file's blocks are rarely contiguous, and tend to be scattered all over a disk:

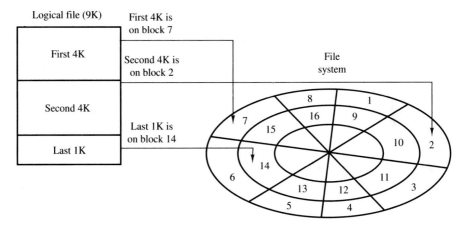

Figure 11.15   A file's blocks are scattered

Block I/O

I/O is always done in terms of blocks. If you issue a read ( ) system call to read the first byte of data from a file, the device driver issues an I/O request to the disk controller to read the first 4K block into a kernel buffer, and then copies the first byte from the buffer to your process. More information about I/O buffering is presented later in this chapter.

Most disk controllers handle one block I/O request at a time. When a disk controller completes the current block I/O request, it issues a hardware interrupt back to the device driver to signal completion. At this point, the device driver usually makes the next block I/O request. Figure 11.16 is a diagram that illustrates the sequence of events that might occur during a 9K read ( ).

Inodes

UNIX uses a structure called an *inode* (**I**ndex **Node**) to store information about each file. The inode of a regular or directory file contains the locations of its disk blocks, and the inode of a special file contains information that allows the peripheral to be identified. An inode also holds other information associated with a file, such as its permission flags, owner, group, and last modification time. An inode is

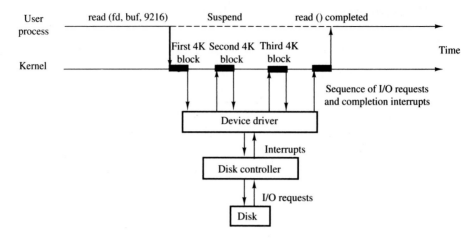

Figure 11.16   Block I/O

a fixed size structure of about 120 bytes. Every inode in a particular file system is allocated a unique inode number starting from 1, and every file has exactly one inode. All of the inodes associated with the files on a disk are stored in a special area at the start of the disk called the *inode list*:

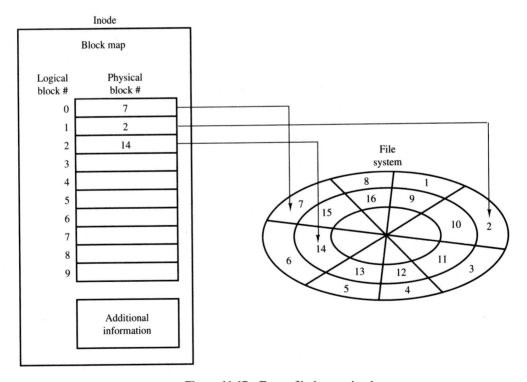

Figure 11.17   Every file has an inode

Inode Contents

Here's a list of the file information contained within each inode:

- the type of the file: regular, directory, block special, character special, etc.
- file permissions
- the owner and group ids
- a hard link count (described later in this chapter)
- the last modification and last access times
- if it's a regular or directory file, the location of the blocks
- if it's a special file, the major and minor device numbers (described later in this chapter)
- if it's a symbolic link, the value of the symbolic link

In other words, an inode contains all of the information that you see when you perform an "ls -l," except for the filename.

The Block Map

Only the locations of the first ten blocks of a file are stored directly in the inode. Most UNIX files are less than 40K in size, so this is sufficient for a majority of cases. An indirect access scheme is used for addressing larger files. In this scheme, a single user block is used to hold the location of up to 1024 user blocks. When used in this manner, a block is called an *indirect block*. Its location is stored in the inode, and is used to address the next 1024 blocks. This approach allows files up to 4 megabytes to be addressed.

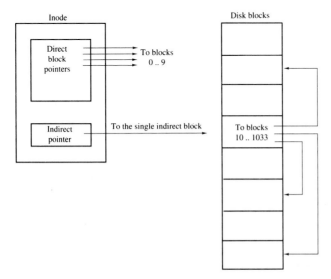

Figure 11.18 The single indirect block

For files greater than 4 megabytes in size, a similar double-indirect scheme is used. A user block is used to hold the location of up to 1024 indirect blocks, each of which points to a maximum of 1024 user blocks. The inode holds the location of the double-indirect user block.

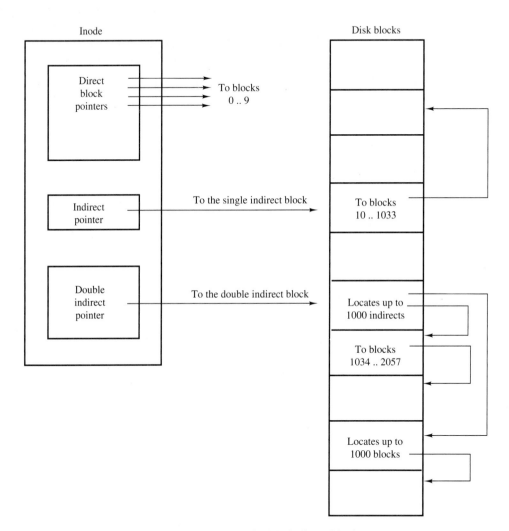

Figure 11.19   The double indirect block

Note that as the file gets larger, the amount of indirection required to access a particular block increases. This overhead is minimized by buffering the contents of the inode and commonly referenced indirect blocks in RAM. The buffering mechanism is described later in this chapter.

File System Layout

The first logical block of a disk is termed the *boot block*, and contains some executable code that is used when UNIX is first activated. See chapter 12 for more information. The second logical block is known as the *superblock*, and contains information concerning the disk itself. Following this is a fixed size set of blocks called the *inode list* that holds all of the inodes associated with the files on the disk. Each block in the inode list can normally hold about 40 inodes. The remaining blocks on the disk are available for storing file blocks, and contain both directories and user files.

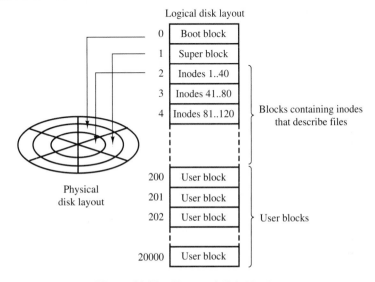

Figure 11.20   Usage of disk blocks

The Superblock

The superblock contains information pertaining to the entire file system. It includes a bitmap of free blocks, which is a linear sequence of bits, one per disk block. A one indicates that the corresponding block is free, and a zero means it's being used.

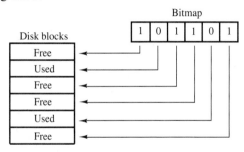

Figure 11.21   The free block bitmap

The information in the superblock includes the following:

- the total number of blocks in the file system
- the number of inodes in the inode free list
- the free block bitmap
- the size of a block in bytes
- the number of free blocks
- the number of used blocks

Bad Blocks

A disk always contain several blocks that for one reason or another are not fit for use. The utility that creates a new file system, described in chapter 12, creates a single "worst nightmare" file that is comprised of all the bad blocks in the disk, and records the locations of all these blocks in inode number 1. This prevents the blocks from being allocated to other files.

Directories

Inode number 2 contains the location of the block(s) containing the root directory. A UNIX directory contains a list of associations between filenames and inode numbers. When a directory is created, it is automatically allocated entries for "..", its parent directory, and ".", itself. Since a >filename, inode number < pair effectively links a name to a file, these associations are termed "hard links." Since filenames are stored in the directory blocks, they are not stored in a file's inode. In fact, it wouldn't make any sense to store the name in the inode, as a file may have more than one name. Because of this observation, it's more accurate to think of the directory hierarchy as being a hierarchy of *file labels*, rather than a hierarchy of *files*.

All UNIX systems allow a filename to be at least 14 characters, and most support much longer names.

Here's an illustration of the root inode corresponding to a simple root directory. The inode numbers associated with each filename are shown as subscripts:

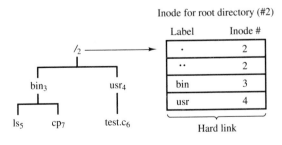

Figure 11.22 The root directory is associated with inode two

Translating Pathnames Into Inode Numbers

System calls such as open ( ) must obtain a file's inode from its pathname. They perform the translation as follows:

1. The inode from which to start the pathname search is located. If the pathname is absolute, the search starts from inode #2. If the pathname is relative, the search starts from the inode corresponding to the process's current working directory. See the "Process Management" section of this chapter for more information.

2. The components of the pathname are then processed from left to right. Every component except the last should correspond to either a directory or a symbolic link. Let's call the inode from which the pathname search is started the *current inode*.

3. If the current inode corresponds to a directory, the current pathname component is looked for in the directory corresponding to the current inode. If it's not found, an error occurs—otherwise, the value of the current inode number becomes the inode number associated with the located pathname component.

4. If the current inode corresponds to a symbolic link, the pathname up to and including the current path component is replaced by the contents of the symbolic link, and the pathname is reprocessed.

5. The inode corresponding to the final pathname component is the inode of the file referenced by the entire pathname.

To illustrate this algorithm, I'll list the steps required to translate the pathname "/usr/test.c" into an inode number. Figure 11.23 contains the disk layout that I assume during the translation process. It indicates the translation path using bold lines, and the final destination using a circle.

Sample Pathname To Inode Translation

Here's the logic that the kernel uses to translate the pathname "/usr/test.c" into an inode number:

1. The pathname is absolute, so the current inode number is 2.

2. The directory corresponding to inode 2 is searched for the pathname component "usr." The matching entry is found, and the current inode number is set to 4.

3. The directory corresponding to inode 4 is searched for the pathname component "test.c". The matching entry is found, and the current inode number is set to 6.

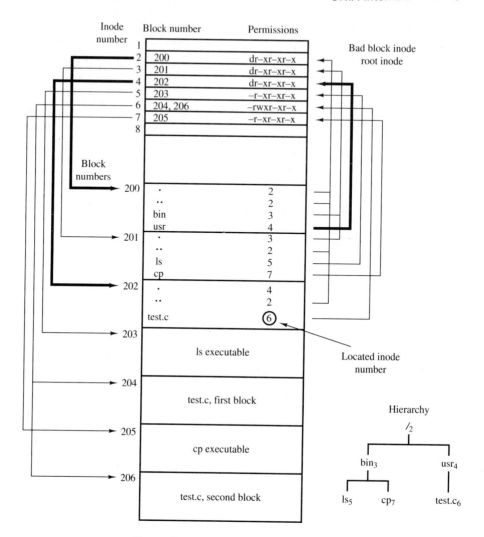

Figure 11.23 A sample directory layout

4. "test.c" is the final pathname component, so the algorithm returns the inode number 6.

As you can see, the translation bounces between inodes and directory blocks until the pathname is fully processed.

Mounting File Systems

When UNIX is started, the directory hierarchy corresponds to the file system located on a single disk called the *root device*. UNIX allows you to create file systems on other devices and attach them to the original directory hierarchy using a mechanism termed *mounting*. The **mount** utility allows a super-user to splice the root directory of a file system into the existing directory hierarchy. The hierarchy of a large UNIX system is typically spread over many devices, each containing a subtree of the total hierarchy. For example, the "/usr" subtree is commonly stored on a device other than the root device. Non-root file systems are usually mounted automatically at boot time. See chapter 12 for more details. For example, assume that a file system is stored on a floppy disk in the "/dev/flp" device. To attach it to the "/mnt" subdirectory of the main hierarchy, you'd execute the command:

```
$ mount /dev/flp /mnt
```

Here's a diagram that illustrates the effect of this command:

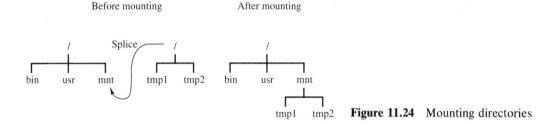

Figure 11.24   Mounting directories

File systems may be detached from the main hierarchy by using the **umount** utility. The following command would detach the file system stored in "/dev/flp":

```
$ umount /dev/flp
```

File System I/O

For details about the kernel implementation of file system I/O, refer to the "Input/Output" section later in this chapter.

PROCESS MANAGEMENT

In this section, I describe the way that the kernel shares the CPU and RAM among competing processes. The area of the kernel that shares the CPU is called the *scheduler*, and the area of the kernel that shares RAM is called the *memory manager*. This section also contains information about process-oriented system calls, including exec (), fork (), and exit ().

Executable Files

When the source code of a program is compiled, it is stored in a special format on disk. The first few bytes of the file are known as the *magic number*, and are used by the kernel to identify the type of the executable file. For example, if the first two bytes of the file are the characters "#!", the kernel knows that the executable file contains shell text, and invokes a shell to execute the text. Another sequence identifies the file as being a regular load image containing machine code and data. This kind of file is divided into several sections containing code or data, with a separate header for each section. The headers are used by the kernel for preparing the memory management system described shortly. Here's an illustration of a typical executable file:

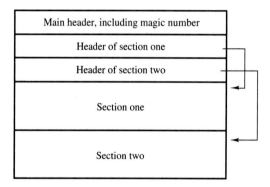

Figure 11.25   Layout of an executable file

The First Processes

UNIX runs a program by creating a process and then associating it with a named executable file. Surprisingly enough, there's no system call that allows you to say "create a new process to run program X"; instead, you must duplicate an existing process and then associate the newly created child process with the executable file "X."

The first process, with process id (PID) 0, is created by UNIX during boot time. This process immediately fork/execs twice, creating two processes with PID 1 and 2. The names of these processes are usually as follows:

PID	Name
0	swapper
1	init
2	pagedaemon

The purpose of these processes is described later in this chapter. All other processes in the system are descendants of the *init* process. For more information concerning the boot sequence, see chapter 12.

Kernel Processes And User Processes

Most processes execute in user mode except when they make a system call, at which point they flip temporarily into kernel mode. However, the swapper (PID 0) and pagedaemon (PID 2) processes execute permanently in kernel mode due to their importance, and are termed *kernel processes*. In contrast to user processes, their code is linked directly into the kernel and does not reside in a separate executable file. In addition, kernel processes are never preempted.

The Process Hierarchy

When a process duplicates by using fork ( ), the original process is known as the *parent* of the child process. The *init* process, PID 1, is the process from which all user processes are descended. Parent and child processes are therefore related in a hierarchy, with the *init* process as the root process. Here's an illustration of a process hierarchy involving four processes:

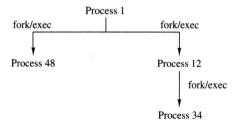

Figure 11.26   Process hierarchy

Process States

Every process in the system can be in one of six states. The six possible states are as follows:

- *Running*, which means that the process is currently using the CPU.
- *Runnable*, which means that the process can make use of the CPU as soon as it becomes available.
- *Sleeping*, which means that the process is waiting for an event to occur. For example, if a process executes a read ( ) system call, it sleeps until the I/O request completes.

- *Suspended*, which means that the process has been "frozen" by a signal such as SIGSTOP. It will resume only when sent a SIGCONT signal. For example, a *Control-Z* from the keyboard suspends all of the processes in the foreground job.
- *Idle*, which means that the process is being created by a fork ( ) system call, and is not yet runnable.
- *Zombified*, which means that the process has terminated but has not yet returned its exit code to its parent. A process remains a zombie until its parent accepts its return code using the wait ( ) system call.

Here's a diagram that illustrates the possible state changes that can occur during the lifetime of a process:

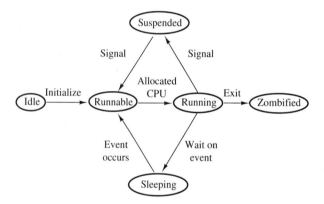

Figure 11.27   Process states

Process Composition

Every process is comprised of several different pieces:

- a *code area*, which contains the executable portion of a process
- a *data area*, which is used by a process to contain static data
- a *stack area*, which is used by a process to store temporary data
- a *user area*, which holds housekeeping information about a process
- *page tables*, which are used by the memory management system

The uses of the first three areas should be familiar to you, and I'm going to leave a discussion of page tables until later. The next subsection contains a description of the user area.

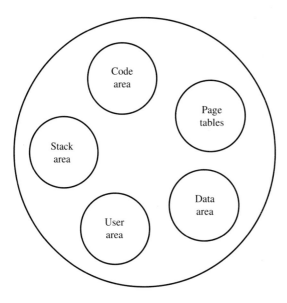

Figure 11.28 Process composition

The User Area

Every process in the system has some associated "housekeeping" information that is used by the kernel for process management. This information is stored in a data structure called a *user area*. Every process has its own user area. User areas are created in the kernel's data region and are only accessible by the kernel; user processes may not access their user areas. Fields within a process's user area include:

- a record of how the process should react to each kind of signal
- a record of the process's open file descriptors
- a record of how much CPU time the process has used recently

The contents of a user area are described in more detail later in this chapter.

The Process Table

There is a single fixed-size kernel data structure called the *process table* that contains one entry for every process in the system. The process table is created in the kernel's data region and is only accessible by the kernel. Each entry contains the following information about each process:

- its process id (PID) and parent process id (PPID)
- its real and effective user id (UID) and group id (GID)
- its state (running, runnable, sleeping, suspended, idle, zombified)
- the location of its code, data, stack, and user areas
- a list of all pending signals

Here's the process table that would result from the small process hierarchy that I illustrated earlier in this chapter. It assumes that the process with PID 48 is currently waiting for I/O completion:

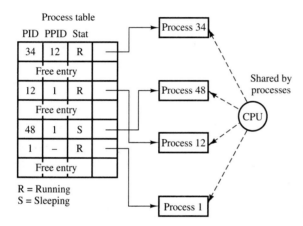

Figure 11.29 The process table

The Scheduler

The kernel is responsible for sharing CPU time between competing processes. A section of the kernel code called the *scheduler* performs this duty, and maintains a special data structure called a *multi-level priority queue* that allows it to schedule processes efficiently. A priority queue is a linked list of the runnable processes that have similar priorities. The way that the kernel calculates a process's priority is discussed later in this chapter.

Processes are allocated CPU time in proportion to their importance. CPU time is allocated in fixed size units called *time quantums*. On most systems, each time quantum is 1/10 second. Here's an illustration of the queues in relation to the process table, based on the small process hierarchy illustrated earlier in this chapter:

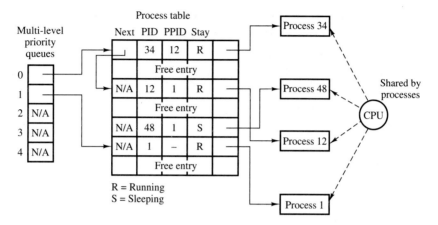

Figure 11.30   The process table and priority queues

Scheduling Rules

Here are the rules that describe the way that the scheduler works:

- Every second, the scheduler calculates the priorities of all the runnable processes in the system and organizes them into several priority queues. The queues are stratified based on the process's priority values.
- Every 1/10 second, the scheduler selects the highest-priority process in the priority queues and allocates it the CPU.
- If a process is still runnable at the end of its time quantum, it's placed at the end of its priority queue.
- If a process sleeps on an event during its time quantum, the scheduler immediately selects another process to run and allocates it the CPU.
- If a process returns from a system call during its time quantum and a higher-priority process is ready to run, the lower-priority process is preempted by the higher-priority process.
- Every hardware clock interrupt (which typically occurs one hundred times a second), the process's clock tick count is incremented. Every fourth tick, the scheduler recalculates the process's priority value. This tends to reduce a process's priority during its time quantum.

The formula for calculating a process's priority may be stated roughly as follows:

```
priority = constant1 / (Recent CPU usage) + constant2 / (nice setting)
```

where *constant1* and *constant2* are calculated based on particular system-wide characteristics. The "nice setting" is the value set by the nice () system call. This formula ensures that a process's priority diminishes if it uses a lot of CPU time in a particular "window" of time. It also ensures that processes that have a high nice setting will have a lower priority. A spin-off from this formula is that interactive processes will tend to have a good response time; as an interactive process waits for a user to press a key, it uses no CPU time and therefore its priority level rises rapidly.

The act of switching from one process to another is termed a *context switch*. To "freeze" a process, the kernel saves its program counter, stack pointer, and other important details into the process's user area. To "thaw" a process, the kernel reinstates this information from the process's user area.

The result of these rules is that during every second, processes in the highest non-empty priority queue are allocated the CPU in a round-robin fashion. At the end of each second, the processes are repositioned in the queues depending on their new priorities, and the round-robin allocation repeats. Here are some illustrations of the scheduling rules in action:

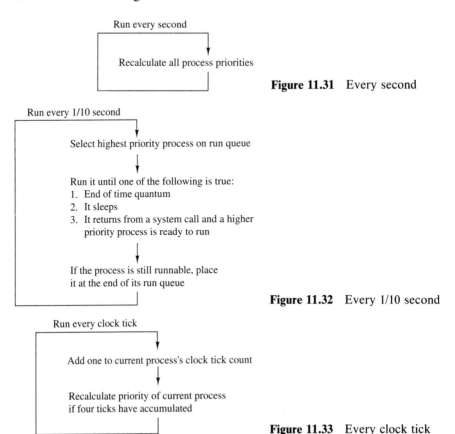

Run every second

Recalculate all process priorities

Figure 11.31   Every second

Run every 1/10 second

Select highest priority process on run queue

Run it until one of the following is true:
1. End of time quantum
2. It sleeps
3. It returns from a system call and a higher
   priority process is ready to run

If the process is still runnable, place
it at the end of its run queue

Figure 11.32   Every 1/10 second

Run every clock tick

Add one to current process's clock tick count

Recalculate priority of current process
if four ticks have accumulated

Figure 11.33   Every clock tick

Memory Management

In addition to scheduling, the kernel is responsible for sharing RAM between processes in a secure and efficient manner. The next few sections describe the UNIX memory management system.

Memory Pages

The UNIX memory management system allows processes that are bigger than the total RAM capacity to execute. In order to achieve this, it divides RAM, code, data, and stack areas into fixed-size chunks of memory called *pages*. This is analogous to the way that a disk is divided up into fixed-size blocks. The size of a memory page is set to be equal to the size of a disk block, typically 4K. The reason for this relationship will soon become evident. Only the pages of a process that are currently being accessed or were recently accessed are stored in RAM pages; the rest are stored on disk.

Page Tables And Regions

The code, data, and stack areas of a process do not have to reside in logically contiguous memory. For example, the compiler might generate a program whose code, data, and stack occupy the following logical areas of address space:

Section	Logical address
code	0K..15K
data	64K..72K
stack	64K..72K

Each area of contiguous logical address space is termed a *region*, and therefore most processes have three regions. The pages of a region do not have to be stored contiguously in RAM; every region has an associated data structure called a *page table* that records the location of each of its pages. A process's page tables are created in the kernel's data region and are only accessible by the kernel. The locations of a process's page tables are stored in the process's user area. A page table in the memory management system is analogous to an inode in the file system, as each tracks the location of individual storage units.

Figure 11.34 is an illustration of the relationship among the process table, user areas, and page tables.

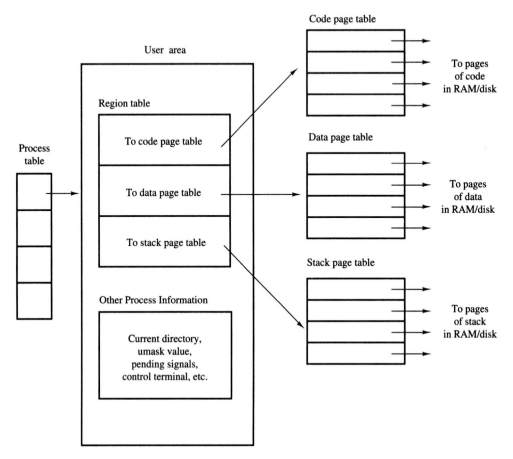

Figure 11.34   The user area, regions, and page tables

The RAM Table

The memory manager allocates pages of RAM to a process only when it needs them. A single fixed-size kernel data structure called the *RAM table* records information about each page of RAM, such as whether the page is currently being used and whether it's "locked" into memory. Locked pages are never transferred to disk; for example, all of the pages that contain the UNIX kernel are locked.

Loading An Executable: exec ( )

When a process performs an exec ( ), the kernel allocates page tables for the process's code, data, and stack regions. At this point, all of the code and initialized data resides on disk in the executable file, and so the code and data page table entries are set to contain the locations of their corresponding disk blocks. These locations are extracted from the executable file's inode and header. When the process accesses one of these pages for the first time, its corresponding block is copied from disk into RAM and the page table entry is updated with the physical RAM page number.

The stack and uninitialized data regions do not have a corresponding disk location. The kernel therefore marks their corresponding page table entries as *zeroed*. When a zeroed page is accessed for the first time, the kernel allocates a page of RAM and fills it with zeroes *without* loading anything from disk. It then updates the page table entry with the physical RAM page number.

Assuming that the first eight pages of RAM were originally free, here's an illustration of a process's memory layout immediately after an exec ():

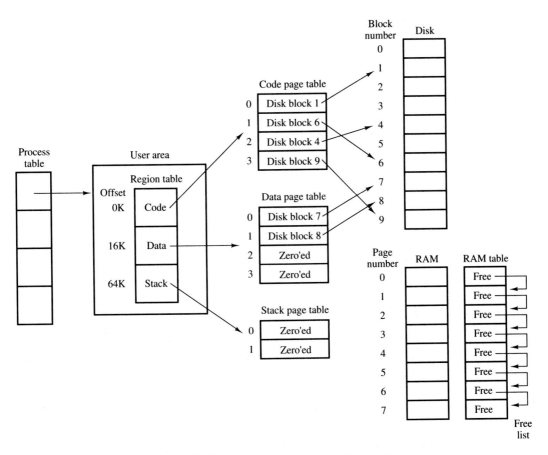

Figure 11.35   Memory layout immediately after an exec ( )

Address Translation

All of the logical addresses that travel down the hardware address bus from a process must be mapped to a physical address using the information contained in the process's region and page tables. This translation process is aided by a special piece of hardware called a *memory management unit (MMU)*. Assuming that every page of RAM is 4K and that all addresses are 32-bit values, the memory management unit works as follows:

- When a process is scheduled, several hardware-specific registers in the MMU are set to point to the process's region and page tables. The MMU uses these registers to access these data structures during the address translation process.
- When an address appears on the hardware address bus, the MMU is activated and starts the translation process. I'll call the incoming address **ADDR**.
- The MMU then determines which region the incoming address **ADDR** lies within; either the code, data, or stack region.
- The MMU then subtracts the starting virtual address (**SVA**) of the region from the incoming address **ADDR**. This yields the offset of the incoming address from the start of the region (**OSR**).
- **OSR** is then split into two pieces. The most significant 20 bits correspond to the region page number of the incoming address (**RPN**), and the least significant 12 bits are equal to the offset within this region page (**ORP**).
- The MMU then consults the region's page table to determine the current location of the logical page **RPN**. If the page is currently in RAM, the incoming logical address is translated into a physical address by replacing the logical page number by the physical RAM number. If the page is not in RAM, the MMU gives up trying to translate the logical address, generates a page validity interrupt, and then processes other incoming logical addresses.
- When UNIX receives a page validity interrupt, it issues an I/O request that loads the page from disk into a free page of RAM. When the page is loaded, the appropriate page table entry is updated with the RAM page number, and the address translation is restarted.

Illustration Of MMU Algorithm

Here's an illustration of the MMU mapping algorithm:

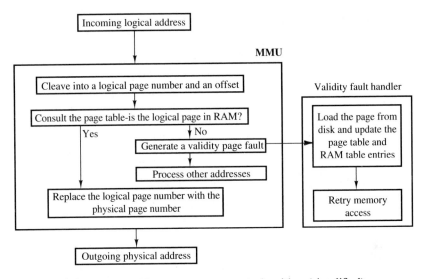

Figure 11.36   Memory management algorithm (simplified)

The MMU And The Page Table

Each page table entry contains a number of fields that are used by various facets of the memory management system. Some of these fields are set automatically by the MMU under certain circumstances:

- The *modified bit* is set when a process writes to the page.
- The *referenced bit* is set when a process reads from or writes to the page.

Some of the other fields are automatically used by the MMU when translating an incoming logical address:

- If the *valid bit* is set, the MMU replaces the logical page number of the incoming address with the *physical page number* field.
- If the *valid bit* is not set, the MMU generates a page fault.
- If the *copy on write bit* is set and a process attempts to modify the page, the MMU generates a page fault regardless of the state of the *valid bit*.

The Memory Layout After The First Instruction

An exec () causes the first instruction of the executable to be fetched from memory, which in turn causes the MMU to fault in the first page. The address of the first instruction is stored in the executable's header, and tends to be a low memory address. In the following diagram, I assumed that the first instruction was located at logical address 0 and that page 0 of the code region was paged into physical RAM page 0:

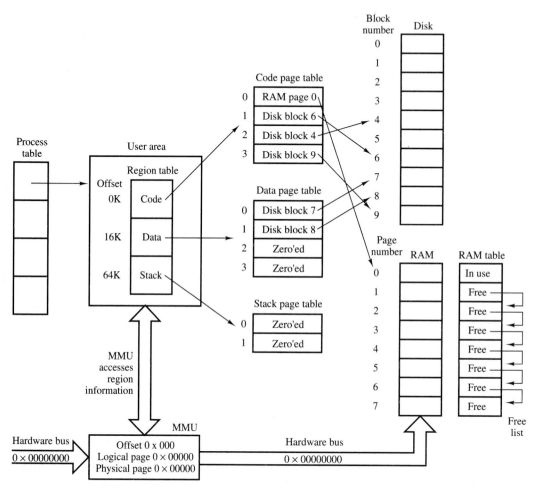

Figure 11.37 Memory layout after the first instruction executes

The Memory Layout After Many Instructions

When a process continues to execute after an exec ( ), it tends to fault in more of its code, data, and stack pages. The following diagram illustrates a situation in which all of the physical pages of RAM have been filled by a single process. This can never happen in a real UNIX system, as the kernel occupies low RAM addresses and several other daemon processes will always occupy portions of high RAM, but it does show how the page tables of a process gradually get filled in with RAM addresses.

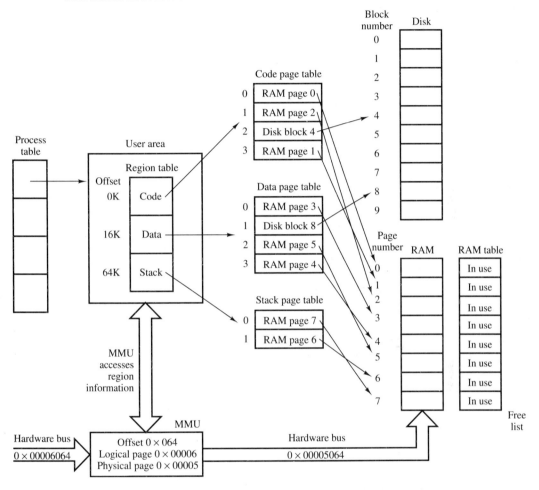

Figure 11.38 Memory layout after several instructions

The Page Stealer

The previous diagram illustrated a situation in which all the physical pages of RAM were filled. If a process tried to fault in another one of its pages, the system could save one or more of the RAM pages onto disk to make room for the incoming page. In practice, it works out much better if the memory management system always keeps a certain number of RAM pages free for pages that wish to fault in. The minimum number of pages that it tries to keep free is called the *low-water mark*. When the number of free pages drops below this level, the memory management system wakes up a process called the *page stealer* (sometimes called the *page daemon*) to free up some RAM pages. The page stealer uses an algorithm that is described shortly to save pages to a special area of disk called the *swap space* until the number of free pages rises above a *high-water mark*. It then goes to sleep until it's needed again.

Swap Space

Swap space is a special contiguous area of disk set aside for the efficient transfer of pages to and from RAM. Although it can reside on the root device, it is often allocated on a separate disk so that regular file access and paging can occur simultaneously. The swap space is supported by a special kernel data structure called the *swap map* that is used to track the usage of its blocks. The swap map is used to find free contiguous chunks of blocks in the swap space, and is updated whenever swap space is allocated or deallocated. When two neighboring chunks of swap space become free, the swap map automatically combines them into a single, larger chunk of free space.

The Page Stealer Algorithm

Every page table entry includes three fields called the *modified bit*, the *referenced bit,* and the *age*. Whenever a process accesses a particular page, its referenced bit is set and its age is set to zero. The page stealer uses these two fields in order to free the pages that have been least recently used. It cycles through every page table in the system, performing the following operation:

- If the referenced bit of a page is set, it resets it and sets the age field to zero; otherwise, it increments the age field.

The age fields of pages that are currently being accessed will hardly increase at all, as they're continually being reset back to zero; however, the age fields of pages that are inactive will continue to grow. When the age field reaches a certain system-dependent value, the page stealer attempts to free the page using the following rules:

- If the page has never been paged out to the swap device, the page is placed on a list of pages to be paged out and its RAM table entry is marked as "ready to page out."
- If the page has been paged out before and hasn't been modified since, its valid bit is reset and its RAM table entry is immediately marked as "free" and placed on the free page list.
- If the page has been paged out before and has been modified since, it's

placed on the list of pages to be paged out, its RAM table entry is marked as "ready to page out," and its previous swap space area is deallocated.

When the list of pages to page out reaches a certain size, the kernel locates a suitable chunk of swap space by consulting the swap map and then schedules the pages to be written to swap space. When a page is written, its valid bit is reset and its RAM table entry is marked as "free" and placed on the free list.

The result of this algorithm is that the least recently used pages are gradually paged to swap space until the number of free pages rises above the preset high-water mark.

The Memory Layout After Some Page Outs

The following diagram illustrates the state of the example process's memory map after code page 1, data page 0, and stack page 1 were paged to swap space:

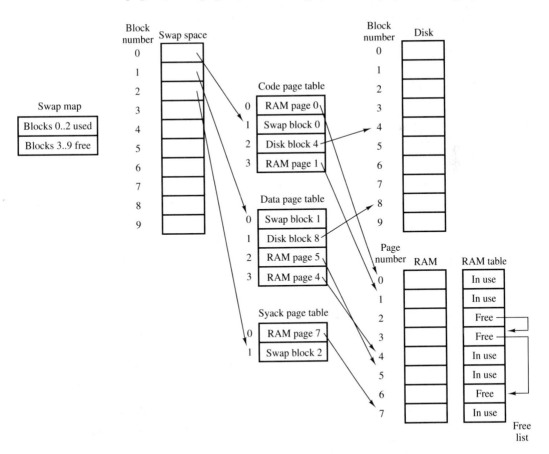

Figure 11.39 Memory layout after some page outs

Accessing A Page That's Stored In Swap Space

When the MMU attempts to access a page whose valid bit is not set, it generates a page fault. Before requesting that the page is read from disk, the kernel checks to see if the page is still in RAM, having been freed by the page stealer but not yet overwritten by another page. It can do this quickly because it maintains a hash table that maps disk block addresses onto RAM page numbers. If it finds that the page is still cached in RAM, it simply updates the page table entry and sets the valid bit. If the page is not found in RAM, one of two cases is possible:

- If the page has never been loaded into RAM, the kernel requests that the page is loaded in from the executable file.
- If the page is stored in swap space, the kernel requests that the page is loaded in from the swap device.

One consequence of this algorithm is that a page is only ever loaded once from the executable file; from then on, it spends the rest of its lifetime travelling between RAM and swap space. This is illustrated by the following diagram:

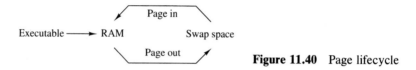

Figure 11.40   Page lifecycle

Duplicating A Process: fork ( )

When a process forks, the child process must be allocated a copy of its parents code, data, and stack areas. Unfortunately, a process often immediately follows a fork () by an exec (), thereby deallocating its previous memory areas. To avoid any unnecessary and costly copying suggested by these two observations, the kernel processes a fork () in a crafty way:

- It sets the child's code region entry to point to the parent's code page table and increments a reference count associated with the page table to indicate that it's being shared.
- It creates a data page table and a stack page table for the child that are duplicates of the parent's, and sets the *copy on write* bit for every page table entry of both processes' data and stack tables. If the parent's page table entry points into RAM, the child's page table entry is set to point to the same location and a reference count associated with the RAM page is incremented to indicate that it's being shared. Similarly, if a parent's page table entry points into swap space, the child's page table entry is set to point to the same location and a reference count associated with the swap space location is incremented to indicate that it's being shared.

The copy on write flag is used by UNIX to process shared RAM and swap pages in a special way, described shortly. Following is an illustration of the parent and child memory maps immediately following a fork (). The small numbers next to the region tables, RAM table, and swap table are reference counts maintained by the kernel.

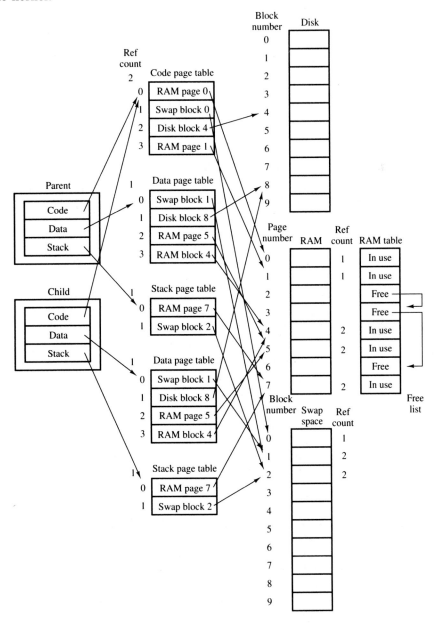

Figure 11.41 Layout after fork

Processing References To Shared RAM And Swap Pages

Shared pages are processed by UNIX as follows:

- If a process reads a shared RAM page, nothing special happens at all.
- If the page stealer decides to page out a shared RAM page, the page's reference count is decremented and a copy of the page is transferred to swap space. The process whose page was transferred has its page table entry updated to reflect the transfer, but the other processes that share the same page still reference the RAM page. If the RAM page reference count is still non-zero after it's decremented, the RAM page is not added to the free list.
- If a process accesses a shared swap page, it's paged in from swap space and the process whose page was transferred has its page table entry updated to relect the page in. The other processes who share the same swap page still reference the swap space.
- If a process attempts to modify a page whose copy on write bit is set, the MMU automatically generates a page fault. The page fault handler looks to see if the RAM page's reference count is greater than one; if it is, it means that a process is writing to a shared page. In this situation, the fault handler copies the page into another page of RAM and updates the child's page table entry to point to the new copy. The child's page table entry copy-on-write bit is reset. It then decrements the original RAM page's reference count and resets its copy-on-write bit if the count dropped to one. If a process attempts to modify a copy on write page and its reference count is equal to one, the fault handler allows the process to use the physical page and resets the copy-on-write flag, but also disassociates the page from its current swap copy. This is because it's possible that another process related by a fork is also sharing the same swap copy.

Thrashing And Swapping

If a large number of processes are running at the same time, it's possible that the rate of page faulting causes most of the CPU time to be spent transferring pages to and from swap space. This situation is called *thrashing*, and results in poor system performance. When the memory management system detects thrashing, it wakes up the *swapper* process, which chooses processes to deactivate and transfer to disk. It selects processes based on their priority and memory usage, marks them as "swapped," and pages all of their RAM pages to swap space. The swapper continues to swap processes to swap space until thrashing stops, at which point it goes back to sleep. Once a pre-determined time period has elapsed, a swapped process is marked as "ready to run," and its pages are faulted back into RAM in the normal manner.

Terminating A Process: exit ( )

When a process terminates, the following events occur:

- Its exit code is placed in its process table entry.
- Its file descriptors are closed.
- The reference count of each of its regions are decremented.
- If the reference count of a region drops to zero, the reference count of all of its RAM pages and swap pages (if appropriate) are decremented.
- Any RAM or swap pages that have a zero reference count are deallocated.

Its process table entry is deallocated only when its parent accepts its termination code via a wait ( ).

Signals

Signals inform processes of asynchronous events. The data structures that support signals are stored in the process table and the user areas. Every process has three pieces of information associated with signal handling:

- an array of entries called the *signal handler array* in its user area that describes what it should do when it receives a particular type of signal
- an array of bits in its process table entry called the *pending signal bitmap*, one per type of signal, that records whether a particular type of signal has arrived for processing
- a process group id, which is used when distributing signals

Figure 11.42 is a diagram of these signal-related kernel data structures. I'll describe the implementation of signals by describing the implementation of the system calls that are related to signals.

setpgrp ( )

setpgrp ( ) sets the calling process's process group number to its own PID, thereby placing it in its own unique process group. A fork'ed process inherits its parent's process group. setpgrp ( ) works by changing the process group number entry in the system-wide process table. The process group number is used by kill ( ), as you'll see later.

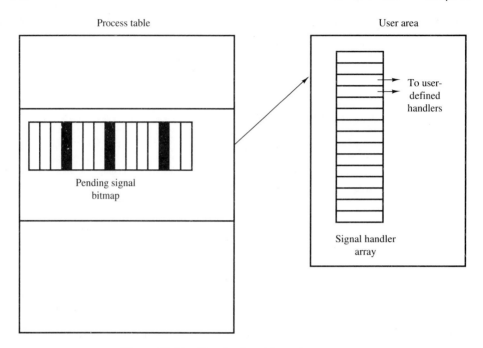

Figure 11.42   Signal-related kernel structures

signal ( )

signal ( ) sets the way that a process responds to a particular type of signal. There are three options: ignore the signal, perform the default kernel action, or execute a user-installed signal handler. The entries in the signal handler array are set as follows:

- If the signal is to be ignored, the entry is set to 1.
- If the signal is to cause the default action, the entry is set to 0.
- If the signal is to be processed using a user-installed handler, the entry is set to the address of the handler.

When a signal is sent to a process, the kernel sets the appropriate bit in the receiving process's signal bitmap. If the receiving process is sleeping at an interruptible priority, it is awakened so that it may process the signal. The kernel checks a process's signal bitmap for pending signals whenever the process returns from kernel mode to user mode (i.e., when returning from a system call) or when the process enters or leaves a sleep state. Note therefore that a signal is hardly ever processed immediately; the receiving process deals with pending signals only when it's scheduled to do so. This makes signals a relatively poor mechanism for realtime applications. Note also that the pending signal bitmap does not keep a *count* of how many of a particular type of signal are pending. This means that if three SIGINT signals arrive in close succession, it's possible that only one of them will be noticed.

Signals after a fork or an exec

A fork'ed process inherits the contents of its parent's signal handler array. When a process execs, the signals that were originally ignored continue to be ignored, and all others are set to their default setting. In other words, all entries equal to 1 are unchanged, and all others are set to 0.

Processing a signal

When the kernel detects that a process has a pending signal, it either ignores it, performs the default action, or invokes a user-installed handler. To invoke the handler, it appends a new stack frame to the process's stack and modifies the process's program counter to make the receiving process act as if it had called the signal handler from its current program location. When the kernel returns the process to user mode, the process executes the handler and then returns from the function back to the previous program location. The "death of a child" signal (SIGCHLD) is processed slightly differently, as you'll see when I describe the wait () system call.

exit ()

When a process terminates, it leaves its exit code in a field in its process table entry, and is marked as a zombie process. This exit code is obtainable by the parent process via the wait () system call. The kernel always informs a parent process that one of its children has died by sending it a "death of child" (SIGCHLD) signal.

wait ()

wait () returns only under one of two conditions; either the calling process has no children, in which case it returns an error code, or one of the calling process's children has terminated, in which case it returns the child process's PID and exit code. The way that the kernel processes a wait () system call may be split up into a three-step algorithm:

1. If a process calls wait () and doesn't have any children, it returns an error code.
2. If a process calls wait () and one or more of its children is already a zombie, the kernel picks a child at random, removes it from the process table, and returns its PID and exit code.

3. If a process calls wait ( ) and none of its children is a zombie, it goes to sleep. It is awoken by the kernel when *any* signals are received, at which point it resumes from step 1.

Although this algorithm would work as it stands, there's one small problem; if a process chose to ignore SIGCHLD signals, all of its children would remain zombies and this could clog up the process table. To avoid this problem, the kernel deals treats ignorance of the SIGCHLD signal as a special case. If a SIGCHLD signal is received and the signal is ignored, the kernel immediately removes all the parent's zombie children from the process table and then allows the wait ( ) system call to proceed as normal. When the wait ( ) call resumes, it doesn't find any zombie children, and so it goes back to sleep. Eventually, when the last child's death signal is ignored, the wait ( ) system call returns with an error code to signify that the calling process has no child processes.

kill ( )

kill ( ) makes use of the real user id and process group id fields in the process table. For example, when the following line of code is executed:

```
kill (0, SIGINT);
```

the kernel sets the bit in the pending signal bitmap corresponding to SIGINT in every process table entry whose process group id matches that of the calling process. UNIX uses this facility to distribute the signals triggered by *Control-C* and *Control-Z* to all of the processes in the control terminal's process group.

INPUT/OUTPUT

In this section, I'll describe the data structures and algorithms that the UNIX kernel uses to support I/O-related system calls. Specifically, I'll look at the UNIX implementation of these calls in relation to three main categories of file:

- *regular* files
- *directory* files
- *special* files (i.e., peripherals, pipes, and sockets)

I/O Objects

I like to think of files as being special kinds of objects that have I/O capabilities. UNIX I/O objects may be arranged according to the following hierarchy:

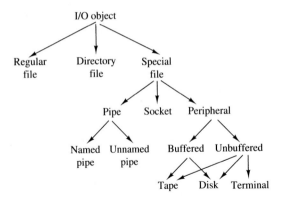

Figure 11.43 The I/O object hierarchy

I/O System Calls

As I described in chapter 10, the I/O system calls may be applied in a uniform way to all I/O objects. A few exceptions exist; for example, you can't use lseek ( ) on a pipe or a socket. Here's a complete list of the system calls that are described in this section:

- sync
- open
- read
- write
- lseek
- close
- dup
- unlink
- ioctl
- mknod
- link
- mount
- umount

I/O Buffering

The kernel avoids unnecessary device I/O by buffering most I/O in a fixed-size system-wide data structure call the *buffer pool*. The buffer pool is a collection of buffers that are used for caching file blocks in RAM.

When a process reads from a block for the very first time, the block is copied from the file into the buffer pool and then copied from there into the process's data space. Subsequent reads from the same block are serviced directly from RAM. Similarly, if a process writes to a block that isn't in the buffer pool, the block is copied from the file into the pool and then the buffered copy is modified. If the block is already in the pool, the buffered version is modified without any need for physical I/O. Several hash lists based on the block's device and block number are maintained for the buffers in the pool so that the kernel can quickly locate a buffered block.

When a process accesses a buffer during an I/O system call, the buffer is locked to prevent other processes from using it. If another process attempts to access a locked buffer, it is put to sleep by the kernel until the buffer is unlocked. When UNIX is booted, all buffers in the pool are marked as *unlocked* and placed on an *unlocked buffer list*.

When the kernel services a process's I/O system call and needs to copy a block from an I/O object into the buffer pool, it selects the first buffer on the unlocked buffer list, marks it as *locked*, removes it from the unlocked buffer list, issues an asynchronous read request to the appropriate device driver, and then sends the process to sleep. When the read request has been serviced, the process is awakened and the kernel continues to execute the system call. If the unlocked buffer list is empty, the process is sent to sleep until an unlocked buffer becomes available. If the block is already buffered, the kernel simply locks the existing buffer. When the system call is finished with the buffer, it is unlocked and placed on the end of the unlocked buffer list. This scheme ensures that the least recently used buffer is selected each time a new buffer is required.

It's tempting to think that the kernel copies all of a file's modified buffered blocks back to disk when the file is closed. It doesn't. Instead, the kernel sets a ''delayed-write'' flag in a buffer's header whenever it is modified by a write (). The buffered block is only physically written to disk when another process attempts to remove it from the unlocked block list due to the algorithm described in the previous paragraph. This scheme delays physical I/O until the last possible moment.

Figure 11.44 is an illustration of buffering in action.

sync ()

sync () causes the kernel to flush all of the delayed-write buffers to disk. System administrators arrange for the **sync** utility, which invokes sync (), to run regularly. This ensures that the contents of the disk are kept up to date.

Regular File I/O

The next few sections describe the implementation of *regular* file I/O, including the implementations of open (), read (), write (), lseek (), close (), dup (), and unlink ().

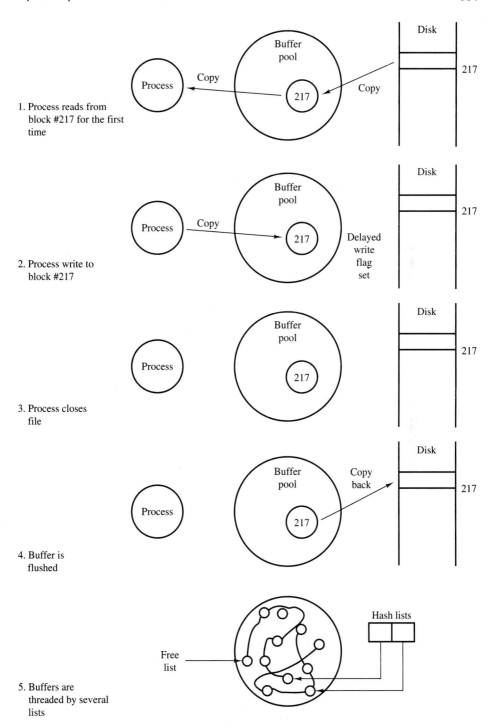

1. Process reads from block #217 for the first time

2. Process write to block #217

3. Process closes file

4. Buffer is flushed

5. Buffers are threaded by several lists

Figure 11.44 Buffering in action

open ()

Let's take a look at what happens when a process opens an existing regular file for read-only. Later, we'll examine the way that the kernel creates a new file. Assume that the process is the first process to open the file since the system was last rebooted, and that it executes the following code:

```
fd = open ("/usr/glass/sample.txt", O_RDONLY);
```

The kernel begins by translating the filename into an inode number, using the algorithm described earlier in this chapter. If the inode of the file is not found, an error code is returned. Otherwise, the kernel allocates an entry in a fixed-size system-wide data structure called the *active inode table* and copies the inode from disk into this entry. The kernel also stores several other values in this entry, which are described later. The kernel caches active inodes and recently used inodes in this table to avoid unnecessary disk access.

Next, the kernel allocates an entry in another fixed-size system-wide data structure called the *open file table*. It fills this entry with several useful values, including:

- a pointer to the new entry in the active inode table
- the read/write permission flags specified in the open () system call
- the process's current file position, set to 0 by default

Finally, the kernel allocates an entry in the per-process file descriptor array, points this entry to the new entry in the open file table, and returns the index of this file descriptor entry as the return value of open (). Following is an illustration of the process and kernel data structures that result from this example.

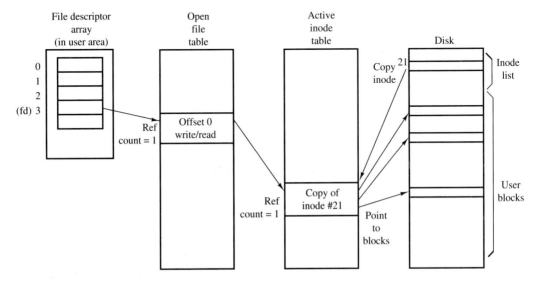

Figure 11.45 Kernel file structures

If a process opens a non-existent file and specifies the O_CREAT option, the kernel creates the named file. To do this, it allocates a free inode from the file system's inode list, sets the fields within it to indicate that the file is empty, and then adds a hard link to the appropriate directory file. Recall that a hard link is an entry consisting of a filename and its associated inode number.

Now that you've seen the way that the kernel handles an open () system call, I'll describe the read (), write (), lseek (), and close () system calls. For simplicity, assume that the example file is being accessed by just one process. I'll describe the kernel support for multiple users of the same file later on in this chapter.

read ()

Let's see what happens when the example process executes the following sequence of read () system calls:

```
read (fd, buf1, 100);   /* read 100 bytes into buffer buf1 */
read (fd, buf2, 200);   /* read 200 bytes into buffer buf2 */
read (fd, buf3, 5000);  /* read 5000 bytes into buffer buf3 */
```

Here's the sequence of events that would occur during the execution of the example:

- The data requested by the first read () resides in the first block of the file. The kernel determines that the block is not in the buffer pool, and so copies it from disk into an unlocked buffer. It then copies the first hundred bytes from the buffer into **buf1**. Finally, the file position stored in the open file table is updated to its new value of 100.
- The data requested by the second read () also resides in the first block of the file. The kernel finds that the block is already in the buffer pool, and so copies the next 200 bytes from the buffer into **buf2**. It then updates the file position to 300.
- The data requested by the third read resides partly in the first block of the file and partly in the second block. The kernel transfers the remainder of the first block (3796 bytes) from the buffer pool into **buf3**. It then copies the second block from disk into an unlocked buffer in the pool and copies the remaining data (1204 bytes) from the buffer pool into **buf3**. Finally, it updates the file position to 5300.

Note that a single read may cause more than one block to be copied from disk into the buffer pool. If a process reads from a block that does not have an allocated user block (see chapter 10 for a discussion of sparse files), then read () doesn't buffer anything, but instead treats the block as if it were filled with ASCII null (0) characters.

write ( )

The example process now executes the following series of write ( ) system calls:

```
write (fd, buf4, 100);        /* write 100 bytes from buffer buf4 */
write (fd, buf5, 4000);       /* write 4000 bytes from buffer buf5 */
```

Recall that the current value of the file position is 5300, which is situated near the start of the file's second block. Recall also that this block is currently buffered, courtesy of the last read ( ). Here's the sequence of events that would occur during the execution of our example:

- The data to be overwritten by the first write ( ) resides entirely in the second block. This block is already in the buffer pool, and so 100 bytes of **buf4** are copied into the appropriate bytes of the buffered second block.
- The data to be overwritten by the second write ( ) resides partly in the second block and partly in the third block. The kernel copies the first 3792 bytes of **buf5** into the remaining 3792 bytes of the buffered second block, copies the third block from the file into an unlocked buffer, and then copies the remaining 208 bytes of **buf5** into the first 208 bytes of the buffered third block.

lseek ( )

The implementation of lseek ( ) is trivial. The kernel simply changes the value of the descriptor's associated file position, located in the open file table. Note that no physical I/O is necessary. Here's a diagram that illustrates the result of the following code:

```
lseek (fd, 3000, L_SET);
```

Figure 11.46　lseek changes the file offset

close ()

When a file descriptor is closed and it's the only one associated with a particular file, the kernel copies the file's inode back to disk and then marks the corresponding open file table and active inode table entries as *free*. When a process terminates, the kernel automatically closes all of its file descriptors.

As I mentioned earlier, the kernel has special mechanisms to support multiple file descriptors associated with the same file. To implement these mechanisms, the kernel keeps a *reference count* field for each open file table entry and each active inode entry. When a file is opened for the first time, both of these counts are set to one. There are three ways that a file can be shared by several file descriptors:

1. The file is explicitly opened more than once, either by the same process or by different processes.
2. The file descriptor is duplicated by dup (), dup2 (), or fctnl ().
3. A process forks, which causes all of its file descriptor entries to be duplicated.

When a file descriptor is created by the first method, the kernel creates a new open file table entry that points to the same active inode, and increments the reference count field in the file's active inode:

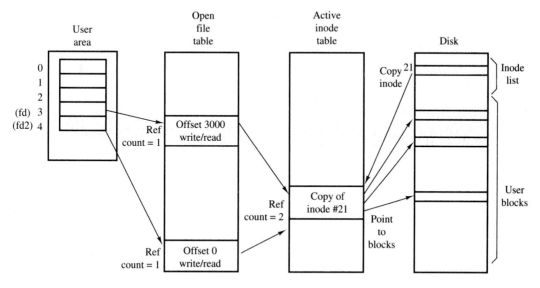

Figure 11.47 Open creates a new open file table entry

When a file descriptor is created by either of the latter two methods, the kernel sets the new file descriptor to point to the same open file table entry as the original file descriptor, and increments the reference count field in the descriptor's open file table entry.

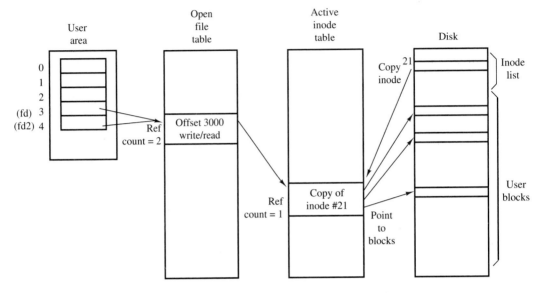

Figure 11.48   Duplicating a file descriptor

The algorithm for close () handles the reference count fields as follows: when a file descriptor is closed, the kernel decrements the reference count field in its associated open file table. If the open file table reference count remains greater than zero, nothing else occurs. If the reference count drops to zero, the open file table entry is marked as free and the reference count field in the file's active inode is decremented. If the active inode reference count remains greater than zero, nothing else happens. If the reference count drops to zero, the inode is copied back to disk and the active inode entry is marked as free.

dup ()

The implementation of dup () is simple; it copies the specified file descriptor into the next free file descriptor array entry and increments the corresponding open file table reference count.

unlink ()

unlink () removes a hard link from a directory and decrements its associated inode's hard link count. If the hard link count drops to zero, the file's inode and user blocks are deallocated when the last process that is using it exits. Notice that this means that a process may unlink a file and continue to access it until it exits.

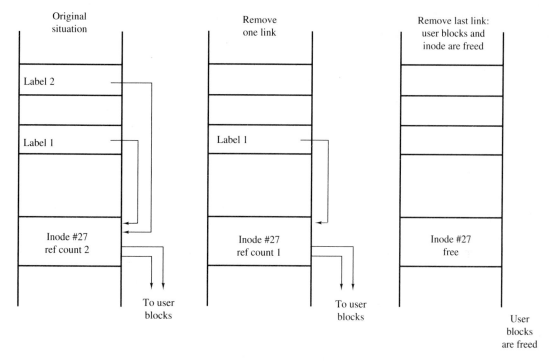

Figure 11.49   Unlinking

Directory File I/O

Directory files are different from regular files in a few ways:

- They may only be created using mknod ( ).
- They may only be read using getdents ( ).
- They may only be modified using link ( )

This ensures the integrity of the directory hierarchy. Directory files may be opened just like regular files. Let's take a look at the implementation of mknod ( ) and link ( ).

mknod ( )

mknod ( ) creates a directory, named pipe, or special file. In every case, the system call starts by allocating a new inode on disk, setting its type field accordingly, and adding it via a hard link into the directory hierarchy. If a directory is being created, a user block is associated with the inode and filled with the default

"." and ".." entries. If a special file is being created, the appropriate major and minor device numbers are stored in the inode; more on this later.

link ()

link () adds a hard link into a directory. Here's an example of link ():

```
link ("/usr/glass/file1.c", "/usr/glass/file2.c");
```

In this example, the kernel would find the inode number of the source filename "/usr/glass/file1.c" and then associate it with the label "file2.c" in the destination directory "/usr/glass." It would then increment the inode's hard link count. Only a super-user may link directories, to prevent unwary users from creating circular directory structures.

Mounting File Systems

The kernel maintains a single fixed-size system-wide data structure called the *mount table* that allows multiple file systems to be accessed via a single directory hierarchy. The mount () and umount () system calls modify this table, and are only executable by a super-user.

mount ()

When a file system is mounted using mount (), an entry is added to the mount table containing the following fields:

- the number of the device that contains the newly mounted file system
- a pointer to the root inode of the newly mounted file system
- a pointer to the inode of the mount point
- a pointer to the buffered superblock of the newly mounted file system

The directory associated with the mount point becomes synonymous with the root node of the newly mounted file system, and its previous contents become inaccessible to processes until the file system is later unmounted. To enable the correct translation of pathnames that cross mount points, the active inode of the mount directory is marked as a *mount point*, and is set to point to the associated mount table entry. For example, Figure 11.50 is a diagram showing the effect of the following system call, which mounts the file system contained on the "/dev/da1" device onto the "/mnt" directory:

```
mount ("/dev/da1", "/mnt", 0);
```

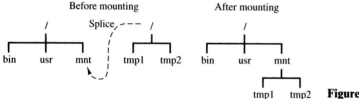

Figure 11.50 Mounting direct

Translation Of Filenames

The name translation algorithm uses the contents of the mount table when translating pathnames that cross mount points. This can occur when moving up or down the directory hierarchy. For example, consider the following example:

```
$ cd /mnt/tmp1
$ cd ../../bin
```

The first **cd** command crosses from the root device to the "/dev/da0" device, and the second **cd** command crosses back across to the root device. Here's how the algorithm incorporates mounted file systems into the translation process:

- When an inode is encountered during the translation process that is a mount point, a pointer to the root inode of the mounted file system is returned instead. For example, when the "/mnt" portion of the "/mnt/dir1" is translated, a pointer to the root node of the mounted file system is returned. This pointer is used as the starting point for the rest of the pathname translation.
- When a ".." pathname component is encountered, the kernel checks to see whether a mount point is about to be crossed. If the current inode pointer of the translation process points to a root node and ".." also points to a root node, then a crossing point has been reached. It replaces the current inode pointer of the translation process with a pointer to the inode of the parent file system, which it finds by scanning the mount table for the entry corresponding to the device number of the current inode.

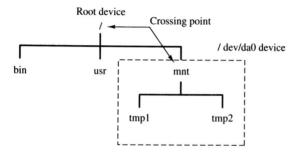

Figure 11.51 Crossing point

umount ( )

When unmounting a file system, there are several things that the kernel must do:

- It checks that there are no open files in the file system about to be unmounted. It can do this by scanning the active inode table for entries that contain the file system's device number. If any active inodes are found, the system call fails.
- It flushes the superblock, delayed-write blocks, and buffered inodes back to the file system. Once this is done, the invalidated blocks are placed on the head of the unlocked buffer list, as they are the least necessary of all the buffers to cache.
- It removes the mount table entry and removes the "mount point" mark from the mount point directory.

Special File I/O

Most special files correspond to peripherals such as printers, terminals, and disk drives, so for the rest of this section I'll use the terms *special file* and *peripheral* synonymously.

Every peripheral in the system has an associated *device driver*, which is a custom-crafted piece of software that contains all of the peripheral-specific code. For example, a tape drive's device driver contains the code for rewinding and retensioning the tape. All instances of a particular kind of peripheral may be controlled by a single device driver. In other words, three tape drives of the same type can share a single device driver. The device drivers for every peripheral in the system must be linked into the kernel when the kernel is configured by the system administrator. For more information, consult chapter 12.

Device Interface

A peripheral's device driver supplies the peripheral's *interface*, which can come in two flavors:

- *block-oriented*, which means that I/O is buffered, and that physical I/O is performed on a block-by-block basis. Disk drives and tape drives have a block-oriented interface.
- *character-oriented*, which means that I/O is unbuffered, and that physical I/O occurs on a character-by-character basis. A character-oriented interface is sometimes known as a *raw* interface. All peripherals usually have a raw interface, including disk drives and tape drives.

A peripheral's device driver sometimes contains both kinds of interfaces. The kind of interface that you choose depends on how you're going to access the device. When performing random access and repeated access to a common set of blocks, it makes good sense to access the peripheral via its block-oriented interface. However, if you're going to access the blocks in a single linear sequence, as you would when making a backup tape, it makes more sense to access the peripheral via its character-oriented interface. This avoids the overhead of the kernel's internal buffering mechanism and sometimes allows the kernel to use the hardware's DMA capabilities.

It's perfectly possible, although not advisable, to access a single device simultaneously via both interfaces. The trouble with this is that the character-oriented interface bypasses the buffering system, possibly leading to confusing I/O results. Here's an example:

- Process A opens a floppy disk using its block-oriented interface, "/dev/flp." It then writes 1000 bytes to the disk. This output is stored in the buffer pool, and marked for delayed writing.
- Process B then opens the same floppy disk using its character-oriented interface, "/dev/rflp." When it reads 1000 bytes from the disk, the data that was written by process A is ignored, since it's still in the buffer pool.

The solution to this problem is easy—don't do it!

Switch tables

All UNIX device drivers must follow a predefined format, which includes a set of standard entry points for functions that open, close, and access the peripheral. Block-oriented device drivers also contain an entry point called *strategy* that is used by the kernel for performing block-oriented I/O to the physical device. The entry points of each block-oriented interface and each character-oriented interface are stored in system-wide tables called the *block device switch table* and the *character device switch table*. These tables are stored as arrays of pointers to functions, and are created automatically when UNIX is configured. One dimension of the array is indexed by a peripheral's major number, and the other dimension is indexed by a function code. Here's an illustration of a small sample switch table:

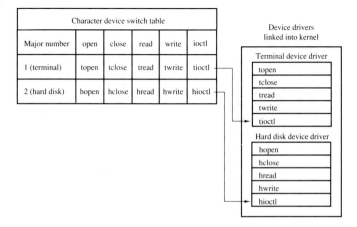

Figure 11.52 A small sample switch table

Here's a diagram that illustrates the kernel data structures that might be formed after the following bit of code is executed:

```
fd = open ("/dev/tty2", O_RDWR);
```

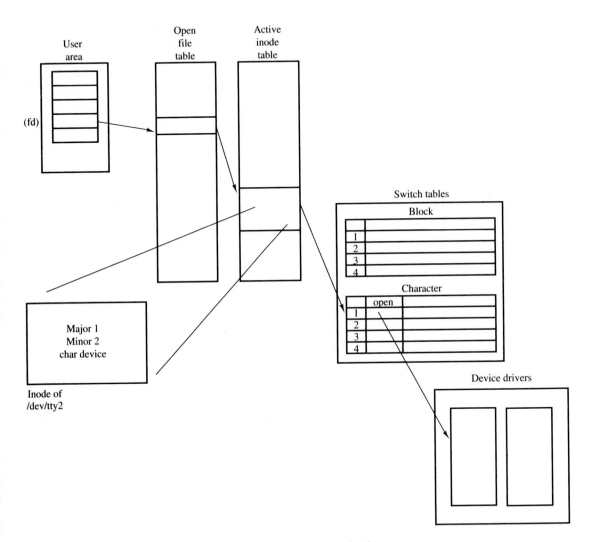

Figure 11.53   Special file access

lseek (), chmod (), and stat () work the same way for special files as they do for regular files. open (), read (), write (), and close () work slightly differently, and make use of the block/character switch tables. In each case, their operation may be split into a peripheral-independent part and a peripheral-dependent part. There now follows a description of each system call.

open ( )

When a process opens a file, the kernel can tell that it's a peripheral by examining the type field of the file's inode. If the field indicates a block-oriented or character-oriented device, it reads the major and minor numbers to determine the class of the device and the instance of the device that is being opened.

When processing open ( ), the kernel performs peripheral-independent actions followed by peripheral-dependent actions. The peripheral-independent part of open ( ) works just like a regular file open ( ); the file's inode is cached in the active inode table and an open file table entry is created. The peripheral-dependent part of open ( ) invokes the device driver's open ( ) routine. For example, a tape driver's open ( ) routine usually retensions and rewinds the tape, whereas a terminal driver's open ( ) routine sets the device's baud rate and default terminal settings. Since every successful open ( ) increments the active inode's reference count, a device driver may use this information to limit the number of users of the device. For example, a printer's device driver usually prevents more than one process from using the printer at any given time.

read ( )

When reading from a character-oriented device, read ( ) invokes the *read* function in the device driver to perform the physical I/O.

When reading from a block-oriented device, read ( ) makes use of the standard I/O buffering mechanism. If a block needs to be physically copied from the device to the buffer pool, the *strategy* function in the device driver is invoked. This function combines both read and write capabilities.

write ( )

When writing to a character-oriented device, write ( ) executes the *write* function in the device driver to perform the physical I/O.

When writing to a block-oriented device, write ( ) uses the I/O buffering system. When a delayed-write eventually takes place, the device's *strategy* function is used to perform the physical I/O.

close ( )

The kernel closes a peripheral in the same way as it closes a regular file, except when the process that performs the close ( ) is the last process that was accessing the device. In this special case, the device driver's close ( ) routine is executed, followed by the series of actions for closing a regular file.

The kernel cannot determine that a special file has been closed by its last user by simply examining the active inode's reference count, as a single device may be accessed via more than one inode. Such a situation occurs if one process accesses a device via its block-oriented interface, and another accesses the same file via its character-oriented interface. In this case, the active inode list must be searched for other inodes associated with the same physical device.

ioctl ( )

ioctl ( ) controls device-specific features via a file descriptor. It simply passes on its arguments to the *ioctl* entry point of the device driver. Examples of device-specific operations include setting a terminal's baud rate, selecting a printer's font, and rewinding a tape drive.

Terminal I/O

Although terminals are a kind of peripheral, terminal device drivers are interesting and different enough that I'm devoting a separate section here for their discussion. The main difference between terminal device drivers and other device drivers is that they must support several different kinds of pre- and post-processing on their input and output, respectively. Each variety of processing is termed a *line discipline*. A terminal's line discipline can be set using ioctl ( ). Most terminal drivers support the following three common line disciplines:

- *raw mode*, which performs no special processing at all. Characters entered at the keyboard are made available to the reading process based on the ioctl ( ) parameters. Key sequences such as *Control-C* do not generate any kind of special action, and are passed as regular ASCII characters. For example, *Control-C* would be read as the character with ASCII value 3. Raw mode is used by applications such as editors that prefer to do all of their own character processing.
- *cbreak mode*, which only processes some key sequences specially. For example, flow control via *Control-S* and *Control-Q* remains active. Similarly, *Control-C* generates an interrupt signal for every process in the foreground job. As with raw mode, all other characters are available to the reading process based on the ioctl ( ) parameters.
- *cooked mode* (sometimes known as *canonical mode*), which performs full pre- and post-processing. In this mode, the delete and backspace keys take on their special meanings, together with the less common word-erase and line-erase characters. Input is made available to a reading process only when the *Enter* key is pressed. Similarly, tabs have a special meaning when output, and are expanded by the line discipline to the correct number of spaces. A newline character is expanded into a carriage return/newline pair.

Terminal data structures

The main data structures that the kernel uses to implement line disciplines are:

- *clists*, which are linked lists of fixed-size character arrays. It uses these structures to buffer the pre-processed input, the post-processed input, and the output associated with each terminal.
- *tty structures*, which contain the state of a terminal including pointers to its clists, the currently selected line discipline, a list of the characters that are to be processed specially, and the options set by ioctl ( ). There is one tty structure per terminal.

Here's an illustration of a tty structure and its associated clists:

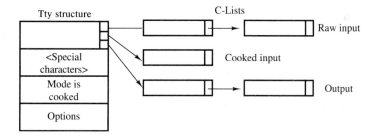

Figure 11.54   Tty structure and C-lists

Reading from a terminal

When a key is pressed, the keyboard interrupt handler performs the following operations, depending on the mode of the terminal:

- *raw mode*: the character is copied onto the end of the raw clist and the process waiting on the read is awakened so that it may read from the raw clist. When the process awakens, all characters on the raw clist are moved into the process's address space.
- *cbreak mode*: if the character is a flow control or break character, it is processed specially; otherwise, the character is copied onto the end of the raw clist and the process waiting on the read is awakened. When the process awakens, all characters on the raw clist are moved into the process's address space.
- *cooked mode*: if the character is a flow control or break character, it is processed specially; otherwise, the character is copied onto the end of the raw clist. If the character is a carriage return, the contents of the raw clist

are moved onto the end of the cooked input clist and the process waiting on the read is awakened. When the process awakens, the special characters such as backspace and delete in the cooked input clist are processed, and then the post-processed contents are copied into the process's address space.

ioctl ( ) allows you to specify conditions that must be satisfied before a reading process is awakened. Conditions include the number of characters in the raw clist and an elapsed time since the last read ( ). If two or more processes try to read from the same terminal, it's up to them to synchronize; otherwise, the input will be shared indiscriminately between the competing processes. Signals generated by special characters in cbreak and cooked modes go to the processes associated with the *control terminal*. For more information about control terminals, consult chapter 10.

Writing to a terminal

When a process writes to a terminal, any special characters are processed according to the currently selected line discipline and then placed onto the end of the terminal's output clist. The terminal driver invokes hardware interrupts to output the contents of this list to the screen. If the output clist becomes full, the writing process is sent to sleep until some of the output drains to the screen.

INTERPROCESS COMMUNICATION

In this section I describe the data structures and algorithms that the UNIX kernel uses to support pipes and sockets.

Pipes

The implementation of pipes differs significantly between System V and BSD, so I'll begin by describing System V pipes.

System V pipes

There are two kinds of pipes in System V—*named* pipes and *unnamed* pipes. Unnamed pipes are created by pipe ( ), and unnamed pipes are created using mknod ( ). Data written to a pipe is stored in the file system. When either kind of pipe is created, the kernel allocates an inode, two open file entries, and two file descriptors. Originally, the inode describes an empty file. If the pipe is named, a hard link is made from the specified directory to the pipe's inode; otherwise, no hard link is created and the pipe remains anonymous.

Pipe data structures

The kernel maintains the current write position and current read position of each pipe in its inode, rather than in the open file table entry. This ensures that each byte in the pipe is read by exactly one process. It also keeps track of the number of processes reading from the pipe and writing to the pipe. As you'll soon see, it needs both of these counts to process a close ( ) properly.

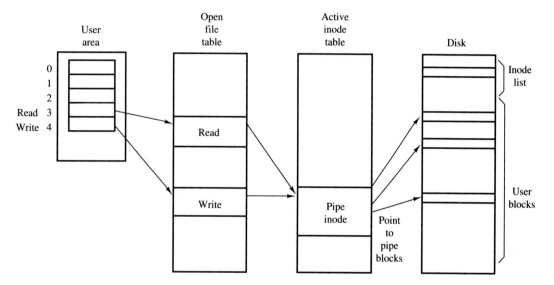

Figure 11.55   System V pipes are stored in the file system

Writing to a pipe

When data is written to a pipe, the kernel allocates disk blocks and increments the current write position as necessary, until the last direct block has been allocated. For reasons of simplicity and efficiency, a pipe is never allocated indirect blocks, thereby limited the size of a pipe to about 40K, depending on the file system's block size. If a write to a pipe would overflow its storage capacity, the writing process writes as much as it can to the pipe and then sleeps until some of the data is drained by reader processes. If a writer tries to write past the end of the last direct block, the write position "wraps around" to the beginning of the file, starting at offset 0. Thus the direct blocks are treated like a circular buffer. Although it might seem that using the file system for implementing pipes would be slow, remember that disk blocks are buffered in the buffer pool, and so most pipe I/O is buffered in RAM.

Reading from a pipe

As data is read from a pipe, its current read position is updated accordingly. The kernel ensures that the read position never overtakes the write position. If a process attempts to read from an empty pipe, it is sent to sleep until output becomes available.

Closing a pipe

When a pipe's file descriptor is closed, the kernel does some special processing:

- It updates the count of the pipe's reader and writer processes.
- If the writer count drops to zero and there are processes trying to read from the pipe, they return from read ( ) with an error condition.
- If the reader count drops to zero and there are processes trying to write to the pipe, they are sent a signal.
- If the reader and writer counts drop to zero, all of the pipe's blocks are deallocated and the inode's current write and read positions are reset. If the pipe is unnamed, the inode is also deallocated.

BSD pipes

BSD pipes are implemented in terms of sockets. The write and read file descriptors are each connected to an anonymous socket's end point within the UNIX system domain.

Sockets

A complete description of the implementation of sockets would be rather lengthy, as it would require an explanation of the workings of Internet addressing, routing, and communication. For this reason, I supply only a brief overview of the socket system in terms of its memory management and interface to the Internet protocols.

Memory management

When data is transferred between socket end points, the data is buffered using a dynamic memory allocation system that uses fixed-size data packets called *mbufs*. Each *mbuf* is 128 bytes long, broken down as follows:

- a 112-byte buffer
- a field that records the size of the data in the buffer
- a field that records the offset of the data in the buffer

Routines that read buffers can strip off protocol headers by simply adjusting the data size and offset fields, rather than having to shift the valid data in memory. The *mbuf* memory manager is relatively efficient, and several other kernel routines use it for non-socket-related uses.

Sockets and the open file table

When a socket is created using socket ( ), the system creates a socket structure that records all of the information pertaining to the socket, including the following fields:

- the socket domain
- the socket protocol
- a pointer to the socket's *mbuf* lists

In order to tie the file descriptor system to the socket system, the kernel keeps a pointer from the socket's open file table entry to its associated socket structure. This structure is accessed when performing socket I/O. Following is a diagram of this arrangement.

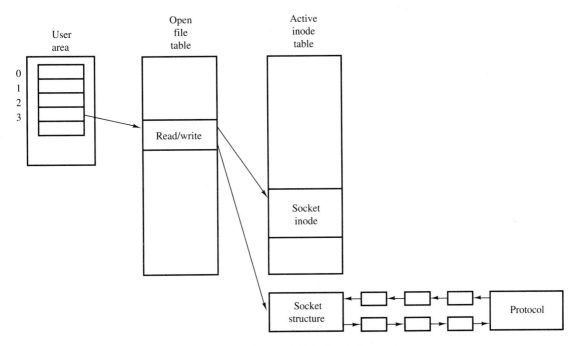

Figure 11.56   Berkeley sockets

Writing to a socket

When a socket is written to using write ( ), the data is placed onto the output *mbuf* list for transmission by the protocol module.

Reading from a socket

When data arrives at the protocol module, it is placed onto the input *mbuf* list for consumption by the process. When the process performs a read ( ), the data is transferred from the input *mbuf* list into the process's address space.

CHAPTER REVIEW

Checklist

In this chapter, I described:

- the layering of kernel subsystems
- the difference between user mode and kernel mode.
- the implementation of system calls and interrupt handlers
- the physical and logical layout of the file system
- inodes
- the algorithm that the kernel uses for translating pathnames into inode numbers
- the process hierarchy
- the six process states
- how the scheduler decides to allocate the CPU
- memory management and the MMU
- the I/O subsystem, including buffering
- interprocess communication via pipes and sockets

Quiz

1. Why does the kernel maintain multiple priority queues?
2. Why do system calls make use of kernel mode?

3. What happens when an interrupt interrupts another interrupt?
4. How do modern disk designs attempt to increase total storage capacity?
5. Where is the name of a file stored?
6. What information does the superblock contain?
7. How does UNIX avoid using bad blocks?
8. Why is inode #2 special?
9. What is the meaning of the term *magic number*?
10. What is the meaning of the term *context switch*?
11. What information is stored in a process's user area?
12. If a signal is sent to a process that is suspended, where is it stored?
13. Describe an overview of the memory mapping that the MMU performs.
14. What does the page stealer do?
15. How does UNIX copy a parent's data to its child?
16. What is the meaning of the term "delayed-write"?
17. What is the purpose of the open file table?
18. What is the use of the I/O switch tables?
19. Why does the UNIX terminal driver use clists?
20. What is the main implementation difference between BSD and System V pipes?

Exercises

1. How could you avoid having to link the device drivers into the kernel? Why do you think UNIX has this restriction? [level: *medium*]
2. A low priority interrupt may be lost if it occurs during the servicing of a higher priority interrupt. How do you think the systems software deals with lost interrupts? [level: *hard*]
3. The superblock contains a lot of important information. Suggest some ways to minimize disruption to the file system in the case that the superblock gets corrupted. [level: *medium*]
4. When very small files are created, some disk space is lost due to the minimum allocation unit size. This wasted space is called internal fragmentation. Suggest some ways to minimize internal fragmentation. [level: *medium*]
5. Delayed writing normally causes a modified buffer to be flushed when its RAM is needed, and not when its file is closed. An alternative method is to flush modified buffers when disk traffic is low, thereby making the best use of the idle time. Critique this strategy. [level: *medium*]

Projects

1. If you know object-oriented techniques, design a basic object-oriented kernel where system services are provided by a collection of system objects. How does the design of your kernel differ from the UNIX kernel? [level: *hard*]

2. Investigate some microkernel operating systems such as ''Mach'', ''Plan 9'', and ''Windows NT.'' How do they compare against UNIX? [level: *medium*]

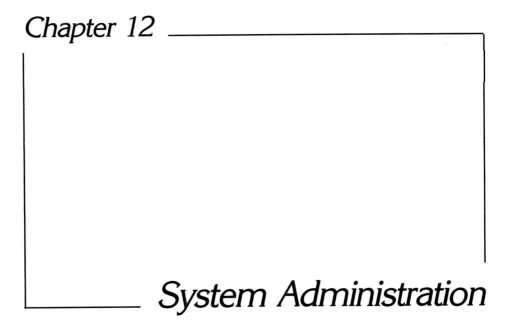

Chapter 12

System Administration

Motivation

There are a number of administrative duties that must be performed on a UNIX system to keep it running smoothly. Without them, files may be irrecoverably lost, utilities may become out of date, and the system may run slower than its potential speed. Many UNIX installations are large enough that they warrant a full-time system administrator; other UNIX systems, such as my home system, do not. Regardless of whether you're destined to perform administrative duties, this chapter contains valuable information on how to oversee a UNIX installation.

Prerequisites

In order to understand this chapter, you should have read chapters 1 and 2. It also helps if you've read chapters 3 and 8.

Objectives

In this chapter, I describe the main tasks that a system administrator must perform in order to keep a UNIX system running smoothly.

Presentation

The information presented in this section is in the form of several small, self-contained subsections.

Utilities

This section mentions the following utilities, listed in alphabetical order:

ac	fsck	newfs
accton	halt	pac
config	last	reboot
df	mkfs	shutdown
du	mknod	

INTRODUCTION

There are many tasks that a system administrator must sometimes perform in order to keep a UNIX system running properly, including the following:

- maintaining user accounts
- maintaining the file system
- performing system accounting
- installing new software
- installing and configuring peripherals
- configuring the kernel
- automating repetitive tasks
- checking system security

Almost all of these tasks require the administrator to be in super-user mode, as they access and modify privileged information. If you haven't got access to the super-user password, you'll just have to use your imagination. Here's a diagram that illustrates the tasks in a hierarchical fashion:

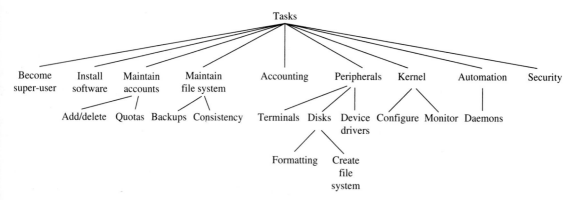

Figure 12.1 System administrator tasks

To cover each of these topics in depth would require an entire book, so this chapter simply presents an overview of system administration. For more detailed information, I thoroughly recommend the *UNIX System Administration Handbook* [16].

BECOMING A SUPER-USER

Most administration tasks require that you have super-user powers, and there are two ways to get them:

- Log in as "root," the user id of a super-user.
- Use the **su** utility, described in chapter 7, to create a child shell owned by "root."

Although the first method is very direct, there are some dangers associated with it. If you log in as "root," every single command that you execute will have super-user privileges - even the ones with errors in them. Imagine typing "rm -r * .bak" instead of "rm -r *.bak" whilst in the "/" directory! Because of this problem, I strongly recommend that you always use the second method. Log in to UNIX as a regular user, and only become a super-user when you need to.

STARTING UNIX

UNIX is usually in one of two modes:

- *Single-user mode*, which means that a single user may log in from the system console and execute commands from a shell. This mode has no active system daemons, and is generally used for system maintenance, backups, and kernel reconfiguration.
- *Multi-user mode*, which means that many users may log in from different terminals. This mode has active system daemons, and is the default mode for most systems.

Some machines allow you to choose the mode by toggling a front panel switch; other machines enter multi-user mode by default unless the boot sequence is interrupted by a *Control-C*. The only way to tell what your own system does is to read the manual.

When you turn on the computer, the following sequence of events occurs:

1. The hardware performs diagnostic self-tests.
2. The UNIX kernel is loaded from the root device.
3. The kernel starts running and initializes itself.
4. The kernel starts *init*, the first user-mode process.

init starts by checking the consistency of the file system using **fsck**, which is described later in this chapter. If single-user mode was chosen, *init* then creates a Bourne shell associated with the system console. If multi-user mode was chosen, *init* performs the following actions:

- It executes the commands in "/etc/rc," which perform site-nonspecific initialization tasks such as starting the mail daemon and clearing the "/tmp" directory.
- It then executes the commands in "/etc/rc.local," which perform site-specific initialization tasks such as setting the local host name.
- Finally, it creates a "getty" process for every terminal in the "/etc/ttytab" file. "/etc/ttytab" contains one line of information for every terminal on the system, including its baud rate and pathname.

A "getty" process listens for activity on its associated terminal and replaces itself by a "login" process if it detects that someone's trying to log in. "login" accepts a user id and a password, checks them against the entries in the "/etc/passwd" file, and replaces itself with the user's startup program if the password is correct. The startup program is usually a shell.

When a user logs out, *init* receives a SIGCHLD signal from the dying shell. When this happens, *init* removes the user from the "/etc/utmp" file, which contains a list of all the current users, and appends an entry to the "/var/adm/wtmp" file, which contains a list of all the recent logins and logouts. *init* then creates a new "getty" process for the freed terminal.

init's behavior may be modified by sending it a signal:

- SIGHUP causes *init* to rescan the "/etc/ttytab" file and create "getty" processes for all the terminals in the file that need them. It also kills "getty" processes that don't have an associated terminal. This facility allows you to add and remove terminals without rebooting the system.
- SIGTERM causes *init* to take UNIX to single-user mode.
- SIGTSTP tells *init* not to create a new "getty" process when a user logs out. This allows the system to gradually phase out terminals.

init is vital to the functioning of UNIX, as it's responsible for creating and maintaining login shells. If *init* dies for any reason, the system reboots automatically.

STOPPING THE SYSTEM

A modern computer prefers to run all the time; turning it on and off causes it stress. However, there are some circumstances where it's a good idea to turn it off. For example, if a storm is coming, you should disconnect your computer from its power source to avoid high-voltage surges. UNIX should not be shut down directly; instead, you should use one of the **shutdown**, **halt**, or **reboot** utilities.

    shutdown can be used to either halt UNIX, place it into single-user mode, or place it into multi-user mode. It emits warning messages prior to the shutdown so that users may log out before the system changes state.

Utility: **shutdown** -hkrn *time* [*message*]

shutdown shuts down the system in a graceful way. The shutdown time may be specified in one of three ways:

- *now*: the system is shut down immediately.
- *+minutes*: the system is shut down in the specified numbers of minutes.
- *hours:minutes*: the system is shut down at the specified time (24-hour format).

    The specified warning message (or a default one if none is specified) is displayed periodically as the time of shutdown approaches. logins are disabled five minutes prior to shutdown.

    When the shutdown time arrives, **shutdown** executes **sync** and then sends *init* a SIGTERM signal; this causes *init* to take UNIX to single-user mode. The **-h** option causes **shutdown** to execute **halt** instead of sending the signal. The **-r** option causes **shutdown** to execute **reboot** instead of sending the signal. The **-n** option prevents **shutdown** from performing its default sync. The **-k** option is funny; it causes **shutdown** to behave as if were going to shut down the system, but when the shutdown time arrives, it does nothing. "k" stands for "just kidding"!

---

halt causes an immediate system shutdown with no warning messages:

Utility: **halt**

halt performs a sync and then halts the CPU. It appends a record of the shutdown to the "/var/adm/wtmp" log file.

---

reboot may be used to force the system to reboot:

Utility: **reboot** -q

reboot terminates all user processes, performs a sync, loads the UNIX kernel from disk, initializes the system, and then takes UNIX to multi-user mode. A record of the reboot is appended to the "/var/adm/wtmp" log file. To perform a quick reboot, use the **-q** option. This option instructs reboot not to bother to kill the current processes before rebooting.

MAINTAINING THE FILE SYSTEM

This section describes the file system-related administrative tasks:

- ensuring the integrity of the file system
- checking disk usage
- assigning quotas
- creating new file systems

File System Integrity

One of the first things that *init* does is to run a utility called **fsck** to check the integrity of the file system. **fsck** works like this:

Utility: **fsck** -p [*fileSystem*]*

fsck (file system check) scans the specified file systems and checks them for consistency. The kind of constistency errors that can exist include:

- A block is marked as free in the bitmap but is also referenced from an inode.
- A block is marked as used in the bitmap but is never referenced from an inode.
- More than one inode refers to the same block.
- An invalid block number.
- An inode's link count is incorrect.
- A used inode is not referenced from any directory.

> For information about inodes, see chapter 11.
>
> If the **-p** option is used, **fsck** automatically corrects any errors that it finds. Without the **-p** option, it prompts the user for confirmation of any corrections that it suggests. If **fsck** finds a block that is used but is not associated with a named file, it connects it to a file whose name is equal to the block's inode number in the "/lost+found" directory.
>
> If no file systems are specified, **fsck** checks the standard file systems listed in "/etc/fstab."

Fortunately, **fsck** is very good at correcting errors. This means that you'll never have the joy of hand-patching disk errors.

Disk Usage

As I just mentioned, disk errors are uncommon and are corrected automatically. Disk usage problems, on the other hand, are very common. Many users treat the file system as if it's infinitely large, and create huge numbers of files without much thought. When I taught UNIX at UT Dallas, the disks would invariably fill up on the last day of the semester, just as everyone was trying to complete their projects. Students would try to save their work from **vi**, and **vi** would respond with a "disk full" message. When they quit from **vi**, they would find that their file had been deleted.

To avoid running out of disk space, it's wise to run a shell script from **cron** that periodically runs the **df** utility to check the available disk space. **df** works like this:

> *Utility:* **df** [*fileSystem*]*
>
> **df** displays a table of used and available disk space, in kilobytes, on the specified mounted file systems. If no file system is specified, all mounted file systems are described.

Here's an example of **df** in action:

```
$ df                     ...list information about all file systems.
Filesystem          kbytes     used    avail capacity  Mounted on
/dev/sd3a            16415    10767     4006     73%    /
/dev/sd3g           201631   125513    55954     69%    /usr
/dev/sd3d            60015    34773    19240     64%    /export
$ df /dev/sd3a           ...list a specific file system.
Filesystem          kbytes     used    avail capacity  Mounted on
/dev/sd3a            16415    10767     4006     73%    /
$ _
```

If **df** reports that a disk is greater than 95% full, your script could detect this and send you some warning mail. Even better, your script could then run the **du** utility to determine which users are using the most disk space, and then automatically send them mail suggesting that they remove some files. **du** works like this:

Utility: **du** -s [*fileName*]*

du displays the number of kilobytes (BSD) or 512-byte blocks (System V) that are allocated to each of the specified filenames. If a filename refers to a directory, its files are recursively described. When used with the **-s** option, **du** only displays the grand total for each file. If no filenames are specified, the current directory is scanned.

In the following example, I used **du** to find out how many kilobytes my current directory and all its files were using up. I then obtained a file-by-file breakdown of the disk usage:

```
$ du -s .              ...obtain grand total of current directory.
9291  .
$ du .                 ...obtain file-by-file listing.
91    ./proj/fall.89
158   ./proj/summer.89/proj4
159   ./proj/summer.89
181   ./proj/spring.90/proj2
21    ./proj/spring.90/proj1
204   ./proj/spring.90
455   ./proj
...                    ...other files were listed here.
38    ./sys5
859   ./sys6
9291  .
$ _
```

Assigning Quotas

Some systems allow a system administrator to set disk quotas for individual users. You may specify the maximum number of files and the maximum number of blocks that a particular user is allowed to create. It's fairly complicated to add quotas, and involves reconfiguring the kernel, updating the "/etc/rc" file, modifying the "/etc/fstab" file, and creating the "/users/quotas" quota control file.

Creating New File Systems

If you buy a new disk drive, you must perform the following tasks before your file system can use it:

1. Format the media.
2. Create a new file system on the media.
3. Mount the disk into the root hierarchy.

The manufacturer of the device will supply you with a formatting utility. Use this to perform step 1. Next, create a file system on the media using **mkfs** or **newfs**. Here's a description of **mkfs**:

Utility: **mkfs** *specialFile* [*sectorCount*]

mkfs creates a new file system on the specified special file. A new file system consists of a superblock, an inode list, a root directory, and a "lost+found" directory. The file system is built to be *sectorCount* sectors in size. Only a super-user can use this command.

Because it's unlikely that you'll know the correct value of *sectorCount* without looking it up in the manufacturer's handbook, the **newfs** utility was designed as a user-friendly front end to **mkfs**:

Utility: **newfs** *specialFile deviceType*

newfs invokes **mkfs** after looking up the *deviceType's* sector count from the "/etc/disktab" file, which contains information about standard device characteristics.

Once the file system is created, it may be connected to the root file system by using the **mount** utility that is described in chapter 7.

Backing Up File Systems

The procedure and utilities for backing up the file system are described in chapter 7.

MAINTAINING USER ACCOUNTS

One of a system administrator's most common tasks is to add a new user to the system. To do this, you must:

- Add a new entry to the password file "/etc/passwd."
- Add a new entry to the group file "/etc/group."
- Create a home directory for the user.
- Provide the user with some appropriate startup files.

The Password File

Every user of the system has an entry in the password file of the following format:

```
username:password:userId:groupId:personal:homedir:startup
```

where each field has the following meaning:

Field	Meaning
username	the user's login name
password	the encoded version of the user's password
userId	the unique integer allocated to the user
groupId	the unique integer corresponding to the user's group
personal	the description of the user that is displayed by the **finger** utility
homedir	the home directory of the user
startup	the program that is run for the user at login

A $ in the password field indicates that no login is allowed. Here's a snippet from the UT Dallas password file:

```
$ head -5 /etc/passwd                    ...look at first five lines.
root:rcfsmtio:0:0:Operator:/:/bin/csh
daemon:$:1:1::/:
sync:$:1:1::/:/bin/sync
sys:$:2:2::/:/bin/csh
bin:$:3:3::/bin:
$ _
```

I used **grep** to find my own entry:

```
$ grep glass /etc/passwd              ...find my line.
glass:dorbnla:496:62:Graham Glass:/usr/glass:/bin/ksh
$ _
```

The Group File

To add a new user, you must first decide which group it's in and then search the group file to find its associated group id. As an example, I'll show you how to add a new user called "simon" into the "cs4395" group.

Every group in the system has an entry in the "/etc/group" file of the following format:

```
groupname:groupPassword:groupId:users
```

where each field is defined as follows:

Field	Meaning
groupname	the name of the group
groupPassword	the password for the group (not used, and often filled with an *)
groupId	the unique integer corresponding to the group.
users	a list of the users in the group, separated by commas

Here's a snippet from the UT Dallas "/etc/group" file:

```
$ head -5 /etc/group             ...look at start of group file.
cs4395:*:91:glass
cs5381:*:92:glass
wheel:*:0:posey,aicklen,shrid,dth,moore,lippke,rsd,garner
daemon:*:1:daemon
sys:*:3:
$ _
```

As you can see, the "cs4395" group has an associated group id number of 91. To add Simon as a new user, I allocated him the unique user id number 10, a group id of 91, and left his password field empty. Here's what his entry looked like:

```
simon::101:91:Simon Pritchard:/usr/simon:/bin/ksh
```

Once the entry was added to the password file, I added Simon onto the end of the "cs4395" list in the "/etc/group" file, created his home directory, and gave him some default startup files such as "`.kshrc`" and "`.profile`". I copied these files from a directory called "`/usr/template`" that I made to keep the default versions of user startup files.

```
$ mkdir /usr/simon                          ...create home directory.
$ cp /usr/template/.* /usr/simon            ...copy across startup files.
$ chown simon /usr/simon /usr/simon/.*      ...give them to simon.
$ chgrp cs4395 /usr/simon /usr/simon/.*     ...set the correct group.
$ _
```

Finally, I logged in as Simon and used **passwd** to change his password to a sensible default value.

To delete a user, simply reverse these actions: delete the users's password entry, group file entry, and home directory.

DEVICES

Let's assume that you've just bought a new device and you wish to connect it to your system. How do you install it? And if it's a terminal, which terminal-specific files must be updated? This section presents an overview of device installation and a list of the terminal-related files.

Installing A Device

The basic steps of device installation are as follows:

1. Install the device driver if it isn't currently in the kernel.
2. Determine the device's major and minor numbers.
3. Use **mknod** to associate a filename in "`/dev`" with the new device.

Once the device driver is installed and the major and minor numbers are known, you must use **mknod** to create the special file:

Utility: **mknod** *fileName* [c] [b] *majorNumber minorNumber*
       mknod *fileName* p

mknod creates the special file *fileName* in the file system. The first form of **mknod** allows a super-user to create either a character- or block- oriented special file with the specified major and minor numbers. The major number identifies the class of the device, and the minor number identifies the in-stance of the device. The second form of **mknod** creates a named pipe, and may be used by anyone.

In the following example, I installed the thirteenth instance of a terminal whose major number was 1:

```
$ mknod /dev/tty12 c 1 12        ...note that 13th instance is index 12.
$ _
```

The "c" indicated that the terminal was a character-oriented device. In the next example, I installed the first instance of a disk drive whose major number was 2:

```
$ mknod /dev/dk1 b 2 0           ...note that 1st instance is index 0.
$ _
```

The "b" indicated that the terminal was a block-oriented device.

Major and minor numbers are the fourth and fifth fields, respectively, in an "ls -l" listing. In the following example, I obtained a long listing of the "/dev" directory:

```
$ ls -l /dev                 ...get a long listing of the device directory.
crw--w--w-  1     root  1,  0 Feb13 14:21 /dev/tty0
crw--w--w-  1     root  1,  1 Feb13 14:27 /dev/tty1
brw--w--w-  1     root  2,  0 Feb13 14:29 /dev/dk0
crw--w--w-  1     root  3,  0 Feb13 14:27 /dev/rmt0
...
$ _
```

Terminal Files

There are several files that contain terminal-specific information. Here's a list of them, together with a brief description of their function:

Name	Description
/etc/termcap	An encoded list of every standard terminal's capabilities and control codes. The UNIX editors use the value of the environment variable $TERM to index into this file and fetch your terminal's characteristics.
/etc/ttys	A list of every terminal on the system together with the program that should be associated with it when the system is initialized (usually "getty"). If the terminal's type is constant and known, this information is also included.
/etc/gettytab	A list of baud rate information that is used by "getty" when deciding how to listen to a login terminal.

AUTOMATING TASKS

There are several system tasks that are fairly simple but tedious to perform. For example:

- adding a user account
- deleting a user account
- checking for full disks
- generating reports of logins and logouts
- performing incremental backups
- system accounting
- removing old "core" files
- killing zombie processes

I recommend that you automate as many of these chores as you can, using shell scripts and C programs. Tasks that must be executed on a periodic basis can be scheduled by the **cron** utility. Many system administrators swap useful scripts at weekly meetings.

ACCOUNTING

The UNIX accounting facilities allow you to track the activity of its subsystems. Each subsystem of BSD UNIX keeps a record of its own history in a special file, as follows:

- *Process management*: a record of the user id, memory usage, and CPU usage of every process is appended to the "/usr/adm/acct" file. The **sa** utility may be used to report on the information in this file. Process accounting is toggled by the **accton** utility.
- *Connections*: a record of the login time, user id, and logout time of every connection is appended to the "/usr/adm/wtmp" file. The **ac** and **last** utilities may be used to report on the information in this file. Connection accounting is enabled by the presence of the "/usr/adm/wtmp" file.
- *Printer usage*: every printer records information about its print jobs in the "/usr/adm" directory. The **pac** utility can generate reports from this information. Printer accounting is toggled by an entry in the "/etc/printcap" file.
- Other subsystems such as **uucp** and **quota** also produce log files.

System V system accounting works in a similar way: different subsystems generate files that are converted into reports by utilities and shell scripts. The system administrator is responsible for maintaining accounting records for the target subsystems, and for purging/archiving the accounting files periodically.

CONFIGURING THE KERNEL

The UNIX kernel is a program written mostly in C with a few assembly language sections. When you purchase a UNIX system, the manufacturer includes several pieces of software related to the kernel:

- a generic executable kernel
- a library of object modules that correspond to the parts of the kernel that never change
- a library of C modules that correspond to the parts of the kernel that may be changed
- a configuration file that describes the current kernel setup
- a **config** utility that allows you to recompile the kernel when the configuration file is changed

The kernel configuration files are kept in either the ''/usr/conf'' (BSD) or the ''/usr/src/uts/cf'' (System V) directories. The facets of the kernel that may be changed include the following:

- the device drivers
- the maximum number of open files, clists, quotas, and processes
- the size of the I/O buffer pool and system page tables
- some important networking information
- the physical addresses of devices
- the name of the machine
- the time zone of the machine

To recompile a new kernel, you must follow a multi-step process:

1. Edit the configuration file and change the parameters to their new values.
2. Run the **config** utility, which creates some header files, some C source code, and a makefile.
3. Run the **make** utility, passing it the name of the makefile created by **config**. **make** recompiles the newly created source code and links it with the unchanging portion of the kernel to produce a new executable.
4. Rename the old UNIX kernel.

5. Rename the new UNIX kernel to take the place of the old one.

6. Reboot the system.

SECURITY ISSUES

The UNIX security mechanisms such as file protection and passwording are tough for a regular user to break but not so hard for experienced hackers. The best that a system administrator can do is to read about as many of the known security loopholes as possible and adopt strategies to stop them all. To give you an idea of what you're up against, here are a couple of common password-nabbing techniques:

- If you have a regular account and desire a super-user account, you begin by obtaining a copy of the one-way encryption algorithm that is used by the UNIX **passwd** utility. You also buy an electronic dictionary. Next, you copy the "/etc/passwd" file to your home PC and compare the encrypted versions of every word in the dictionary against the encrypted root password. If one of the dictionary entries matches, you've cracked the password! Other common passwords to test for include names and words spelled backward. This brute force technique is very powerful, and may be defended against by asking everyone to pick non-English, non-backward, non-trivial passwords.

- A scheming user can use the command overloading technique described earlier to trick a super-user into executing the wrong version of **su**. To use this Trojan horse technique, set $PATH so that the shell looks in your own "bin" directory before the standard "bin" directories. Next, write a shell script called **su** that pretends to offer a super-user login, but really stores the super-user password in a safe place, displays "wrong password", and then erases itself. When this script is prepared, call a super-user and tell him/her that there's a nasty problem with your terminal that requires super-user powers to fix. When the administrator types **su** to enter super-user mode, *your* **su** script executes instead of the standard **su** utility, and the super-user password is captured. The super-user sees the "wrong password" message and tries **su** again. This time, it succeeds, as your Trojan horse script has already erased itself. The super-user password is now yours! The way to defeat this technique is never to execute commands using a relative pathname when you're at an unfamiliar terminal. In other words, execute "/bin/su" instead of just "su".

The best ways to improve your knowledge of cunning schemes is to network with other system administrators and to read specialized system administrator books [16].

CHAPTER REVIEW

Checklist

In this chapter, I described:

- the main system administration tasks
- how to obtain super-user powers
- how to start and stop UNIX.
- the difference between single- and multi-user modes
- some useful disk-utilization utilities
- how to create a new file system
- how to add and delete user accounts
- an overview of how a device is installed
- the process of creating a new kernel
- some common security problems

Quiz

1. Under what situations is it appropriate to shut down a UNIX system?
2. What does a ``getty'' process do?
3. How can you put UNIX into single-user mode?
4. When is the file system checked for integrity?
5. Which files must be modified when you add a new user?
6. Which UNIX subsystems generate accounting records?
7. Which kernel parameters may be modified?
8. Describe the ``Trojan horse'' technique for capturing a super-user password.

Exercises

1. Use du to examine your disk usage. Write a script that prints out the full pathnames of your files that are over a specified size. [level: *medium*]
2. Obtain a floppy disk, format it, create a file system on it, mount it, and copy some files onto it. You'll almost certainly need a system administrator to help you through this process. [level: *medium*]
3. Try using cpio and tar to transfer some files to and from a floppy disk. Which of these utilities do you prefer? [level: *easy*]
4. Write a ``Trojan Horse'' script to capture a super-user password, but don't use it for malicious purposes! [level: *medium*]

Project

1. Ask your system administrator what he/she belives to be the strengths and weaknesses of UNIX from a system administrator's standpoint. Are these issues being addressed by current UNIX releases and research? [level: *medium*]

Chapter 13

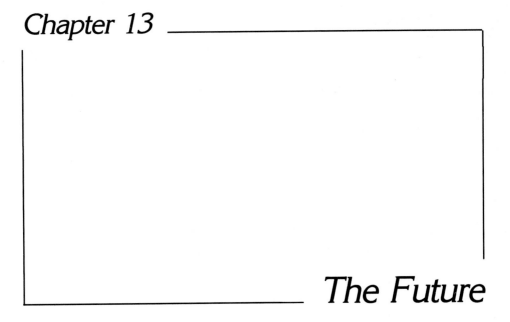

The Future

Motivation

Operating systems continue to develop and improve as software and hardware technology expands. Although old, stagnant systems will inevitably hang around for quite a while, systems that incorporate the best concepts and philosophies will eventually replace them. UNIX is over 20 years old, and is already beginning to show its age in terms of its internal architecture. Knowledge of operating system trends will help you to understand the changes that will occur in UNIX over the next few years, as well as allowing you to place the role of UNIX in perspective.

Prerequisites

You should have read chapter 11. It is also helps if you have some knowledge of object-oriented concepts.

Objectives

In this chapter, I'll describe the latest research that aims to improve the performance and capabilities of UNIX, as well as looking at operating system concepts that will provide stiff competition for UNIX.

Presentation

This chapter is comprised of several fairly self-contained sections, each of which examines a different aspect of operating system research.

INTRODUCTION

To set the scene for this chapter, let's take a look at the latest trends in software and hardware. The hottest software topics include the following:

- object-oriented systems
- distributed parallel processing
- high-bandwidth communication systems

Hardware advances include the following:

- chips designed especially for parallel processing
- optical processors
- advanced digital signal processing (DSP) chips

Both sets of trends may be extrapolated to an exciting and interesting future. In order to fit these subjects into a coherent framework, I'll begin by painting a scenario that will appear at first glance to be in the realm of science fiction. Remember, however, that the same was true of stories that talked about rocket ships and space travel! I personally believe that most of the technology that I'm about to describe will exist in less than thirty years.

THE GRID

One of the most successful and influencial computer systems of the present is the telephone network. It's a good example of a parallel distributed system, since phone calls are handled by local exchanges rather than by a single central call-processing center. Areas of a phone system can malfunction without affecting the rest of the system. Modern civilizations rely on the telephone system for communication of voice and data, making it indispensable for everyday business. As companies expand and new technologies such as fiber-optic cable become readily available, the phone system is being required to handle much higher capacities of data. Frame relay systems, for example, are one of the latest improvements in switching systems that allow high-bandwidth communication over the phone network. Telephone companies are also designing telephones that can take advantage of the improved performance. For example, AT&T and Northern Telecom recently announced telephones that incorporate a keyboard and a screen so that they can be used to communicate more easily with remote computer systems. The MINITEL system is a similar keyboard-based telephone that has been very successful in France for several years.

As the telephone network becomes more pervasive and is integrated into more areas of life, it will be looked at more as a medium for data communication rather than for voice communication. It's likely that all kinds of household appliances such as televisions and heating systems will become hooked up to the network so that they can be controlled remotely. For the rest of this section, I'll refer to this "telephone network of the future" as "The Grid."

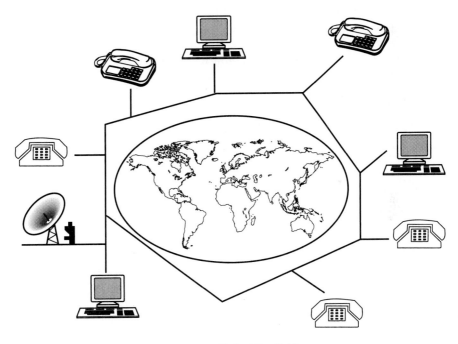

Figure 13.1   The Grid

VIRTUAL REALITY

One of the latest applications of high technology is called virtual reality (VR for short). A user of VR can don a pair of goggles, a headset, and optional special clothing that supplies an alternative set of sensory inputs, effectively creating another reality for the user. For example, pilots using VR equipment can experience combat situations that are synthesized by computers. For realism, the feeling of acceleration can be approximated by appropriate pressure pads connected to the pilot's body. Similar systems are under development to allow chemists to see and feel molecules and their reactions, and for architects to explore synthetic versions of their creations. If you've seen "Star Trek: The Next Generation," then you'll recogonize VR as an inferior version of the holodeck. The synthetic environment that VR machines create is sometimes termed *cyberspace*.

As virtual reality machines become more commercially available, I think it's likely that they will gradually replace telephones and televisions as the preferred means of communication. VR machines will be in every home, connected together via the global "grid." Home applicances, cars, industrial robots, and other machines will also be part of the grid. In other words, everything will be able to talk to everything. Resources and their interconnectivity will be greater than ever before. The theme of the 21st century will be *collaboration*.

Rather than simply listening to someone over the phone system, you'll be able to see them and even shake their hand using VR. Similarly, rather than watch a 2D television program, you'll experience the show in 3D. Virtual offices will be created to allow workers in many countries to form businesses overnight. A Japanese person could knock on the door of a VR office, open it, and talk to a person in Australia. The implications of VR on the education system are enormous - rather than simply talk about the Grand Canyon, the class members could all don VR equipment and actually "fly" through it. A single master teacher could give a lecture to thousands of students at the same time by communicating through cyberspace. Peripherals such as the Hubble space telescope could be part of the grid, allowing wealthy individuals to peer into space as if they were suspended far above the earth. Millions of people could experience Space Shuttle missions without any danger.

As the power and flexibility of virtual reality systems allows more personal transactions to take place in cyberspace, the need for physical travel will become less. Industries will create virtual products in virtual reality that won't actually exist in the normal physical sense. For example, a company might market virtual "appearances" so that a VR user could look quite different in cyberspace than he or she does in the real world. The potential for entertainment is incredible. It's very likely that many users will become addicted to VR for this very reason.

BUILDING CYBERSPACE

The future that I just painted has already begun. There are several companies that are actively developing machines capable of supporting simple VR systems. I believe that it's just a matter of time before mainstream telecommunication companies get very interested in VR. The big question is: how do you implement it? Systems capable of supporting VR must have the following properties:

- They must be fault tolerant.
- They must supply a huge amount of computing power.
- They must have a high-communication bandwidth.

Fault tolerant systems are generally distributed, so that many computers can work simultaneously on overlapping parts of the same problem. This ensures that the total performance degrades proportionately to the number of working units. The grid will contain at least twenty million computers, each with about 100 MIPS of power (100 million instructions per second), which should provide a fair amount of computer power. This kind of computing power is already within reach - in ten years, these figures will be much higher. In order to achieve the kind of intercommunication that VR requires, the topology of the grid will be more interconnected than traditional systems, rather like the high-level topology of biological nervous systems.

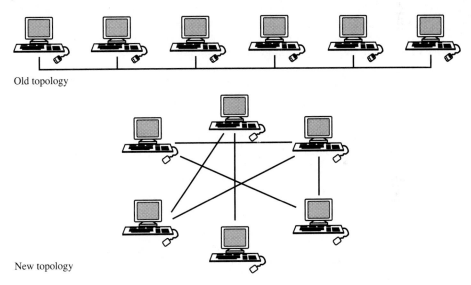

Old topology

New topology

Figure 13.2   Old and new topologies

One of the most promising hardware devices that would be able to support such a system is a processor from Inmos called a "transputer." Let's take look at what transputers can do....

TRANSPUTERS

Transputers are CPUs that were designed from the ground up to support parallel processing. Imagine that your job is to design and build a circuit board that contains four CPUs for parallel processing. There are several ways you could

design your board topology. One possible architecture connects all of the CPUs
to a single bus that accesses a single block of shared memory:

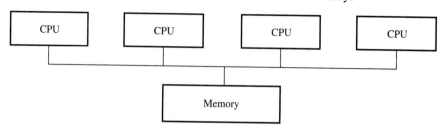

Figure 13.3   Single bus architecture

This architecture is terrible for at least two main reasons:

1. Since the bus is shared, only two CPUs can talk to each other at any one
time, which keeps the bandwidth fairly low.

2. Since the memory is shared, only one CPU can access it at any one time.
This once again keeps the bandwidth low.

In both cases, the restricted bandwidth is a result of what is usually termed a
bottleneck, a single resource that cannot be used simultaneously by those who
need it.

   The solution to this problem is to remove both bottlenecks. This can be
done by allocating each CPU its own local memory and by increasing the interconnectivity of the CPUs. Regular CPUs require between 16 and 32 wires to form
one inter-CPU connection; transputers require only 3 wires. This means that the
board construction for connected transputers is much easier. Transputers communicate by converting parallel data into serial data and then sending the serial
information between the CPUs at rates between 20 Mbits/s (old transputers) and
200 Mbits/s (new transputers). Each transputer contains up to 4 links, which
means that a single CPU can talk at up to 800 Mbits/s at peak rates.

   Here's an illustration of a small multiple bus architecture:

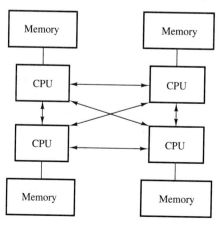

Figure 13.4   Multiple bus architecture

It's not necessary for every CPU to be connected directly to every other CPU; indeed, this is very impractical for all but the smallest networks. However, typical transputer networks are highly interconnected, thereby avoiding the shared bus bottleneck.

I already mentioned that future systems must support parallel processing, and transputers have been built from the ground up to support such systems. Each transputer has a timesharing multiprocessing system *built into silicon*. No operating system is necessary to run parallel programs. In addition to this, interprocess communication mechanisms that allow a process on one transputer to talk to another process on a different transputer *are also built into silicon*. This low-level support of basic parallel processing and communication is very handy for advanced software development. Transputer chips come in several flavors:

Family	Characteristics
T400	20 MIPs, 4 × 20 Mbit/s links, no floating point
T800	20 MIPs, 4 × 20 Mbit/s links, floating point
T9000	200 MIPs, 4 × 200 Mbit/s links, floating point (due late 1992)

One problem that many older parallel systems had is that the CPUs had to be synchronized to a single global clock. Transputer chips each generate their own clock signal, and don't even have to be running at the same speed. A T9000 chip can communicate with a T400 chip with no problems at all.

In summary, transputers are ideal building blocks for the next generation of parallel processing systems.

PARALLEL OBJECT-ORIENTED SYSTEMS

Object-oriented systems are taking traditional systems by storm. Industry has found them to be easier to design, understand, and maintain than traditional systems. Object-oriented programming languages such as C++ and Smalltalk are already commonly used in industry. However, all of the commercially available languages have the following weaknesses:

- None of them conveniently supports multi-user access to objects.
- None of them supports flexible parallel distributed processing of messages.

I use the word *convenient* here because there are several "hacked" attempts to synthesize these features, none of which are smoothly integrated into the object-oriented paradigm.

The current technique for sharing objects between multiple users is to use an object-oriented database (OODB). OO applications may save objects into an

OODB in native format and load them back at a later time. Most OODBs have several language interfaces.

The common solution to parallel distributed processing of messages is to network PCs or workstations, each of which is running a standalone OO application, and then to write some special software that acts as a go-between for the transfer of messages and objects between the computers. In other words, the applications programmer ends up writing a lot of code that should really be transparently incorporated into the programming system.

In response to the current state of affairs, several companies are working on object-oriented platforms that directly and transparently support object sharing and parallel distributed processing. Examples of these systems include the new Apple/IBM joint venture to develop the object-oriented operating system "Pink," and a Canadian consortium that is developing "Utopia," a complete object-oriented environment.

Sharing Objects

The rewards of going to an O/S that directly supports objects are tremendous. To show you why this is, let's examine a sample problem and its solution in a traditional O/S and an object-oriented O/S.

Imagine that you're writing a program that uses a 200K graphics library, a 100K data structures library, a 100K C runtime library, and 100K of your own code. On a UNIX system without dynamic link libraries, you'd link all of these libraries together, yielding an executable file of size 500K. Let's assume that your system contains 50 programs that follow a similar pattern; they all use 400K of standard library routines, and then 100K of application-specific code. The total disk requirement to store the 50 programs on a traditional system is therefore 50 × 400K = 20,000K. If we assume a main memory size of 10 megabytes, the ratio of RAM to total executable size is 1 : 2.

In an object-oriented system, a standard hierarchy of classes is available to all users. This hierarchy would contain the classes corresponding to the various libraries available on a traditional system. Each user can also add classes to the hierarchy and share classes added by other users. Programs are not "linked" in the traditional sense. Instead, when a message is sent to an object, the system checks to see whether the code corresponding to the message is already in RAM. If it isn't, it's loaded from disk; otherwise, the copy in RAM is used. This ensures that only a single copy of any message code ever resides in RAM, shared by all users that need it. The total disk requirement for 50 "programs" constructed in this manner is therefore equal to 200 + 100 + 100 + (50 × 100) = 5400K, a considerable improvement over the traditional system. In reality, the savings would be even greater, as a good percentage of the application-specific code would be reusable from the hierarchy. Note also that the ratio of RAM to total executable size has improved to 2:1, allowing all of the code of all the programs to be memory-resident. The larger the number of programs on the system, the larger the savings of RAM and disk space.

Another advantage of having a hierarchy that is shared between all users is that it makes code reuse much more practical. All of the code in the entire system is accessible from one location and arranged in an orderly fashion.

Object Communication

Communication between processes in traditional systems has evolved over time, yielding several different approaches. For example, UNIX includes the following methods of interprocess communication:

- signals
- unnamed pipes
- named pipes
- sockets
- streams
- shared memory
- semaphores

Object-oriented systems, on the other hand, support just one means of IPC, the *message*. Any object may send any other object a message using a standard protocol, regardless of whether the object is in the same machine, or in a machine on the other side of the world. This simplification allows the kernel to be much smaller, and makes life easier for programmers.

Another boon of object-oriented operating systems is that they don't need a file system. This surprises many people who have grown up being used to the idea that computer systems and files go hand in hand. To understand why file systems will become obsolete, you must first become familiar with the idea of persistent objects. Traditional programming languages allow you to create global variables that last the lifetime of the program, but require you to save variables to disk in an intermediate format if you wish to use them in future applications. An object created in an object-oriented operating system lives forever until you explicitly delete it or remove all references to it. This means that you never have to save or load objects; they're simply "there." This is a much better metaphor of the real world than the file metaphor. When you build an object in the real world, it stays around until you pull it apart. Since objects no longer have to be saved, there is no need for a file system. Objects that are actively being accessed are kept in RAM, and all other objects are stored on disk. Objects are transferred to and from disk depending on their usage.

There are at least a couple of advantages of replacing the file system with the persistent object paradigm: the kernel becomes smaller, and programmers no longer have to worry about saving and loading objects to disk. Incidentally, the fact that objects will be easily accessible to all programmers means that object-oriented databases will no longer be necessary, since their main use is to support object-persistence and multi-user access in traditional operating systems.

CURRENT TRENDS

There are several developments that are taking us in the direction that I just described:

- *Helios* is a transputer-based version of UNIX that uses the transputer's abilities to implement the UNIX multitasking capabilities efficiently.
- *Plan 9* is a distributed operating system being designed by some of the original UNIX designers that stores different kernel functions in different machines. For example, one machine might be a file server and contain a copy of the file system portion of the kernel, whereas another machine might not have any disks and thus not require the file system portion. By contrast, every UNIX system contains a full copy of the kernel.
- Some researchers are constructing a multi-user Smalltalk system that allows many programmers to share and operate upon the same hierarchy, and allows objects to operate in parallel across multiple platforms.
- Apple and IBM are working on an object-oriented operating system based on an older system called "Pink" that will work on current architectures and the powerful PowerPC chip that IBM intends to manufacture.

THE REALITY METAPHOR

The parallel object-oriented programming systems (*POOPS*) that I just described are one more step in a trend that began long ago; a trend toward computer systems that model reality:

- *Traditional systems* divide the world up into passive data and active functions. Functions truly become active, however, only when executed by a single CPU.
- *Parallel traditional systems* keep the division of code and data, but allow more than one function to be truly active at any one time. Functions can communicate data via one of several interprocess communication mecha-

nisms. Functions are always chunked into programs, and when a program finishes, all of its data is lost unless the programmer explicitly saves it to a secondary storage medium.

- *Object-oriented systems* merge data and code into a single entity, an object. If two objects are in the same program, they can communicate via messages; otherwise, they must use a secondary IPC mechanism. Objects must still be saved between invocations of programs. Some operating systems such as Windows 3.0 allow objects in different programs to talk, but the IPC mechanism is still fairly clumsy and non-transparent.
- *Parallel object-oriented systems* allow many messages to be processed in parallel.
- *Parallel distributed object-oriented systems* allow objects to communicate freely across machines via messages, and objects remain in the system after they're created until they're explicitly destroyed.

The last kind of system is closest to the real world; the universe is built out of an incredible number of components, each of which performs its own local processing in parallel with the others.

BIOLOGICALLY INSPIRED SYSTEMS

The kinds of systems that computer scientists dream of already exist; they're called *biological organisms*. Lifeforms exhibit all of the properties that we're striving for:

- fault tolerant
- massively parallel
- distributed
- well organized
- self-repairing
- designed in a layered fashion
- designed out of simple components

I believe that computer scientists could learn a lot about how to design advanced computer systems by studying the biological systems that already exist. The area of neural networks is one area in which biologists, physiologists, and computer scientists are actively collaborating, but is only one facet of the intersection of these topics.

THE OBJECT SOCIETY

In the same way that biological systems exhibit beautiful properties, so does our own society. A society is a collection of collaborating individuals, each with his/her own value system, and each striving for his/her own goals. The actions of a society are determined by the actions of the individuals.

For example, take a group of scientists and citizens who are all interested in building a spaceship to travel to Mars. No single individual has the money, skills, or lifespan to achieve this on his/her own, but working together it's a reasonable goal. The individuals each use their own specialized skills to develop a piece of the project, and collaborate and coordinate with the others so that their work is integrated into the final product. Managers perform the coordination, scientists develop the technology, and industrialists build the hardware.

Let's have a look at how a society is like a single organism:

- It's *fault tolerant*, as the skills and knowledge of the individuals overlap. The death of a single individual would not cause the project to stop.
- It's *massively parallel*, as the individuals perform their tasks at the same time.
- It's *distributed*, as the components of the spaceship are designed and produced in different areas of the world.
- It's *well organized*, thanks to a layered management system that coordinates the logical phases of each operation.
- It's *self-repairing*, as individuals who leave are replaced by other retrained individuals. As faults in the spaceship are discovered, the design is improved.
- It's *designed in a layered fashion*, with some individuals assigned to highly specialized tasks and others to more general coordination.
- It's *designed out of simple components*. Relative to the complexity of an entire society, an individual is rather straightforward.

There's a book by Marvin Minsky called *The Society Of Mind* that describes how a mind may be viewed as a society built out of small, relatively simple agents. An agent in the society of mind is analogous to a human in the society of earth; much simpler, and acting on its own accord.

I believe that the computer systems of the future will be societies of objects, each with individual strengths and weaknesses, and each collaborating with other objects to achieve its own goals.

To illustrate my point, imagine a situation where three high-level objects are simultaneously trying to achieve their goals. One object wants to move a robot arm, one wants to predict stock market movement, and the other wants to create some electronic art. Assume that each object requires the services of a "quadratic equation solver" object. Each of the three objects places a bid for the services of such an object, depending on how badly it needs it. The currency that objects use for competing in the object market is immaterial, but for now I'll use dollars. The robot arm object bids $10 for a quadratic object, and the others bid $5 and $2. The quadratic objects work for the highest bidders, and then use the currency that they receive in order to gather their own resources. For example, a quadratic object might need a subtraction, multiplication, square, and square root object in order to achieve its goal. Here's an illustration of the object marketplace:

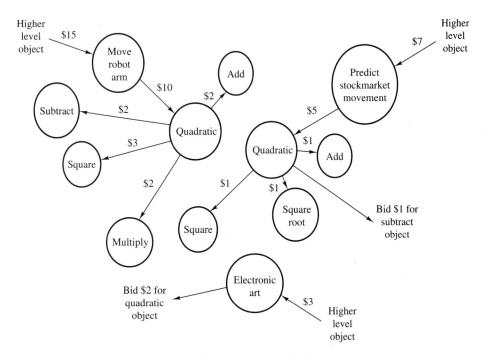

Figure 13.5   A society of objects

If objects could change their behaviors based on the current market demand for services, this kind of free market object system would exhibit some very interesting behaviors:

- If the demand for a particular type of object exceeded the supply, some objects would have to wait for the services or pay more. This would result in an increased profit for the objects in short supply. Other objects that were not in demand would start to duplicate the services of those making a large profit, resulting in an increase in the supply of the object and a decrease in profit. Fewer objects would have to wait for the service, resulting in an increase in parallelism and a different mix of object services.

- If the demand for a particular type of object was much less than the supply, objects that were part of the over-supply would change their behaviors to something more profitable.
- Multiple copies of useful services ensure a fault-tolerant system, as the failing of an individual object does not affect the system very much.
- An object may boost its priority by increasing the amount that it bids for services. For example, if a stock market object decided that it needed to process information very quickly, it could increase its bid and steal away the services of objects from other bidders.

I realize that this kind of system is radically different from those of today, but a great deal of research trends indicate that these are the kinds of systems that we're heading toward. I think the next decade of computer science is going to be amazing.

CHAPTER REVIEW

Checklist

In this chapter, I described:

- an advanced CPU called a "transputer"
- several different network architectures
- the benefit of parallel systems
- the benefit of distributed systems
- the future use of telecommunication networks
- virtual reality
- the requirements for the construction of cyberspace
- parallel object-oriented operating systems
- Helios, Pink, and Plan 9
- the real-world metaphor
- the powerful biological metaphor
- a free market object paradigm

Quiz

1. What O/S features will a virtual reality system require?
2. What are the advantages of a multiple bus architecture over a single bus system?

3. Why are transputers well suited for parallel architectures?
4. Name some companies that are investing in object-oriented operating systems.
5. What is the purpose of object-oriented databases?
6. Describe the "free market" object model.
7. What are the most powerful parallel systems known to us?

Projects

1. Write a paper that explains the trend in computer science toward systems that more closely model reality. [level: *hard*]
2. Write a paper that describes the pros and cons of a free market system of objects versus the traditional computational models. [level: *hard*]

REGULAR EXPRESSIONS

Regular expressions are character sequences that describe a family of matching strings. They are accepted as arguments to many UNIX utilities, such as **grep**, **egrep**, **awk**, **sed**, and **vi**. Note that the filename substitution wildcards used by the shells are _not_ examples of regular expressions, as they use different matching rules.

Regular expressions are formed out of a sequence of normal character and special characters. Here is a list of special characters, sometimes called _meta-characters,_ together with their meaning:

Metacharacter	Meaning
.	Matches any single character.
[ ]	Matches any of the single characters enclosed in brackets. A hyphen may be used to represent a range of characters. If the first character after the [is a ^, then any character *not* enclosed in brackets is matched. The *, ^, $, and \ metacharacters lose their special meaning when used inside brackets.
*	May precede any character, and denotes zero or more occurrences of the character that it precedes.
^	Matches the beginning of a line only.
$	Matches the end of a line only.
\	The meaning of any metacharacter may be inhibited by preceding it with a \.

A regular expression matches the longest pattern that it can. For example, when the pattern "y.*ba" is searched for in the string "yabadabadoo", the match occurs against the substring "yabadaba" and not "yaba". The next page contains some examples of regular expressions in action.

To illustrate the use of these metacharacters, here is a piece of text followed by the lines of text that would match various regular expressions. The portion of each line that satisfies the regular expression is italicized.

Text

```
Well you know it's your bedtime,
So turn off the light,
Say all your prayers and then,
Oh you sleepy young heads dream of wonderful things,
Beautiful mermaids will swim through the sea,
And you will be swimming there too.
```

Patterns

Pattern	Lines that match
the	So turn off *the* light, Say all your prayers and *the*n, Beautiful mermaids will swim through *the* sea, And you will be swimming *the*re too.
.nd	Say all your prayers *and* then, Oh you sleepy young heads dream of w*onder*ful things, *And* you will be swimming there too.

Pattern	Lines that match
^.nd	*And* you will be swimming there too.
sw.*ng	And you will be *swimming* there too.
[A-D]	*B*eautiful mermaids will swim through the sea, *A*nd you will be swimming there too.
\.	And you will be swimming there too.
a.	S*ay* all your prayers and then, Oh you sleepy young he*ad*s dream of wonderful things, Be*au*tiful mermaids will swim through the sea,
a.$	Beautiful mermaids will swim through the se*a,*
[a-m]nd	Say all your prayers *and* then,
[^a-m]nd	Oh you sleepy young heads dream of w*ond*erful things, *And* you will be swimming there too.

Extended Regular Expressions

Some utilities such as **egrep** support an extended set of metacharacters, which are described below:

Metacharacter	Meaning
+	Matches one or more occurrences of the single character that it precedes.
?	Matches zero or one occurrence of the single character that it precedes.
| (pipe symbol)	If you place a pipe symbol between two regular expressions, a string that matches either expression will be accepted. In other words, a | acts like an "or" operator.
( )	If you place a regular expression in parentheses, you may use the *, +, or ? metacharacters to operate on the entire expression, rather than just a single character.

Here are some examples of full regular expressions, using the example file from the previous page:

Pattern	Lines that match
s.*w	Oh you *sleepy young heads dream of w*onderful things, Beautiful mermaid*s will sw*im through the sea, And you will be *sw*imming there too.
s.+w	Oh you *sleepy young heads dream of w*onderful things, Beautiful mermaid*s will sw*im through the sea,
off|will	So turn *off* the light, Beautiful mermaids *will* swim through the sea, And you *will* be swimming there too.
im*ing	And you will be swimming there too.
im?ing	\<no matches\>

MODIFIED-FOR-UNIX BACKUS-NAUR NOTATION

The syntax of the UNIX utilities and system calls in this book are presented in a modified version of a language known as Backus-Naur notation, or BNF for short. In a BNF description, the following sequences have a special meaning:

Sequence	Meaning
[strings]	Strings may appear zero or one time.
{ strings }*	Strings may appear zero or more times.
{ strings }+	Strings may appear one or more times.
string1|string2	string1 or string2 may appear.
-optionlist	Zero or more options may follow a dash.

The last sequence is the UNIX-oriented modification, which allows me to avoid placing large numbers of brackets around command line options. To indicate a [, {, |, or - without its special meaning, I precede it with a \ character.

Some variations of commands depend on which option you choose. I indicate this by supplying a separate syntax description for each variation. For example, take a look at the syntax description of the **at** utility:

Utility: **at** -csm *time* [*date* [, *year*]][+*increment*][*script*]
       at -r { *jobId*}+
       at -l { *jobId*}*

The first version of the **at** utility is selected by any combination of the command line options **-c**, **-s**, and **-m**. These must then be followed by a time and an optional date specifier. The optional date specifier may be followed by an optional year specifier. Additionally, an increment may be specified and/or a script name.

The second version of **at** is selected by a **-r** option, and may be followed by one or more job id numbers.

The third version of **at** is selected by a **-l** option, and may be followed by zero or more job id numbers.

SYSTEM CALLS: An Alphabetical Cross-Reference

Here is a list of references to each system call. The page number of the system call description is in boldface.

Name	Synopsis	Examples
accept	accepts a connection request from a client socket	453, **458**, 459, 469, 498
bind	binds a socket to a name	453, **457**, 469, 498
chdir	changes a process's current working directory	**418**
chmod	changes a file's permission settings	**401**, 402, 446, 447
chown	changes a file's owner and/or group	**400**, 401
close	closes a file	372, 379, 386, **387**, 395, 403, 404, 423, 425, 443, 444, 447, 453, 454, 459, 464, 489, 494, 496, 498
connect	connects to a named server socket	454, **460**, 461, 464, 468, 496
dup	duplicates a file descriptor	**402**, 403, 489
dup2	similar to dup	**402**, 403, 425, 444, 488, 489, 494, 496, 498
execl	replaces the calling process's code, data, and stack from an executable file	**417**, 418
execle	similar to execl	**417**
execlp	similar to execl	**417**, 444

Name	Synopsis	Examples
execv	similar to execl	**417**
execve	similar to execl	**417**
execvp	similar to execl	**417**, 421, 425, 434, 489
exit	terminates a process	380, 393, 397, **413**, 414, 415, 416, 423, 434, 439, 440, 453, 454, 459, 464, 486, 487, 488
fchmod	similar to chmod	**401**
fchown	similar to chown	**400**
fcntl	gives access to miscellaneous file characteristics	372, **403**, 404
fork	duplicates a process	**410**, 411, 412, 414, 416, 421, 434, 435, 438, 439, 440, 443, 444, 459, 486, 487, 488
fstat	similar to stat	**398**
ftruncate	similar to truncate	**407**
getdents	obtains directory entries	394, **399**, 423
getegid	returns a process's effective group id	**420**
geteuid	returns a process's effective user id	**420**
getgid	returns a process's real group id	**420**
gethost-name	returns the name of the host	465, **467**
gethost--by-name	returns a structure describing an Internet host	465, **467**
getpgrp	returns a process's process group id	**438**
getpid	returns a process's id number	**411**, 412, 416, 438, 439
getppid	returns a parent process's id number	**411**, 412, 416
getuid	returns a process's real user id	**420**
ioctl	controls a device	**405**

Name	Synopsis	Examples
kill	sends a signal to a specified process or group of processes	**432**, 434, 435
link	creates a hard link	**405**
listen	sets the maximum number of pending socket connections	453, **458**, 469, 498
lseek	moves to a particular offset in a file	372, 380, **385**, 386, 395, 404, 423
mknod	creates a special file	**406**, 446, 447
nice	changes a process's priority	**419**
open	opens/creates a file	370, 372, 378, **381**, 382, 383, 386, 394, 403, 404, 423, 425, 447, 448, 494
pause	suspends the calling process and returns when a signal is received	**430**, 431, 438
pipe	creates an unnamed pipe	**441**, 443, 444, 488
read	reads bytes from a file into a buffer	372, 378, 380, **383**, 384, 385, 386, 443, 448, 455, 461, 466
setegid	sets a process's effective group id	**420**
seteuid	sets a process's effective user id	**420**
setgid	sets a process's real and effective group id	**420**
setpgrp	sets a process's process group id	**437**, 439, 440, 486
setrgid	sets a process's real group id	**420**
setruid	sets a process's real user id	**420**
setuid	sets a process's real and effective user id	**420**
signal	specifies the action that will be taken when a particular signal arrives	**429**, 430, 431, 433, 439, 440, 453, 480, 486
socket	creates an unnamed socket	453, 454, **456**, 460, 464, 468, 469, 496, 497

Name	Synopsis	Examples
stat	returns status information about a file	394, **398**, 399, 422
sync	schedules all file buffers to be flushed to disk	**407**
truncate	truncates a file	**407**
unlink	removes a file	**387**, 388, 447, 453, 457, 498
wait	waits for a child process	**415**, 416, 423, 434, 440, 488
write	writes bytes from a buffer to a file	372, 378, 380, **384**, 385, 386, 404, 443, 448, 461

Bibliography

Here's a list of the books that I refer to in this book. The number that precedes the title of the book is the index number that I use in my references. I've included the ISBN and edition numbers just in case they're useful.

1. **A Practical Guide To The UNIX System**, second edition
   Sobell
   ISBN 0-8053-0243-3
2. **Advanced UNIX Programming**
   Rochkind
   ISBN 0-13-011800-1
3. **C Programming In The Berkeley UNIX Environment**
   Kernighan
   ISBN 0-13-109760-1
4. **DOS|UNIX - Becoming A Super User**
   Seyer, Mills
   ISBN 0-13-218645-4
5. **The Design Of The UNIX Operating System**
   Bach
   ISBN 0-13-201799-7

6. **The Korn Shell**
   Bolsky, Korn
   ISBN 0-13-516972-0

7. **The UNIX C Shell Field Guide**
   Anderson, Anderson
   ISBN 0-13-937468-X

8. **The UNIX Operating System**, second edition
   Christian
   ISBN 0-471-84782-8

9. **The UNIX Programming Environment**
   Kernighan, Pike
   ISBN 0-13-937681-X

10. **The X Window System Programming And Applications With Xt**
    Young
    ISBN 0-13-497074-8

11. **Tricks Of The UNIX Masters**
    Sage
    ISBN 0-672-22449-6

12. **UNIX Communications**
    The Waite Group
    ISBN 0-672-22511-5

13. **UNIX Network Programming**
    Stevens
    ISBN 0-13-949876-1

14. **UNIX Papers**
    The Waite Group
    ISBN 0-672-22578-6

15. **UNIX RefGuide**
    McNulty Development Inc.
    ISBN 0-13-938957-0

16. **UNIX System Administration Handbook**
    Nemeth, Snyder, Seebass
    ISBN 0-13-933441-6

17. **UNIX System Architecture**
    Andleigh
    ISBN 0-13-949843-5

18. **4.3 BSD UNIX Operating System**
    Leffler, McKusick, Karels, Quarterman
    ISBN 0-201-06196-1

19. **UNIX Desktop Guide To EMACS**
    Ralph Roberts
    ISBN 0-672-30171-7

Index

*A boldface page number indicates the definition of a term.

M

N